Augustus J. Thébaud

The Church and the Moral World

Considerations on the Holiness of the Church

Augustus J. Thébaud

The Church and the Moral World
Considerations on the Holiness of the Church

ISBN/EAN: 9783337313487

Printed in Europe, USA, Canada, Australia, Japan

Cover: Foto ©Lupo / pixelio.de

More available books at **www.hansebooks.com**

AND

THE MORAL WORLD

CONSIDERATIONS ON THE HOLINESS

OF THE CHURCH.

BY THE

Rev. AUG. J. THÉBAUD, S.J.

"*Estote ergo vos perfecti, sicut et Pater vester cælestis perfectus est.*"
—Matt. v. 48.

New York, Cincinnati, and St. Louis:
BENZIGER BROTHERS,
Printers to the Holy Apostolic See.
1881.

PREFACE

In describing in a previous work the rapid extension of the Christian Church at the time of its first establishment, the intention of the writer was to insist on its instantaneous universality as a proof of its divine origin. This is what theologians call a mark or note of the true Church, and they say that any religious organization which is not catholic or universal cannot be the Spouse of Christ, whom He espoused when He died on the Cross for all men.

Many well-known circumstances of that mighty event sufficiently indicated that, at the same time, a great moral change took place among the converted nations. Not only was polytheism destroyed and a pure worship everywhere introduced in place of a debased superstition; not only a complete revolution in the annals of mankind marked the advent of the God-man, and left the footprints of His Church deeply impressed forever after in history; but a new code of morals was given to the world, and Christian holiness began to spread the fragrance of pure virtue wherever moral corruption had prevailed and unblushing vice had openly unveiled its depravity.

Sanctity, therefore, was one of the most prominent characters of the new and universal religion, and sanctity naturally followed its introduction among all nations of the globe. As, however, the chief object of our former work was to describe the rapidity and universality of the early Christian movement, the character of holiness was left, as it were, in the background; it must now be brought forward.

For it is as great a proof of a divine origin as any other mark that can be proposed. Nay, it can be maintained that it is the greatest and the most absolute sign that it comes from heaven. God is not only *Maximus;* He is chiefly *Optimus.* His power strikes with awe, His goodness attracts with an irresistible force. The same is true with regard to the Church. Her extraordinary strength, her magnanimous deeds, her universal dominion, impose even on the unbeliever the task of bowing his head before her. But the mild and pure virtues which spring up under her feet in her pilgrimage through the world have a much greater power to subdue the heart and bring men to her. The important point is to place that character of sanctity in a strong and vivid light, so that no one can refuse to acknowledge it.

This was scarcely possible when all the strength of the argument lay in the character of *universality*. For this reason it is important to take here that of *holiness* apart, and concentrate on it alone all the reflections the subject naturally suggests. Chiefly is this necessary in this age when on every side the purity of Christian morals is openly assailed; and some go even so far as to pretend that the moral world since Christ appeared is not of a very different character from what it was in the most pagan times, yea, when the first Roman emperors horrified mankind by their inconceivable immorality. The task of demonstrating the folly of this assumption appears easy, and does not require great effort to convince a candid mind; but unfortunately in our day the more bold an assertion is, though altogether unsupported, the more it finds a following among men for whom everything is a matter of opinion, and who willingly embrace the most extreme doctrines, extreme even to the verge of absurdity.

The question, however, must rest on its own merits; and in the present case the proofs are so overwhelming that little attention can be paid to the insane clamor of adversaries. We may occasionally discuss their objections and show the weakness of their attacks. But our chief concern will be to place before the reader the solid ground on which the Christian moralist rests, and the profound reason he has to repeat every day in his prayers, *Credo in Unam, Sanctam Ecclesiam*.

The volume is naturally divided into two Books, and the first would suffice to demonstrate the Holiness of the Church. For its only object is to place before the reader the *principles* or *sources* of sanctity evidently possessed in their fulness by the Catholic Church. Any institution endowed with such privileges as those cannot but be holy, and it would be the duty of opponents to prove that the Church does not possess them. They never have attempted to do so; and if they were to try it, the whole religious history of mankind in modern times would protest against their boldness. But the attempt would be futile chiefly on account of the incontrovertible *facts* contained in the Second Book. That the Church has been holy, and continues to be holy to this day, is now a matter of simple history, and the Catholic can proudly offer those facts even to an unbelieving world.

The second branch of the subject embraces both the first centuries of Christianity under the sway of Rome, and the ages which followed the barbarian invasions until recent times. Less details will naturally be furnished for the primitive epoch, down to the fifth century, than for the subsequent period of time. Much has already been said on the subject of this first part, in the "Church and Gentile World," which it would be unnecessary to repeat. But the matter which embraces the conversion of barbarians, the middle ages, and our own day is altogether new, and was not even touched in the previous work. On this account it required on our part a greater amount of effort to give as thorough an idea of it as space and time permitted.

The whole of this r̥e must bring the conviction that if ever sanctity has flou..̥ed on earth it was under the wings of the Catholic Church, and that she alone has spread in the entire universe the "kingdom of God" which Christ came to establish forever. All ages have equally contributed to the work, and all nations have gloried in the "legions of saints" which their annals contain. Yea, the great majority of European families known to history have placed their "canonized ancestors" among the most precious links of their lineage. Many kingly races particularly have set a higher value on those of their own kin who have practised an heroic virtue on the throne than on the mighty conquerors or wise lawgivers their pedigree could show. Germany has boasted of her Henry II., France of her Louis IX., England of her Edward the Confessor, Castile of her Ferdinand III., more than of their greatest legislators and warriors. Of all the images of ancestors that were then kept in the glorious houses of princes, dukes, and barons, those that were most honored and preserved with greatest reverence were the mild portraits of saintly popes and bishops, humble and zealous monks, pure and pious nuns, all having the nimbus of sanctity encircling their heads. All the cities of Europe, during many ages, offered also to the traveller, in their courts of justice, town halls, or places of records, the portraitures on canvas of innumerable "blessed" or "saints" who had honored their country by the perfect fulfilment of the Gospel precepts.

If all this is now gone, it is, however, a glorious memory. It is well known that an attempt has been made, and is still going on at this hour, to publish all the lives of those who have deserved a place of honor in the annals of the Catholic Church; and the *Acta Sanctorum*, by the Bollandists, are now found in all the libraries of Europe and this country. The full list of their names alone fills a large folio volume; still the collection is far from being complete. It is doubtful if the next century will witness the achievement of a task of which Boilandus himself, the originator of the scheme, had certainly no conception when he began. Meanwhile this immense compilation fills with delight all Catholics who can peruse its pages The rationalists, unbelievers,—nay, atheists,—if they have any taste for the beautiful, often go so far as to profess the greatest admiration for that noble work; and among them M. Ernest Renan acknowledges that in the sixty large folios of which the work is now composed he always finds a delightful reading, a sound erudition, and an inexhaustible source of the feelings naturally engendered by "the true, the good, and the beautiful."

In conclusion, the only remark on which we must insist is the noteworthy fact that the *Acta Sanctorum* present to the eye of the reader a panorama of holiness from which *no age* of the Church is excluded. What is called by many modern writers the *dark* period of Catholicism offers in those pages to the admiration of mankind as glorious a galaxy of moral heroes as those ages which are confessedly recognized as the purest and holiest in Christianity. It can be, therefore, maintained that the priceless compilation of the Bollandists contains the irrefragable demonstration of one of the most important parts of this volume; namely, that in which the author vindicates the middle ages and the fourteenth and fifteenth centuries from the rash aspersions of open enemies or doubtful friends. Would to God that more copious details could have been furnished! The blind themselves would have been constrained to see and acknowledge this solemn truth, that there is not a single moment in the life of the Church when she was shorn of the ray of sanctity.

Meanwhile the reader will easily understand that the "moral world" in the Catholic Church is far superior, purer, and more comprehensive than out of it. From the beginning, it is true, the *Eternal Word*, as St. John says at the head of his gospel, has "enlightened every man that cometh into the world," and has given to the human conscience the true principles of right. But as this "enlightenment" took place only through our human faculties, it could not produce more than natural effects, and the virtues that man could thus know and practise belonged of necessity to the natural order. But since the Eternal Word became incarnate, and the God-man began His mission of *grace* among us, He adopted us into His own Sonship, and raised us to a supernatural plane in which morality as well as belief was transformed, so as to give to the moral world a completely different meaning. There was a new lawgiver, Christ; a new sanction, His own promise of life eternal; a new code, formed on the model of the sublime virtues practised by the Redeemer; a new view of life, based on the firm ground of eternal truths; a substantial sanctity, resulting from the influence of Christ over His members; a mystic body, in fine, partaking both of heaven and earth, endowed with new powers, and with a higher aptitude for virtue, ending at last in holiness.

Sanctity in the Catholic Church is consequently peculiar; and it is necessary it should be so, since, according to St. Peter, God has given us through Christ "the highest and most precious promises, so that we become through them partakers of the divine nature" (2 Pet. 4).

TABLE OF CONTENTS.

FIRST BOOK.

DOCTRINE OR PRINCIPLES.

CHAPTER I.

THE FIRST SOURCE OF HOLINESS IN THE CHURCH IS DERIVED FROM THE BELIEF IN THE ORIGINAL RIGHTEOUSNESS OF MAN AT HIS CREATION.

1. Place of man in creation	16
2. Of man's creation in general	23
3. Mr. Darwin's hypothesis	25
4. Man was created to the image and likeness of God	37

CHAPTER II.

SECOND PRINCIPLE OF HOLINESS IN THE CHURCH—THE PRESERVATION OF THE DECALOGUE AS INTERPRETED BY CHRIST, AND ITS EXTENSION TO THE WHOLE HUMAN RACE.

1. Necessity of the written precepts of the Decalogue	51
2. The Decalogue as explained by Christ	60
3. The Decalogue, as explained by the Saviour in his Sermon, was confirmed on the day of Pentecost for the whole human race	65

CHAPTER III.

THE CHURCH PROPOSES THE LIFE OF JESUS AS THE CHRISTIAN IDEAL—THIRD SOURCE OF HOLINESS.

1. Christ as pattern of sanctity	71
2. The Evangelical Counsels, as derived from the life of Christ, open a new and higher source of holiness in the Church	79

CHAPTER IV.

CATHOLIC DOCTRINE ON THE MORAL AND INDEFINITE PERFECTIBILITY OF MAN—AIMING AT PERFECTION—FOURTH PRINCIPLE OF HOLINESS IN THE CHURCH.

		PAGE
1.	Unreliable systems of human perfectibility	95
2.	The true theory of the moral perfectibility of man	99
3.	The moral perfectibility of man is unfolded in the Christian life even in the common path of the Commandments	107
4.	The best development of human perfectibility is carried out in the practice of the Evangelical Counsels	119
5.	Aiming at perfection	130

CHAPTER V.

THE ETERNAL DESTINY OF MAN, CONTRASTED WITH TEMPORAL THINGS, GIVES TO THE FOREGOING PRINCIPLES THEIR MAIN STRENGTH AND EFFICACY WITH REGARD TO THE PURSUIT OF HOLINESS ON EARTH.

1. The irremediable defect of all moral codes which are not founded on Christian principles comes from the want of a sanction, in the absence of a hereafter.. 145
2. Can there be a solid objection made against the Christian code of morals? 153
3. The contrast of temporal with eternal things is promotive of good morals and holiness.. 160

SECOND BOOK.

FACTS.

CHAPTER I.

MORAL CHANGE EFFECTED BY THE APOSTLES OF CHRIST IN JERUSALEM AND THE JEWISH RACE.

1. What is to be understood by the "kingdom of God" which Christ our Lord came to establish?.. 167
2. First establishment of God's kingdom on earth—Origin of the Church at Jerusalem.. 175
3. Extraordinary characteristics of the Judeo-Christian congregations..... 182
4. Did the first Judeo-Christians hate those of their countrymen who did not embrace the faith?.. 186
5. Character of the community of goods among the first Christians in Jerusalem.. 192

6. Was ever the virtue of charity practised in any other religion or institution as well as in the Catholic Church?............................. 196
7. Holiness was fostered among the first Judeo-Christians by the observance of the Mosaic law—A word on the Essenes..................... 206

CHAPTER II.

CHRISTIAN HOLINESS IN THE EAST—THE THERAPEUTÆ IN EGYPT, AND THEIR RELATIONS WITH THE CHURCH AT JERUSALEM—FIRST DEVELOPMENTS OF MONASTICISM.

1. Who were the Therapeutæ?—Their connection with Jerusalem.......... 213
2. Description of the primitive Christian life in Egypt..................... 219

CHAPTER III.

HOLINESS IN UPPER SYRIA AND MESOPOTAMIA—EDESSA, THE CENTRE OF THE MOVEMENT.

1. Christianity was preached at Edessa in the Apostolic age.............. 225
2. Monasticism and theology, two sources of holiness at Edessa........... 227
3. The theology and poetry of Edessa were eminently conducive to holiness. 235
4. Some objections are answered and conclusions drawn.................. 241

CHAPTER IV.

CHRISTIAN HOLINESS IN THE WEST—MORAL CHANGE EFFECTED IN ROME AT THE FIRST PREACHING OF CHRISTIANITY.

1. This moral change began very early................................... 249
2. Can this moral change be explained by natural causes?................ 259
3. This is confirmed by the new moral doctrine which could not be derived from any previous religion or philosophy........................... 269
4. Some further proofs of the Church's holiness in Rome................. 278
5. The moral change effected in Rome during the Apostolic age was permanent... 282

CHAPTER V.

THE BARBARIAN WORLD CONFRONTED BY THE CHURCH AND BROUGHT TO THE PRACTICE OF THE HIGHEST CHRISTIAN VIRTUES.

1. A short sketch of German and Scandinavian tribes before their conversion.. 297
2. Remarkable moral change effected in all German and Scandinavian nations by Christianity... 314
3. Holiness among the Anglo-Saxons in Great Britain, a sufficient test of the previous opinion.. 324
4. A few words on the conversion of the Germans to Christianity.......... 340

CHAPTER VI.

CHRISTIAN HOLINESS DURING THE MIDDLE AGES.

1. Difference of opinion on the subject..................................	348
2. The first period of the Middle Ages consisted on the part of the Church in a rude training of wild tribes; hence violence, crime, immorality, were to be expected from the greatest number: the ages of faith had not really commenced	356
3. Formation of Christian congregations in cities mainly by bishops; in the country particularly by monks...............................	370
4. The true foundation of holiness laid down in redeemed Europe	380
5. The ages of faith were likewise ages of holiness.......................	390
6. The dark side of the Middle Ages is briefly explained..................	425

CHAPTER VII.

SUPPLEMENTARY.

1. A short summary of facts so far unfolded............................	451
2. How far did corruption invade the sanctuary previous to the so-called Reformation?...	453
3. The moral teaching of the Church was at that time as firm as ever........	456
4. A large array of facts proves that the principle of regeneration in the Church was always active in the midst of a widespread corruption.....	459
5. Holiness continued in the Church during the darkest period of the great schism	464
6. The Catholic Church in the present age continues its work of regeneration with the vigor of renewed youth.................................	473

THE CHURCH AND THE MORAL WORLD.

FIRST BOOK.

DOCTRINE OR PRINCIPLES.

CHAPTER I.

THE FIRST SOURCE OF HOLINESS IN THE CHURCH IS DERIVED FROM THE BELIEF IN THE ORIGINAL RIGHTEOUSNESS OF MAN AT HIS CREATION.

THE Church is "the kingdom of God on earth." One of its first characteristics, on this account, must be holiness; and since it is composed of men, man himseif within her precincts must be holy. Not only the *facts* of the Church's history must reflect *a posteriori* this attribute; but all her doctrine, all the *principles* she inculcates, considered *a priori*, must deeply lay the foundation of virtue. For this reason the present volume affects naturally a two-fold division: *principles* and *facts*.

We place at the head of the first the Church's doctrine on the origin of man, because it is chiefly at his *origin* that the design of God in creating him must have appeared. In the very act of giving him existence, God declared what he was to be. Had human nature been destined only to be placed at the head of the animal kingdom, it would have been circumscribed within the limits of animality, and the physical laws of sensation and emotion would have sufficed to guide human destiny. But according to Scripture and the Church's doctrine, man came out of the hands of his Creator a moral person, created in integrity and holiness; and by the very initial movement of his being, he was above all preordained to the practice of sublime virtues. By his moral nature he was to be chiefly distinguished from animals.

This is called a principle, though it is not an axiom but a fact. It is, however, a fact declaring on the part of the Creator what must be the spring of all human actions. From it the whole destiny of man on earth is derived; and the necessity of actual holiness follows as a strict conclusion from an indubitable premiss. Let us, therefore, briefly discuss what the Church teaches on our origin, as being from her a first declaration of the duty of holiness on the part of man; and to do so more effectually, it is proper to begin by considering man's position in the universe.

1. *Place of Man in Creation.*

The doctrine of the Church on this subject is, as usual, derived from Scripture and the Fathers. For besides reason there are only two sources of truth; namely, the written word of God, consigned in the sacred records of the Old and New Testament, and the unwritten revelation of the same divine word, transmitted orally by the Apostles and their successors whom we call eminently the Fathers. Both testimonies may give us a more accurate means of knowing man's nature than the simple discoveries of naturalists on the same subject. Still we must not discard this last means of information, since natural truth is the handmaid of revealed truth, and both come from God.

Consider first, therefore, how Scripture anticipated science in the order it assigned to the appearance of man on earth. He came only after his dwelling had been prepared and the whole inorganic, vegetable, and animal creation had been settled in permanent order. This precise statement of Moses in the first chapter of Genesis distinguishes his narrative from all ancient cosmogonies outside of his own.

The Fathers insisted principally on this remarkable disposition described in Genesis to prove that there was a providential design from the very beginning. God had prepared the dwelling of man before introducing him into it, the same as a palace of a king is furnished with everything necessary or convenient previous to the monarch coming on to sit on his throne and issue his commands. Many Fathers, in fact, compare man to a ruler for whom this world was made, as he was himself made for God. Hence he has been called "the king of creation," though this title is unjustly denied him by many scientists of our day. Some Fathers, however, were not satisfied with this, and Gregory of Nyssa did not scruple to pen the following words: " It was proper that man, ordained beforehand to enjoy in heaven all divine gifts, should possess on earth in his nature some attributes of Him whose partner he was destined to be. Hence was he adorned with life, speech, wisdom, all possible heavenly graces."* Cyril of Alexandria † says on the same subject: "The earth was first filled to repletion with everything which could glorify man, in order that when he finally came he could from their beauty judge of the Creator's glory." Gregory Nazianzen, on this account, gives to man at the moment of his creation the highest titles and prerogatives.‡ He calls him "a second world placed in an inferior one; standing on earth an angel in greatness; alone able truly to adore, to contemplate intelligently the visible creation, to penetrate the mysteries of the invisible world; king of every earthly thing, at the same time earthly and heavenly." Gregory of Nyssa again wrote the following words on the same subject, in a book which he purposely composed on the "Creation of Man" (ch. 2): "The prince and ruler could not appear when there was yet nothing over which he could rule. But as soon as the empire had been set in order, the coming of the monarch was announced." Among the Latin Fathers, Lactantius, opening a new view of the same object, draws a proof that the world was created for man "from his erect position, owing to which his eyes are directed toward heaven, his face looks toward God, and the proud attitude of his head is common to him and to his Maker. For, in the act of raising him from the ground, God enabled him to contemplate the divine Majesty face to face." ‖

Many other texts of the Fathers on the same chapter of Genesis could be quoted. These are sufficient for the purpose. If they differ so completely as they do from the appreciations of modern naturalists, it must not be directly concluded that the Fathers' judgment was based merely on fancy, and the recent one of scientists on facts. But the first argued from Scripture, and the second from a supposed identity of human physical nature with that of inferior animals. If on the one side Scripture is the

---

* Cathech. cap. 5.   † Glaph. 1.   ‡ Oratio 38.   ‖ Inst. Divin. cap. 7.

word of God, as Christians give strong proofs of it, and if on the other the modern naturalists judge of man only from his physical nature, as is evident from many of their books, it is not difficult to decide on which side truth must be. And many other reflections on which we are going to enter will abundantly prove it.

The Fathers, arguing from Scripture, had acknowledged in man a master of the world which was made for *him*, a ruler, a king of creation, an angel in moral stature, a partner of God in the government of this earth; but they also stated the rational ground of all those titles, by calling him a *microcosm*—an epitome of the universe. On this account they said that he was the last created, because it was proper that the creative power should *rest* after having given him birth, as the Book of Genesis positively affirms.

But because their knowledge of nature was far less extensive and sure than ours, this concept is much better adapted to the men of our age, who besides the word of God have a far more accurate knowledge of physical facts which must agree with God's word. It is proper consequently to examine what is known from reason of man's nature, and to see the harmony of both revealed and rational truths. It is certain that all the chief organs of inferior animals are reproduced in man; but how far more perfect they are in him than in all their prototypes! Comparative anatomy alone could prove this superiority in many points at least; the demonstration of it is still far more convincing when physiology intervenes, even without taking any account of man's spiritual faculties. The main object, however, which must be kept in view here is the universal plan of the animal kingdom altogether culminating in man; so that after him our mind cannot conceive any physical organized being more perfect which could give rise to the addition of a single higher individual species over and above what already exists. Hence man is the last, and a compendium of the whole.

It is well known that the establishment of what is called the "natural system in zoology" has cost long years of labor to a number of great scientists in France, England, Germany, and Italy. All those labors had for their object to study and ascertain the place assigned by God to each being in the universal scheme. Have they not all agreed that with respect to animals, starting from the lowest insect or worm, and going successively through all classes, orders, families, genera, and species, man is reached at last, above whom nothing more can be found or even supposed? This is the object of all treatises on natural history.

Strange to say, it is true, this stupendous fact, which must be for a reasonable man the strongest proof of a design in nature, has given rise to the pretended system of evolution, which by many at least is intended to do away with the need of a designer; but this aberration can no more invalidate the cogency of the proof itself than the light of the sun can be denied on account of some clouds which obscure it temporarily. There is no need of entering extensively into those considerations, since the present object is to state plainly and fully what the Church teaches, not what men have imagined on the same subject. A few paragraphs, however, of Agassiz* may clear away some prejudices which the theory of evolution has created in many minds. Hear him on the classification of animated beings. We retranslate from the French:

"Nature," he says, "proves the existence of a thinking God as surely as man manifests the faculty of thinking, when he acknowledges the natural concatenation of things. The existing correlation of all the parts of nature embraced into a system reduced to fact reveals an intellect which far surpasses the highest faculties of which man is proud. The actual division of the animal kingdom into branches, classes, orders, families, genera, and species, represent the categories of divine thought; they are the headings of chapters in the great book of creation, which the naturalist is only bound to interpret. The systems invented by the masters of science are thus the simple translation in human speech of the Creative Thought.

"The whole universe can be considered as a school where man learns to know himself, his relation to other creatures, and the First Cause of every thing that exists. . . . If it is proved that the plan of creation has not originated from the *necessary* action of physical laws, but has been *freely* conceived by an Almighty Intellect, there will be an end of the theories which refer only to material laws in order to explain all the wonders of the universe. Now the laws which suffice to explain the phenomena of the *inorganic* material world are perfectly incompetent to account for the existence of *living* beings, even when they have a body. . . .

---

* On Species and Classification in Zoology. French translation by F. Vogeli; Paris, 1869.

"The student of nature experiences a profound surprise when he sees how far animals are independent from the physical forces in the midst of which their life is developed and maintained. That independence is so great that it can be attributed only to a Sovereign Power ruling at once the physical forces, the plants, and the animals, and preserving among them all an harmonious relation by a mutual adaptation. The modifications which result from the influence of physical causes on living beings have only a secondary importance with regard to animal life, and scarcely touch the general plan and the various complications of the physical structure. Almost all those things which are generally ascribed to the influence of physical agents on organized beings prove only *correlations* resulting from the general plan of nature.

"Nothing is more striking than the unity of plan in the structure of the most divers types. From pole to pole mammalia, birds, reptiles, fishes, reveal a single plan of formation. This plan denotes conceptions of the highest order, and surpasses by far the vastest generalizations of human thought. It has required the most laborious researches for man to merely recognize the simple idea of it. . . . Those rational relations, that admirable harmony, that infinite variety in unity, could not have for their origin forces incapable of thinking, of combining ideas, of realizing them in time and space. . . . How could that system of which man is only a fragment have been produced at all, except by a Sovereign Intellect, a Designer and Creator?"

These few reflections of Agassiz, well pondered and developed, suffice by themselves to show the perfect inanity of Darwinism. We will only add that the great Swiss naturalist in calling man a *fragment* meant surely that man enters into the system as an individual element. But he would not have denied that man is not only the highest of them, but the *résumé* of the whole and the compendium of creation, and he says so in several beautiful passages of his writings.

From the very origin man's position in the whole scheme has been so high that he cannot be included in any branch or class common to him with other animals. The doctrine of the Fathers has been mentioned which makes of him a ruler, a king, a partner with God. We hail with joy the open declaration of many scientists, in France particularly, who place him in a commanding position *apart* from all other animal classes over which he is appointed to rule. M. de Quatrefages has been for many years a powerful advocate of this opinion, which it is to be hoped the majority of scientists will soon adopt. This belief is predicated first on the moral character of man, which raises him far above any class of mere animals whatever, and second on the unity of his personality. The naturalist (M. de Quatrefages contends) cannot separate the intellectual and moral faculties in man from those that are purely physical, because man would not be any more what he is if his intellectual and moral faculties were taken away. To find his place in creation both his physical and spiritual natures have to be considered as united in a single personality. M. Isidore Geoffroy St. Hilaire, when living, was also strongly of this opinion, which was in ancient times that of Aristotle, and in the middle ages that of Albert the Great. But when this is done and man is studied in his complexity, it is evident that he cannot be entirely included in the animal kingdom, from which he is divided by the whole abyss of the spiritual world. There is as much distance, at least, between him and the highest animals as there is between the animal and the vegetable kingdoms, as there is even between the vegetable and the mineral. Man, therefore, must be placed in a *kingdom* apart, which must be called the *human kingdom*. These ideas are so clear, so simple and true that there can be no doubt of their adoption in a near future by all reasonable and sincere scientists who care more for truth than for the success of some pet theory or other. M. de Quatrefages has clearly proved it in his last book, *L'Espèce Humaine*.

That this hope is not delusive but, on the contrary, probable follows from the recent conversion to spiritualistic ideas of former Darwinists; yea, of ardent supporters of the gradual physical development of man, Mr. A. R. Wallace in particular. For a long time this gentleman appeared to have adopted the most advanced, that is atheistic, ideas of the evolutionists. He shared entirely the notions of Mr. Darwin, and was thought even by many to have anticipated them. The supposed immense influence of natural selection for the production of new species was a doctrine which he conceived simultaneously with Mr. Darwin himself. As early as 1855 and 1858, consequently before this last author had published his "Origin of Species," Mr. A. R. Wallace had developed the same ideas in two essays which made a great sensation at the time. But in 1871 his "Contributions to the theory of natural selection" announced an important change in his views, since he openly professed that these supposed laws—of natural selection—could not be claimed for the development of *man*. In his new opinion he declared, first, that the size of the skull in man and the distribution of the hair on his body supposed a totally different cause, and simple evolution could not have produced them. Secondly, he proved the same to be the fact from the shape of the foot and of the hand in man, as well as from his larynx and his æsthetic taste for music. All this, he thought, supposed a preparation formally *designed* for a future state of civilization, because, he continued to admit, the primitive state of man had been barbarous. But in a third place he went much farther still in considering the intellectual and moral faculties of man; and he proved triumphantly that evolution could have no share in them. He touched particularly the right key when he said that "although the practice of benevolence, of honesty, of veracity, etc., may have been *useful* to primitive human tribes"—this is the great argument of Mr. Darwin to evolve morality from mere matter—"yet this does not explain why the idea of *sanctity*, *holiness*, is attached to those actions which men even in the tribal state consider as good and moral, in contradistinction to those which are simply useful." This Mr. Wallace developed admirably; and we cannot be surprised that in a pamphlet anterior to the *Contributions* he had mainly for his object to show "that in nature man occupies a *place apart*, is not only the head and the highest point in the grand series of organized beings, but a new being in some degree." In all those considerations the gifted author is not yet a Christian, and is far from admitting what the Church teaches on the origin of man; but he is on the way to it. At least he has fairly begun to prove the incompetency of *natural selection* alone to explain the nature and position of man in creation; and from the day of this first attack on Darwinism, the manifold deficiencies not only of natural but likewise of sexual selection have been eagerly canvassed, and are now fully admitted by such writers as Mr. Peschel himself and other Germans of the same rationalistic school.

The Christian, therefore, cannot be called any longer an obscurantist, because he believes in the primitive dignity of man. All in the end will be bound to admit it. But enough of this; let us come back to the Fathers and Scripture, leaving aside the scientists and *reason*. Scripture says that man was created "to the image and likeness of God," and it is from this simple text particularly that most of the Fathers conclude that he was created holy, and destined to the most sublime sanctity; namely, to copy that of God Himself. This is the great characteristic of his origin, which includes all those of true civilization.

2. *Of Man's Creation in General.*

Holy Scripture enunciates an axiom of simple good sense in stating that God *created* the universe and man. Neither the one nor the other could have ever existed without Him; and creation is the only simple and rational way of accounting for their appearance. God is the only Infinite and *necessary* being; and what we call the universe cannot be any more infinite in time than in space. To suppose either is puerile; still it is the opinion of many pretended scientists. A child only can believe that to be limitless to which his imagination can assign no limit. The *mind* of a man tells him that whatever is contingent in the philosophical sense — that is, not absolutely necessary — must have depended on another for its existence. That other is the only Infinite Being, and He could not communicate His attributes in full to those things which He might have refused to create. Whoever objects to even pronounce the name of God, and acknowledges the existence only of what falls under his senses, is bound indeed to believe them eternal and infinite; but in doing so he abjures the possession of human intellect, which says that whatever can be supposed not to exist has not subsisted from all eternity. There must, moreover, have been a beginning for whatever is subject to change, because change supposes the non-possession of full reality, and only what is immutable can exist *a se*.

Again, the men who call themselves positivists, in order to explain their cosmogony, have to suppose a *protoplasm;* and this very word—plasma—includes the notion of creation. In fact, matter is absolutely incomprehensible without a previous designer. As the human mind alone can discuss it and use it, so the divine mind was necessary to give it existence. Who can imagine matter existing alone? It is at best an instrument; and an instrument supposes necessarily an artisan or an artist. Still every strict evolutionist pretends that at the beginning matter existed alone. Are they conscious that they themselves have a mind who speak so? The bee, in constructing her cell, could give them a lesson which they should not forget, if the wish to escape from their responsibility to God has not made them perfectly unreasonable.

In speaking of man's creation, the first thing to be remarked is that, according to Genesis, God Himself acted not only consciously— the contrary would be absurd—but most deliberately, since He is represented as holding counsel within Himself, *Faciamus hominem.* The previous creation of the inorganic and organic world, though far inferior to that of man, cannot be supposed to have been left to the action of unconscious forces. We have heard Mr. Agassiz on the subject: "The rational relations, the admirable harmony, that infinite variety in unity, visible everywhere in nature, could not have had for their origin forces incapable of thinking, of combining ideas, of realizing them in time and space." But if this is true of the world outside of man, it is much more so of man himself, who, according to Mr. A. R. Wallace, though he is a positivist, is "not only the head and the highest point in the grand series of organized beings, but a new being in some degree, so that in nature man occupies *a place apart.*" This phrase he had previously explained by man's moral nature, and by the idea of *sanctity* which even savages attach to the precepts of human ethics, without stopping at their *usefulness,* though this is the only principle of morality recognized by strict evolutionists.

Thus Genesis, in narrating the formation of all things previous to man, had attributed it directly to God, but to a simple *fiat* of His infinite power. Not so when there was question of the creation of man, for which an unconscious cause can be called the most absurd of all suppositions. How could consciousness have appeared in man unless it had been derived from an all-conscious power? Hence Holy Scripture expressly mentions a sort of deliberation on the part of the divine mind, which, it seems, was not needed for the production of unconscious beings. *Faciamus hominem ad imaginem nostram.* But before this text is fully explained, it is important to briefly discuss the theory which has been broached in our day, in opposition to the dogma of creation. A few words on this will be useful the better to understand the true theory. A short discussion of this question cannot be omitted, owing to the efforts made on all sides to substitute for creation an array of unreflecting and blind forces which many suppose can replace God.

3. *Mr. Darwin's Hypothesis.*

Listen to Mr. Darwin, and you will hear that the world's formation was the most simple affair, provided sufficient time is granted. This time must be long indeed, but have we not eternity to fall upon; the eternity, namely, of matter which could not have had any beginning? There is, no doubt, already a deep mystery here, and our reason is perfectly unable to understand it. The word *eternity* should be expunged from the rationalist's vocabulary. On this account, surely, Mr. Darwin uses it, if ever, as sparingly as he can; still he cannot do without it, since his system absolutely needs it and supposes it. He prefers, nevertheless, to use the less objectionable phrase, *the deep recesses of time*. We object to this as too poetical in a philosophical book.

It has just been said that his system needs eternity and supposes it, because, since he discards creation alogether, there cannot have been any beginning to what exists, and the whole of it resolves itself into an endless chain. It is preferable, in our opinion, to come at once to the old pagan principle that matter is eternal, though this is absolutely incomprehensible.

That system, moreover, cannot admit any but spontaneous causes; and conscious design is always strictly set aside by Mr. Darwin from any operation which brings on the endless variety of effects. It is consequently important to deal, from the very beginning, with this aspect of it, and expose the irrationality of the attempt by a closer look at it. For it is a mighty effort to exclude mind entirely from the origin and government of this world; and certainly man himself is supposed by it to owe his existence not to the benevolent will of a superior being, but to an innumerable set of "unthinking and unconscious forces," as Mr. Agassiz calls them.

A short sketch of the whole scheme is on that account necessary, in order to know if by its supposed agency reason explains more satisfactorily the origin of the universe than by merely stating that "God created it." This will not take too much time, because it can be reduced to a few bold assertions of the inventor of the system. It is true that in the numerous volumes published by him, particularly in his "Origin of Species," in his "Expression of the Emotions in Man and Animals," and finally in his "Descent of Man," there is brought forward an immense number of facts of natural history which often bewilder the reader and incline him to suppose that they prove his main assertions. It is not difficult to prove that the greatest number of those facts have scarcely any bearing on the true question, and that some of them might be taken as proofs of the contrary. But this would require a great labor which does not seem necessary for the object presently intended; and it will be sufficient, we think, to look simply at the assertions themselves in order to convince any rational mind how gratuitous they are in the main, considering the conclusions which are drawn from them.

This is the Darwinian scheme in its simplicity, as far as we were able to understand it after a close and most attentive reading:

1. The classification of organized beings forming the various groups called classes, orders, families, genera, and species is altogether arbitrary and conventional, unless it is based on "the amount of difference between the several groups; that is, the amount of modification which each has undergone; and as we have no record of the lines of descent, these lines can be discovered only by observing the degrees of resemblance between the beings which are to be classified." Moreover the various groups, exclusive of species, depending on this last element, and species being essentially variable, the whole of it is constantly on the move toward the production of higher beings which result from "the struggle for life" and "the survival of the fittest."

2. The two great causes which secure this result of real "progress," are the "natural selection" and the "sexual selection," by which in the struggle for life the fittest only survive, and new species of a higher grade are constantly produced.

3. It all resolves itself into what is called "evolution," by which one being passes into another by insensible and gradual steps.

4. This evolution alone can give a reason for the successive appearance not only of material beings, but also of those belonging to the moral and intellectual orders.

5. Those various operations require an excessively long time; but the study of geology and astronomy has accustomed us to consider the elements of time and space as being practically without limits.

This, I think, is a fair representation of the main ideas of Mr. Darwin; and there is no presumption in calling them mere assertions without adequate proof. A short discussion will convince the reader that they are far from being as rational as is the Christian belief that God created the universe, such as we see it, in the unity of its plan and the immense variety of its details.

First, it is not true that the classification of organized beings into classes, etc., is altogether arbitrary and conventional, unless it is based on the amount of modification which each group has undergone. The great naturalists who with an immense labor have at last agreed, or nearly so, on what they call "the natural system in zoology," never thought that they were merely settling an arbitrary nomenclature, the same, for instance, as shorthand writers have agreed upon for the adoption of arbitrary signs to render easy the work of the transcriber. They—the naturalists—called their system "natural" because it is based on the natural characters of organized beings; and these are called *natural characters* because they were literally bestowed by the Creator on each group, and on every individual being in each group and form, as it were, their essence.

Mr. Agassiz has told us that the great men who founded "the natural system in zoology" had merely translated in human speech the thoughts of God as manifested in creation. Consequently this first assertion of Mr. Darwin is so far from being true that "the natural system in zoology" continues to be taught to this day in France, England, Germany, Italy, and Spain, in fact the whole of Europe, without introducing into it any of those pretended modifications which would certainly have been found out in great number had the opinion of Mr. Darwin on the subject produced any conviction on the European mind.

As to his suggestion that the classification in natural history, in order to cease to be arbitrary and conventional, " must be based only on the amount of modification introduced by evolution in each group" (in the course of ages, no doubt). This was a cool proposition addressed to all European scientists to admit first the Darwinian system and then base their classifications upon it. Their universal silence in answer to this proposition meant purely that they would think of doing so after he had furnished the proof that real and essential modifications had, in the course of ages, been introduced into organized beings. And since this demand of Mr. Darwin included species as well as genera, families, etc., it amounted to the bold assertion that in reality species had been constantly changing; and he thought he had proved it in his "Origin of Species," but the greatest number of scientists did not think so.

This variableness of species is the main prop of the system of evolution. It cannot be denied that a respectable number of naturalists thought that Mr. Darwin had proved it for a certain number of *plants.* And there is nothing very surprising in this. Botany is a vast field comprising millions perhaps of distinct species, independently of an immense number of varieties; and it is sometimes difficult to ascertain if a given plant is a pure specimen of a distinct species or merely a variety of the same. To come to a decision is often hazardous, not only because hybridity is still much more frequent in plants than in animals, but also because the minuteness of many of those small organisms necessitates the use of the microscope, which may often give rise to deception. Thus although we firmly believe, on the strenth of Genesis alone, that God has created all plants, even the smallest, "each after its kind," still we are not surprised that the best botanists are sometimes mistaken as the natural characters of some of them. Let Mr. Darwin and his supporters make the most they can of this concession.

But we demur from admitting that the same obscurity rests on the natural characters of animals, if we except those whose nature cannot be well determined because they form the link between the fields of zoology and botany. They are mainly called, on that account, zoöphytes. As to all those beings which possess evidently the characters of distinct animals, we do not believe that the variableness of species has ever been proved for a single one of them. In France particularly, where the study of natural history has always been pursued with vigor and accuracy, the doctrine of *transformism*, as it is called there, continues, to this day, to be altogether rejected by all the chief leaders in the science. And the same is the case to a great extent in England and Germany. The fossil species are thought by some to have been the origin and cause of many modern ones; but even these writers do not think that the species are constantly changing. They only did so once, they think, on account of the violent revolutions in nature which accompanied the passage from one geological epoch to another.

Secondly, another powerful reason for calling this principle of Darwinism a mere assertion is the fact that the two main causes which are everywhere assigned for the mutability of species—namely, natural selection and sexual selection—are admitted now nearly by all scientists to be a delusion having scarcely any foundation in fact. This requires some development, because if it is well ascertained the consequence must be that Mr. Darwin has altogether lost his time and trouble. His system vanishes in thin air.

To understand this clearly, it is proper to remark that long before

Mr. Darwin began his labors there was an "artificial selection" going on actively in the animal kingdom, and carried out by a class of people who had no great pretension to the title of scientists, but who practically rendered more service to natural science than many "leaders of thought." These were the improvers of the breed of animals. Horses, cattle, dogs, swine, fowls, birds of every description, were the great object of their practical study. And most of them did it not so much for the sake of science as for the sake of gain. A new stallion, having a long genealogy of noble ancestors, born in their stable, with finer characters than any of its progenitors, might be sold in London for many thousand pounds, in Paris for hundreds of thousands of francs, in New York for an incredible amount of dollars. This was the mainspring of their efforts which followed strictly the rules of a judicious "artificial selection." They "selected" well the dam and the sire; the object of their "selection" fell likewise on the season for breeding, on the food, on the drink, on a hundred other circumstances of which we know little, as we never felt any inclination for that kind of craft.

Selection in such cases as these was called artificial, because it was not left to the blind impulse of nature, but was directed by the mind of man, and powerfully helped by the teaching of experience. For this useful art is not of recent origin. The Arabs have carried it on, with regard to the improvement of the horse, from the most remote antiquity. In all ages the breeding of all domesticated animals has been the constant care of pastoral people, and Genesis has told us how Jacob overreached Laban in the production of many-colored sheep and goats.

During so many ages of study and experiment, it is certain that if man could have produced by artificial selection any new species of animals, the same would have been recorded in the annals of mankind; and that very species still existing in our day would be pointed out by everybody as the creation of man and not primarily of God. But it is notorious that from all those attempts at improving the breed of animals nothing has come out but varieties. Varieties, however, without number. For who could count those of the sheep, of the ox, of the horse, of the dog particularly?

Mr. Darwin knew this well, and, afraid that this alone might be fatal to his system, he strongly insisted on the divergences of opinion among naturalists with regard to the characters of species;

and thus introduced some confusion into the whole matter, as if it was really impossible in many cases to distinguish varieties from the original stock. But this was all in vain. Naturalists often differ, it is true, in stating theoretically how species in animals can be distinguished from varieties; but practically they all agree as to the ultimate result; and there are few indeed, if any, who would pretend that artificial selection has in fact introduced any new species into the animal kingdom. Not a single example of it could be stated by Mr. Darwin.

This point being considered as settled, there remains now to examine the next question; namely, If artificial selection has never produced a single new species of animals, could natural selection do it? The statement of the query carries with it its answer. There is no mind to direct natural selection; it is therefore blind and rests only on chance. The improvers of the breed of animals have likewise the benefit of chance, if there is any benefit to be derived from it. They have, besides, their own ingenuity, skill, reflection, coupled with the long experience of those who have preceded them. How is it that with all those advantages human practitioners have never succeeded in creating a single new species, whilst on the other side *all the species* in existence are the result of natural and sexual selection, at least in the system of Mr. Darwin? Only a simpleton can believe it. .

Time and space forbid us any longer discussion of this subject. There is, moreover, scarcely any need of it; since it seems now generally admitted that Mr. Darwin's explanation is perfectly inadequate to the production of the intended effect. Mr. A. R. Wallace himself, to whom the evolutionists' theory owes, it seems, its origin, is now confident that even in case natural selection had sufficed to account for the changes effected in animals, it does not explain the origin of the intellectual and moral faculties of man; and this is sufficient for our present purpose (see his "Contribution to the Theory of Natural Selection"). It has been also previously remarked that Mr. Peschel likewise refuses to admit the adequacy of such cause for the production of organic beings, and this seems to be now the general opinion of scientists.

But Mr. Darwin still insists; and he says that "in the struggle for life the fittest is sure to survive; and in that survival, owing to the law that organs of the greatest advantage must have always the preëminence, new species must be produced, and have been produced from the beginning." The reply is ready and calls for a rejoinder. If they have been produced to the extent which is claimed by Mr. Darwin, the same must continue in our age, and he is unable to show a single case in point except among the doubtful specimens of the vegetable kingdom, on which a sufficient explanation has already been given.

If a single fact of this nature was perfectly authenticated among animals, it would be the beginning of a show of evidence favorable to the new theory; but nothing more. Since the Darwinian pretension consists in claiming this origin for all the species in existence, it must be a universal process going on constantly in the universe, and a single isolated fact, which might be only a monstrosity, could not furnish a sufficient support for establishing a thesis of so extensive a nature. Still Mr. Darwin cannot offer us a single case except within the range of doubtful plants, none certainly among animals. Palæontology, moreover, would show it, if such had been the origin of the world; and this new branch of geology entirely disproves it. But this is by itself a vast subject which cannot be discussed here. Meanwhile it must be maintained that nothing has been proved, and the whole system ends in a mass of pure assertions.

But though evolution rests mainly on the mutability of species through natural selection, it is in itself a vast subject which must be discussed *in abstracto*. And it is good to remark at once that it cannot be proved, and thus becomes *in toto* a simple assertion. A very fatal want of proof is that the first link of its long chain of suppositions is an absurd hypothesis. *Matter has always existed:* this is the starting point. Most of the evolutionists, in order to give it a concrete nature, call it *protoplasm existing ab æterno*. They have no right to use such a word as this which supposes a design; namely, that of serving for the formation of other beings. Since in their opinion there was no Mind at first, protoplasm cannot be admitted. There are here consequently two absurdities: the supposition of eternal matter, which is inconceivable and repugnant to our mind, and the assertion that this primitive substance had an object, being a protoplasm, which is repugnant to the fundamental axiom of evolutionists, since it rejects design.

Out of this protoplasm the whole series of beings is evolved, each new substance coming strictly from the previous one in an unbroken succession. From inorganic substances, they pretend that there arose the first organized cells, and *life was born*. This is particularly the illogical assumption of Mr. Herbert Spencer, who thinks that the homogeneous can become heterogeneous through *differentiation*. This explanation is a mere jumble of words which can have no meaning. An inorganic being cannot produce life, and the living alone generate the living. How can sensible men be satisfied with these first steps of a theory which is announced as the only one acceptable to reason?

Once there is animal life, the rest follows without great difficulty, in the imagination of the evolutionists. Sensation, emotion, consciousness, memory, reason, and at last conscience or some sort of morality, are the spontaneous products from protoplasm through evolution, which at last culminates in man; until the irresistible progress of natural things will probably bring on some new being as superior to man as he is himself above common brutes.

All this, of course, is supposed to be derived from "unconscious and unthinking" forces, without any design, except at the end of the series: the designs, namely, of the hawk against the sparrow, of the sparrow against the worm, of the worm against the foliage of plants, to say nothing of the designs of man against all inferior creatures. This is called the struggle for life, which is said to promote natural selection, and thus generates the only order acknowledged in the universe; namely, that of nomenclature and authorized classification. We remember Mr. Darwin's axiom on this subject.

The reader is begged to believe that there is no exaggeration in all these statements. Condense or develop all the books of Mr. Darwin in order to obtain the pure substance of their products, and I do not believe you will extract anything else of importance. Inorganic beings are supposed to have existed at first without any cause whatever. The life of organized beings is supposed to have sprung up from mere matter. Yet there is an absolutely impassable gulf between both. The same is evidently the case between mere sensation and intellect, particularly because this last attribute is always coupled with a moral conscience. All these axioms of evolutionists are not only simple assertions, but they evidently are absolute impossibilities. Mr. Darwin thinks he has proved them by his natural and sexual selections. A selection, it must be remembered, not directed by mind, but the pure effect of chance, which is called here the struggle for life!

Again, this scheme intended to explain the world supposes no plan whatever, since there cannot be any with unthinking and unconscious forces. The whole, besides, is resumed in a single line of successive formation, and this goes directly against all the facts of creation which we all witness. Not only we see that there is a plan in nature, and consequently a directing Mind; but we cannot close our eyes to the fact that this Supreme and Spiritual Power has not chosen to dispose His creatures on a single line of evolution, though It might have done so. Several of these are visible in the exterior world. I think the naturalists distinguish five of them for animals alone. There may be a kind of evolution for each of them; but there is not evidently a single plan of development comprising the whole. To quote only an example, the *mammalia* and the *radiata* cannot be the result of the same plan. The whole of natural history could be unfolded here as against the system.

The fact is that Darwinism is totally unscientific. It unsettles all the principles of classification as well as of science itself. A book of natural history written and published according to the assumptions of the new system not only would not satisfy the claims of reason and logic, but could not even give any satisfactory account of the universe. It would be the best means of rendering the world incomprehensible, and of retarding the progress of science for centuries.

The strange delusion under which the author of the system evidently labors for reducing the world to a single line of formation has emboldened him to fall upon embryology as a strong proof in his favor; and he seems confident of success when he says, ("Descent of Man," i. 31): "The embryo of a man, dog, seal, bat, reptile, etc., can at first hardly be distinguished from each other." *Hardly* is a convenient expression, which he nevertheless would probably have preferred to replace by a simple *not*. The word *hardly* is sufficient, however, for the destruction of his system, since the smallest possible difference in the embryo contained in the egg suffices as a starting-point for a *different* evolution "in a man, seal, dog, reptile, bat, etc." But he is careful not to mention, though he must have been fully aware of it, that the study of embryology, which has been carried in France farther than anywhere else, has proved that the embryo in animals is not developed, in most cases, according to a single line of increase, but is in fact a stage of various transformations comparable to those of the larva, chrysalis, and winged insect in the butterfly. Very often, in fact, a natural development has nothing to do with those transformations which follow various plans assigned to them by the *Creator*, and are often disconnected from each other.

We are glad to have met almost unexpectedly this mighty word Creator, which brings us back to the question propounded a few pages back. Is it not more rational, as well as more simple, to explain the present world by a strict *creation* dependent on the will of an Infinite Power than leave its production to any atheistic system? Which of the two is more scientific than the other? This is the next thing to be examined.

Science is either the induction of well-ascertained facts going to prove some general principles: this is called *analysis*, that is, the scientific process from the known to the unknown. Or it is the deduction from well-settled principles, or evident axioms, to particular details involved in the premises: this is called *synthesis*, and was preferred by the ancients, who always liked best to start from generalities because their minds were more comprehensive than ours in their first grasp. But whichever scientific process is preferred, Darwinism must be condemned and rejected altogether from the field of science, in the matter of evolution. Synthesis—to begin with it as we like it best—is still followed in our day by all great mathematicians, who invarialy use its process to invent new theorems or to find out laws until their time unknown or not proved. Kepler, among many others, was a master in that magnificent branch of knowledge so fertile in splendid discoveries. We have always been unable to see why this admirable process has been called *mathematical analysis;* for thus all elements of mathematics call it. It would be, in our opinion, much more proper to design it as *mathematical synthesis*. But whatever may be thought of this, it cannot be denied that the usual process followed by modern scientists and naturalists has no point of contact with real synthesis; and Mr. Darwin, in particular, must be pronounced a thorough-going analyst. It would be, consequently, useless to examine his claim to science under this first aspect, of which he does not seem even to be aware. It remains only to inquire if he follows the strict rules of *analysis*, and can hope to reach truth scientifically by the way he applies those rules. The chief of them are, first, that the peculiar facts from which induction has to proceed should be well ascertained and exactly stated; second, that no bias should be given to those facts with the view of making them tell more than they do; third, that their list should be complete, and not opposed by other contrary facts; fourth and last, that no conclusion should be drawn more general than the facts themselves are in their complexity. With these rules analysis is a sure guide.

Now of all of them the first is the only one that Mr. Darwin follows strictly. He and his friend Mr. Huxley are most remarkable men for their painstaking labors in collecting facts of natural history. Their erudition in that line is most wonderful; and not only their followers admire them in that regard, but their opponents even gladly concede that it would be difficult to go farther in industry and care. Mr. Darwin, particularly, has thus obtained the admiration of many scientists opposed to his views. It seems it was for this reason that M. de Quatrefages endeavored to obtain his admission among the honorary and corresponding members of the Academy of Sciences in Paris. But this learned body twice refused, on account, no doubt, of the deficiencies of Mr. Darwin in other respects. Those deficiencies are so glaring, with regard to all the other rules of a strict analysis, that it is impossible to admit his claim to the name of scientist. Thus after having stated the facts accurately, he knows how to accommodate them unduly to the needs of his system. His work on the "Expression of the Emotions in Man and Animals" is an obvious example of it. He may prove in it that the *same* muscles are used by both to express their emotions; but he goes out of his strict province by giving to those emotions the *same* significance, as if they argued exactly the *same* inward principle, and as if the explosion of laughter, for instance, in a monkey and in a man expressed really the same inward feeling. But it is particularly the last rule which is constantly left aside by Mr. Darwin; and often from some very trifling facts, few in number, he concludes rashly, and draws consequences which would excite the smiles of a child as soon as he would understand the question.

Yet this farrago of conjectures, possibilities, unfounded assertions, and occasionally absolute absurdities, is pompously set forth as a system giving a rational and scientific explanation of the world far preferable to the supposition of its production by an Infinite Power. If, nevertheless, science is *a strict and rational deduction of clear consequences from well-ascertained principles*, the dogma of creation can be called perfectly scientific, whilst Darwinism is not. And it precisely falls out that, independently of Revelation and the Word of God contained in Holy Scripture, truth can be elicited most felicitously by both the *synthetic* and the *analytic* methods applied to this belief.

Synthetically first, for the world is a great synthesis where the name of God can be read everywhere. It is all comprised in the text of St. Paul:* *Invisibilia (Dei), a creatura mundi, per ea quæ facta sunt intellecta conspiciuntur.* "The invisible things of God, from the creation of the world, are clearly seen, being understood by the things that He made." God, therefore, manifested Himself by bringing the world into being. We see in it His immensity, omnipotence, justice, love, and providence, in spite of the opinion of a few pessimists. God alone explains rationally the world. Whoever does not suppose Him first can understand nothing of what we all *clearly see*. But as soon as He is acknowledged and adored the great book opened before our eyes speaks to our intellect, and unveils what was before hidden and mysterious. Man particularly, his relations to the universe and to its Author, are no more incomprehensible enigmas. Besides the material world, that part of it so superior to the first which includes the great principles of order, harmony, true beauty, moral feeling, conscience and its sanction, the duty of holiness, sanctity itself as reflected from the bosom of God on the heart of man—all those sublime things and many others become clear at once. Truly indeed our path is strewn with light and glory! The development of the universe as a divine synthesis would require pages of description, and we must hurry on.

The language of analysis is the same. When, satiated finally with a long-protracted look at the world as a whole, we come to pluck a flower on the way, play with a tame bird in an aviary, follow with our eyes a bright insect making its bed of the petals of a rose, it is still God that we perceive in the smallest objects after having admired Him in the infinity of space. But particularly when we analyze our feelings, aspirations, desires, noble aims and leanings, the process attains at once the height of

---

* Rom. i. 20.

demonstration. Our destiny is no more a problem; it is written with the sweetest characters in the deepest recesses of our soul. We know for certain that we have a father in heaven; an eternity of happiness is our blessed lot; and the conviction remains forever firm with us that we were born for immortality.

Is not this the language of reason, of true science, of natural intuition? Yet nothing is said here of the happy privilege of the Christian who relies, besides all this, on the very Word of God to strengthen his faith and hope. Let the reader compare this picture with the fair *exposé* that has been made of Darwinism. It would be useless to speak at length of the fourth and fifth articles of its scheme; those, namely, that regard the evolution of the moral order, and the long time the system must assume for its operations. A word must suffice. For the attempt of Mr. Darwin to account for the evolution of the moral order must be admitted to be an absolute and thorough failure by all those who have a true appreciation of scientific processes. It has been seen that Mr. Wallace himself was obliged to give up evolution in the case of man considered in his moral character; and there is nothing to add to the few words which were said on the subject.

5th. The immense period of time required by the system of strict evolution would not have called for a single remark of ours, had not its greatest advocate insidiously insinuated the idea that these "deep recesses of time" of which he speaks go in fact to an antecedent eternity. The fallacy of the supposition has been sufficiently exposed. The word *eternity* itself being incomprehensible, alone refutes the system.

4. *Man was created to the image and likeness of God.*

Mightier minds and nobler hearts than evolutionists' can be must now be heard speaking of man's creation. They will give us a far higher view of our race; and this alone would be sufficient to assure us that it is true as well as noble. Even since his fall man has preserved so many marks of his original grandeur that whatever lowers him in the scale of beings is repugnant to his nature. Mr. Darwin has felt it; and in his "Descent of Man" in the very book where he pretends to administer the proof that man is descended proximately from an *ape* and remotely from an *ascidian*, he imagines that we can still be proud of our origin, and he writes the following strange lines:* "We have given to man a pedigree of prodigious length, but not, it may be said, of noble quality. The world, it has often been remarked, appears as if it had been long preparing for the advent of man; and this in one sense is strictly true, for he owes his birth to a long line of progenitors. If any single link in this chain had never existed, man would not have been exactly what he now is. Unless we wilfully close our eyes, we may, with our present knowledge, approximately recognize our parentage; nor need we feel ashamed of it. The most humble organism is something much higher than the inorganic dust under our feet; and no one with an unbiassed mind can study any living creature, however humble, without being struck with enthusiasm at its marvellous structure and properties."

The writer of this paragraph evidently laughs at us. In his scheme any organism being the result of "unthinking and unconscious" forces cannot be nobler than mere *inorganic dust;* and to feel any "enthusiasm" for the structure and properties of any object, we must first be persuaded that it comes from an All-wise and All-good Creator. When this is denied, any disposition of matter, however striking and orderly in appearance, cannot excite any feeling of admiration, since it is the work of chance; and an "unthinking" simpleton alone can admire and praise it.

But if anybody is so easily satisfied as to be enraptured at the sight of an "humble organism," the sublime declarations of the highest Doctors of the Church, on the subject of our origin, are much more calculated to excite enthusiasm in our heart than the cold theories of all materialistic philosophers. And since those declarations are based on the testimony of Scripture, they are much better entitled to our respect and belief.

Genesis had first spoken of man's physical organization. He appeared after all the animals, and without any connection with their particular formation except that the ideal of his future bodily frame was evidently the pattern on which all those inferior beings had been previously modelled. For this reason the Fathers called him a *microcosm*. His body, however, was composed only of the inorganic elements of the earth; but the hand of God had raised it up to Himself and placed it in an erect position, so that

---

* Vol. i. p. 205.

at his first moment of existence man could look on God face to face, as Lactantius said; and the animals created for him had to revere him as their *god* who was to rule over them, since they were made for him.

This the Fathers have already told us. But when they speak of the creation of his soul, their language is far more sublime. Following Holy Scripture, they say that it came from the breathing of God Himself, and by this divine insufflation man's soul was "made to the image and likeness of his Creator."

Any one curious of knowing *in extenso* their doctrine on the subject will find the substance of it in Petavius' *Dogmata Theologica*. But there is a view of it entertained by many Fathers which requires of us a particular examination. They make in general a distinction between *imago* and *similitudo*. Man, they say, is the *image* of God in his spiritual nature, and he bears the *similitude* of God by the practice of supernatural virtue. Hence after his fall he is still the *image* of God, because he has not been deprived by it of his natural gifts; but being now a sinner he has lost the *similitude* of God, and does not enjoy any longer the supernatural gifts he had received at his creation.

It is most remarkable that Plato had received, from tradition probably, some insight of this noble truth; and he says in his *Laws* :* "The virtuous man is dear to God, because he *resembles* God; the depraved man is no more like unto God, but *dissimilar* and unjust." And better still in *Theætetos :* "To fly from sin is to *resemble* God as far as is allowed us; and this resemblance consists in being just, holy, and wise." It is precisely the doctrine of Christ, who commands us "to love our enemies that we may be *like* unto our heavenly Father."†

Man at his creation, therefore, bore the similitude of God, because his soul was adorned with all supernatural virtues. The Fathers are unanimous on the subject; and the doctrine of the Church has never varied as to the god-like *integrity* (as it is called) of the father of our race. Holiness was his first characteristic. This holiness, it is true, was lost by the Fall; but man can recover it by the grace of the Spirit; and it must be the object of his best efforts to conquer his passions and re-establish in his soul the reign of virtue, nay, of sanctity, the true similitude of God.

---

* Lib. iv. † Matth. v. 45.

Irenæus declares * " Whoever has lost the life of his soul (by sin) is reduced to animalism. . . . He possesses still the *image* of God impressed on the nature of man at his birth (*plasmate*), but he does not bear any longer the *similitude* of God, through the operation of the Spirit." " The sons of God," says St. Cyprian,† " must be so perfect as to show in their life a heavenly second birth. . . . The divine *similitude*, which Adam had lost by his sin, must shine in their actions and be manifested in their daily work. St. Ambrose, ‡ after having said that the *image* of God is reflected in the three faculties of the human soul, intellect, will, and memory, adds § that the *similitude* of God consists in justice and virtue, and " the more a man practises them the nearer he comes to God and the greater similitude he bears with Him."

It would be tedious to continue the enumeration of those texts. We would find only the repetition of the same thought more or less strongly impressed on the reader. But it is important to insist on a particular remark most appropriate to our present object. The various texts which have been just brought forward, and many others which could be added, give us of the primitive dignity of man a far higher idea than any of the previous passages, where there was question only of the physical condition of man and of his natural gifts. Yet this last view is in our day the only aspect of the question which is taken into consideration. When it has been established that man at his creation was placed far higher than any animal even of the highest grade, that he cannot be included in any order or class such as natural history discusses and sets in order, that his moral nature, independently of his supernatural gifts raises him up to a region above this earth, everything which appears to be required in the present state of our knowledge has been set forth; and if the same is proved, all the modern theories of the materialistic order crumble into dust and disappear. All this certainly is a great deal, and deserves to be insisted upon.

But the Fathers of the Church are not satisfied with raising man up to that region which is merely above our sublunary atmosphere. They must place him as far up as God himself, and represent him as reflecting in his supernatural endowments all the

---

* Lib. v., adv. hær. c. 6.   † De bono patientiæ.
‡ De dignitate condit. hom., c. 2.   § Ibid., cap, 3.

moral grandeur of Deity. He must be wise, virtuous, just, nay, perfect as the Heavenly Father; and through and by *virtue* he must be shown to be really God-like. This is to be examined with more attention, because it is the real foundation of the holiness of the Church; that is, of redeemed man; which is the precise object of this volume. The discussion must necessarily prove that Christian virtue, sanctity, is of a kind which is exalted as far up as the throne of God, so that natural morality remains far below.

And to begin at once, it is proper to ask, What is the most prominent characteristic in human destiny? What is the view we must first take of man? Is he to be appreciated only from his physical qualifications? or from his merely natural though spiritual endowments? For what end chiefly was he made? He was evidently made for God and eternity; and sanctity is the necessary condition for fulfilling this high destiny. Let us look at this with care. Man's aspirations cannot be satisfied short of an eternal companionship with God in heaven, which supposes primarily the most strict holiness on earth. Let us examine this more in detail.

To see in man the lineal descendant of lower beings, destined like them to perish entirely; to derive all his faculties from unthinking and unconscious forces, and place him, by the simple chance of natural selection and the struggle for life, at the head of a materialistic organization, is not only unwarranted by all we know of purely physical laws, and opposed to all the principles of science itself, but must be considered as a most abject doctrine which can find room in its tenets only for the lowest kind of morality. Its abettors, in spite of all their efforts to prove that they do not discard entirely human conscience, know well that its pretended origin from protoplasm through a blind evolution leaves it absolutely without a sanction, and cannot subject man to any moral responsibility. If their system were to prevail, human society could 'not be placed logically under the control of any law; and, the most violent passions remaining unbridled and unamenable to the sense of duty, the society of wild beasts would be preferable to that of man. It would be a kind of insult to keep the reader any longer on these considerations. Simple good sense must tell him that this first way of explaining human destiny is at once degrading and unwarranted by true science.

The second supposition is far above this first one, yet cannot satisfy our real aspirations. It is that of the pure deist, who recognizes the spiritual but not the supernatural order. It consists in admitting the mysterious but not miraculous creation of man by God Himself, and for a merely natural end. Man is made for happiness, but a happiness such as we can enjoy in this life, only in a higher degree. Eternal life is admitted, but of a purely natural order. The future life, if there is one, is merely the continuation of this, which comprises the totality of human aims and aspirations. No supernatural union of God with man can be imagined, as long as we remain in the domain of pure reason; and that of Revelation being discarded in this second system, we are neither the real *image* of God, nor destined to become *similar* with Him by the practice of supernatural virtue.

Still in this system there is room for a true, though limited, morality, accompanied with a real sanction in another world. That system of a holy life comprises all the principles of pure ethics imprinted in the heart of man by its Creator. It is what Mr. Lecky calls "the intuitive school of morals."

This view of human destiny is so far above the first that even Christians must admit that God might have been satisfied with it in creating man. It is not, therefore, absurd as the first. Nay, its conception gives of humankind an exalted idea, so far as the material world is concerned. For everything that was said by the Fathers on the physical creation of Adam according to Genesis, answers admirably to the mere theistic explanation. Man was placed at the head of the world to rule it; his position in the plan of creation is that of leader and master; alone he is endowed with an immortal soul, not destined to perish like the beasts of the field. The Latin pagan poets, except Lucretius, had received from tradition the deposit of those natural truths, and Ovid particularly has transmitted them to us in many beautiful lines. We find room only for the following quotation from I. Metamorph.:

> " Sanctius his animal, mentis que capacius altæ
> Deerat adhuc, et quod dominari in cætera posset ;
> Natus homo est."

This system, however, cannot fulfil the real aspirations of man, because it discards entirely Christianity; and man, such as God has really made him, cannot be supposed without Christ. Neither in history nor in anthropology, itself considered in all its bearings, can the human problem be solved without the dogma of the Incarnation. Not in history first : try to write the history of the earth without the God-man, either expected in the old world or actualized in modern times, and you will have an unaccountable narrative, leaving the universe without plan and object, because deprived of the only bond which can connect it with heaven. The plan of the deist in that regard is not positively degrading, but childish and altogether unable to satisfy human reason as enlightened by history. Christ in fact is the centre of all rational narratives giving a true account of humankind. These considerations could be extended indefinitely ; we leave them to the meditations of an enlightened reader.

But it is particularly when we consider the peculiar nature of each of us—namely, true anthropology—that the plan carried out in Revelation appears indispensable, rationally speaking. The deist admits that God is All-good, All-wise, All-provident ; yet man in his opinion has been left to himself, without any other guide than the feeble glimmer of his reason. He has to secure an eternal happiness in the next world, in which he tries his best to believe ; but he scarcely sees how he can do it, agitated as he is by strong passions all allied together to lead him astray. On many occasions the light of his conscience is at best obscure, and still he has no other guide to follow. His sad experience has taught him that he often fails in his duty, that he has frequently in his life gone openly against the most important commands of his God. He is awfully alive to the fact that he has been many times guilty of what he is bound to consider as sin, and even crime. Yet he cannot be certain of his forgiveness, even should he sincerely repent, because he has not received from Heaven any sure means of reconciliation. The bond between heaven and earth is totally broken in this system, because the God-man alone is that bond and the Deist refuses to acknowledge him. O God ! the more one reflects on it, the more it becomes clear that what is called the supernatural is absolutely necessary to the individual man, as well as to the whole race in the complexity of its annals. The natural order cannot suffice in the supposition of an All-good, All-wise, All-provident Creator ; and the cry of Isaias, repeated substantially by Plato, is after all the most natural cry of the human heart: "Oh, that thou wouldst rend the heavens and come down !"

Thus complete morality and holiness cannot belong to man in

the deistic system ; and consequently it does not fully unveil his real destiny, and the deist cannot appreciate his true dignity. It is in fact by his moral nature that man is primarily distinguished ; and his moral nature, in order to satisfy his aspirations, must be carried up to the height of holiness. Let us see this somewhat leisurely.

That we are made for eternity is a truth which cannot be even obscured by the materialistic systems invented from the time of Lucretius down to our own. The human conscience protests against them ; and as they do not explain our origin by their silly schemes, they cannot be supposed to give the least idea of our real destiny. To their senseless theories we proudly oppose the plan of Revelation as testified to in Scripture and authoritatively developed by the Fathers. It is the only one which renders a true account of the appearance of man on earth, unveils the end of his creation, and reveals his grandeur.

That the moral nature of man is the highest of his charactertics cannot create any difficulty for any one who reflects. Neither his physical endowments, nor his intellectual acumen, nor even his social qualities can compete with the high privilege he enjoys of having a conscience, and through it the means of a strict discrimination between moral good and evil. By this last alone he is totally distinguished from animals, who have certainly great physical qualities, a respectable share of sense, and often a highly developed sociability. But none of them have a conscience, none can be actuated by the sense of moral duty, none can be accountable to any tribunal but that of man on earth, their master and often their tyrant. Mr. Darwin, who in all the productions of his pen does his best to lower man, seems to be bent on doing still more to raise animals above their proper level. He does not shrink often from granting them real virtues or vices ; and the third chapter, on Moral Sense, in his "Descent of Man," is almost a serious attempt at confounding all the notions of virtue and duty by making them common to animals with man. At page 88 (Appletons' edit.), he is bold enough to say : "We hardly use the word *ought* in a metaphorical sense, when we say hounds ought to hunt, pointers to point, and retrievers to retrieve their game. If they fail thus to act, they fail in their duty and act wrongly." Many other expressions of the same kind in the same chapter indicate the deliberate intention of the author to grant to animals a true conscience, a real sense of duty, and the possession of a strict moral sense. But the attempt is too futile to be successful, and only the most infatuated among the strict evolutionists will consent to follow Mr. Darwin in this more than childish attempt. It will continue to remain perfectly certain that on earth moral sense belongs to man alone, and that all animals without exception are altogether deprived of it, whilst they share evidently to a remarkable extent in many other human qualifications.

This being evident, none of us can be surprised that Adam at his creation is represented by Catholic theology as endowed with a perfect moral integrity which impressed upon him the similitude of God, so that he alone on earth shared in the divine virtues of wisdom, justice, temperance, prudence, etc. And these were in him of a supernatural character, because they had been infused into his soul by the Creator when He impressed upon him His similitude.

To better understand this point, it is proper to remark with Bellarmine,* that "human nature consists of a body and a soul. By the first, man comes in contact with animals; by the second, he shares in the spiritual nature of angels. There is naturally a conflict between the inclinations of either; and if Adam had not received a peculiar help of a supernatural character, he would have naturally experienced the effects of that conflict, such as we all feel since the Fall. But the benevolent Creator, to show his peculiar love for man, gave him at the beginning more than his nature strictly required, and developed his moral sense to such a degree that the conflict between body and soul ceased, and the sensual appetite became altogether obedient to reason. This privilege was evidently supernatural, since it could not come from any of the *natural* prerogatives of man."

This was effected in Adam when he was created "to the likeness of God." By this he received much more than was contained in the material frame, by which he resembled mere animals, and even in the spiritual soul, by which he partook of the nature of angels. This supernatural favor continued to bless his existence as long as he remained obedient to the command of God; for he kept all the while his free will, and he could disobey—as he did in fact—though he never experienced any moral conflict. By his dis-

---

* " De Gratia Primi Hom.," cap. 5.

obedience he and his race were deprived only of this supernatural boon, and the integrity of nature was forever preserved for us. Whatever, therefore, the Church teaches of the dignity of man in the present state, it must be far inferior to what we can conceive belonged to it before the Fall.

The whole of it is comprised in a short phrase: "Holiness as derived from similitude with God." It is often expressed in a still shorter compass by calling it "original righteousness." A still greater light is thrown on the subject by St. Paul when he says * that "we are called by Christ to enjoy again that righteousness in which man had been first created." Thus the holiness to which we are invited by the Church is that of Adam at his creation. The same is repeated by the apostle.† The Council of Trent finally has made it a dogma of faith by its decree on original sin in its fifth session.

The consequence of this doctrine is that Adam in paradise was not only a just man but a holy man, owing to his similitude with God and through the operation of the Holy Spirit; and all Christians are called to the practice of the same supernatural virtues.

A long array of texts from the Fathers and mediæval Doctors could be quoted to prove that this belief in primitive righteousness, and in its restoration through Christ, has always been the Christian and Catholic doctrine. This, it is true, is ridiculed in our day as a dream, an utopia, a fable of the supposed golden age, etc. Man, in the opinion of nearly all modern writers, was at first a barbarian, nearly allied to the ape if he was not descended from it. As to virtue—not to speak of holiness—he first completely ignored it, and if he gradually came to acquire the lowest notions of it through a long moral evolution, it was only by strong efforts and severe studies that he reached at last the abstract idea of duty. Mr. Darwin in particular, in his "Descent of Man," derives all possible virtues from "social instincts," which, being common to animals with men, entitles the beasts of the field to a share in the strict notions of conscientious duty. And he glories in the fact, to use his own expression, that, "so far as he knows, no one has [before him] approached it" (the great question of moral sense) "exclusively from the side of natural history." A rational and reliable origin indeed!

We could remain satisfied with this simple exposition of the

---

* Eph. iv. † Col. iii.; also 1 Cor. xv.

two systems, and merely say that at least the believers in natural history must concede that the Catholic Church starts from a higher stand-point than they do.

But we cannot rest contented with this short method of pleading for the truth; and the question itself of the origin of virtue on earth must be briefly discussed on its own merits. For it is difficult to see with equanimity the name of virtue so much abused as to be openly granted to the brutes.

Have we retrograded so far in our backward progress that we do not understand any more that the idea of holiness is far anterior to the creation of the material world? To hear the strict evolutionists, it looks as if the knowledge of it did not exist before "hounds began to hunt, pointers to point, and retrievers to retrieve game." Have they not heard that pagan philosophers, and among them Plato, called all the notions of virtue "eternal ideas"? Where could the actual upholders of strict evolution discover when they were young men the notion they now have of it? In what books of wisdom could they find, even at that recent epoch, the simplest hint that virtue originated in a pack of hounds? In none certainly. They may boast that it is a discovery of their own. Though many Greek philosophers were atheists and materialists, they would not have dared to publish it in case it had come to their own mind. The precious truth that virtue came from heaven was still too fresh in the memory of men to be openly blasphemed in the name of philosophy. This was reserved for our own age, and for a generation of searchers after wisdom in the low regions where animals multiply, live, and perish.

There had been before them, however, ardent investigators of it who made it their delight to hunt after truth, pursue it with ardor, until they finally reached it, and captured it, but only to fall at its feet, and profess their imperishable devotion to it. What would they have said had they heard the pretended discoveries of this nineteenth century? They would have simply repeated to the new scientists the speech of the Egyptian priest to Solon, related by Herodotus: "O foolish babblers, you imagine that all men are like you, children, and that the annals of the world have not been faithfully kept by any people before. You prate about what you know not, and you pretend to be wise, when you are only prattling babes." Listen to the wisdom of the ancients:

From all eternity the only Omnipotent, Infinite, and Necessary

Being existed in the Immensity of its own Essence. To imagine that it was then the reign of emptiness is a thought worthy of him who is nothing but a "natural historian." There was in God as rich a wealth of Greatness, of Power, of Love, as there has ever been since He thought of creating the world. Exterior creation could add nothing substantial to what existed previously; since even human science shows that the addition of any number of finite terms does not change the sum total of an Infinite Series.

Still the Almighty had decreed to give existence to beings distinct from Himself. From that moment time began as an inferior image of eternity. The first works of His hands were pure spirits, because they were the nearest copies of His attributes. But after these He created matter which could not be in His design, but an instrument left to the use of other spiritual beings destined to form the uniting link between Himself and the material world.

Matter itself, moreover, was raised to the dignity of becoming an expression, however inferior, of His own attributes; since He remained always the Great Pan through whose power and by whose design and will would forever subsist and act whatever was created even in the material order. For this reason St. Paul wrote that *Invisibilia Dei per ea quæ creata sunt conspiciuntur.*

Thus we understand that the great *design* extended even to matter, which could not exist *ab æterno* and still sprung out of an "eternal idea" contained in God. When the moment came that the design should be realized, the solar or stellar dust (as the expression has it in modern books of astronomy) was ready to fill the space, and form its concentric rings and orbs revolving in the immense extent of creation. There were already seen in the vast expanse of the heavens His infinity, His power, His love, His beauty, when the stars, as Job said, sang in the morning of their existence a hymn to His greatness. To their song responded that of the angels created long before, who admired in the apparently illimitable space the little orb where the Son of God Himself, the Eternal Word, was to assume our flesh and consecrate matter by His hypostatic union with it.

If this was an "eternal idea" worthy of God, though its object was only an inferior substance, deprived of an inward energy, and productive of effect mainly through the activity of spiritual beings, is it not still more true that all immaterial attributes, such as virtue, holiness, power, love, existed primarily in the "eternal ideas" of God, and could only come from Him as the source of "all good gifts"? How can we conceive the idea of virtue and holiness springing up in the mind of angels or men except from a divine source?

The reader is aware that in speaking of "eternal ideas" in God, and referring them to Plato's doctrine, the intention is not to admit them in the sense of the founder of the Academy. It is known that he fell into a grave error in making of these ideas entities having a self-existence of their own and almost independent of God. When we speak of them, we mean merely the divine thoughts, and not anything distinguished from His essence. They were eternal because God Himself is eternal; and whatever He thinks cannot have begun in time. It is in fact His designing Mind that we suppose all along, and which cannot be imagined as absent whenever there is question of the world. To entirely separate the world from it is to introduce dualism, or what has been justly called Manicheism.

Virtue, holiness, was one of the most important of those "eternal ideas" of God. It is called even one of His attributes, and includes all that we can designate as supreme moral goodness. From the divine bosom a ray of its mild splendor fell on the heart of man at his creation, to bestow on him a conscience impressed with the sense of duty. Man alone, on earth, has received that inestimable boon; but all men, without exception, show that they are the possessors of it. Let a Christian missionary find himself alone in the midst of barbarians who until that moment had never looked on an European face, as soon as the man of God can understand them and be understood by them he will have unmistakable proofs that the moral law has been imprinted on their hearts. It is there, but came from God; and animals even of the highest order have been altogether denied this privilege. As free will has not been bestowed on them, they need no moral guidance, and are left to their instincts, which are never wrong. Man, on the contrary, owing to his freedom of choice between good and evil, is absolutely in want of a guide, and conscience is for him the voice of God by which he is repeatedly invited to follow the path of duty.

But there is still a step farther to go in order to fully understand the divine origin of virtue. As soon as the interior voice of conscience is heeded, and man of whatever race or country follows it, he is not only the happy possessor of a treasure on which he can constantly draw, but if he in fact draws on it and actually practises virtue, then all the Fathers of the Church use a strange expression which they profess to derive from the written word of God. They unanimously say that man has acquired some *similitude* with God; and that all that is needed to resemble Him in truth is to be in our own small measure and capacity what God is essentially and fully; namely, just, charitable, loving, chaste, having sin in horror and detestation, and shunning it as any one shuns the plague.

This admirable prerogative of resembling God as perfectly as our limited nature admits explains the word of Christ, as quoted at the head of this volume, which otherwise would be mysterious, or rather unintelligible: "Be ye perfect as your heavenly Father is perfect." By the practice of virtue man becomes like unto God; and by doing so constantly and adequately so far as he is able, he becomes perfect as God is, not in degree but in kind. This is the abstract of the Church's doctrine on the origin of holiness on earth, and the reader has already been carried to the bosom of God himself, and to the very depths, not of creation, but of eternity. Still we have so far considered only the first source of it, and we must pass on to considerations of a different nature having the same object in view.

CHAPTER II.

SECOND PRINCIPLE OF HOLINESS IN THE CHURCH: THE PRESERVATION OF THE DECALOGUE AS INTERPRETED BY CHRIST, AND ITS EXTENSION TO THE WHOLE HUMAN RACE.

1. *Necessity of the Written Precepts of the Decalogue.*

HOLINESS considered subjectively in man is the exact, nay, perfect conformity of his actions with the moral law. Morality, therefore, is the basis of holiness; and the first question to be considered regards its standard. We maintain that the Church alone places that standard in our hands, and the only compendium of the moral law which can be practically relied upon is contained in the Decalogue. The Church in the Old Law jealously kept it in the ark of the covenant, and has extended it in the New to the whole of mankind, after Christ had explained it more thoroughly than could be done in the old dispensation. This is the first stepping-stone of the Christian moralist.

The moral law is, no doubt, imprinted in our hearts, and this interior promulgation might strictly suffice for our guidance. Its inadequacy, however, must strongly come out in this chapter, on account of the hesitancies and positive errors which naturally follow when there is no other rule than what is called the "intuitive" teaching. It is important to look at this question with care, because many suppose in our day that mankind has scarcely been benefited by the text of the Ten Commandments, and that provided we look into our interior, we must immediately find a sure guide.

And, first, it would be a great error to suppose that the moral precepts followed during the first ages of human history (as was proved in *Gentilism*) came only from the inward consciousness of right and wrong. As this would have been insufficient in our fallen state, it is certain that the patriarchs received from heaven a true revelation embracing the rules of human action as well as of human belief—*credendorum et agendorum*. Outside even of the Hebrew patriarchs from Abraham down to Moses, the Zends afford a strong proof that this was the case for other races besides the Jewish. The Book of Job likewise is not Jewish but patriarchal. But in order not to rely on strong conjectures only like this of Zoroaster, we must come directly to the promulgation of the Ten Commandments as preserved in Exodus and Deuteronomy, and examine first if it were not proper—nay, necessary—that the great principles of the moral law should be written down and not confided solely to human tradition, supposing even its transmission from a previous revelation. This oral method of preserving among mankind the saving precepts imparted by God Himself to the fathers of the race had been mainly followed since Adam and Noe; and for this reason probably, in the time of Moses, moral corruption was already universal, whilst the world was a prey to the debasing doctrines of polytheism. Compare Palestine, for instance, in the days of Abraham with the same country at the epoch of the Exodus. All the details given in the Pentateuch of the promulgation of the Ten Commandments prove also that the Israelites themselves absolutely needed a written code. They would soon have become as debased morally as were the Chanaanites, had not the tables of the law been brought to them by Moses. And it was evidently in order that pure morality should be preserved at least among them that the Decalogue was made, as it were, their private property and privilege, though it contains simply the expression of the moral law binding on all mankind and imprinted on the hearts of all.

It is proper to look somewhat attentively at that great fact witnessed on Mount Sinai so many centuries before Pentecost, and compare it with this last effusion of the Spirit of God. In both it will be easy to perceive a never-failing source of holiness for nations gushing forth from high Heaven, either in the midst of thunder and lightning on Sinai or through the active energy of tongues of fire at Jerusalem; the second being merely a development of the first. Until the gathering of Israel in that arid desert in front of the rugged and burning mountain, the sons of Jacob had not yet been a nation. They were rather a family than a tribe when they entered Egypt; and during the greater part of their sojourn in the country of the Pharaos they had been groaning under oppression and servitude. Before occupying the territory allotted to them in Palestine they were to receive a national existence from a supernatural source; for Moses, their lawgiver, was only the mouth-piece of God. It is to be remarked that this birth of a nation, considering all its circumstances, foreshadows already their cosmopolitan character so striking to the eyes of any one who looks at them without a preconceived bias. As among them, and of their blood, was to be born "the Desired of all nations," so likewise, before His coming, their destiny was to raise in the midst of all the races of man in the ancient world the standard of virtue and holiness. It was not for themselves alone that the precepts of the law engraved by the finger of God were placed in the ark of the covenant, but for all the children of Adam groping so soon as this in moral darkness through the inextricable maze of error and corruption.

At the head of the written moral law was enjoined the majestic belief in the unity of God, because polytheism had been the source of immorality, as St. Paul so justly remarks in his Epistle to the Romans. Still this was called the *law of fear*, because man was yet a child susceptible chiefly of the stern discipline of admonitions and threats. The same law was to take a very different character on Pentecost day, when mankind, prepared for the restoration of all its birthrights, would be thenceforth treated with the affection due to God's sons and placed under the sweet yoke of the *law of love*.

It is important to listen first to the austere voice of Sinai and examine its main identity with the sermon of Christ on the Mount, which the gentle coming down of the Holy Ghost on Pentecost day was to imprint forever on the heart of man.

And, first, "law" is always a restraint on what is called "man's liberty." Consequently law, being distasteful to corrupt human nature, is unavoidably opposed by whomsoever dislikes even the semblance of a restraint. There can be, therefore, nothing surprising in the fact that the Ten Commandments, although so evidently necessary for the well-being of human society, have always found a violent opposition on the part of many men who have refused to admit a lawgiver of any kind over themselves. During many ages that bold opposition was displayed by open heretics, either Gnostics and Manicheans or, later on, Protestant sects which took avowedly the name of *Antinomians* (opposed to law.) In our day the same antagonism takes an apparently milder form, and consists simply in ignoring the Decalogue to substitute for it the "inner moral consciousness" of man; that is, the simple voice of the human conscience with its hesitation and perplexity. This is in fact a return to the previous destitute condition of our race, before the Ten Commandments were given on Mount Sinai. The modern rationalists, therefore, would bring back mankind to a period of four thousand years ago. There seems to be little fear at this day that the immoral theories of Gnosticism and Manicheism should revive, and even that the Antinomianism first preached by Luther, and afterwards violently opposed by him when he saw the consequences drawn from it by Agricola of Eisleben, should produce again the violent commotions so startling to the reader of the religious history of the sixteenth century.

But the supercilious ignoring of the law of God as promulgated by Moses is a much more insidious and deadly evil, deserving at least some observations on the threshold of our inquiry. It takes in our day a practical form whose consequences cannot but be baneful and even fatal. The complete severance in modern education between religious morality and instruction (so that apparently through fear of sectarianism everything bearing the least supernatural character is directly discarded) tends evidently to a total rejection of the morality of the Bible, under the plea of leaving it to family or Church training. Gradually and little by little the Decalogue's text becomes forgotten, and, worse still, the very children appear to be ashamed of it. It is time to point out briefly the plain consequences of this *anti-sectarian* system; and this is certainly the occasion of it. It is important to prove that the simple rehearsal of the Ten Commandments cannot be dispensed with in our day and replaced by the morality of the "intuitive school," as it is called; and that the Church is much more likely to establish among men the true principles of virtue by insisting on the course she has invariably pursued until this time, than in consenting to lay aside the "tables of the law" as they were brought down by Moses after forty days of communication with God on the summit of Sinai.

The solution of this question will be found in the nature of the human conscience, which it is first necessary to analyze thoroughly. Conscience is a most important attribute of our soul; depends on, or uses, all its other faculties without ever communicating to them any real share of itself. The intellect is used by it as a *substratum* to all its acts; still the human conscience does not impart to the intellect anything of its own moral character. The will in man is the peculiar instrument used by conscience in all its decisions, still the will can be imagined as independent from any moral idea; its essence consists in determination, fixedness of purpose; it is only its object which gives it a moral character. Conscience alone, therefore, constitutes the moral world in man. And since it is mainly by his moral nature that man is distinguished not only from the physical universe but also from all other organic beings subjected to our control, conscience may be said to be the first and foremost attribute of the soul. Particularly is it so because free will seems to be the most essential characteristic of our moral nature, and conscience is the only faculty which enlightens human free will and directs it to moral good.

It is in fact a light imparted to man by the Eternal Word, as St. John says at the beginning of his gospel: " Erat lux vera quæ illuminat omnem hominem venientem in hunc mundum." This seems to give a powerful strength to the theory of "the intuitive school," but we advocate only truth, and this is undoubtedly true. Qualifications, however, must come later on, to show the weak point in the "intuitive" doctrine.

And it is also in behalf of truth alone that we think proper to warn the reader against the mistake of many French philosophers who give the name of conscience to any reflex act of the human soul from the internal or external world on to itself. Thus they confound with it self-consciousness, which is totally different and has no part in morality. But the modern evolutionists, Mr. Darwin in particular, err much more egregiously still by confounding conscience with social instinct, and thus making it common to man and all animals, as was previously seen. Jean Jacques Rousseau, with all his errors, came much nearer to the truth when he called the human conscience *un instinct divin, juge du juste et de l'injuste.*

The Catholic moralists conclude from all this that it is the supreme rule of our moral actions, and that we must follow at all times the voice of our conscience, even when it happens to speak falsely. It looks indeed as if the moralist philosophers of "the intuitive school" had gained a decisive point in this discussion, and that after all the text of the Decalogue was not necessary.

Sed contra, as Thomas Aquinas would say; all these principles are firm and true when man is considered in his primitive integrity, but give rise to many difficulties since the Fall; and if even then man is bound to follow his conscience, he must help himself, for following the path of virtue, with exterior adjuncts which he necessarily requires for his safe guidance. The Fall has not only obscured the intellect and weakened the will; it has chiefly rendered the conscience irresolute, vacillating, and faltering. If left alone it cannot be called any longer a safe guide on all occasions. The tempter had deceived Eve by telling her that if she ate the forbidden fruit she would "know good and evil." What is the meaning of these pregnant words? Could she not, could not Adam, know evil without experiencing its fatal effects? What increase of knowledge did concupiscence bring to our first parents when it induced them to remain deaf to the voice of their conscience and to disobey God? St. Augustine examines several of those questions in his treatise, *De Genesi ad Litteram;* and their consideration is most important at this moment, for our present purpose.

He proves (book viii. c. 16) that man could understand what moral evil is before he had made the sad experience of it, merely by arguing from his knowledge of moral good and supposing the very contrary of what this is in itself. He brings on there a multitude of examples to show that this is the usual means of knowing many things of which we cannot judge by the consideration of their own nature. This negative knowledge of moral evil was the great thing required to secure an unbiassed conscience.

In a previous chapter (the fourteenth) Augustine had given what can be called the full analysis of the human conscience, without, however, naming it; and here it is proper to quote his text. "God," he says, "is the immutable Good. Man, considered in the nature he received at his creation, is good but not immutable. He acquires, nevertheless, a greater degree of unchangeableness by adhering to the immutable Good, loving and serving It by his own rational and free will. Consequently his nature is good in a high degree, precisely because he can adhere to the nature of the supreme Good. Should he refuse, he deprives himself of a great good, which is to him a great evil deserving a punishment on the part of the justice of God. It would be in fact very unjust to allow that man to go unpunished who has forsaken the cause of goodness. This cannot be. Sometimes, no doubt, the loss of it is not felt as long as a far inferior good is preferred and possessed. But the divine justice requires that he who willingly has lost what he ought to have loved comes to lose with grief the unworthy object of his love. And this is fair, because even that inferior object contains some degree of goodness. For unless there was something good left in fallen human nature man could not regret the loss of anything good."

In this admirable passage of the great Doctor of Hippo, substitute instead of *nature* and *man* the *human conscience*, and a flood of light is thrown on the subject under discussion. This is evidently his meaning: 'It would have been far preferable to man that his conscience should never have known evil except by its opposition to whatever is good, and never to have acquired that knowledge by a sad and positive experience.' And on this first part of the subject he brings on the fact of the Man Christ who remained obedient to the law of God without any experience of moral evil in his human nature. There was no room to quote that long but splendid paragraph.

Sinful man, however, is in a very different position from that of Christ. 'He keeps still his conscience in his fallen state and could adhere to God; but often he does not, and he prefers an inferior good, which becomes a great evil deserving of punishment. Conscience, nevertheless, is so much blinded by the enjoyment of the inferior good that it generally necessitates the loss of it to bring man to his senses, and win him over to the practice of the divine law.' The holy Doctor might have added that the denunciations and threats of the Decalogue were intended to open the eyes of man even before sinning and strengthen the voice of his conscience, too weak in his present state to guide him safely when passion—which St. Augustine calls the love of an inferior good—speaks to his heart. This shows the necessity of an exterior law.

In many cases, therefore, the admonition of conscience will not suffice, and must be supplemented by a more powerful voice; namely, that of God speaking from Sinai; and this is confirmed by all human experience. Before leaving this subject, however, a few words must be added to give a more thorough understanding of the office of that faculty of our soul, and grant to the philosophers of the "intuitive school" the full advantage of whatever they have a right to, but nothing more.

If we suppose a man naturally passionless, with a great development of a solid mind, and a positive disposition toward virtue, the teaching of the verbal decalogue might not be absolutely necessary for him, though no one can deny that it would not be altogether useless even in this case. But the number of persons is very small indeed to whom all those traits of character belong. The mass of mankind is precisely the reverse, full of passion, with a small mind, and a strong inclination to moral evil. For them conscience alone does not suffice.

Again, there is no doubt that remorse is an integrant part of the human conscience, and that those only have lost all susceptibility of remorse who have destroyed it by the most unblushing and constant practice of vice. We willingly admit that this is a powerful natural help to bring man back to the path of duty. Some one has said with justice, in French: "On éprouve souvent du remords pour des actions qui plaisaient avant qu'on les fît, qu'on approuvait en les faisant, et dont on a tiré profit après les avoir faites." "Man often experiences remorse for actions which pleased him before he consented to them, which he approved during the act itself, and of which he drew profit after they were done." But remorse is not retroactive, and when it takes place virtue has been lost and morality outraged. It cannot, consequently, be a guide, but only a warner.

The question, therefore, remains in all its strength: Can any philosopher of the "intuitive school" boast openly of his attempt at replacing the Decalogue by his theory which supposes man almost sinless and naturally good and holy, though descended either from a barbarian ancestor or from a mere animal of a lower species? This at least many of them pretend to be the case.

Listen first to the Law itself,* and judge what must be its effect on man:

"I am the Lord thy God. . . . Thou shalt not have strange gods before me. . . . Thou shalt not adore them nor serve them. I am the Lord thy God, mighty, jealous, visiting the iniquity of the fathers upon the children. . . . Thou shalt not take the name of the Lord thy God in vain. . . . Six days shalt thou labor. . . . But on the seventh day is the Sabbath of the Lord thy God: thou shalt do no work on it. . . .

"Honor thy father and thy mother. . . .

"Thou shalt not kill.

"Thou shalt not commit adultery.

"Thou shalt not steal.

"Thou shalt not bear false witness against thy neighbor.

"Thou shalt not covet thy neighbor's house; neither shalt thou desire his wife. . . ."

---

* Exod. xx. *passim*.

These precepts belong to the natural order, and every one can know them by only consulting the voice of his conscience. Still, in case he should do so without any bias, and entirely free from the disturbance of passion, had he no other means in his reach he never could clearly perceive the strictness of his obligation, did he not hear the solemn and majestic voice of Deity proclaiming them as His own injunctions. Without this formal proclamation many men might consider those precepts as being only the promptings of nature, over which man is after all more or less master. Virtue is lovable solely when passion is silent. It is not every one on earth who can persuade himself that these natural dicta always vindicate themselves when they are disobeyed; and even those who pretend they can do so may very seldom see in it a sufficient sanction for their observance. In fact, in this case the lawgiver is scarcely visible. Hence it is indubitable that for the great majority of men the threats of God are absolutely required for securing their perfect submission and obedience. Whoever removes from his sight the stupendous spectacle offered to the Hebrews from the heights of Sinai is in great danger of making a small account of the whole moral law.

And not only does it thus remain without a sufficient sanction; its meaning when left to the interpretation of every one becomes at once obscure and liable to perversion. Read in Mr. Lecky's "History of European Morals" the long array of opinions entertained by the most strict philosophers of the "intuitive school" on the foundation of virtue; that is, on the essence of moral principles. Since they so poorly agree on such a subject, it is manifest that practically the natural law is covered with a thick veil for the most acute eyes in point of mind and information. The Decalogue, on the contrary, was by the precise command of God deposited in the tabernacle, and entrusted to the priesthood as to its meaning and practical working, not left to private interpretation. It became eminently so in the new dispensation, and the Church of Christ alone was made the true interpreter of the divine law. Who can believe that humankind has gained nothing by this divine economy? What effect, on the contrary, has ever had in the world the moral teaching of Socrates; of Plato, his disciple; of Zeno; of Seneca; of Epictetus himself (though this last philosopher was already enlightened by the Christian doctrine), compared with the simple teaching of the catechism in the Church? Millions of children, of adult people among the rude and ignorant, to say nothing of the more refined in human society, have been brought to the practice of a holy life by adopting for their rule of conduct the simple text of the Decalogue.

A few concluding words are opportune here, before considering the Decalogue as explained by Christ in His Sermon on the Mount. It was brought down by Moses from Sinai, engraved on two tables of stone. The precepts regarding the worship of God are supposed to have been written on the first; and on the second those that concern man's relations to his fellow-men. The number itself of the Commandments is not the same for all interpreters. These differences are of little importance, and need not be discussed here. We suppose that there were ten, as it is the prevailing opinion; and that the three first filled the first table, the seven others being inscribed on the second. Many Catholic interpreters, however, think that the fourth precept, on the honor due to parents, accompanied on the first table the prescriptions which regarded the worship of God, because in the moral law the parents are the representatives of God himself with regard to their children. Enough of this. Considerations of a far higher importance wait for the reader.

2. *The Decalogue as explained by Christ.*

There are many passages of the gospels in which our Saviour gave some particular explanation of individual points of the Law; none, however, so forcible as are found in the Sermon on the Mount, which comes naturally in the line of the present inquiry. The sermon itself contains matter far superior to any article of the Decalogue understood in the highest meaning; and the beatitudes which form its introduction may be called the code of the purest spirituality and holiness. This will be the subject of further reflections. The evangelical counsels alone, to which the Ten Commandments have no reference, can explain this heavenly doctrine of the Saviour. With justice, consequently, Maldonatus in his admirable interpretation of this part of St. Matthew's gospel proves that the Apostles alone were present when the Saviour delivered this discourse. This was not for the ear of the multitude.

But many passages of the sermon allude to the Law of Moses, and it is to these alone that the present remarks must be confined. There is, however, a preliminary question on which a word only can be said. When our Lord declares that his disciples must follow a doctrine more strict than that of the scribes and Pharisees, and when he explains with a greater rigor what was said to "the men of old," does he intend to supply the deficiencies of the Law, or does he merely wish to correct the abuses introduced by "the traditions of men"? Maldonatus is strongly of the first opinion; and he seems to admit a striking difference between the precepts of Deuteronomy and those of the Gospel. Although far less rigid than Martin Becan, he appears to belong to the same school of exegesis. The question has been discussed in the first chapter of "The Church and the Gentile World," to which the reader is referred. It suffices here to remark that the celebrated Spanish author of the *Commentaria*, in spite of his just-mentioned opinion, sees in the Decalogue and generally in the Mosaic code a pure expression of the moral law and a strict introduction to that of the Gospel. In this he is far superior to Becan and comes very near to Suarez' opinion. In the seventeenth verse of the fifth chapter of St. Matthew, "Do not think that I am come to destroy the law or the prophets. I am not come to destroy, but to fulfil," Maldonatus distinguishes in the old dispensation four things; namely, the prophecies, the Ten Commandments, the ceremonial prescriptions, and the judicial enactments; and he proves that Christ fulfilled them all—*Christus omnia complevit*. In his opinion, therefore, the difference between the Law and the Gospel, though striking, does not touch any essential point.

Taking apart, however, the precepts of the Decalogue, which form the main object of this discussion, the reader must remember what was said in "The Church and the Gentile World" on the inner spirit of Jews and Christians. The reflections made on that occasion prove conclusively that the morality of the Old Law was really conducive to holiness, and that the precept of charity in particular was understood in the Mosaic code as it is by us under the new dispensation. To render this, nevertheless, clearer still, I find in Father H. J. Coleridge's "Sermon on the Mount" (chapter iv,) a remarkable passage which it will suffice to copy for the complete satisfaction of the reader.

"It must be remembered that the Mosaic law was not the first declaration of the will of God as Lawgiver to men, and that even its highest precepts were republications and fresh declarations of the natural law which had existed from the first, and to which the conscience of every man bore witness, whether he were aware or not of the formal promulgations of Mount Sinai. This natural law is unchangeable and everlasting; it requires the service of the heart as well as external obedience, and it did not derive its intrinsic authority from the declarations of the Decalogue. It aimed at making men holy, lovers and servers of God with all their hearts and minds and souls and strength. As far as the Mosaic law was nothing more than a fresh promulgation of the natural law, there could be no question at all of its being relaxed or destroyed by any new legislation. In this sense, therefore, our Lord's words are easily understood. No declaration, however perfect and sublime, as to the will of God or the duty of man could possibly be antagonistic to, or a destruction of, the Law and the Prophets, because the natural law, on which those last were founded, cannot possibly be changed.

"Nor, in the second place, could He possibly undo, though he might certainly fulfil and make perfect, the Law of Moses under that other aspect which we find often spoken of by St. Paul, as when he says that 'the Law is not set for a just man,' or that it was added 'because of transgressions;' that is, in order to brand sin as sin, and to threaten it with punishment in a matter which could not be mistaken or forgotten. For such is the advantage of a written over an unwritten law, of a law which is enshrined in positive enactments, and so made certain and unchangeable, placed in the view of all, and entrusted to definite tribunals and officers and sanctions for its enforcement and vindication. In a perfect state there would be no need for such a written law, because the interior principle of charity would be enough to guide men into all justice. But, in the actual state of mankind, the written and positive law which was given by Moses was one of the greatest blessings ever bestowed upon a nation, as is shown by a comparison of the state of the Jews at the time of our Lord with that of any other nation in the world, however elevated in character and advanced in civilization and mental culture."

This offers a clearer view of the doctrine previously developed.

There can be no question that even at this day, after the preaching of Christ, and under the law of grace, if the written precepts of the Decalogue came to be forgotten or set aside, mankind would soon be in danger of retrograding morally and returning to the state of all the pagan nations at the time of the coming of Christ; and that, consequently, the care taken by the Church to keep alive among men the text itself of the Ten Commandments, accompanied with her interpretation, is one of the most powerful means of preserving among men the purity of public and private morals.

This interpretation of the Church is the same that Christ gave, because the Church is the representative of Christ on earth and has received all His powers. The Sermon on the Mount does not give an exhaustive review of all the Christian moral precepts, and is not properly a theological treatise on the Decalogue; but the particular points examined in it give the key to the interpretation even of those which are not mentioned therein. The reader can consult on the subject, in particular, what Father Coleridge says on the sins of anger and of lust as adverted to in the discourse of the Saviour.

From all this it strictly follows that there is for the Christian, even before he reaches manhood, a strictness of moral precepts which cannot exist for any philosophers of the "intuitive school," and that it is a very sorry attempt on their part to ignore the Decalogue, as they do, and substitute in its place the inner consciousness of man. Christ knew better what were our needs; and by explaining the Mosaic law in His sermon, He has shown the importance of it for all time to come.

What renders this more palpable still is the facility which the text of Exodus or Deuteronomy gives to every one for *examining his conscience*. Men do not sufficiently reflect on this. On the very threshold of these considerations it has been remarked that although the intellect and the will in man have of themselves no moral character, still they are ancillary to the human conscience, which constitutes for us the whole moral world. The necessity of a strict examen of conscience, as a subjective foundation of individual virtue, carries with it, therefore, the use of the intellect and the will, and thus enables every one to obtain an exact and, it may be said, scientific knowledge of himself. This knowledge is the true source of wisdom, and becomes the beacon-light to direct us in the performance of duty. Now it can be maintained that it is not possible to find a surer and shorter way to it than to oblige man from the dawn of his reason to consider the precepts of the Decalogue as a rule of conduct in order to find out, through his intellect, his moral deficiencies and strengthen his will in the determination of correcting them; inspiring us first with a thorough detestation of them, and a firm determination to oppose all evil inclinations. This must carry the assent of a mere philosopher; the Christian knows that, besides this, he can rely on the grace of God, without which, as Christ said, man can do nothing: *Sine me nihil potestis facere.**

These reflections are strongly corroborated by the plain assertion

---

* John xv. 5.

of the Saviour in several passages of the Gospel. He not only said that he had not come to destroy the Law and the Prophets, but to fulfil them. He added on many occasions that the whole moral doctrine of the Law and the Prophets consisted in the love of God above all things, and in the love of the neighbor as ourselves. In saying so, He no doubt referred to the two tables of the Law, the first of which contained the precepts which concerned the worship and love of our Creator, whilst the second prescribed our chief duties toward our fellow-men. Who does not perceive that whenever a human being is solidly grounded in this theoretical system of morals, and in the practical application of those principles to human conduct, he becomes truly wise, and that should he continue during a number of years in a serious practice of this simple method he will become truly virtuous and find little difficulty in overcoming temptation?

This is the natural and daily result of what we Christians call the examen of our conscience, which the constant remembrance of the Decalogue renders of an easy accomplishment; whilst all those who forget it, discard it, and refuse to make use of it, soon find themselves groping in moral darkness, a prey to all base passions, contemptible in their own eyes, however they may pretend to be strict adherents to all the doctrines of the "intuitive school."

This becomes in a high degree striking to all "directors of souls" when they compare the various classes of children, both boys and girls, who apply to them for confession. Those who have received instruction from Christian teachers are in general wonderfully clear in the view they present of themselves, can analyze their feelings, describe their spiritual maladies, are anxious for the correction of their defects, and show a real appreciation of the beauty of virtue and the heinousness of vice, even in a tender age. The others, on the contrary, whose education has been entrusted to mere professors of secular learning, seem often to have no idea whatever of the moral world. Their conscience is a blank in which they cannot see any spot, inasmuch as nothing has yet been written upon it. Duty for them is often a mere word, and the love of God a nonentity. They give already all the signs of the most complete selfishness, and seem to be dead to anything above sense, to any moral consideration whatever. Will sensible people refuse to acknowledge that it would be greatly to their benefit if the threatening voice of Sinai could reach them and impress them with something of the fear of God, since they have been so far altogether out of the reach of His love?

3. *The Decalogue, as explained by the Saviour in his Sermon, was confirmed and consecrated on the Day of Pentecost.*

It is not sufficient for the Christian to consider the Decalogue as a strict but exterior moral code, promulgated with a solemn grandeur calculated to create a feeling of awe and fear. It would not even suffice to add to its prescriptions the explanations of the Saviour on the Mount, if they are viewed only as an *exterior* rule of conduct, though giving to the New dispensation a most remarkable superiority over the Old one. The reflections which have just been made were confined to the passages of the *Sermon* that have a reference to the precepts of the Old Law, and the question of the evangelical counsels was not even touched upon. There will be soon occasion to come back to it. But even should we, so early as this, enter into this most important discussion (which we do not intend to do as yet) and treat at once of the whole moral view of Christianity, embracing the way of common life and the way of perfection, we would have to take, apart from all this, the solemn *interior* promulgation of the law of love on the day of Pentecost. It gives a much stronger view of holiness which is altogether interior, and would be insufficient if it were confined to exterior duties and practices. It has been, moreover, promised, and for a Christian the majestic spectacle of Sinai must always be supplemented by the warm and strengthening radiance of the "tongues of fire" at Jerusalem.

The view generally taken of this solemn scene is faulty. It is supposed that the whole effect of it was confined to the Apostles. By the coming down of the Holy Ghost over them, it is said, they were changed into men full of courage and strength, able to conquer the world even by the shedding of their blood. This is very true, but not adequate. The only thing that can be maintained with regard to the Apostles is that the *immediate* effect of the "descent" of the Holy Spirit was confined to them. They alone had received from the Saviour the injunction to spend ten days in prayer as a preparation; and it is only on them, with the addition of the Blessed Virgin, however, that the "tongues of fire" rested. It would be a suppression of truth not to mention those circumstances. But is it not known from the Book of *Acts* that from that day forth the Holy Ghost descended also, sometimes visibly, on all the faithful as soon as they professed their belief, were baptized, and received confirmation from the Apostles? Was not the pouring out of the Holy Spirit over all, the great feature of those days in the primitive Church? A complete list of all the passages, not only of the *Acts* but likewise of the *Epistles* having more or less reference to it, would surprise perhaps any one who should peruse it.

The fact is that the scene of Pentecost was enacted for all Christians of that age and of the following ages to the end of time. It was the solemn act foretold long before by the Prophets, by which the Spirit of God was to take possession of the whole earth—*Spiritus Domini replevit orbem terrarum.* It was the Eternal, Divine, Overflowing Source of Holiness spreading its waters over the globe to purify and sanctify it. It was the universal promulgation of the *interior* law of love destined to replace forever that of fear promulgated on Mount Sinai.

To thoroughly understand this a few words on *law* and *grace* are absolutely necessary. St. Paul has been made by the Tübingen school the great antagonist of law and the great upholder of grace. St. Peter and St. James, on the other side, were, according to the same school of pretended theologians, strongly in favor of the first against the second. The truth is that those gentlemen have very incomplete notions of both, such as they have always been understood by Christians. Because St. Paul openly pronounced himself against the necessity of subjecting the converted gentiles to the observance of the old ceremonial law, of circumcision in particular, he is represented as entirely opposing the Mosaic code. Should any one ask if ever the Apostle of the gentiles stood up manfully for the entire suppression of the Decalogue, which was not only a part of that code but the very head and substance of it, it is to be hoped that the gentlemen of the Tübingen school would not pretend that such was *his* moral theology. Therefore he was not opposed to the law. Should any one ask, on the other side, if St. Peter and St. James at the council of Jerusalem did not declare that the gentiles should not be subjected to the ceremonial enactments of Moses' law, it is to be hoped that the majority of them would acknowledge it and not take refuge in the last shift of the boldest among them by denying the authority of the book of St. Luke. Therefore the majority of them must acknowledge that even St. Peter and St. James were not upholders of the law in the sense of the Tübingen school.

Why not, therefore, have the good sense to come back to the interpretation of these words *law* and *grace* as given by all theologians from the beginning? Law is a command promulgated by any legitimate authority, and binding all those subjected to its control. Grace is an interior help given by Almighty God to fallen man that he may be profitably able to observe His law. This law is called divine because it came from God, who gave it formerly to the Jews through Moses, and more recently to all men through Christ. It is particularly for the observance of this *divine* law that interior grace is necessary. The human lawgiver has not the power to confer it on those who are subject to his enactments. He is reduced to tell them: "I have jails and hangmen for the law-breakers."

Our actual view, therefore, is restricted to the divine laws, for the observance of which alone grace is bestowed on us from heaven. How stand both dispensations, the old and the new, with respect to the influence of God's grace? It is generally said, and it is true in many respects, that the old law did not give grace, which is abundantly provided in the new. It is certain, however, that the Jews were, to say the least, no more deprived of it than the pagans were; and it is, thank God, an article of our holy faith that no man has ever been left without some interior help from God. It might have happened, nevertheless, that the Jews could have received *interior* grace on many occasions without deriving it from their law, though it was divine, since, according to the common saying of the schools, the Mosaic law did not give it. We must, therefore, examine if there never was any grace for the Jews in their observance of the Mosaic law as such. The question has already been treated to some extent in "The Church and the Gentile World." It was proved there that "if the Mosaic rites, sacraments, and laws could not confer grace and justify *ex opere operato*, as the theologians say, they prescribed and made a strict obligation of many things to which justification was attached, so that this law was to the Jews the source of many spiritual blessings far superior to whatever the gentiles possessed." Owing, however, to many positive declarations of St. Paul, no Catholic can believe that the Mosaic law possessed and gave to the Jews any direct means of justification; and on this account the great event of Sinai bears no resemblance whatever to that of Pentecost. The dogma of the Trinity in God, if adumbrated in the Old Testament, was not sufficiently known to the Jews to become a basis of justification properly so called. There was for them a general hope of a Redeemer, but not sufficiently explained to establish a thorough confidence in His merits as a Saviour. Above all, the diffusion and influence of the Holy Ghost, not only through the whole universe but particularly in the heart of every human individual, was then absolutely unknown; and nothing of it could be said by

Moses when he came down from Sinai and promulgated the law is the people. Still in that very diffusion and influence of the Holy Spirit consists the inward working of grace. Consequently grace was altogether absent from the scene described with such pomp in the Pentateuch. Instead of a promise of help from above, we hear only threats of punishment. It is the rod that is to govern the Jewish world; and this is so much the more remarkable that the Holy Spirit —the Holy Breathing, in Hebrew—as a personality in God is everywhere spoken of in the Old Testament. The prophets announced His coming, His universal diffusion, with the greatest majesty and distinctness. But it was only a prediction, it was an immense future event that the whole earth would one day witness. Grace, therefore, was announced, but not given.

At Pentecost it predominates. St. Peter openly declared it in his first speech on that day: "This is that which was spoken of by the prophet Joel: and it shall come to pass in the last days, saith the Lord, I will pour out of My Spirit upon all flesh; and your sons and your daughters shall prophesy. . . . And it shall come to pass that whosoever shall call upon the name of the Lord shall be saved."

The Son of God had appeared before, clothed in our nature; and St. John afterwards declared that "the Word was made flesh and dwelt among us . . . full of grace and truth; . . . and of His fulness we all have received, and grace for grace." His coming, no doubt, sufficed to establish on earth the everlasting reign of that holy union and co-operation of God with man to which we give the name of grace. Still He wished to do more, and after His Last Supper, just before His passion, he said to His apostles: "I will ask the Father, and He shall give you another Paraclete, that He may abide with you forever. The Spirit of truth, whom the world cannot receive, because it seeth Him not, nor knoweth Him. But you shall know Him; because He shall abide with you and shall be in you." For reasons which we cannot know, the God-man was enjoined by His Father not to stay with us, but go to heaven and remain there till the last day. He said, however, that He *did not wish us to remain orphans*, so He would not only remain invisibly with us, but send us the Holy Ghost to govern His Church and establish *His tabernacle*, according to the strong expression of St. Paul, in the heart—nay, in the body—of each of us.

This immanency of God's presence began on Pentecost day, and gives to it a character altogether different from that of Sinai. The object of both days, however, was in some sense the same, namely, to promulgate the eternal law of God, on the first occasion exteriorly, and on the second inwardly. But even in this last contingency the former text of the law remained; only it was no more engraved on "tables of stone," but, as St. Paul says, "in the fleshy tables of our heart." This could not be done except by purifying and sanctifying it; and thus the text of the law which primitively promoted holiness but did not give it came at last to be impregnated with God's holy breathing which creates sanctity in us, as His first breathing on the body of Adam in paradise created his soul and made him a living, rational, God-like creature. In these few words we have the true analogy of the two Testaments.

Thus was the Decalogue not only confirmed, but also consecrated on the day of Pentecost; and it is proper to speak briefly of this consecration, which alone could establish the reign of sanctity on earth. It will be the best way to prove the existence of the supernatural order in point of morality, and to show the insufficiency of natural ethics.

The Mosaic law, by giving only an exterior promulgation and sanction to the eternal principles of right, had conferred an immense benefit on mankind, since its knowledge was not strictly confined to the Jewish people whom it governed, but it became gradually known to the surrounding nations, and finally through the dispersion of the Jews nearly to the whole earth. Nevertheless, as it was only a clearer enunciation of the natural law, history does not show that the nations learned from it and consequently followed in their life the principles of pure virtue. The process of moral degradation among them continued, on the contrary, without any perceptible change. But as soon as the order of grace was established at Pentecost a universal diffusion of holiness took place, which it will be our agreeable duty to describe in the Second Book of this volume. There must have been a profound reason for this difference; and by looking closely at it, it is easily perceived that it could not come but from a real consecration given on that day to the Decalogue which it did not possess before.

This consecration resulted from the effusion of the Holy Spirit, who thenceforth accompanied with His gifts the exterior promulgation of the moral law. Fallen man required interior help, and this could not come but from a supernatural source. This is admirably described in the Acts of the Apostles. Though the "impetuous wind," the "tongues of fire," the "single meaning" understood by spectators used to "various languages," were as many exterior phenomena speaking only to the senses, it was evident that the chief circumstance of the whole scene consisted in the presence of the Divine Spirit coming down from heaven to take possession of men's hearts, and to give to virtue the supernatural consecration of holiness.

Henceforth a virtuous act was not to be produced by man alone reduced to his natural faculties, and following his inward consciousness of right. God was to act with him, and bestow on him the moral strength he did not possess in his fallen state. He was thus truly redeemed, and that redemption was *interior*. A change would take place in his soul which would give it a higher degree of sanctity than he possessed even in the *integrity* of his first creation.

This was the great result accomplished on that day when the Church was solemnly founded and dedicated, as it were, in presence of the multitude. But to give of it a still clearer idea, it is important to add that at the same time the Mosaic law was replaced by the law of the Gospel, and the Decalogue was thereby sanctified and became the property of the whole human race through the Church. A word will suffice in conclusion. The immense superiority of the Gospel's precepts over those of Judaism strikes every one who compares them. It is, in particular, impossible not to acknowledge it when placing in juxtaposition Christian life in modern times and Jewish morality in former ages. The reader understands that by Christian life is meant here that which is truly inspired by the spirit of the Gospel.

But it is indubitable that the difference between both comes from this, that the Decalogue is not understood in the same way by the modern Christian as it was by the ancient Jew. The superiority of the one over the other comes evidently from the new impress given to the former Ten Commandments by the breathing of the Holy Spirit when He took possession at the same time of the earth itself and of the heart of redeemed man.

CHAPTER III.

THE CHURCH PROPOSES THE LIFE OF JESUS AS THE CHRISTIAN IDEAL. THIRD PRINCIPLE OF HOLINESS.

1. *Christ as Pattern of Sanctity.*

FROM the apostolic age, and throughout the following centuries, the Church has made a positive precept of the Saviour's imitation. All must partake of His inner life according to the degree of their calling. In the Sermon on the Mount Jesus Himself commands His disciples "to be perfect as their heavenly Father is perfect."* Both prescriptions agree, because of the identity of Christ with his Father. Thus are we invited to a holiness far superior to the morality simply derived from the precepts of the Decalogue. This, consequently, is of a much higher importance than anything contained in the previous considerations. It partakes, as Cornelius a Lapide remarks on this text, of the nature both of precepts and of counsels, as many passages of the Sermon on the Mount evidently do. A greater degree of attention, therefore, is required of the reader who must be brought to the consideration of a virtue which far transcends the order of nature, and cannot be even thought of by the mere philosopher. It will be, however, the most simple way to teach us why the Christian religion is called supernatural; and by knowing how far above the Mosaic law it must be placed, we will by the very fact understand that the purest morals derived only from "our inner consciousness" sink into insignificance when they are compared with the holiness to which the Christian is called.

St. Paul has spoken magnificently in many passages of his epistles of the necessity for all Christians to copy in their lives that of Christ, and to rise gradually to perfection, until they reach the age of spiritual manhood in that holy attempt to become like

---

* Matt. v. 48.

unto their model. In three of them particularly—namely, to the Galatians the Colossians, and the Ephesians—he has established the true characters of the sublime sanctity whereto the Church herself and her disciples are invited. The only difficulty is for our mind to reach the height of this doctrine, since the moral perfection of the God-man is the point aimed at, and according to St. Paul himself: "In him dwelleth all the fulness of the Godhead corporally."*

The details, however, given by the apostle of the gentiles prove that this is not only possible for man, but becomes easy, simple, and natural, if we may use this expression in a matter which belongs entirely to the supernatural order. This invitation to copy Christ, to aim at the perfection of Christ, is addressed sometimes to "babes;" that is, to new Christians, still weak in the faith, and walking with tottering steps in the path of a holy life. This results evidently from the wonderful expressions of St. Paul to the Galatians: "My little children, of whom I am in labor again until Christ be formed in you." The new disciples of Galatia had so little understood the doctrine of St. Paul when he had appeared and labored among them, though they were apparently full of enthusiasm and love for him, that many among them thought they were bound by the precepts of the Mosaic law, and they expressed the intention of submitting to the right of circumcision, as if the painful subduing of the passions through a sincere imitation of Christ did not now replace the obsolete Jewish rite, simply typical in its character. The apostle naturally felt a sort of indignation at the absurd construction they had given to his words, and he exclaimed: "O senseless Galatians, who hath bewitched you that you should not obey the truth?" Still, directly after, he addresses endearing terms of affection to them, and declares that he is engaged in giving them a new birth, "until Christ be formed in them." No language could be stronger to prove that Christ's life is the true pattern for the humblest and less intelligent disciples, as well as for the highest and most advanced in virtue. And there can be nothing surprising in this, since all, to whatever rank they belong in the Church, are *sons of God* through the Incarnation; and on this account they are bound to copy the perfection of their heavenly Father. This must appear incomprehensible to

---

* Col. ii. 9.

'men of the world, who, having no other standard of holiness than the "intuitive teaching of their inner consciousness," cannot but feel that there is too infinite an abyss between God and man, to be thus bridged over by the simple moral considerations addressed afterwards by the apostle to his "little children."* "The works of the flesh are manifest, which are fornication, uncleanness, immodesty, luxury. . . . But the fruit of the spirit is charity, joy, peace, patience, . . . modesty, continency, chastity. Against such there is no law. And they that are Christ's have crucified their flesh with its vices and concupiscences." This by the apostle is attributed to Christ's influence, derived consequently from heaven.

These prescriptions in fact, though so simple and plain, directly belong to the highest order, and raise the man who follows them to the very level of God, because Christ, who gave us the example of them all, possessed "the fulness of the Godhead corporally." Consequently, though the doctrine of the Incarnation is a deep mystery, it is nevertheless radiant with light, because it is the only way to fully understand and satisfy the highest, (which are also the simplest) aspirations of our nature; by which we are powerfully drawn toward whatever is above it. Let us see this more in detail.

The whole of it is comprised in the simple reflection that the "natural order" is limited to this world, but "our essential aims" cannot be satisfied with it; and to bring us up to a level such as they demand, a superior economy of means required the Incarnation of the Son of God, whom we are bound to imitate. This briefly developed will prove that the natural order in man must be supplemented by the supernatural, and will demonstrate the high degree of holiness to which we are called. This is to be briefly examined. The natural order cannot satisfy our aspirations, because *our heart is too great to be filled by it*. Those only who have succeeded in deadening their moral sense by a gross and sensual life can imagine the contrary. It is probably on this account that often man gives himself over to *unnatural* passions of which animals are never guilty. These passions are most degrading, but at the same time they attest the insatiable avidity of our souls, since man is often carried by them beyond all *natural* limits, and they show the extraordinary extent of its desires. The awful crime of suicide also might be given as another strong proof of the same truth. This

---

* Gal. iv. 19. *seq.*

must be admitted by all reflecting men, and the whole history of our race can be said to furnish its full demonstration. The insatiability of our nature is written in all the pages of mankind's annals.

At the same time that man is so great by his soul, he falls almost to the level of the brutes by his body. The union of both in a single personality is one of the most admirable works of the Creator; but it has been the source of untold evils owing to the disorder introduced into the human economy by the fall of our first parents. This, as was seen above, is the only way of explaining our present moral condition. Henceforth the soul instead of commanding often obeys, or rather submits to the slavery of the senses.

God through His infinite mercy decreed our reconciliation with Him; and as He had Himself created us, He wished also personally to work our redemption. This second great act on His part may be said to be as high above the first as our soul is above the material universe. To redeem man—in the supposition that man was to be redeemed—could not consist on the part of God in merely issuing a *decree*, as Calvin imagined; and then declaring that man, totally depraved (as he was and always *remained*) was nevertheless worthy of being called the son of God. This is the monstrous theology of the great patriarch of Presbyterianism. It has never been that of the Church. Man was to be redeemed in *fact* and not by imputation; and his *nature* was to be really restored to its primitive purity. What is called concupiscence was to remain because our soul's faculties had been weakened by sin; but *remedies* of concupiscence, as theologians say, were to be found, so as to restore the original harmony between man's soul and body. Man would thus be able to *practise* virtue, and would not *remain* depraved. For on this condition alone could he be readmitted unto God's friendship—nay, sonship.

A new father of the human race was necessary for this mighty purpose. For the race itself was to be *new*. Adam, who had lost for himself and his posterity the chief privileges of his first birth, could not be the head of a renewed race. Not only did he not deserve it; but he was justly condemned to "eat his bread at the sweat of his brow," to spend his long earthly career in mourning and tears. The infinite love of God the Father solved the problem by decreeing the incarnation of His Son. God had personally created the world and man; it was proper that personally He should redeem and renew both. The reason assigned for it by St. John, or rather Jesus Himself, is so resplendent with light, that a single phrase of the Gospel suffices to put an end to all the twaddle of infidels past, present, or future on the subject—"God has so loved the world that He gave His only begotten Son."

Christ, therefore, is the new head of our race. In Him the natural and supernatural orders are closely combined in the same person, because he is true Man and true God. By His union with us He has given us a title which we could not receive from the first Adam. We are called, and we are indeed, the adopted sons of God. Admitting this "adoption" can there be a single aspiration of our soul, however high and sublime, which will remain unfulfilled? These aspirations have been called "essential aims," and it was said that on account of them the natural order did not suffice any more, and that it must be supplemented by the supernatural. We need this most imperiously. Nothing in this world can altogether satisfy us, and we must look up to a higher one. This higher world Christ, in coming down from heaven, has in truth brought on earth, without, however, disturbing the natural order which he has assumed in His own person. We feel instinctively that our greatness as Christians is so inconceivable that nothing under God can entirely fill our hearts. Wealth, power, knowledge, everything we can conceive, leaves us positively empty as long as we have not the hope of heaven. But with that hope, the most wretched condition on earth is not only tolerable; it has been often preferred by many men to the most brilliant position that any one can covet. But if we examine well what it is that produces such a prodigious change in our estimation; that makes us, for instance, choose poverty rather than wealth in order to obtain heaven; that causes us consequently to give the preference to our heavenly aspirations over the earthly ones, we will find that it is *supernatural virtue*. Christ has brought it in His own person; He is our pattern by His example, and our helper by His grace, and thus the even balance of our being is restored between soul and body. The natural order remains, and we do not lose it, because Christ has assumed and purified it. But the supernatural prevails over it not only in our aspirations but practically in our deeds. Thus we become through Christ truly—nay, personally—virtuous, and as such we can be embraced again by Almighty God as His sons. This is the great result of the mystery of the Incarnation.

All this process goes on constantly in the Church under the inspiration and guidance of God's grace; but the view we must take of it here, as it was promised at the head of this section, is to consider particularly that Christ is the true and adequate pattern for his disciples, who find thus in His life a true source of holiness of so exalted a nature that the precepts of the Decalogue could not give us an idea of it. Being the God-man, He has adopted us as partners in His moral greatness; and remaining on earth we can soar up to heaven in practising the highest virtues. Not only the passions of the human heart are thus subdued, tamed, and purified; but by looking on Christ, our elder brother, we see in Him the model who "taking the form of a servant, being made in the likeness of men, ... humbled himself, becoming obedient unto death, even to the death of the cross." *

To embrace at once the whole of this imitation of the Saviour, it is evident from the Gospel's narrative that the admirable and perfect life of the God-man is most easy and simple to copy, either in childhood, when "He went down with His parents and came to Nazareth, and was subject to them;" † or during His youth when His own countrymen, the people of His town, would not believe in the reality of His wonderful deeds, exclaiming, "Is not this the carpenter, the son of Mary?" ‡ or even during His public career, when He appeared subject to all the laws which govern humanity, suffering from hunger and thirst, opposed by many, followed by a few, and these of the humblest sort; at all times reaching the highest self-sacrifice in the midst of the most common occurrences. This is the pattern proposed to all men, and which all men can evidently imitate. God shows His goodness in nature by covering the earth with blossoms and fruits, which all can admire and use. In the moral world He shows His love by rendering the path of sanctity accessible to all of us through Jesus, and thus strews over it attractiveness and charm. What can be more attractive than to copy the virtues of the Saviour, and what more charming than to look at the sweet effusion of His love?

And it is not only through a simple and easy imitation that the inner life of the disciple copies that of Christ, but chiefly through a divine influence, proceeding from the union of both in the reception of the sacraments. This powerful means of holiness is explained by St. Paul in his epistle to the Colossians, where he opens before

---

* Phil. ii. 7, 8.   † Luke ii. 51.   ‡ Mark vi. 3.

our eyes a new horizon which we regret not to be able to survey thoroughly, but only briefly and inadequately. Simple imitation, in fact, would be incompetent for the task, because it supposes man struggling with only his natural powers to attain an end far above them. How can man truly imitate God, when there is such a moral abyss between both? He can at best copy exteriorly whatever he sees has been practised by his model, the Divine Being manifested in the flesh. But the interior act of virtue resplendent in the soul of Christ, with its perfect disinterestedness, purity, and sublime aim because divine, cannot be imagined as being communicated to man by a simple act of imitation, because it far transcends the mightiest effort of the human will. A real union of that will with God must identify in us, as it were, both the divine and human natures. The Christian cannot understand holiness otherwise; for him it would not be real and substantial sanctity; although this is precisely what is incomprehensible to mere philosophy. It is proper to remark on this subject that Christianity from the beginning has fully taught to man the doctrine of grace, as it is called in theology. Yet, even since it has been explained so thoroughly by our great writers, the Fathers and Doctors of the Church, philosophical writers appear never to have had their eyes opened to the great truth, that in order to be truly holy we must be raised to a level far above any human scope; and this cannot take place without help from heaven and a real union with God which supposes the order of grace. This is true at least in our fallen state.

Christ alone, by uniting both natures in Himself, has rendered this possible; and so again it is owing to the Incarnation that true holiness is practicable. St. Paul knew it when he told the Colossians:* "Christ is the head of the body, the Church. He is the beginning, the first born from the dead; that in all things he may hold the primacy. Because in Him it has well pleased the Father that all fulness should dwell. And through Him to reconcile all things unto Himself, making peace through the blood of His cross. . . . And you, whereas you were some time alienated and enemies in mind, in evil works; yet now He hath reconciled. . . . to present you holy and unspotted and blameless before Him."

This, the apostle directly remarks, is a doctrine far above philosophy, whose aim is to *cheat* the Christian of his knowledge of and

---

* Col. i. 18.

union with Christ.* But he adds: "In Him dwelleth all the fulness of the Godhead corporally; and you are filled in Him who is the head. . . . And when you were dead in your sins, He hath quickened you together with Him in baptism, forgiving all your offences."

The divine reason of it he gives a little farther on † "Let no man seduce you" (through philosophy), "not holding the Head" (Christ Jesus) "from which the whole body" (the Church) "by joints and bands being supplied with nourishment, and firmly united together, groweth unto the increase of God."

These surprising words in their extreme condensation require for an ordinary reader, even a Christian, at least a short commentary, and nothing better, we think, can be adduced than the few words of Cornelius a Lapide which we translate: "As the vital force necessary in the body for life, sensation, and motion flows down from the head through the nerves and their ramifications, through the articulations of the limbs and all the physical organs, so as to communicate to all parts of the body the faculties of sensation and motion; so likewise the spirit of *grace*, as a divine force, flowing from Christ, the Head, into all the members of the mystic body—that is, all the faithful Christians (through the articulations of a mutual union and charity)—imparts to them all spiritual life and motion, so that the whole body of the Church increases in God, that is to say in faith and the spirit of God, according to the plainer text of the Peshito." If every word of this short commentary is well weighed, the doctrine will be sufficiently known.

This is still better explained by St. Paul in the third chapter of the same epistle where he speaks of the necessity for the Christian "of stripping himself of the old man with his deeds, and putting on the new." ‡

The new man here is Christ Himself, the second Adam, as the same apostle explains in some other part of his epistles. The Christian thereby is taught that in order to practise holiness he must be united to Christ, from whom alone true virtue must flow. Philosophy, therefore, is altogether incompetent to give us an adequate code of morals, and more incompetent still to bestow on us the moral strength required for the practice of true virtue. If the philosophers of the "intuitive school" refuse to admit this, they must at least confess that their doctrine can never reach on this subject the elevation

---

* Col. ii. 8. † Ib. 18, 19. ‡ Col. iii. 9, 10.

of that of Christianity. Virtue with them cannot be divine, cannot rest on an eternal foundation, is fluctuating with the mind of man, subject to the same errors and miseries, has consequently never found yet a uniform expression among them, leaves thus their disciples at the mercy of opinion, cannot support them efficiently in times of temptation and doubt, and cannot possibly act with the same power as does the conviction of the Christian, independently of its truth. How can any one pretend that the holiness prescribed and fostered by the Church is not greater than that of the worldly philosopher? Who can refuse to admit that the pattern offered by the Church in the life of the Lord Jesus Christ is unapproachable to mere philosophy? If rationalists could well understand and persuade themselves that the imitation of an irreproachable model must be accompanied by a divine help which we call grace, in order to produce fruits of substantial holiness, they would be far nearer the true system of human ethics than they are at present, or have ever been since philosophy was born.

This shall appear more evident still by considering a further explanation of the same sublime doctrine contained in the epistle of St. Paul to the Ephesians.* The new details this will place under our eyes shall bring us on to the consideration of the various degrees of Christian holiness; so as not to be satisfied with keeping the precepts of the law, but follow likewise the counsels of the Gospel. This will open for us a new prospect of higher questions.

2. *The Evangelical Counsels as Derived from the life of Christ Open a New and Higher Source of Holiness in the Church.*

So far the foundation of virtue has been considered only as resting on the precepts of the Decalogue, and on those prescriptions of the Sermon on the Mount which more strictly explain the text of the Mosaic law. The effects of the life of the Saviour, both as a model for imitation and a source of grace, has been also pointed out as the great treasure of holiness open to all Christians. To this free gift on the part of heaven all were invited; nay, all were declared as bound to use it. The epistle of St. Paul to the Ephesians opens a new view on the subject, by establishing gradations and distinctions among the followers of the Saviour.

---

* Chap. iv.

In order that those Christians who are called to a higher holiness might not fancy for themselves a proud superiority over their brethren, the apostle begins by declaring that in the Church there is "one body and one Spirit; . . . one Lord, one faith, one baptism; one God and Father of all, who is above all, and through all, and in us all." These last words are evidently an allusion to the influence of divine grace on all Christians indiscriminately by which they are all made partakers of the inner life of the God-man, or as St. Peter expressed it, somewhat differently, *divinæ consortes naturæ*, "partakers of the divine nature." It is impossible to conceive anything more sublime; and the highest rulers in the Church, even if penetrated with the deepest sense of their dignity, and supposing them worthy of it by their virtues, cannot but look with complacency on the humblest of their flock, admire the simplicity and purity of their lives, and rejoice that they are really the children of God, animated with the divine Spirit, and copying in their daily actions those of their Saviour and model. How could a prelate, a metropolitan, a pope, despise any of them as below himself, when he knows that they have the authority of St. Peter for firmly believing that they truly "partake of the divine nature"?

All, therefore, as St. Paul says,* must be "careful to keep the unity of the Spirit in the bond of peace." Still he declares immediately after † that to every one of us is given grace, according to the measure of the giving of Christ." In the following lines he enters into fuller details by saying that "He gave some [to be] apostles, and some prophets, and other some evangelists, and other some pastors and doctors ; for the perfecting of the saints, for the work of the ministry, for the edifying of the body of Christ; until we all meet into the unity of faith, and of the knowledge of the Son of God, unto a perfect man, unto the measure of the age of the fulness of Christ.",

In this passage there is a positive distinction made between Christians, which does not appear in the epistles to the Galatians and to the Colossians. And it is herein stated that it is based upon the fact that "to every one of us is given grace, according to the measure of the giving of Christ." The God-man, therefore, does not grant the same measure of grace to every one. To some more is afforded, to others less; but all belong to the same

---

* Col. iv. 3. † Ib. 7.

mystic body, and have "one Lord, one faith, one baptism." The question is to know what kind of grace that is; namely, if it is simply a gift embracing only exterior privileges, such as the power of ruling in the Church, of administering validly the sacraments, even of prophesying and performing miracles, such as the apostles had certainly received from Christ. This kind of privilege is called by theologians *gratia gratis data*, is compatible with the state of sin; and although it imposes on the recipient the duty of a holy life, it is separable from it, and it has too often happened that "the bestower of the gifts of God" to other men was at the same time the slave of Satan. It seems at first sight as if St. Paul spoke only of this; and the enumeration contained in the eleventh verse of the fourth chapter of this epistle refers certainly to the exterior offices of apostles, prophets, evangelists, pastors, and doctors. But must we admit that the other superior kind of grace, called by theologians *gratum faciens*, by which those offices are performed holily, so that "the bestower of the gifts of God" is God-like himself, and worthy of his ministry, is here excluded by St. Paul? By no means; and the whole text of the epistle to the Ephesians would protest against this supposition. From the first line to the last the apostle unveils the cardinal mystery of the Christian religion, which consists in the divine influence of the God-man on the whole Church and on each one of the faithful, in order that true holiness should be possible on earth. He speaks everywhere of holiness and of nothing else. He shows that philosophy could not give it; that Christ alone, the thrice-holy, is the true bestower of it, not only by the exterior example of His actions on earth, but above all by the communication of His own inner life to the Church in general and to each Christian in particular; and in the sixteenth verse of the same chapter he repeats in equivalent terms what he said to the Colossians on that sublime mystery of the oneness and holiness of the Church through Christ, as imparted to the members of His mystic body.

It is, therefore, but natural to understand of the second kind of grace mentioned above—*gratia gratum faciens*—what the writer had affirmed previously; namely, that "to every one is given grace, according to the measure of the giving of Christ." This evidently means that God does not bestow on every one the same degree of interior grace. Some are called to a higher perfection; others must be satisfied with a common degree of sanctity. Still all belong to the same body; all are holy according to the measure granted them; none can despise the other; all must be "careful to keep the unity of the Spirit in the bond of peace."

It is important, consequently, to examine in what precisely consists that distinction between Christians, and what kind of holiness it introduces on earth above what is common to all. The same must be derived from Christ, who is the only source and perfect model of sanctity. A few paragraphs back some particulars of His life have been mentioned, as being a mirror and pattern for all indiscrimately, in his childhood, youth, and manhood. Cannot a number of other peculiarities be found in the same God-like career which evidently were not intended to be copied by the majority of men, but only by a few comparatively of His most fervent disciples? Nothing is more easy and simple, especially for this reason, that the Church herself has pointed them out by her subsequent institutions, and the Church in doing so could not deceive us, since she is the Bride of Christ, invested with all His powers. We must here enter into some details which will be illustrated by several remarkable passages of the Sermon on the Mount.

The life of the Redeemer, as portrayed through the Gospel, is at the same time most simple and easy of imitation by all His disciples, and also offering the highest character of holiness, of most difficult performance, such as a God-like being alone could present. He certainly reached the most eminent perfection that a human being can be supposed to attain. Not only in all the actions of His life the least defect cannot be ever detected; but in all circumstances, even the most trying and sudden, His exterior acts, as well as whatever we can discover of His motives and purposes, disclose the utmost excellence our mind is able to appreciate. Nay, His whole life transcends whatever our human ability in point of discovery of character can even imagine, because we cannot go beyond the natural order, and the life of Christ must be admitted to be far superior to it.

Although it is important to illustrate this point by some details at least, there is scarcely any need of it when the appreciation of the true blessedness He promises by the very first words of His discourse on the Mount is considered. All these extraordinary blessings which he pronounces on the head of His disciples He exemplified first in His own person. It is impossible to give a more truthful picture of His whole life than is condensed by St.

Matthew in a few phrases. Does He not invite us to the very summit of moral perfection which He first practised Himself? He was truly poor in spirit, meek and humble, mourning and sorrowful, hungering and thirsting after justice, merciful, clean of heart, a peace-maker, and persecuted. If these are blessings, He was undoubtedly blessed above all other human beings; and all His disciples must, in their own degree of grace, aspire to be His imitators under all those respects. No one certainly will deny that the whole of this enumeration lies outside of the natural order, and that Christ by giving Himself as the pattern, and inviting all to follow Him, wished to establish on earth a society altogether different from any other society, and raised far above whatever is purely natural and earthly.

But did the Saviour impose on all the precept of practising virtue to the degree of perfection He reached Himself? Evidently no; there can be no difference of opinion on the subject. Did He require that all His disciples should practise it to the same degree of perfection among themselves? The text of St. Paul previously quoted proves that He did not.* It strictly follows that the perfection of the Beatitudes is not "of precept," since whatever has this character is of strict obligation for all men. Some theologians and able writers of our time think that all Christians are bound to the practice of the Beatitudes, which are, they say, the code of the New Law as the Decalogue was that of the Old Law, and the main reason they give of it is that the Sermon on the Mount contains the essential spirit of Christianity, as the precepts promulgated from Sinai embraced the substance of the Mosaic dispensation. Much could be said in opposition to this; one single remark will suffice here: The precepts of the Decalogue belong to the New as well as to the Old Law, and no real opposition can be supposed between them. That the Beatitudes breathe the sweetest aroma of the religion of Christ, and that no sincere disciple of the Saviour can be imagined as living in opposition to them; that, moreover, during the ages of faith, when the maxims of the Gospel prevailed generally, human society presented a near approach to the sublime realization of that sublime code, cannot be denied. This demonstrates the error of those who pretend that Christianity is opposed to the welfare of mankind and to human

---

* Eph. iv. 7.

nature itself. But all these remarks do not prove that the Saviour made it a duty on all His disciples to reach the same degree of perfection in the observance of that holy code. As He knew that all His followers, without exception, would fall back far behind Himself in the path which He was the first personally to pursue, so He allowed the plasticity of human nature, of which He was the author, to have its way; and St. Paul, inspired by Him, declared that "to every one of us is given grace, according to the measure of the giving of Christ."

Consequently Cornelius a Lapide is right when he states in his "Commentary on St. Matthew's Gospel" that in the Sermon on the Mount, particularly in the Beatitudes, "there are some things which are of precept," and others which are "of counsel." On this account he thought, as well as Maldonatus, that the apostles alone were present when He spoke on the Mount. At least He believed that the multitude was not present the whole time; but Jesus spoke *partim ad discipulos, partim ad turbam*, and we may suppose that to the apostles alone He unfolded what was to be "of counsel" in the Christian law.

At any rate it is certain that Christ practised all His life what we now call the evangelical "counsels" as well as "precepts," and that His apostles followed Him in both, each one according to his own degree of grace. The Church in her subsequent institutions consecrated the distinction between them. All theologians and canonists are agreed on this subject; and it is known, moreover, that they all condense the "counsels" of the Gospel into the three vows of religious poverty, chastity, and obedience. It is evident, besides, that those vows as explained by the Church, and practised by devout religious when they follow the rules laid down by their founders, realize in human life the sublime scheme of Christian society as portrayed by Christ Himself in the Beatitudes. For what is the essence of "religious" life in the Church if not poverty of spirit, meekness, mercy, mourning, thirst after justice, purity of heart, and readiness to suffer persecution? Read the history of religious orders, such as they have arisen successively in the various ages since the beginning; examine attentively all the circumstances of their origin, the divers objects they had in view, and the way they set at it; the terms of the approval they received from Popes and Councils and Bishops; everything, in fact, that went to form their first establishment; and it will not be difficult to find in all those particulars a realization of the entrancing picture presented to us by St. Matthew and St. Luke in the Beatitudes. Should any one object to the falling off of many of these orders from their primitive fervor, the sad degeneracy of the children from the fathers, gold turned into lead, and virtue unto corruption: this very picture of human frailty would but confirm the truth that they were in reality founded in order to give actuality and being to the Beatitudes preached by Christ. As soon as the spirit of their institution was forgotten their former blessed state disappeared; they did no more receive the approval of God and men. The Church had to labor earnestly to bring them back to their first fervor. She often employed for it reproaches, threats, censures; and the solicitude of Christian rulers did not rest until a *reformation* was accomplished.

We must, however, consider the *strict* practice of the evangelical counsels by our Lord, in order to understand something of the sublime holiness He brought on earth, and of the ever-flowing source of sanctity issuing from His sacred heart to fertilize and beautify the garden of His Church.

Of what kind of poverty do the Beatitudes speak? Interpreters may vary on the subject. But it cannot be difficult to understand the text accurately by considering the life of Christ. We all know that He was born poor, although descended from a long line of kings. The grotto of Bethlehem speaks eloquently to the Christian heart whenever the Christmas season recurs. Look on the Son of God Himself, wrapped up in rags and laid in a manger. Read in St. Luke's gospel all the details of that wonderful birth, and say how it was that angels came proclaiming "glory to God on high, and on earth peace to men of good will." This was the first glorification of poverty. There will henceforth be peace on earth, since the greatest cause of contestation has always been the acquisition of wealth. A God, born of an humble virgin, calls around His cradle shepherds and kings, that the first may not complain of the many needs which they cannot satisfy, nor the second refuse to their poorer brethren the superfluous gold they possess.

But see how firm was the purpose of our great Model to inspire men with the abhorrence of superfluity. He is a young man, and can direct His course in whatever channel He likes. Still He hides Himself in Nazareth, a mere village, and leads a poor life in the midst of poor people. Until He reaches manhood He will toil at a carpenter's bench, and He bows down willingly under the sentence pronounced on man at his fall: "Thou shalt eat thy bread at the sweat of thy brow." How can the poor complain at the sight of their Lord and God working like an humble artisan for the support of Himself and His mother? If that astonishing spectacle were better heeded how different would be the world in which we live in this age! We would not hear of those guilty conspiracies which now threaten the universal peace and portend ages of woe. The angels knew it when they proclaimed peace to men of good will; namely, to those who would strive to imitate the humility of their Saviour, and to no other.

But either in Bethlehem or at Nazareth Jesus preached the love of poverty to all men without exception. The immense majority of mankind is doomed to toil and labor. It will continue to be so to the end of time; and all the vain theories of modern thinkers and economists will never change this decree of Fate. On this account did Christ spend nearly the whole of His' life to preach by His example submission to an inexorable law. During the last three years and a half of it He became chiefly the pattern of those who would, in the course of ages, embrace the same kind of ministry as He did and become His apostles to the end of time. For them it must be a voluntary poverty, as it was for Him. It is no more the involuntary distress to which most men are condemned. Contemplate the strictness of it as He embraced it of His own free will, and say if it could be greater. He declared Himself that "the foxes have holes, and the birds of the air nests; but the Son of man hath not where to lay His head.* Always travelling on foot through towns and villages, reduced to live on alms, He would not carry Himself the purse which contained the humble sums of money absolutely necessary for His support and that of His apostles. He often suffered from hunger and thirst, and never used for His own needs the miraculous power He possessed by which He was once enabled to feed five thousand persons with a few loaves and fishes. This lasted strictly to the last day of His life, when a much more thorough poverty was exacted from Him by the will of His Father. All Christians must often deeply meditate on

---

* Luke ix. 58.

the complete destitution of the Saviour on the cross, when even His garments became by lot the property of His tormentors.

These few details would be sufficient to prove that the Beatitudes contain many things which are " of counsel," not "of precept." For although certainly, as was said, Christ intended in this simple code to give us a thorough idea of the spirit of His religion, and wished to exemplify it in His own person in all its strictness. Still no one can pretend that He made it a duty to all His disciples to do exactly as He had done, and to carry it to the same degree of perfection. His dearest friends, those who would endeavor to follow more closely in His footsteps, and embrace after Him an apostolic life, might also, like Francis of Assisium, proclaim holy and voluntary poverty their queen, and divest themselves of property of any kind; but the great bulk of Christians would follow the more ordinary road. For them the poverty of spirit preached in the Beatitudes would consist in being detached from this world although still encumbered with some of its wealth. They would be the providers of their poorer brethren; but in giving abundant alms they would bestow on others what belonged truly to themselves, and on that account would it be meritorious.

But the great truth advocated at this moment requires many more details from the life of Christ. It is proper, in a second place, to see how the Saviour became the model of His nearest followers by His voluntary obedience, as it has just been proved that He was by His voluntary poverty. He declared in so many words by the inspired pen of St. John that "He came down from heaven not to do His own will, but the will of Him that sent him."* Any one who reads the four gospels attentively cannot but be convinced that the God-man had truly resigned His human will into that of His Father. He always considered the prophecies which had announced His coming ages before, and minutely described the chief circumstances of His life as the expression of Heaven's will in His regard, and He was most careful to see that they were accomplished in His person, with all the peculiarities they contained. This is particularly true of His passion; and His very last word would suffice to prove it. The passage of St. John's gospel where it is narrated is most striking, and cannot offer any loophole for a

---

* John vi. 38.

difference of interpretation : "Jesus knowing that all things were now accomplished, that the scripture might be fulfilled, said : I thirst. Now there was a vessel set there full of vinegar ; and they, putting a sponge full of vinegar about hyssop, brought it to His mouth. Jesus therefore, when He had taken the vinegar, said: It is *consummated*. And bowing His head, He gave up the ghost." The passage of the Psalms in which this peculiarity of the passion of Christ is foretold is well known : " They gave me gall for my food, and in my thirst they gave me vinegar to drink." It is one of the less important details contained in the prophecies of the Old Testament. Still Christ would not die before He had accomplished it, because it was the will of His Father that He should.

Go through the Gospel narrative, and you will find only one occasion when the Redeemer appeared to hesitate a moment in His perfect submission to the will of Heaven. It was in the garden of Gethsemani when He exclaimed: "My Father, if it be possible, let this chalice pass from me." * St. Luke relates the same circumstance in equivalent terms. But that hesitation lasted but a moment, for He added directly, " nevertheless not as I will, but as Thou wilt." Catholics know well that in fact there was not the least irresolution in the will of Christ, and it was merely for our sake, and in order to be a perfect model against temptation on account of our want of determination, and of our hesitancies, that He voluntarily submitted to that momentary weakness; but this is not to be examined here, and the passage is quoted only because there can be no better proof of the thorough and constant obedience of the Incarnate Son of God to the will of His Father. But in another chapter of the gospel of St. John there is an expression of our Lord which renders it perfectly certain that during *all* His human life He had present to His mind the hand of God, as directing and leading Him from the height of heaven, to whose guidance He committed Himself unreservedly. It is found directly after the long conversation of Christ with the Samaritan woman, when the disciples, knowing that He was fatigued and must feel hunger, offered Him the food they had just brought from the city: " I have food to eat," He said, which you know not. The disciples therefore said one to another: Hath any man brought Him to eat? Jesus saith to them: My food is to do the will of Him

---

* Matth. xxvi. 39.

that sent me, that I may perfect His work." As man needs constantly food, and cannot spend a single day without it, so the Saviour needed always the guiding hand of His Father. This of course is understood of His human will, which alone He could submit to another's; but from these words it is evident that His obedience was always perfect, and this is most remarkable, for it does not appear to have been altogether necessary for the work of our redemption. We can suppose that Christ might have done in perfection the great thing for which He came, without surrendering His human will, which was always hypostatically united to the personality of the Eternal Word. Then He would have acted from His own human impulse; and this is more easily understood by our mind than the contrary supposition of a complete subjection in everything. Subjection in Christ is, in fact, a mystery which we have to explain by that of the Incarnation. It was for Him a work of supererogation, if we can use such a word in His regard. It was a real and profound act of humility on His part; and if we can understand it at all, it is as a consequence of the doctrine by which, according to St. Paul, "being in the form of God . . . He annihilated Himself, taking the form of a servant, being made in the likeness of men. . . . He humbled Himself, becoming obedient unto death, even to the death of the cross."*

Christ became thus the model of those who, being called to a higher perfection than ordinary Christians, resign their own will into that of their superiors, and consent to have no will of their own with regard to their position in life, their occupations, their place of dwelling, and the like. But this, again, is only "of counsel," not "of precept." Still it is evidently embraced in the blessing conferred on the "meek," which is the second of the Beatitudes. Meekness is opposed in a direct manner to pride, and nothing is more calculated to do away with it than the surrendering of one's will. There can be no pride possible in any one who constantly and absolutely does the will of another and not his own.

Finally, in a third place, the most unsullied chastity, resplendent in the life of the Saviour, becomes the beacon-light of those who feel an instinctive attraction towards an angelic purity rather than remain wedded to even innocent pleasures. The most cur-

---

* Phil. ii. 6. *seq.*

sory perusal of the Gospel impresses the reader with the soaring aloft of the Saviour over the world of sense, and every pure-minded man feels an innate repugnance to bring together even in imagination the idea of the God-man and that of sensual indulgence of any kind. It cannot, therefore, be the intention here to awaken, although remotely, any image bordering on the sensuous. It would be indeed sacrilegious to do so. But chastity is so attractive a virtue in itself, particularly when every contrary suggestion is sternly removed, that there is nothing so calculated to exalt the character of Christ as looking at Him in the perfection of His purity. What renders it more sublime and wonderful is the deep tenderness of His heart, the acuteness of His affection, the perfect sensibility of His whole being, closely united with the total absence of self-indulgence of any sort.

To prove this with entire satisfaction it would be necessary to unfold all the circumstances related in the Gospel when the Saviour ever came in contact with women; beginning by His most pure mother and ending by the penitent Magdalen, or better still by the suddenly converted adulteress rescued from a just condemnation without any wound inflicted on justice. A large volume could be composed on the subject, if all proper details were laid down; and it might be made one of the most interesting and instructive books ever written. How many entrancing pages could not be penned on the single fact related by St. Luke in his seventh chapter? It is indeed a strange spectacle to see Jesus reclining at table in the *triclinium* of a rich man, allowing a woman, *a sinner*, to come behind, to shed tears over His naked feet, to wash them with the flood running from her eyes, to wipe them with the long tresses of her hair, and anoint them with the perfume she has brought with her. The Pharisee is scandalized. It is the only circumstance of His life which ever excited suspicion. Nowhere else is it found that anything He did or allowed to be done to Him could give rise to the most remote doubt of the purity of His soul. But as soon as He condescends to answer to the foul thought of His accuser, who could refuse to admire in Him the transcendant height of the most sublime virtue? Not only this woman was no more a sinner, but she had already reached the summit of true divine love, far above the pretended holiness of the Pharisee. On this account only had the Saviour allowed her this surprising familiarity.

Read again in St. John's and St. Luke's gospels what preceded the resurrection of Lazarus, particularly the mention made by the first of these evangelists that "Jesus loved Martha, and her sister Mary, and Lazarus." Human affection, consequently, had entered His heart, or rather burned brightly in it, and never for a moment grew cold or turned into indifference. All the details given by St. John,* together with several circumstances mentioned by St. Luke,† show that the inclination of our Lord for the two sisters was not only most tender, but likewise discriminating and not equally balanced. He preferred Mary, and openly said so, but gave the reason for it: "Martha, Martha, thou art full of cares, and art troubled about many things. But one thing is necessary. Mary hath chosen the best part which shall not be taken away from her." In His affections what He looks to is the heart; the purity of the soul is the only thing that can move Him. No exterior excellence of any kind seems to attract His attention. No one will ever find in the Gospel any word, hint, allusion, of the Saviour having any reference to the world of sense in anything which excited His human feelings. Even in the surroundings of a happy and comfortable home like that of Lazarus, in the midst of its graceful inmates surrounded by many objects of taste if not of luxury, the reader will never find a word intimating that Jesus minded in the least the attractive world of art or physical beauty; although this also comes from Him as the primary source of the beautiful. Not only the slightest impropriety and the faintest approach to sinfulness cannot be even thought of; but what is purely of a worldly character, altogether indifferent to virtue or its opposite, cannot be brought in as a part of the scene, nor enter as the remotest element of the world in which Jesus moves. Though He lives on earth, His soul is always in heaven. Placed in front of Martha and Mary, or holding, if you like, both by the hand, it looks as if He could not perceive any object except what is spiritual and heavenly.

These considerations present themselves still with greater force, when meditating on another slight incident of the life of Christ, mentioned by St. John. It is certain that the Saviour after His resurrection appeared first to several holy women, among them to Mary Magdalen. They were commanded by Him to go and announce it to the apostles, chiefly to Peter. Thus our Lord

---

* Ch. xi. † Ch. x.

showed a real predilection for the female sex, even compared with His most intimate apostles. But in His apparition to Magdalen there is an expression on which interpreters, it is true, do not agree, yet which can very well be understood as strongly corroborative of the previous reflections. Mary had been looking into the empty sepulchre, and had been asked by the angels, whom she saw and mistook for ordinary men, why she was shedding tears. Turning round to go away, Jesus appeared to her without, however, unveiling Himself, so that she mistook Him for the gardener. It is only when He pronounced her name, "Mary," that her eyes were opened, and she rushed toward Him to prostrate herself and embrace His feet. But suddenly the Saviour checks her and forbids her to touch Him, as she had been wont to do before His resurrection. "Do not touch me," He says, "for I am not yet ascended to my Father." These expressions are certainly strange, and are understood quite differently by many Fathers. Justin Martyr's interpretation is to our mind one of the most sensible and probable, although Cornelius a Lapide discards it to introduce his own. The good Christian philosopher thought that by these words, which were the very first uttered to any disciple after His resurrection, Jesus wished to establish between Himself and His faithful friends during the following forty days a different mode of intercourse from the one He had admitted in His previous life. At that time He permitted them to remain with Him as long as they chose, and Mary Magdalen particularly during His public career was one of those holy women who followed Him everywhere. But during the forty days which were to elapse before His ascension he prescribed to their familiarity more narrow limits, in order to prepare them for a total separation after His final departure. He would thenceforth appear to them occasionally, but for a very little while each time; they could not follow Him during the short period that would elapse between His various apparitions. Thus Mary Magdalen could not be allowed to remain with Him and embrace His feet as formerly. *Noli me tangere.*

This interpretation is evidently extremely natural, and very probably true. It opens a long vista of most impressive considerations on the holy freedom our Lord allowed His apostles to take with Him, during His mortal life, not excluding the simple women who accompanied Him. But together with all this familiarity of intercourse, the infinite elevation of the Saviour over the world of sense looms up as the great feature of the intimate companionship between Jesus and His friends. He saw their souls and loved them; they admired His goodness and would have given their life for Him. Holy purity, such as it had never yet appeared on earth, spread its lustre as a divine halo around that little company of a few disciples which then formed the Church of Christ.

But the author of the "Commentaries on Holy Scripture," Cornelius a Lapide, finds fault chiefly with the interpretation of this passage by Justin Martyr, on account of the meaning he attaches to the words "I am not yet ascended to my Father," which are certainly explained by the Christian philosopher with less acumen than is usual with him, and for this reason we will not refer to them here with more detail. But what could prevent any one from interpreting them in quite a different manner, connected, however, much more strictly with what Justin had said so far? For instance, cannot the idea be proposed that the Saviour, in establishing between Himself and His apostles during the forty days previous to His ascension a mode of intercourse less familiar than the one usual before His passion, wished to induce them to submit to it willingly by announcing at the same time that He would act with more apparent affection after taking possession of heaven, and when He would, at the end of their lives, call them all to Himself? Who can imagine the intimate union of Christ in eternity with His saints: a union in which the body itself, spiritualized and almost divinized, as St. Paul describes so eloquently, will have its part as well as the soul? "Do not touch me, because I have not yet ascended into heaven." When this will happen, and I have brought you around me, then I will not prevent you from touching me, from embracing me; but as, during the remainder of your lives, you will not be able to enjoy that privilege after my final departure from you, it is better you should be weaned gradually from it, as long as I remain still on earth and appear occasionally among you.

This interpretation is offered for what it is worth in the opinion of any Christian reader. But the reflections that have been so far insinuated on this subject, independently of many more which could be suggested by other passages of the gospels, give to Jesus' character a transcendent lustre of purity. He came to establish it on earth among His disciples of every degree. The greatest number of them would follow an ordinary path and enter the bonds of marriage. No one can refuse to admit that the inflexible laws which He established, particularly in His Sermon on the Mount, with regard to the marriage state could never have been imagined by any human lawgiver before Him, and that as to the Jews themselves, though living under a divine code, His new doctrine made a profound alteration in their ideas. He brought at once the first element of human society—namely, the family—to the ideal standard of elevation so remarkable in Christian society; raised woman from her previous degradation, and placed her hand into that of man; gave henceforth to the general intercourse between both sexes that varnish of purity, simplicity, and taste which has always distinguished the Christian nations; and from that time forward, good breeding alone obliged the vicious among men to cover at least their foul thoughts under the appearance of innocence and courtesy.

But Christ did much more. He preached perfect celibacy by His own example, and by some very clear expressions which the Gospel contains. We would here refer the reader to a passage of St. Matthew which can have but one meaning, and clearly proves that our Saviour wished that a certain number of His disciples at least should endeavor to imitate, after Him, the angels in their purity. It is needless to repeat that this could not be made a precept for all, and was consequently to remain an "evangelical counsel."

This has been invariably, likewise, the doctrine of the Church, and it has become for her a principle, an axiom, on which she has never varied, and which suffices alone to give her a pre-eminence of holiness over any other earthly institution. When we come to consider the facts which her whole history displays, we may be able to prove that her principles are not utopias and theories only, but have in fact been, and are every day, reduced into practice. Meanwhile we must consider this new system of ethics introducing among men the idea of moral perfection, altogether unknown before Christ. Moral perfection, in fact, is the whole aim and scope of the evangelical counsels.

---

xix. 12.

CHAPTER IV.

CATHOLIC DOCTRINE ON THE MORAL AND INDEFINITE PERFECTIBILITY OF MAN—AIMING AT PERFECTION—FOURTH PRINCIPLE OF HOLINESS IN THE CHURCH.

1. *Unreliable Systems on Human Perfectibility.*

DURING the last hundred years many theories have been advanced on the perfectibility of man, but not in the Christian sense. There was first the attempt made to prove that the human mind had constantly progressed since the time of primitive and universal barbarism; and the conclusion was drawn that it would continue to progress until it reached perfection. Man henceforth being thoroughly civilized, enlightened, intelligent, and wise, nature would be entirely subdued by him, and human society would offer the spectacle of perfect harmony and peace. The most ardent advocate of this opinion was, in France, the Marquis de Condorcet, and he developed his ideas in his *Essai d'un tableau historique des progrès de l'esprit humain.* It was written after his proscription by the Convention, on account of his being a Girondin, and during a concealment of nine months in the house of a friend. France was then rapidly going back to barbarism, and the horrors so well described by M. Ternaux and M. Taine were daily spreading dismay all over the world. Still the Marquis de Condorcet continued hoping against hope. He could dream of a continuous social and mental progress, whilst he had under his eyes the spectacle of universal disorganization and ruin. He was still under the spell of a rose-colored vision, such as had before him guided the pen of a Voltaire and a Turgot. Had they both lived to see what Condorcet witnessed, they would most probably have modified their ideas and ceased to expatiate on the constantly increasing happiness and knowledge of mankind, precisely when faith was weakened or, better still, totally destroyed. The Marquis de Condorcet was too much wedded to his anti-Christian fanaticism to confess his error under the iron rule which then oppressed France. He persevered in it even to the last day of his life, when he took poison to escape the guillotine. The apostles of unbelief often have a faith far more unreasonable and obstinate than the Christians, to whom both epithets are applied in spite of many proofs to the contrary.

That the amount of our knowledge increases with time is undoubtedly true. That our mind itself becomes day by day, or rather century by century, stronger is as certainly false. If human progress, as understood by Condorcet, is absolutely true, no greater and stronger minds could have existed, say, three thousand years ago than are known in our age; and at the present period the average human mind would be far above that of primitive times. But the reverse is precisely the fact. To quote only a few instances, sufficient for our purpose: In philosophy, was not the mind of Aristotle far greater and stronger than that of Emanuel Kant? In medicine, was not Hippocrates a greater man than any practising physician of our day? In poetry, was not Job, independently of his inspiration, far superior to any poet of our age, taken in any country you choose? In architecture, were not the builders of the pyramids above the greatest architects of the present age? In art—that is, painting, sculpture, and ornamental work—did not the ancient Greeks perform wonders which the best artists of our age cannot so much as imitate? In fertility of invention, were not the discovery of writing, of working in metals, of music, vocal and instrumental, of solving intricate problems in geometry and arithmetic, on a par at least with the most wonderful discoveries of the present day? The enumeration and comparison might be made much longer.

With regard to *fertility of invention*, antiquity does not appear at first sight as being far superior to modern times, owing to the innumerable little conveniences which have been lately added to our stock of knowledge, and which certainly increase considerably our comfort. But when one reflects that in antiquity man had to discover everything by the strength of his own mind, that he knew scarcely anything to start from, whilst in our day the knowledge previously acquired serves as a point of vantage to advance constantly further; when, moreover, the remark is made that every new invention comes naturally as a consequence from the anterior ones, it is seen at a glance that in this last case it is not so much a strong mind that is required as a keen sense of observation, helped by innumerable and almost perfect instruments. But the actual question is to compare the *mind* of primitive man with our own, and not the facility we possess of progressing farther.

We feel instinctively that our intellect is not growing and developing itself from an innate power of evolution; but that it has come from God with all its faculties and all its native energy. It is not, therefore, surprising that it was as strong at least at the beginning as at the present moment. The impression made upon us by the examples quoted a moment ago, would even make us believe that it was then stronger. But this comes merely from the fact that in ancient times man was less preoccupied than he is now by a thousand cares and thoughts, which fill our days with distracting objects almost without number. It is nevertheless false to say that the human mind has materially progressed in its essence. We know that every human soul is created immediately by the Almighty; and if soul differs from soul according as God thinks proper to create them, still at all the epochs of man's history we find that great minds have suddenly appeared: more of them formerly than to-day.

It has been said also that the average human intellect was stronger in ancient times. This is evident to every one who reads attentively what is recorded of ancient nations, as nations, either in the interior of Asia and Africa, compared with those who live in the same continents in our time, or even in Europe, where the phenomenon is not so striking owing to causes which cannot be enumerated at the present moment. Was not the Pelasgic mind stronger than the Hellenic? Did not the Celtic nations show more mental power at the beginning, when they covered a great part of Europe, than they did later on, when their spread became contracted and opposed by surrounding tribes? The same may be said of all ancient races, and has been sufficiently proved in *Gentilism*.

The foundation of Condorcet's theory on the perfectibility of man is thus unable to stand; and the writers best inclined toward him admit that his *Essai* is devoid of criticism and erudition. They try to excuse this fatal defect in a subject which requires both by the circumstances in which he wrote, being then proscribed and in concealment, deprived of books and references of any kind. But, even so, the best that can be said in his favor is that his theory is not, but might have been proved in different circumstances. The attempt at doing so has not been renewed by any writer that we know, although Condorcet's thesis is generally supposed to be true, and is for a great number of men a demonstrated axiom. It is maintained by them that the mind of man is better developed and stronger than formerly; that society is laid consequently on better foundations; that the happiness of the greater number is better attended to and realized; that man by rising constantly by his own innate efforts will surely reach a very high degree of perfection and self-control, etc. etc. To whomsoever reflects on the subject this seems to be a bitter irony contradicted by all the facts we witness. We can safely leave the conclusion to the reader.

Another system on the perfectibility of man has arisen in this century which requires only a passing notice. Man's *moral* nature is undoubtedly supposed by the originators of the scheme to be advancing and ameliorating; but they seem to attach more importance to the *physical* progress and well-being of man. It all resolves itself into the doctrine of evolution which has been briefly commented upon in a previous chapter. The delusion has been sufficiently exposed, and we cannot come back to it *ex professo*. There has been no more *physical* than *mental* continuous progress for mankind. The men we read of in primitive history were as active, energetic, and powerful as men are to-day, if they were not even more athletic, more strongly constituted, and longer-lived than the average men of our age. In spite of all the prehistoric discoveries, which must at best be regarded as conflicting, unreliable, and local, the records of Holy Scripture have not been contradicted, and cannot be. Innumerable discoveries, besides, are being made every day, confirming powerfully the most marvellous assertions of our Bible. So that it is not true that man has been gradually evolved in body from a low-built barbarian, if not from an ape, to the stature and form he assumes under our eyes—a puny being indeed!—and that he can hope to rise still much higher—how much higher!—in the scale of organized beings. Among these, they say, he has reached at last the first rank in creation after millions of years of a successful struggle for life, and after the innumerable physical and organic combinations he has successively entered into through natural and sexual selection. This dream of Mr. Darwin and his followers is still less substantial and less likely to be true than the previous one of Condorcet; and since we have to propose to the consideration of the reader a scheme of human perfectibility far preferable to any other, we must hasten on to its exposition and elaboration, leaving behind all those fanciful opinions.

2. *The True Theory of the Moral Perfectibility of Man.*

It is pointedly expressed by our Lord in the following phrase: "*Be ye perfect, as also your heavenly Father is perfect.*" * By exhorting man to perfection, Jesus Christ intimates that *perfection* is possible for him. It is evident, however, that the last part of the proposition, "*as also your,*" etc., means *on the model of*, etc., the Saviour could not intend to excite in us the hope of ever reaching the moral height of the Godhead. All that the most ardent of His disciples can expect is to be able to rise gradually and constantly along the straight line of holiness, whose last term is God Himself, who remains meanwhile at an infinite distance from the most perfect of His creatures.

Was this exhortation addressed to all, or only to the chosen few who are called on to follow the evangelical counsels, as explained in the last chapter? If the Sermon on the Mount, in which the text under consideration is found, was addressed to the apostles only, as Maldonatus and Cornelius a Lapide think, then the second supposition may be true. Another passage of the Gospel might be brought forward in support of this opinion. A young man having said to Jesus that he had kept from his youth the commandments of God, and asking what was yet wanting to him, Jesus replied: "*If thou wilt be perfect, go sell what thou hast . . . and come follow me.*" † No text could be clearer to establish the difference between the path of the Commandments and that of the evangelical counsels, and to this last class of men alone the exhortation to perfection seems to be attached. Many Fathers, however, and in general the orthodox interpreters of Holy Scripture, think that the Sermon on the Mount was not spoken by our Lord before the apostles alone but before the multitude, and that the doctrine it contains is obligatory on all Christians, as it is certainly the purest expression of the spirit He came to spread on earth. This exegetical

---

* Matth. v. 48.   † Matth. xix. 21.

difficulty might give rise to some controversy on the subject. But there is no need of discussing this matter, because all Christians are agreed that every follower of Christ, to whatever degree he may belong, is constantly exhorted in the Church to aim at perfection in his own state of life; and it is not only the "religious," as they are called—namely, those who have freely embraced the practice of the evangelical counsels—who are bound to advance every day more and more in the path of virtue, but all more or less are directed to do so, according to the degree of grace granted them. The Christian belief of the strict account all will have to render to God after death would suffice to render this duty imperative for all without distinction. Let us, therefore, examine to what height of holiness all Christians are called, and how it is true that man is indefinitely perfectible, in a sense far superior to whatever has been imagined by philosophers and naturalists.

To treat this subject so as to render it evident and conclusive, some preliminary remarks are required on the differences which exist between the civil and religious orders in society, on their correlations, and on the necessary superiority of one above the other. The *civil* order (the life of the citizen) must be considered first; afterwards, the *religious* order (the life of the Christian) must be discussed, to thoroughly understand the perfection it leads us to, either in the common path—that of the Commandments—or along the extraordinary road of the evangelical counsels. The discussion must clearly indicate how far the moral perfectibility of man can be carried in the Church, under Christ's influence.

And first let us examine the most important question of our day; namely, would it be possible and advantageous, in considering man's perfectibility, to separate altogether the civil from the religious order? Many men think it would; and they imagine that it might be the best means of procuring at the same time peace to society. To prove that it is a fallacy a very simple remark will suffice. Man is composed of soul and body, and he has but one personality. To separate both is death; and if it is true of the individual, it must be true likewise of any agglomeration of individuals. In human society the civil order is the body; the religious, the soul. This simple assertion must at this moment suffice; and to draw instruction from it, it is proper to consider apart this soul and this body: their needs, aims, and ultimate destiny. The body craves for food, raiment, the preservation of health, and the prolongation of life; the body, again, aims at enjoyment—let us suppose that it will be without excess, as wisdom and good sense requires; finally, the natural destiny of the body is to perish, to return into its primitive elements and disappear. Is it for this alone that civil order is established among men? Those who wish to separate entirely the civil from the religious order would have to be satisfied with it, if they were logical. For it can be demonstrated that the civil order, in its necessary limits, cannot go beyond the concerns of the body. The department of the human soul, with all its adjuncts, escapes from its control absolutely and entirely, in the supposition of a total separation from religious life, which is here the case. The State, having in its possession an armed force, can command my exterior compliance to its orders, never my interior obedience. How can it pretend to regulate, for instance, the development of my mind by its laws on education? It would be sheer tyranny; because the development of my mind is the expansion of my soul, and my soul belongs to me alone. Considering only the natural laws in the social state, I am the perfect master of my spiritual faculties as soon as I have reached the full age of reason. And this is so true that God Himself has limited His omnipotence with regard to my free will; and—awful to say!—I can disobey His positive commands. The most the State can do with regard to my human acts is to restrain me by its armed force when I violate public order, as they say. It can shut me up in its jails, feed me on bread and water, and even deprive me of life; but it cannot mould my soul—that is, my mind, my will, my interior acts of any sort—according to its pretensions. This is as clear as sunlight; no one can answer to that argument; and it remains true that to separate both orders renders the civil one incompetent in many ways.

Has this theory of total separation ever been carried into effect somewhere on earth? And if so, what has been the result? It would be impossible to find a perfect example of it in the annals of mankind; and this alone would prove that there cannot be a total separation of both orders in human society. But the Chinese have come as near as can be to perfection in the establishment of this system; and it is worth while to examine its effects in the Flowery Kingdom. When Matthew Ricci reached Peking and began that apostleship of patience and good sense which so nearly, at one time, resulted in complete success, he found that immense empire, under the last emperors of the Ming dynasty, in an apparently flourishing condition without any

State religion worth naming; the State power enforcing a morality of its own, and ending all its decrees with the dread formula, *Tremble and obey*. The missionaries did not understand the complete working of those strange institutions, because nothing of the kind could tally with the ideas of Europeans in their age, and thus the men of God took a rather rose-colored view of the subject, particularly because the exquisite politeness of the Chinese won them over completely. It is much more easy for us at this moment to take in an intelligent survey of the whole social field in China such as it was at that time; and it fortunately happens that it has not changed since the sixteenth century.

In that empire, the first in the world in point of population, beside the single million of Catholics lost among the three hundred millions of pagans, two numerous religions or sects divide at this day the people, outside of the official worship of the mandarins. They are the sects of Lao-tseu and of Fo or Buddha; both of which may as well be left aside because they have nothing to do with the religion of the State which tolerates and protects them, without allowing its own officials to take part in their rites and ceremonies, at least in their official capacity. Buddhism, therefore, and the religion founded by Lao-tseu, called by him *Tao*, or *Reason*, are altogether foreign to our present purpose. The State openly professes only the religious doctrine of Confucius, if it can be called religious in any sense. China consequently does not offer in appearance a complete separation, but a union rather, of Church and State. It is, however, only an appearance and nothing more. For it is simply a system of moral philosophy, taught not by a priesthood but by the State, in which the four cardinal virtues, according to State theology—that is, piety, morality, justice, and wisdom—combine with purely physical attributes or energies of matter, such as moisture, fire, wind, water, thunder, earth, etc. Heaven and Earth, with Man, form the heads of a three-fold classification of beings. But it is very difficult to know if originally, in the doctrine of Confucius, Heaven, called in the Chinese tongue *Tien* or *Shanti*, was only the material heaven or in truth the God of heaven. We say originally, for at this time it is certainly the material heaven alone, and the name Tien or Shanti cannot be given to the Christian's God, as many missionaries had done previous to the decision of Rome on the subject.

In consequence of this there is not in the mandarin or State religion of the empire any worship of God properly so called. The official cult is atheistic. The worship of ancestors, which has exteriorly all the characters of a religious act, partakes more of a superstition than of a religion, unless it is a purely civil ceremony, as some imagine. It strictly follows that there is in China neither a union nor a separation of the civil and the spiritual orders, as previously explained. The State has absorbed the whole of it, and the spiritual order has entirely disappeared.

This is so true that it is now admitted generally that for the Chinese who follow the supposed worship of the State there is nothing above this earth nor after this life. The upper classes of society are left absolutely without a religion of any kind, except the vague and undefined veneration of ancestors; they do not believe in a personal God, nor in the immortality of the soul; they live brutally in this world, and die with a complete indifference as expecting no other. The Emperor is evidently the god of the State. He enforces by his decrees the natural morality of Confucius, and never appeals, that we know, to superior powers. It is precisely what modern European radicals would wish to establish by having openly proclaimed the total separation of Church and State. The Church might enjoy liberty or not; for it is known that there are among the supporters of this scheme two distinct opinions on the subject. The State, nevertheless, in either case, would be paramount and would enforce what is called morality. But this morality could not have any supernatural sanction, and would be reduced to securing public order, as it is called, by the simple instrumentality of the police.

The question from which we started is now to be examined, and in its simplicity it is expressed in two words: Is this possible, and what would it produce? The remark has been made and cannot be set aside: Man is composed of soul and body, and his spiritual nature has aims and needs as well as the material part of his being. Nay, the first is far superior to the second; and if the State cannot look to it directly and by its own action, it must see that man is not deprived of his rights as clearly defined by the needs and aims of his spiritual nature. And if there is reason to think that those needs and aims have been placed under the guardianship of a heavenly constituted authority, it is the duty of the State to concur with it for the attainment of its spiritual object. The necessity of concurrence for securing this right is derived from the oneness of man. The two natures of which he is composed form but one person. The whole cannot possibly be divided, so that a part of it might be given to the State and the other to the Church. The State has to take care of man in his complexity, as well as the Church. The impossibility of an actual division obliges them to concur in their respective action; and the civil part of it regarding only this life whilst the religious one regards eternity, the first can be, with regard to spiritual matters, only subsidiary to the second, the same as the present life, on account of its probational character, is primarily nothing more than a means of securing the happiness of heaven. Unless the State goes so far as to repudiate and condemn altogether Christian ideas and turn its back upon them by open persecution, this is logically certain; and it becomes evident that the total separation of Church and State is logically impossible.

In case, however, this fatal determination be taken (which is far from improbable), what will be the result? This is the second branch of the proposed question. We can have some idea of it by looking on China, where the doctrine has been for a long time in full sway. It will be shown afterwards, however, that with respect to former Christian nations the result would be far worse, and the reasons of this difference will be given.

Yes, look at China, and examine attentively what has there resulted from neglecting entirely the spiritual nature of man, treating him merely as a social animal, and sternly refusing to concur for his guidance with any supernatural authority. The natives of the country are certainly docile, intelligent, fond of peace and good order. There are among them all the elements of a well-regulated State. They show their good sense by refusing stubbornly to adopt the atheistic maxims enforced upon them by law. The doctrine of Confucius remains confined to the class of officials, a small minority of the nation, and the mandarins themselves follow it, probably, because it is attached to their office and they cannot help it. The mass of the people are either Buddhists or disciples of Lao-tseu. Still, the open atheism and materialism of the State is for them a source of moral corruption and degradation. They have become practically atheists and materialists *en masse.* If they address any prayers to their idols, it is only to obtain favors in this life; they do not think of another. The State showing the most complete indifference for their soul, it is doubtful if they think they have any. Their spiritual nature has been almost totally obliterated; and the State can boast that it rules over them without any opposition, because in fact they have become mere machines or lumps of gross matter. This could be developed indefinitely; it is better to leave it to the meditation of the reader. It is evident, however, that the moral state of China comes from the theory adopted by the State.

For such a state of society there is only one government possible; and we see it flourishing in China, but in China alone of all nations. As there is in the whole country only one man, the Emperor—all the others are his tools—all powers are concentrated in his hands. There is not even the possibility of an aristocracy to help him. The highest mandarins are absolutely his creatures, none of them lords by birthright; and they receive only from him the ephemeral authority they enjoy. He has made them, and can unmake them at will; and they can exercise no control over his absolute autocracy. Imagine, if you wish, the government of three hundred millions of people absolutely entrusted to a single individual, and this often weak in intellect and body. But it might be demonstrated that with the system which prevails in that empire—namely, the total absorption of the spiritual order by the State, or rather its total abrogation—there is no other government possible. Nothing is so easy to prove. If an aristocracy, at least, was possible in any way (there can be no question of a democracy at all), it would be a spiritual aristocracy; namely, that of a priesthood. It has always been the first order of nobility in all ancient nations; and if Europe has obtained in modern times the hegemony of the world, it can be proved that it was originally due to its clergy, which has ruled Christendom for several hundred years. But the system which prevails in China debars forever the nation from the hope of having a spiritual aristocracy, and consequently a nobility of any kind, to temper the Emperor's authority. And this would certainly result in all European nations if a total separation of Church and State were carried out. We cannot see any other power than what we call a clergy able to check that of the ruler, unless it were that of the mob. But this would be open anarchy. The universal opposition of all European governments to the Church springs certainly from an inward feeling that it is so.

Oh! let modern thinkers reflect, and see whither their theories are hurrying them on. Let them not imagine that what has been the case in China for several centuries would be the worst they could fear. The evil would be far greater in the west of the old continent than in the far Orient. There is not in China any other government possible than that of an autocrat. An aristocracy cannot exist, and a democracy cannot be thought of. The European populations on the other side, if such a thing were attempted among them, would not be so submissive as the Chinese flock. The materialistic doctrines spread through all the classes of society would not result only, as it does in China, in creating a stolid indifference to live or die. The immense activity of the former Christian mind would not run smoothly through the ordinary channels of agriculture and industry, as is the case with these eastern Mongolians. Europeans would do something else besides improving their manufactures of porcelain, or their fabrics of cotton and silk. It is useless to speculate on the subject. But the heart recoils with horror at the prospect which the mind could disclose as the sure fate of the European nations in such a supposition as this.

It is time, however, to come back strictly to the object considered in this chapter. These few words must suffice on the nature of the civil order when it is entirely free from the concurrence of any spiritual authority. The perfection of man being the actual subject of consideration, it is evident that the civil order alone cannot procure in any degree that perfection to which human nature must aspire. The very character of the State limits its action to the temporal order, and this cannot satisfy human aspirations. For man is evidently made for heaven. We must, therefore, turn our eyes toward the spiritual power which is alone established to rule over the better part of our nature; and for us there is no other than the Church. The life to which she invites us is called the Christian life. What is it? What system of perfectibility does it offer to man, either in the path of the Commandments or in that of the counsels, and how is this carried out? This brings us naturally to the subject announced in the heading of this chapter.

3. *The Moral Perfectibility of Man is unfolded in the Christian Life, even in the Common Path of the Commandments.*

The Church alone guides man in the road of Christian life, and inspires him with the desire of aiming at perfection. On this the attention of the reader must be concentrated. The civil power can have no authority whatever in this matter, except so far as to concur with the Church. The God-man who came down from heaven for this purpose, who alone could promise celestial bliss, and wished to found the "kingdom of God" on earth as a preparation for it, passed over His authority to the Church when He left this world. He did not entrust it to the State. It was, however, a visible Church that He came to organize, and He gave it all the characters of an exterior and visible power. It has human rulers; particularly the successors of Peter, with whom originates the episcopate. It has an exterior law, the Gospel, which regulates Christian life; an exterior polity in the sacraments, visible as to the rites and invisible as to the grace; an exterior sanction for its laws in its *forum externum*, by which its subjects are either acknowledged as being in good standing and participating in all the privileges of its citizenship, or as having fallen under censure—which can even go so far as cutting them off from the visible body of the faithful.

It forms thus a vast republic, embracing the whole world, which it claims as its own. But the ultimate object is always the salvation of souls and their preparation for heaven. No civil power evidently can encroach on such sacred ground except as a helper. But the present object is to examine this Christian life around which everything else revolves, since it is the only means of attaining the end. And the first aspect in which it is to be studied is the one offered by the great mass of the faithful, who are satisfied with a common life. That common life was so *uncommon* when it was first proposed to mankind that the very sight of it produced then a wonderful revolution in all the minds of men, or rather a general upheaving of the whole moral world. It could not be adopted without changing entirely the framework of human society; and nothing can better express its first effect than the simple words, *total opposition of heathendom to Christendom.*

All of us had the happiness of being born in a land (wherever that was) in which for many centuries the maxims and precepts of Christ had resounded with power, even if some discordant voices could be heard. We can therefore with great difficulty form any idea of the strangeness of the occurrence when the Ten Commandments were published to mankind, and from the dead contents of the Hebrew or Greek Bible took the living form which the tongue of authorized preachers could give them. Looking back on what we know of the apostolic age, let us compare the fierce opposition they met at first from the great majority of men, and, on the other side, the sudden awakening to the contemplation of a "new creation" by the far smaller number of the first disciples. The solemn tone with which they were ushered in, first on Mount Sinai and afterwards from the lips of Christ, started a ferocious war which lasted several centuries: "I am the Lord thy God; thou shalt not have strange gods before Me!" What torrents of blood began to flow and continued to drench the earth on account of these simple words, until victory crowned at last the martyrdom of the Christians, and idols fell prostrate!

Still it is said with justice that the Decalogue is engraved on the heart of man. Unfortunately the impress of it was then thickly covered with the text of the adversary. Instead of the adoration of the true God, the world had adopted the worship of demons. This mockery of religion did not allow any rest to man, and labor being confined to slaves, they had to toil the whole year round to support their masters in idleness and debauchery. No day of rest, no Sabbath for them! To believe in the sacredness of labor and the necessity of rest was the first blow given to the universal system of human slavery, and this again brought on war. The simple and open proscription of anger, hatred, murder, was the absolute condemnation of a world governed hitherto tyrannically by the devil, who "was a murderer from the beginning."* The condemnation of adultery and lust was a clear denunciation of a society given up entirely to it. To forbid the use even of the tongue against a brother-man argued a simplicity so obsolete as to be despised. But particularly to denounce an open anathema against stealing and covetousness was to blaspheme the modern policy of Rome. She might have been in former times honest in her dealings with foreign nations. But this belonged to a long-

---

* John viii. 44.

forgotten age, when her dictators were taken from the plough and her great generals ate radishes dipped in salt, refusing haughtily the bribes of the enemy. Her modern refinement had turned proudly its back on such rustic notions as those. The palaces of her patricians were now adorned with spoils openly stolen from Sicilians, Greeks, Asiatics, and Africans. You could not open your eyes in the capital of the world without witnessing the consecration and success of public theft and robbery. It is true this took the name of the "right of conquest;" but whatever name it took, it was the enriching of a city at the expense of the whole world. And this was strictly forbidden by the text which said, "Thou shalt not steal." As to "covetousness," who could bear to hear that the new religion anathematized it? Was it not lawful for any man to desire what he did not possess, if the object was pleasant and would increase his enjoyments? This was for pagans the great law of aspirations natural to the heart of man; and to forbid it was an attempt to destroy the spring of life and the only means to attain happiness; namely, a noble ambition. Thus all the precepts of the Decalogue could not but meet with the fiercest opposition.

This may appear exaggerated to many men who imagine that the pagans in ancient times possessed a conscience as keen as ours. We, thank God, have been fashioned and moulded by eighteen hundred years of Christianity; the heathen of the old world had inherited from their ancestors, during many ages, a bluntness of moral perception of which we can scarcely form an exact idea in our day.

It may be said, however, that even at that epoch the human laws condemned murder, theft, adultery. They did; and these crimes were punished with a savage legislative cruelty. Retaliation was the law of that age, and barbarous punishments were inscribed in the codes of all nations. It is certain, nevertheless, that human conscience had lost so much of its primitive keenness and sense of right that few saw anything else in those grave injunctions and threats than simple penal enactments. Every one felt at liberty to ward off the consequences by concealing his evil deeds from the eyes of man. Whoever could escape being found out had nothing to fear from the remorse of his conscience. He was the more happy that he not only enjoyed what he had coveted, but he, moreover, had obtained it at the price of some danger, which always enhances the taste of stolen fruit. In case those human laws had not then existed and been occasionally enforced, human society would have altogether perished. But it is evident that the true sense of morality, which in a well-organized commonwealth must always precede and accompany the observance of law, had almost entirely disappeared.

Otherwise the establishment of Christian morals derived from the Decalogue would not have met in heathendom the opposition it met. It is undoubtedly true that it was, on the other side, its enforcement by the Church which mainly attracted toward her all those choice spirits for whom the Gospel of Christ was a *genuine* treasure-trove, and who embraced it with so great an ardor. But for the great majority of pagans, that very holiness of the new religion was the main reason which turned them against it irretrievably. The first outburst of that hatred is generally ascribed by historians to the calumnies spread broadcast against the Christians. It was said that they were atheists, they were cannibals, they were given up to an unbridled lust. This is true, but it was most probably a mere pretext, and in their inmost souls the pagans knew better. Who can imagine that they had become all at once the open advocates of religion and morality, and hated the Christians only because the new religionists offended against both?

Tacitus assigns to it a much more probable cause: *the Christians hated mankind*—"*odium generis humani.*" They showed bluntly their opposition to the loose manners of the age. *Inde iræ*. This is a more rational explanation of the fact, and comes very near to our own. If the popular pretext had had any reality, it would soon have given way before a more exact knowledge of the truth; and this would have produced a revulsion of feeling in favor of Christianity which never took place. All things considered, the practice of the Decalogue's precepts was directly opposed to heathen nature, and this must have been the true cause of the fierce antagonism which has just been described. We shall be still better convinced of it by considering to what height of holiness the practice of the Ten Commandments carried directly the new converts, even those who followed the common life proposed to all the disciples of Christ: the natural antagonism of pagans will come out in a bolder relief.

The first aspect it took was towards God Himself. The Saviour has declared that to love God above all things is the first and the greatest commandment. This had never been so openly proclaimed before to mankind, and alone it would have sufficed to bring back holiness on earth. For the love which is here prescribed embraces all the faculties of the human soul, and consecrates the entire man to God: "Thou shalt love the Lord thy God with thy whole heart, and with thy whole soul, and with thy whole mind." * The old law had already commanded it,† but it had so far been known almost exclusively to the Jews; Christ extended its knowledge to all nations, and by it He proposed to them at once an eminence of holiness which otherwise could not have been so much as imagined by man. For the love of God, carried to the perfection contained in these words of Christ, suffices to enable any one to reach the very summit of virtue on earth. This is to be seen somewhat in detail.

First, God is to be loved as Creator, Redeemer, and Sanctifier. The mystery of the Most Holy Trinity is the fundamental dogma of the Christian; and the simplest meaning of it is this three-fold aspect under which God has condescended to be known by us. These concepts are not abstract notions only, and metaphysical ideas dimly perceived in God's unity; they are substantial perceptions proved to be in fact three distinct persons. We call them the Father, the Son, and the Holy Ghost. Can we even conceive how far up that love must go which is to embrace our Creator, our Redeemer, and the Sanctifier of our souls; that is, the Almighty Father of all, the Saviour of mankind, the Bestower of all spiritual gifts? A large volume has been written by Faber to express only the relations of the Creator towards His creatures; and there is not a page of the book which does not breathe feelings of the deepest affection on the part of man towards his Author. Yet who can suppose that this mighty subject has been exhausted by the tender-hearted Oratorian? The very idea of creation supposes that we owe to God the Father absolutely everything we possess or claim; if love is to be measured by its mutual communication of everything that is good, can there be any limit to the human love for God, when we know that from His liberality the immensity of creation is ours; since we can claim as of right not this earth only, but whatever the universe contains? Measure, if you can, the height of holiness to which this love alone is able to carry us up.

But the particular feature of this holy subject which must be considered apart is the total submission to God which the title of creature imposes on man, as the mightiest step he can take toward perfect sanctity. There can be no question of independence in any degree,

---

* Matt. xxii. 37.   † Deut. vi. 5.

when the very name of creature is analyzed. When it is considered that no faculty of the soul, no organ or function of the body, no outward advantage of any kind, can be claimed by us as derived either from ourselves or from any other source than the infinite goodness of the Almighty Father, how can we lose for a single moment the consciousness of belonging entirely to God? This simple consideration imposes upon man the absolute necessity of a constant self-repression, lest he should offend the most pure eye of the Father, which is all the time beaming on him. And let no one fancy that this must engender fear. As nothing comes from the infinite source of all goodness but what is the offspring of divine love, so likewise every throb of the human heart, every instinctive feeling of the creature we call a human being, every reflex thought of the human soul, and every active emotion of the human personality, cannot but resolve itself into an ardent love which, as a Father has said, "drives away all fear." Then the loss of independence is sweet; the absolute subjection of our whole being to the divine influence is the highest happiness; and nothing thereby is more easy and simple than the practice of the most perfect holiness. For every one who loves God with "his whole heart, his whole soul, and his whole mind," cannot but be holy; and this is after all the shortest road to sanctity.

Thus far this doctrine does not suppose even revelation. Without it, no doubt, man might have scarcely been able to soar so high in the spiritual regions; still unassisted reason can deduce the whole doctrine from the truths engraved on the human heart. But the love of God as Redeemer transcends entirely what reason teaches us; and because this new insight into the higher world is far brighter, the love and the holiness it suggests is still in a certain sense higher and purer.

Our title of creature is here replaced by that of son; and we could never have understood the dignity to which we are raised by it, unless the true and natural Son of God had condescended to reveal it to us by becoming Incarnate in our own human nature. This, therefore, of necessity belongs to revealed doctrine, and cannot be fathomed or even dimly discovered by unassisted human reason. To be the rational creature of the Almighty Father, to belong to Him entirely, and, by a total submission to Him, to claim as a right the possession of the immensity of creation towards which our whole being aspires, is apparently the highest limit of our most ambitious aims. But God can do infinitely more than we can imagine or desire; and by the temporal birth of His Eternal Son from one of the children of men—a Virgin Mother—He has made us all His adopted sons, and given us a right not only to material creation in all its immensity as seen above, but likewise to the incomprehensible spiritual creation of heaven itself which revelation alone can unfold. This is the strict consequence of the dogma of the Incarnation; and for this reason, also, Christ in the New Testament calls Himself indiscriminately the Son of man and the Son of God, to show how both are merged into one.

Look at Him, either in the cave of Bethlehem, a babe just born on earth, whilst his heavenly generation is eternal and divine; or under the humble roof of Nazareth, a young man toiling and living at the sweat of his brow, clothed in our weak humanity, yet enjoying heavenly rest in His most divine personality; or at last on the cross, bearing in His humanity all the sins of mankind, but conqueror of hell in His death, and sure that according to prophecy "His sepulchre should be glorious."

It is on account of all the circumstances of this birth, this life, this death, that Christians must and do love Him. And in loving Him they love their God, the Incarnate Son of the Father. In taking up our nature and appearing as a man among us, He has rendered easy for all the children of Adam, even the most humble and uninformed, the love of the Creator, who has consented to become our Redeemer. For this the Christian is not reduced to metaphysical considerations of the highest order, deduced from whatever the reason of man can know of the nature of the Infinite. A very few intellects can penetrate into the secrets of heaven, where Scripture says that the angels themselves veil their faces when looking on the Lord.* We are, besides, warned by the wise man that "the searcher of majesty shall be overwhelmed by glory."† But there is no fear of falling through intellectual pride, when the Christian on his knees adores the humble Son of Mary, and feels emboldened even to kiss His feet and bedew His divine hands with his tears. Abstract reflections on the infinite attributes of God, supposing them to be guarded and accurate, can scarcely warm the heart, where alone love nestles and expands; and the safest metaphysicians, armed with all the subtlety of philosophy, seldom feel their imagination entranced and their bosom agitated by any emotion of rapture, any warmth even of tender affection. The whole is almost concentrated in the intellect.

---

* Is. vi. 2.   † Prov. xxv. 27.

But the life of Christ seems to have been purposely planned for drawing from the heart of man, even if naturally hard as adamant and cold as ice, an ever-gushing source of deep devotion and an ardent flame of persistent enthusiasm. The more a man is unaffected and simple (however limited his knowledge may be) the more is he fit to be strongly affected by the reading of the Gospel. There is no need of a strong reasoning power, of an acute mind, to detect sure principles and draw from them infallible consequences. An unvarnished fact briefly told, a phrase fallen carelessly in appearance from the lips of the God-man, a word only of His disciple John, kindle directly in the heart a soft and gentle fire, active enough to mettle the hardest nature, yet so harmless as only to vivify, not to burn; to draw tears from the eye, no pain from the frame; to create a new soul endowed with new affections, not to destroy anything worth keeping in whatever belongs to our humanity. An habitual reading of the inspired volume serves but to confirm a first impression. Soon the life of the Saviour becomes so deeply impressed in the human heart that to look simply on His image—either as beaming with joy in His infancy and resting on the knees of His mother; or dwelling with Joseph and Mary in the cottage of Nazareth; or walking through Judea in the midst of His apostles, sitting with them at His last supper, and finally expiring ignominiously on Calvary—suffices for entrancing the Christian soul with delight and devotion, filling our solitude with the company of the angels who once ministered to Him on earth, and changing our dull life into an ever-revolving circle of festive or tender devotions. Innumerable generations of men, chiefly in the middle ages, have had scarcely any other food for their soul but what was then called "the poor man's Bible;" namely, the various circumstances of Christ's life painted on the windows of their churches or sculptured on the walls of their cathedrals, or, finally, engraved on wood and printed for the use of those who could not read. This sufficed for kindling in those simple souls a fire of deep piety resolving itself entirely into the love of Christ as their God. Then religion was not a mere name, but a strong and lasting feeling; it was a tree deeply planted in their hearts, producing, besides leaves and flowers, a profusion of fruits, called then good works, works of mercy, scarcely remembered in our day, but whose precious list formed the holy staple of the morality of those ages.

How many millions of men, women, and children have thus ardently loved their Redeemer! They have abundantly fulfilled the first precept of the law: "Thou shalt love the Lord thy God with thy whole heart, and thy whole soul, and thy whole mind." Many of them have carried that love to a degree of perfection which puts to the blush the men of our age, who have certainly a far greater degree of knowledge and enjoy, also, the privilege of reading the same Gospel, but imagine, in their blindness, that they have many better things to do in this life than reduce the mental food of their souls to the simple diet of their forefathers.

The present age, however, must not be made worse than it is. There are still people who love Christ; and the world will never be without them, because His life sheds on earth too strong a light to be ever entirely obscured by the "shadow of death." These ardent disciples of the Saviour sanctify still in our day all the walks of human activity even in the higher classes of society; though they are far more numerous in the humbler ranks of life. How often does not the minister of God wonder that after the Saviour has pronounced that awful "woe to the rich," there are still so many of them who try at least to keep within the line of the strict Commandments! They submit willingly to Christian discipline in order to save their soul; and if too often "the cares of this world and the deceitfulness of riches choketh up the word" in their heart, and renders them unfaithful to duty, they repent after a while, and humble themselves so far as to acknowledge their guilt at the feet of a man, and thus they are not unworthy of pardon.

But the most precious jewels of Christ's crown are His humble followers in the path of despised poverty. For them the love of the Saviour is everything, since they cannot love the world which disowns them. The whole life of many of them has scarcely ever been touched by mortal sin; and they cannot remember the time when their heart was altogether cold towards their Redeemer. Is not this true of a large proportion of the humble classes of society in the Catholic Church? If a number of them have not been blameless during their youth, and even have for a considerable time disregarded the clearest precepts of religion, they will tell you that this was long ago. During many years of a penitent life they have endeavored to obtain a pardon of which they are always afraid of not being worthy; and having nothing to reproach themselves since their first conversion to God, they continue to accuse themselves of former transgressions which they consider as a load on their conscience, after having so often thrown it away. Is it not evident, therefore, that the first precept of the Decalogue, so comprehensive and weighty, keeping embalmed in itself the strongest, and surest, and most absolute test of sanctity, is still followed by innumerable thousands of people, for whom the love of God in Christ is more important than any other concern of human life?

We have not, however, considered so far the whole extent of this "kingdom of God on earth." Besides the love of the Creator and of the Redeemer, it embraces likewise that of the "Sanctifier," and suggests considerations as important perhaps as those which have preceded, though they must be very shortly suggested.

The benefits of creation and redemption are truly marvellous and cannot be explained in words, because they are in fact, chiefly the second, incomprehensible. The divine love which they excite in the hearts of those who reflect upon them surpasses human comprehension, and calls forth particularly the wonder of the happy men who feel it. Still God has found in His infinite goodness a closer bond of union with us, by consenting to make His dwelling in our hearts and granting us the permanent and familiar presence of His Holy Spirit. He is called the "Sanctifier, the "Consoler," the "Bestower of spiritual gifts." Christ had promised Him before leaving the earth; and St. Paul in particular has spoken eloquently of the fulfilment of that promise. This indwelling of the Spirit of God in man, in the state of grace, is very different from the assistance granted to the Church at large, by bestowing upon her the gifts of infallibility and sanctity. We here speak of the individual influence of the Holy Ghost over each of us, of which we are assured by many words of Christ and by numerous texts contained in apostolic epistles. This is the third part of the economy of grace, the benefits of creation and redemption being the two first ones. This last is peculiar, altogether confined in the interior of man, but on this account most precious and promotive of the love of God. In fact, the chief object of this interior mission of the Holy Ghost, as it is called, is to create and nourish in our soul that supernatural love which is the main end for which we have been created and redeemed. After this new proof of divine liberality towards us, nothing more can be imagined which the infinite power of the Almighty could do. The Most Holy Trinity has exhausted itself in enriching man, since the Holy Ghost is the third and last person composing it. The reader can see at a glance that it is the highest source of holiness for man, because the only possible object of the indwelling of the Holy Spirit in His rational creatures is to make them holy. Volumes upon volumes could be written on this the highest prerogative of the Christian, since by the virtue of it he is not only a creature of God, not only a Son of God, but a partaker of all the gifts of God; of His very nature, as St. Peter says.*

But we are forced to leave these sublime considerations to the meditation of the reader, in order to enter into a general view of their consequences with regard to the whole Decalogue in its complexity. So far we have spoken only of the great precept which forms the main object of the first table of the law.

In general it can be said that the class of precepts contained in the second table is intimately derived from those of the first. If man "loves God with his whole heart, his whole soul, and his whole mind," he will love his neighbor as himself on account of Christ's command, and himself only according to the strict injunctions of the divine law. But the detail of whatever is enjoined by the seven last commandments belongs as well to the natural as to the supernatural order. As belonging to the first they are in fact engraved in the heart of all men, as St. Paul remarks. As belonging to the second they were surely promulgated on Mount Sinai first, but afterwards they were reasserted and explained by Christ Himself as part and parcel of what He came to reveal. If we love God with the perfection required by the "first and greatest commandment," we cannot but be faithful to what He has so clearly written in our hearts and decreed with such power on the Mount of the Beatitudes. As author of nature, as Creator consequently, we owe Him that perfect love described previously as a necessity of our being. The precious deposit of His law contained in the inmost recess of our hearts must be, therefore, considered as the most inestimable heirloom left us by His condescension after the fall of Adam. Had He altogether rejected us, we would not have in our possession such a priceless advantage as the testimony of our conscience undoubtedly is. Its voice is the echo of that of God Himself. We feel it, we know it; the pagans themselves have acknowledged it.

But this second table of the law, which evidently comes from God as the author of nature, comes from Him likewise as the author of grace. The Divine Redeemer has from His own lips repeated the injunctions contained in the Mosaic Decalogue. He has explained them, left them to His Church as a sacred deposit, to be interpreted

---
* 2 Peter i. 4.

by her whenever some particular point should appear obscure owing to the passions of men. He has consequently, as Redeemer, secured forever their usefulness on all occasions, and for all moral purposes. It is a far superior advantage to the one possessed by the Jews, who had only the synagogue to listen to in time of doubt and hesitation. The Commandments have thus become, owing particularly to their clearness, one of the most important results of the scheme of redemption; and since the title of Redeemer assumed by our God in the person of His Son is one of the highest incentives of love towards Him on the part of man, this love, being now supremely in our possession, carries with it the necessity of fulfilling His precepts of the second class, which are, as He says, "like the first."

Finally, the consecration of this holy doctrine by the indwelling of the Holy Spirit in us, as previously explained, extends also to this second branch. For if the heart of the Christian in the state of grace becomes the dwelling of the Holy Ghost, that divine Spirit's gifts must be applied to the fulfilment of the whole law and the establishment of a supreme holiness. This could not be possible unless the precepts of the divine law even of the second class, which were at first merely natural and moral precepts, become elevated to the higher plane of a supernatural influence. And it is for this reason certainly that Christ said that the second precept (to love our neighbor) was "like unto the first."

It is, therefore, easy to understand how all Christians, even those who follow the common life of the precepts, are called to the practice of a real and supreme holiness. The general considerations just offered to the reader suffice for it without entering into a detailed and successive account of each and all these Commandments. What remains to be done for the complete elucidation of this question consists in explaining briefly how the most simple Christian is thus placed on the high-road of *perfection*, and truly fulfils the injunction of our Lord, "Be ye perfect as also your heavenly Father is perfect." To do this requires evidently a real and constant progress in the way of God. For as it is impossible to reach in reality perfection in this life, the injunction of Christ must mean that His disciples are bound to aim at it, and consequently to perfect themselves more and more in the practice of virtue, to progress consequently day after day, as long as human life lasts.

To judge of it easily and thoroughly it is sufficient to consider for a moment in what a Christian life consists. Nothing is more simple and clear; and a child will say that a Christian life is merely the imitation of Christ. All His disciples are bound to it, but not all in the same degree. Whatever that degree may be, however, it always partakes more or less of *perfection*. To imitate Christ, the most humble and uneducated of His disciples must constantly rise above nature and enter the superior regions of a moral world incomprehensible outside of Christianity. He must love his enemies and do them good when he can; he must despise lucre if it involves in the least dishonesty; he must bow his head resignedly when afflicted by sickness, poverty, and all the other natural ills of life; he must endeavor to subdue the passions of lust, avarice, ambition, hatred; he must constantly remember that life is short, eternity long, death sure, and heaven to be reached only through a hard and narrow road. Pages of this kind could be written to describe the Christian life such as it is, without gloss and varnish and in all the nakedness of truth. In this, in a few words, consists for all the imitation of Christ. And it is not a work of supererogation, but it is a duty incumbent on all those who wish to be sincerely the followers of the God-man. They must aim at *perfection*.

Is not all this the road to supreme holiness on earth? Is it not far superior to the path followed by the great majority of men?

No one can do it unless he keeps his eyes constantly on Christ, and tries to copy in his own person the model left us nineteen-hundred years ago and preserved in the pages of the eternal Gospel. The Church has always endeavored to foster among men the thorough imitation of that heavenly model, because it is the most sure and easy way of attaining holiness on earth; and the most common life of the Christian is holiness itself compared to that of those men who are not.

4. *The Best Development of Human Perfectibility is carried out in the Practice of the Evangelical Counsels.*

The short sketch of a few particulars of the Saviour's life given a moment ago was intended to illustrate some of the examples He gave having no reference to what is generally called the evangelical counsels. But if He is the perfect model of all Christians, even of those who follow a common path; if He thus invites them all to perfection according to their degree of grace, His life furnishes likewise the true pattern of a heroic holiness to those who, like the young man in the

Gospel, do not feel satisfied with keeping the Commandments and wish to advance farther on perfection's road. Should any one try to analyze those "counsels," denounced by Luther as encouraging superstition and openly opposed to the law of God, he will easily discern that they resolve themselves into the spirit of *self-sacrifice*.

A simple glance at them will show that to submit our will to that of another is undoubtedly the sacrifice of our will; to subdue the sexual desire by continency and render it submissive to reason supposes the same constant surrender of our sensual leanings; to deprive one's self of the possibility of acquiring and possessing property is a third manner of self-immolation, as unpalatable to human nature as the two others. But many men in our day refuse to admit that human perfectibility is in the least concerned in either of these. They think that Christian holiness cannot be promoted at the expense of all that is dear to man; and some of them go even so far as to pretend that such practices as these are disgraceful to humanity, loathsome in the eyes of God, and the outcome of barbarism rather than of genuine Christianity.

Our object cannot be to convince men who refuse to be convinced, and to bring them to the admission of principles altogether repugnant to their *nature*. They understand this last word in a way peculiar to them, and they must be left in the firm persuasion that they are right. But it will be profitable, we hope, to a great number of candid and sincere people to open before the eyes of all what is in fact the highest and most abundant fountain-head of true holiness on earth, and the irrefragable proof that man is indeed indefinitely perfectible in his moral nature. To place this beyond the reach of contradiction, the most simple and at the same time forcible way is to consider virtue in its various degrees from the lowest to the highest, and attentively examine, first, the difficulty it finds in establishing itself in the human heart and, secondly, the masterly manner with which it finally subdues it and perfects it through Christ's *counsels*. The agency of divine grace in the whole process is always to be supposed in the Christian understanding of it, but here it seems better not to insist on this peculiarity, and develop only what is visible and sensible in the arduous struggle which invariably takes place in the human soul.

1. Virtue is a moral force, and force supposes a resistance to be overcome. All men know that there is no greater resistance to virtue than is found in the evil inclinations to which we are all naturally subject. In thoughts, words, or actions we morally fail at every moment

of our lives, unless we are extremely cautious at first in a kind of desultory warfare against all possible temptations without any apparent order and system, and afterwards apply ourselves to the task with more energy and success, when principles have been finally recognized and some virtuous habits have been at last acquired. The lowest degree of virtue consists in that first supposed fight at random against a number of spiritual enemies by which we are at once assailed. This happens chiefly in the first bloom of youth, when, prompted by a holy but still vague desire of keeping himself pure, a young man resists evil almost instinctively, and without much order and precision in his efforts. Virtue is not yet solidly established in the soul; evil inclinations are strong; and there is nothing surprising in the fact that with the best intentions this young man often experiences humiliating defeats, and at times despairs almost of conquering peace by the most valiant struggles.

No one who has studied himself during his whole life will refuse to recognize his own history in this short description of what has been called a *desultory warfare.* Each act of virtue may be a brave one, but—to continue the simile—the whole campaign is often a failure. Let us examine a moment some particular point of this moral encounter; and as the great epic poet, in the midst of a general description of an universal battle, brings on suddenly the individual fight of two of his heroes, so likewise it will be profitable to analyze more fully some single moral combat in which we remember that we have been formerly engaged, in order to know the fearful difficulty that always meets those who propose to themselves not to allow animalism to prevail through life over their best instincts.

A young man, for instance, has remarked his almost unconquerable inclination to idleness and sloth: either for rising early in the morning, accepting and following the order of the day assigned by parents and teachers, applying his mind to a systematic study, keeping a firm purpose of steady progress and advance; or, in a quite different line, for discarding a friend who comes to entice him away from his actual duty, putting away the occasion he meets of indulging his leaning to idleness—conquering himself, in fact. Imagining at first that few, if any, will be aware of his weakness, he feels an invincible repugnance, an almost unconquerable opposition. He is fully aware, consequently, of the immense difficulty there is for him in practising the virtue of steadfastness or abstaining from the vice of sloth. Being still a novice in both, he too often finds out that after many strong resolves and promises he is the same wavering boy that he has always been; he has not yet acquired a positive habit of the virtue of which he feels the need, without which he knows his life will be ill-spent and end perhaps in disgrace and dishonor.

The example which has been chosen here is one of the most pardonable in a boy, when it is not carried to extreme. There are many other defects or vices which could present a much stronger case for the object in view. But some private reflections on the subject will enable any one to see that nothing is so difficult as to establish solidly the reign of holiness in the heart of man, at the very beginning.

2. The result will be more conclusive still by considering a higher degree of virtue, after having analyzed a single case belonging to a lower class of facts. The boy has now become almost a man; life assumes for him a more serious aspect. Let us suppose that he reflects often on the consequences of his acts, and that he begins to more thoroughly understand the baneful effects of a single immoral habit. He takes an honest resolution not to allow himself to be enslaved like the great number of his companions, whom he daily sees addicted to vices on account of which they often blush without having the courage of freeing themselves from their tyranny. He is besides fully aware of the difficulty of the task. For there are dangers on all sides, and snares laid for his fall all around him. His natural inclinations conspire against him with the allurements of a corrupt world; and he shudders at the sight of so many bad examples, so many loose maxims of conduct, so many scandalous successes in life, which go to form the aggregate of human society. He, therefore understands that if he wishes to preserve himself from moral corruption, he must adopt strict principles of conduct and never deviate from them. He begins to lay under his feet solid foundations of virtue. Aside from the power which man receives from God when he asks it, and which we purposely lay aside in these considerations, the supposed efforts of this young man are the only means that can be imagined of acquiring a firm virtue through life. But does it not suppose a constant practice of *self-sacrifice?* Can a well-ordered and persistent conduct be founded on any other ground than on the immolation of self at all times and on all occasions? Virtue and self-sacrifice are, therefore, identical; and the more complete is the last the more exalted will be the first.

From this single example it is easy to understand that the submission of the individual will to a higher one, the total subjection of the senses to reason, and the abdication of worldly goods and worldly hopes for the sake of charity, being in their combination the most absolute expression of self-renouncement, must be also for man the highest means of acquiring virtue, or rather the very essence of moral perfection on earth, and the highest exponent of the moral perfectibility of man. This, however, must be more clearly brought out, in order that it may offer no difficulty to the understanding of any one.

There can be no more absolute generalization of manhood and its surroundings than what embraces our spiritual faculties, our bodily leanings, and our exterior advantages. The sacrifice of all these at once is that of the whole man. All man's spiritual faculties are evidently concentrated in his will, which naturally supposes his understanding. His bodily leanings mean here the sensible and sensuous part of his being, which, when it is altogether subjected to reason by a particular vow, is made a total sacrifice of, in the presence of God. Finally, the totality of his exterior advantages, as they relate to worldly possessions or the hope of them, comprises whatever is generally understood by the object of the vow of poverty. On this account the solemn pronouncing of the "religious vows" has often been called a holocaust of the whole man on God's altar. A longer explanation is not required, because, under this simple and short expression, it is evident at once that there can be no higher and no more universal self-sacrifice for man than what is understood by "religious vows," and self-sacrifice is the essence of virtue. The only difficulty relates to matters of detail, and can be better disposed of by stating with simplicity some objections of unorthodox writers who not only refuse to admit that the matter of these vows constitutes a way of perfection but pretend, on the contrary, that they are unnatural, unholy, and offensive to God and to man. These objections, so far as they have any strength, rest altogether on misconceptions, and it will require a very short discussion to establish it.

3. A first general observation may be sufficient for the Christian. The religious vows are commended in the Gospel by Christ Himself, and the Church has always highly approved the firm determination of those who freely embrace their practice. The counsels of voluntary poverty and continency are as clearly expressed by the Saviour as it is possible for the human language to do it; and as to the submission of man's will to a higher one, the

whole life of Christ, as was seen, is but a commentary on it, and no better example of "religious" obedience can be offered than that of the God-man during his whole mortal career. This has already been touched upon, but here is the place to prove it beyond contradiction.

First, therefore, nothing but voluntary poverty, such as is practised by the "religious" in the Catholic Church, can answer to the advice given by the Saviour to the young man who had all his life kept the Commandments and wished to do more in order "to have life everlasting." "If thou wilt be perfect, go sell what thou hast, and give to the poor, and thou shalt have a treasure in heaven; and come follow me."* There is here no need of a commentary. From the very words used by Christ it is evident that this is an advice or counsel which is not proposed to all, but only to a few—to those who wish to be *perfect*. It is not a commandment like those of the Decalogue, and no individual in the Church is absolutely required to do it. It is true that when God gives to a soul an inward and strong leaning to it, so that it looks truly like a divine call, it becomes a sort of commandment to that particular soul, who may endanger its salvation by remaining deaf to the call, like this very young man who after receiving this advice from Christ did not follow it, but "went away sad, for he had great possessions." Admitting all this, however, it cannot be included in the line of "precepts," and remains for all an evangelical "counsel."

Secondly, the same must be said of continency, of which the Saviour speaks absolutely in equivalent terms. For after He had explained at length the unity and indissolubility of marriage, such as it was to remain forever in the Church, the disciples themselves were surprised at the strictness of the bond of matrimony, and exclaimed at once: "If the case of a man with his wife be so, it is not expedient to marry."† The Saviour answered: "All men accept not this word, but they to whom it is given. For there are eunuchs who were born so from their mother's womb; and there are others who were made so by men; and there are some who have made themselves eunuchs for the kingdom of heaven. He that can take [or understand], let him take it [that is, understand it]."‡ This passage of the Gospel cannot possibly have reference to anything but the practice of volun-

---

* Matt. xix. 21. † Ibid. 10. ‡ Ibid. 11, 12.

tary continency. St. Paul understood it so when he recommended virginity to the Corinthian Christians, "not as a precept, but a counsel." * A great part of this chapter of St. Paul is but a song in honor of voluntary virginity. But at the same time marriage is honored as an institution necessary for many who otherwise "would burn." That a Christian, after having heard these words of Christ and of St. Paul, could speak disparagingly of holy celibacy must always remain incomprehensible. There are, however, objections often made to it which have an appearance of foundation, of which a few words must be said.

The apostle of the gentiles, in explaining with a supreme good sense the Church's doctrine on the subject, referred to a peculiarity which is precisely the only reason assigned by those who object to the practice of celibacy. Mind! he seems to say, "I speak for your profit, not to cast a snare upon you; but for that which is decent." † Had he made a precept of virginity for all, the objection would have been proper. All cannot keep it, and he had said it himself equivalently. He did not want "to cast a snare upon them." But he had repeatedly declared that the advice he gave was only for those who had reason to think that God called them to that state of comparative perfection, and that the same God would continue to help them. The Church has always likewise put the same limitation to the practice of voluntary celibacy, and has done her best to ascertain the vocation of those who embrace it. There is no doubt that some at least of the examples quoted by the opponents of the Catholic doctrine as incentive to immorality have really taken place, and belong unfortunately to history. But what does it all prove? Only this, that the best things in the world are subject to abuse; nothing more. If a certain number of men have embraced the religious or ecclesiastical state without any of the virtues required for it, it cannot be imputed to the religious state itself, but to the base passions of ambition, avarice, luxury, which naturally corrupt the best institutions when they are secretly indulged by hypocrites and sycophants. That in general the rulers of the Church, chiefly the popes, have been indefatigable in the pursuit of those monsters, and have done all that it was possible to do for preserving holy purity in those who make a public profession of it, is easily ascertainable by history, and becomes every day better and better proved by the earnest endeavors of modern historians.

---

* 1 Cor. vii.   † 1 Cor. vii. 33.

That in times of the greatest corruption there were always in the Church a large number of holy souls living in austerity, and keeping their senses in due subjection to reason and the law of God, can as little be disputed by those who have sufficiently investigated the matter. With these simple remarks the objection under consideration can very well be left for what it is worth. It cannot weaken in the least the strength of the argument derived from the Gospel itself in favor of virginity.

But, in a third place, nothing has yet been said of the submission of the will required of the "religious" in the Church, and on this the adversaries of monastic vows are particularly ardent in their opposition. Why has God given us a will, if not to use it ourselves and not to subject it to the will of another? How can man perfect himself if he discards at once the best means he possesses for the development of his own perfectibility? Can the Almighty be honored by the acts of a mere machine, and is not man simply a machine when he has surrendered his will? And much more is said of the same import. But it is as clear as daylight that all this has no bearing whatever on the question. The practice of "religious" obedience does not deprive a man of his will. To subject it to that of another in all cases required by the rule is not, and cannot be, to destroy it and entirely lose it. It remains as strong in the best "religious" in the world as in the most independent man you can choose. Nay, it is much stronger because it is more perfect, less subject to vacillation and inconstancy, better grounded on principle, and conseqently more firm in its resolve: all things which are precisely the best characteristics of a strong will. The objection just mentioned in detail supposes always that the more the human will is wavering, capricious, liable to change, *because left to the inspiration of the moment,* in the individual, the more it deserves its name. In this case the word itself is simply a misnomer. The precept of obedience is moreover imposed on the "religious" chiefly to give efficiency to the arduous labor undertaken by his Order. If each one acted according to his views there would be in reality no head to the whole community, no unity of purpose, and consequently no result worth naming. But does the impulse given by the one who commands deprive each member of his own activity? The man is altogether blind who does not see that the action of each individual will be much more effective because combined with that of many others. And the consciousness in each of the effect produced by all cannot but increase individual strength and give an immense power to the *will* of the lowest member of the community. Do not deceive yourselves, gentlemen, and particularly do not undertake to deceive others. "Religious" are no more machines than you ; and it is probably on that very account that there are in our age so many men ardent in their efforts to destroy religious orders and congregations.

After all, to what does that dreaded submission of the will amount? To this simply, that the religious cannot dispose at will of his person and surroundings. He cannot choose the place of his residence, arrange his order of the day as he would like, follow his bent for amusement or perhaps worse, idle away his time in unprofitable employments—show, in fine, his want of wisdom in a thousand ways, just as the great majority of men do in all the pretended careers they follow. For this is generally the way for men to show that they have a will. Who can imagine that because they have happily deprived themselves of all those pretended advantages, the religious are reduced to the state of machines and have no more will than the dog trained to obey its master? The will they have is of a very different nature. Its consecration to God and to holy purposes not only does not diminish its strength, but powerfully increases it. Look at the work many of them have done, and say, if you dare, that they were deprived of a will. Xavier was ready at any moment to obey Ignatius, leave India or Japan, and come back to teach children in any college of Biscay or Guipuscoa. Who could pretend that he had no will in all his undertakings, and did not splendidly show it during the ten short years of his missions in the far Orient?

But this is more than sufficient to lay forever at rest the strongest objection that has ever been raised against the practice of the evangelical counsels. It is time to look at them independently of what men often say on the subject without much reflection, and to bring to bear upon the vow of obedience in particular the bright example of Christ Himself. For holiness precisely consists in imitating the Redeemer, and the nearer man comes to His perfection the more he deserves to be called holy.

In a previous passage of this chapter many texts of the Gospel were brought forward to prove that Christ in His humanity considered Himself as strictly bound to obey the will of His Father, not only in a general manner and by a sort of habitual inspiration, but concretely, as metaphysicians say, and in each particular event of His life. To use a comprehensive phrase, it can be maintained that He applied in prayer to God in each of His undertakings, in order, as it were, to know His will; and as soon as it was ascertained He followed it implicitly. This, at least, is the best interpretation that can be given of a great number of passages of the New Testament. It was previously remarked that He appeared to hesitate only once—namely, in the Garden of Olives—and the explanation of the difficulty was given according to the best interpreters.

That He intended this should be a rule for all men is proved not only from the fact that it was perfectly unnecessary for Him on account of His own divine nature, and that consequently He could have no other object in doing so than to afford us a powerful example. But moreover the clause of the prayer which He left us—"Thy will be done on earth," etc.—shows that He wished us to think constantly of the will of God in order to do it, and not to abide too much by the individual will the Creator has given us.

But it is also evident that the holiness which He came to establish on earth among men would always find in him a perfect pattern; and no Christian will deny that to copy that pattern is the highest virtue which a man can practise. This peculiarity of the life of Christ consequently—namely, His constant and unreserved obedience to the will of His Father—teaches us that we must submit our will at least to the will of God, in all and each of our actions, as He did. Here a serious difficulty presents itself. Our communication with God even in the most fervent prayer is not, like that of Christ, above the danger of misconception and delusion. To suppose that each attraction of our mind and heart consequent upon prayer comes surely from heaven would directly lead to fanaticism; and the sad history of religious aberrations of this kind is too well ascertained to leave any doubt on the subject. The only way to be sure of the will of God, and not to be deluded by our fancy, is to take the means which His providence furnishes us by listening to the voice of those appointed to rule over us, and think that God governs us by our civil and ecclesiastical superiors. To be sure, they are men and can command what is wrong. Hence we are warned that should they prescribe what is evidently forbidden by some well-ascertained divine law, not only are we not bound to comply, but we must positively disobey, even at the peril of our life. Outside of these extraordinary cases their voice must be considered as the voice of God, whom we obey by obeying them.

This is the plain and simple "way of precepts" for all men whatsoever; and the "way of counsels" naturally follows for the guidance of those who wish to imitate Christ more perfectly. They submit their will to that of some particular man established over them by the prescriptions of ecclesiastical law. Simple good sense entitles them to consider the commands thus enjoined upon them as coming from God Himself, whenever there is nothing in those commands evidently opposed to the divine law. Their object is to place themselves under a stricter discipline with a view to doing more good. Their individual will, as a human interior faculty, becomes thereby much stronger and more effective; they put under restraint only the part of it which might play false and lead them into error. They deprive themselves of many whims which are left to the free choice of other men; but they lose nothing of what truly ennobles a man. Quite the contrary; they make the sacrifice—a holocaust it has been called—of mere dross, in order to possess the pure and refined gold of a strong will altogether devoted to God and the cause of humanity. They, in fine, rejoice to think that if in order to obtain that result they submit themselves to many acts of self-restraint unpleasant to human nature, Christ, their Model, has done it before them much more absolutely still and effectually.

It is time now at last to come to the precise object of this chapter, and prove that in the process just described of "evangelical counsels" there is a sure means of attaining the highest degree of moral perfectibility in man, and that perfect holiness expands from it as a flower from a bud. This will naturally explain the meaning of the phrase, *aiming at perfection*, which is said to be the particular duty of the "religious." It is an expression altogether and exclusively Christian, which alone would go to prove that Christianity has at least a theory on the subject of the indefinite perfectibility of man in morals, and that this theory is constantly reduced in the Catholic Church into a serious practice, so far as a well-meant attempt is concerned. In the second part of this volume, in which *facts* shall be considered, another step in advance will be taken, and the reader will be able to judge if holiness among

Christians is only a Utopia. Let us proceed with order, and examine first what is indefinite perfectibility in morals, and how far it can be carried out in human life.

5. *Aiming at Perfection.*

Our scheme confines us here to the consideration of the *progress* of the soul towards *holiness*. There can be question neither of physical man as one of the special objects of natural history, nor even of the *summum bonum* within the limits of this life, such as the Greek and Roman philosophers undertook to define, and which is also the only scope of modern moralists. The soul for us is both spiritual and immortal, and its perfectibility must partake of both characteristics. Instead of bodily organs and functions (the only thing considered by naturalists) we have before us an immaterial substance whose aims tend constantly towards the infinite, and whose faculties of intellect and will reflect in their essence the image of God Himself. Instead of an exterior harmony and beauty as seen in man's mortal frame, or, on the other side, of an unseemly deformity introduced by the author of all evil, we either assist at the spectacle of sublime virtues born of self-sacrifice and adorning the earth with something of the radiance of heaven, or we are forced to contemplate with sorrow the degradation of sinful man changing the earth into the abode of demons. Finally, in place of the natural satisfaction produced *during this life* by a simple adherence to the moral laws of the created world, or of the temporary well-being resulting from the mere subjection of animalism without any further object of a higher nature, we have the sublime evolution of an immortal spirit born in the bosom of God in heaven, exiled a moment for probation on this earth, and starting on its forward career toward the goal of perfection, endowed consequently with the noble prerogative of an indefinite perfectibility.

The mere concerns of human life as illustrated in the world of politics, of science, of art, of civilization, pale before the effulgence of the human soul as it is revealed before us by the doctrines of Christianity. The simple ideas of spirituality and immortality transport us at once to heaven; the earth cannot be called any longer our country; the whole of creation itself is too narrow for our dwelling, since the bosom of God is infinitely larger than creation.

It is now demonstrated that the universe must be limited; what is material is absolutely confined ; God alone is without limits ; but He has communicated to us something of His own infinity by creating us immortal and giving to our aspirations, even on earth, infinite aims and a boundless extension. On this is firmly grounded the doctrine of the indefinite perfectibility of the human soul; and it becomes clearer still when some other dogmas of our holy faith are considered.

The image of God was already impressed on man's soul in the very act of creation; but this became much truer still in the act of redemption by which we were made sons of God through Christ. Both ideas have been previously developed, and the whole circle of the doctrine was completed by considering the work of the Holy Ghost in the rehabilitation of fallen man. Sanctification, holiness, the peculiar object of the Holy Spirit's mission, became the ultimate result of the whole plan of the Christian religion; and that holiness must be such as becomes the adopted sons of God.

This is the sublime object which is to be attained, and which the Christian faith places constantly before our eyes. Yet in order to reach such a height of moral goodness man must start from very humble beginnings, and gradually follow a line of constant progression, always aiming higher and higher.

The commencement indeed must be humble, because man unfortunately, born in sin, is inclined to evil, and this leaning is chiefly visible when he has not yet conquered himself ; that is, at the beginning of his career. It is at the price of constant efforts, never to be relaxed, always to be renewed, that he can indulge the hope of advancing. Endowed with free will, loaded with a heavy moral responsibility, he must co-operate with the divine grace in his own sanctification ; and since the ultimate term is perfection itself, and the highest degree ends in God from whom it all originated, it is clear that there is no limit to the exertions of the soul for so sublime an object.

To understand fully, therefore, what is called "aiming at perfection" it is necessary to reflect on the difficulties which are encountered from the very starting point, and to examine how they have to be gradually smoothed down and removed.

Consider a moment, better still than it could be done in a previous passage, how strong are the fetters which bind us to sin. They have been called by the Catholic masters of spiritual life the three concupiscences, derived from a celebrated passage of St. John.* "All that is in the world," says the apostle of love, "is the concupiscence of the flesh, and the concupiscence of the eyes, and the pride of life." Catholic exegetists agree that the second of these, the concupiscence of the eyes, which alone offers a difficulty, means here the love of gold, with which man procures everything calculated to please the senses, and particularly that of sight: fine houses, pictures, statues, furniture, elegant dresses, etc. St. John, therefore, teaches us that the sources of all worldly temptations by which we are enticed into sin can be referred to *lust, avarice,* and *pride.* And it was not difficult to those who have analyzed the human heart to show that all offences against morality are derived from these three heads, as from three prolific and adequate sources. This is the starting point of progression.

Every one is aware of the sort of fatality which pursues the man given to lewdness. No consideration of honor, of health, of respect for the rights of others, of anything which must make impression even on mere worldings, can check him a moment in his wild career. How many fearful crimes have stained the annals of mankind, all traceable to that degrading vice! It kills the body and debases the mind. It ruins the most prosperous families and destroys the hopes of thousands. It is as loathsome as calamitous. Yet few indeed are happy enough to avoid its snares, and to remain all their life pure from its hateful embrace. It is the first obstacle which young men always meet when they generously resolve to enter the path of virtue, and it is often the last heavy yoke which old men have to drag along before they rest finally in their grave.

St. Augustine knew it well, and on this account he intoned in his Confessions a song to holy Chastity: † "Powerful habits kept me wedded to pleasure, and in the midst of my hesitations seemed to tell me: 'Canst thou live without us?' But it was already a faint voice. For on the opposite side, in the direction toward which I had just turned my face (irresolute, however, and trembling still with apprehension), the chaste and noble figure of Continence appeared to my eyes, beaming with serenity and a joy altogether different from that of dissoluteness. Looking honestly into my face, she emboldened me to go to her and not

---

* 1 John ii. 16.   † Lib. viii. c. xi.

to fear. She outstretched her arms, and her holy hands prepared to press me on her bosom, her hands so rich in good works, so full of attractive examples of virtue. Around thee, O lady (I thought), I see a multitude of children, both boys and girls: I see young people, and men of every age, and venerable widows, and pure maidens that have already reached an old age. In the midst of that graceful throng, thou art not barren, O prolific and chaste mother of so many sons! Thy holy womb bore them to the Lord who wedded thee. And the noble figure smiled as if to mock at what she had read in my thoughts, and she appeared to say: 'Canst thou not do what these boys and girls, these men and women, accomplish so easily? They are not reduced to their own strength, they have the Lord God to help them. The Lord God gave them to me.'"

Thus self-sacrifice shows already its power in opposition to the first and greatest obstacle to perfection. But from impurity the text of St. John takes us to *avarice*, to the greed of gold, which he calls " the concupiscence of the eyes." For, as Cornelius a Lapide justly remarks on this passage (*omne quod est in mundo*), the word *mundus*, in the mind of the apostle, may have had several meanings; the most natural is here "the whole universe," embracing chiefly the part of it which entices man to evil, in the sense of another passage of St John where he says that *mundus totus in maligno positus est*—" the whole world is seated in wickedness." After considering, therefore, whatever in it leads to the carnal gratification of sense, he passes to the brilliant part of it, which is the result of wealth; and he calls it " the concupiscence of the eyes." It is undoubtedly one of the greatest sources of moral evil; not only because it gives to man all the means of satisfying his passions, but chiefly because it makes him forget that he has another and better country. The greed of gold, when it is gratified, throws a veil, as it were, on the spiritual part of man, and allows him to see only what is perishable in his nature. He becomes entirely wedded to this world, so beautiful in appearance, and remains altogether indifferent to a hereafter. The consideration of a future life becomes unwelcome and burdensome. We are led to try our best not to believe in it; and this is the main reason why so many people in our day live in this world as if there was no other. Have not the means of sensual gratification been fearfully increased of late by a greater diffusion of wealth? and is not the persuasion of a large number of men 'that wealth is everything' the source of the degrading materialism which prevails? What are the principles of morality good for, when its sanction has disappeared in the universal forgetfulness of a hereafter, if not in a positive disbelief in its existence? If the law of God is after all the only true support of human society, we must shudder at the idea of what this human society will become when the law of God is altogether forgotten in the insane pursuit after money.

Even in a human point of view see what has been the fate of the most powerful nations which have ever existed, as soon as all the attention of their citizens was engrossed by the worship of Mammon. They fell ingloriously under the blows of barbarians who were poor, whose only property consisted in having strong arms and sharp weapons. In reading history we are naturally struck by the outward view of these contests, and we seldom reflect on the true cause of the victory which invariably sides with the uncouth and naked against the refined and pompously attired combatant. On the one side the soldiers have muscles of steel fed by a substantial but coarse fare; on the other the pampered bodies of their would-be rivals have lost all the generous blood which ran of old in the veins of the nation. They can scarcely stand on their feet: how could they answer blows by equally strong blows. The praise of poverty came from the lips of Roman dictators during the glorious age of the republic; their effeminate posterity lived in palaces, boasted of their immense wealth, and could not resist any longer the impetuosity of hungry savages.

Such being the result of effeminacy produced by wealth and, on the contrary, the strength given to nations by abstemiousness, the fruit of poverty, it is possible to calculate the powerful effect of self-renouncement applied to the goods of this life. Thus the evangelical counsels prove their strength in this second branch of inquiry, as much as they did in the first with regard to chastity. Evangelical, that is voluntary, poverty gives an effective blow to the "concupiscence of the eyes;" the second baneful source of evil on earth is dried up at once, and a most powerful obstacle to perfection is instantly removed.

That perfection, the reader knows, is spiritual and belongs to an immortal soul. By accepting willingly poverty as a queen and a mistress, as St. Francis called her, the infinite superiority of a higher sphere is asserted at once over and against all the glitter of the pomps of this world. The soul is directly freed from the fetters which enchained her as a slave *adscripta glebæ,* " made fast to this world;" she can henceforth soar toward a better one and acknowledge it with joy as her true country. Attachment to the goods of the present life, therefore, is renounced as a drag on the natural aspirations of an immortal spirit; and the source of a thousand cares, anxieties, nay, sins and crimes, is altogether drained and exhausted. The first step to perfection is undoubtedly to throw away all hinderances to it; its ulterior goal will be manifested before long, when the whole power of Christian and apostolic poverty will be unfolded, as a ladder on which man ascends to the highest perfection.

There remains to be briefly considered the third baneful characteristic of this world, according to St. John, which is "the pride of life "—*superbia vitæ.* Pride, or the undue estimate of one's greatness, was the primitive cause of Lucifer's fall. It brought to perdition at once a third part of heaven. What must be its effect on poor puny man! That so wretched a creature as any of the unredeemed sons of Adam should lose sight of his deplorable condition and indulge in dreams of superiority, is a mystery which can be explained only by the blindness incident to the Fall itself, by which every faculty of man was distorted and dwarfed so as to appear to the angels a very mockery of his original condition. Still man is proud! Every one must know it by this time, after so long a period of his history. Without entering into a long enumeration of all the aberrations of human arrogance, and denouncing by the mere statement of them the ridiculous features of its innumerable manifestations, it is more than sufficient to briefly allude to the inconceivable proofs of it we all have in this age. Are they not proud, those powerful statesmen of Europe to whom seems to have been entrusted the guidance of the modern world? Yes, they know well, or rather they are fully persuaded, that their wisdom rules it. And that no one should remain ignorant that it is so, they openly announce that heaven has no share in the affairs of this world! It is their own exclusive department! It is only in this age that politics has been openly set free from the divine laws of morality. For it is now an axiom with human rulers that power does not come from God. As according to the new theories He has not presided at the origin of human society, it is useless to apply to Him for guidance on any particular occasion. Human force is all-sufficient to rule the world; and prayer to obtain divine help for that object is childish prejudice, which may have been good for the infancy of political associations, but can have no place in our improved theories of government. This is the corner-stone of the edifice of "modern liberalism," on which the whole fabric stands and must stand forever. This is a proud affirmation which at once disconnects earth from heaven, and gives to political talent a splendid occasion for showing its wisdom and securing the happiness of nations without the interference of priests.

This admirable project has been sufficiently tested by this time. And what do we see? Complaints everywhere, dark conspiracies plotted in the bosom of the most prosperous nations; the word *revolution* inscribed at the head of the programme set forth by numerous political parties. This ominous word, first introduced in France with a new meaning a hundred years ago, has now gone round the world, and is heralded everywhere as destined to stand forever in a constant succession of fierce uprisings before the eyes of the people. No rest, consequently, is to be expected on any spot cursed by the new theories. It is an endless chain of woes, whose circle begins anew as soon as it has gone round. Still the bewildered leaders of the nations affirm that they are competent for the task; and at the very moment that the clouds lower down and threaten another frightful storm, they announce that a new sun is just on the point of dawning, and that after the atmosphere is purified by lightning the zephyrs will blow gently and the eternal peace of the elements shall be proclaimed.

Can blindness and folly go farther? Yes, they must, since the very claps of popular thunder do not awaken those sleepy fools. They would further proclaim that everybody is happy under their rule, and that they are "the beloved of the nations" at the very moment that all are enraged against them and preparing to tear them to pieces. See at this moment the antics of European statesmen with the socialists in front of them, and say if there is any exaggeration in this picture.

But this is only one sample of human pride in this age together with the exposure of its folly. What could not be said of scientific arrogance when it is carried to the point of materialism and atheism, as is so often the case under our eyes? The more true science advances the more is resplendent the glory of God, because

He is the infinite source of knowledge, and away from Him there is only darkness and error. Yet see how the very idea of religion is scouted by many who think they know everything because they deny God. They have openly proclaimed in their pride "an antagonism between science and religion;" and their meaning can scarcely be misunderstood. They declare that any one who believes in a personal God cannot be a scientific man. They think they can explain everything in the universe without the need of a Creator and Preserver. The object here cannot be to discuss their pretensions. Its mere statement is another proof of the folly which always follows pride. Science without God is light without a cause. By denying its origin they turn it into darkness. They become afflicted with a disease which a contributor to the *Revue des questions scientifiques* of Bruxelles has called, with much precision and justice, "scientific blindness." See how they grope their way in the dark, and look for truth where it cannot be found. They announce boldly the demonstration of their system, and they fail ludicrously. Their generalizations are senseless because the first link is always wanting. They walk cautiously at first, and seem to throw a flood of light in the eyes of their admiring listeners; they group phenomena together, and show a sad talent in arranging them so as to prepare the way for the great object they have in view, which is nothing else than the total exclusion of God from His domain; they here and there throw an innuendo or two as stepping-stones going towards an abyss which they intend to fill afterwards with the empty bag of sonorous words; and finally, when the massive scientific construction is all complete except the head concealed in the clouds, they make a bold use of an unmeaning word like *protoplasm* or such like, and everybody must be satisfied or consent to remain among the unscientific crowd. Did ever the world witness in previous ages a higher and at the same time emptier pretension in the noble ranks of the learned? And what would be the result of the attempt if it could succeed? It would take away from mankind its hopes and highest aspirations; deprive human society of all principles on which it can securely rest; destroy morality, religion, virtue—everything which must be dear to man; give us no other heirloom on the day we are born than "the survival of the fittest" in this world and "nothingness" in the next.

If pride produces such fatal results among the highest classes of mankind, such as are political rulers and scientists; if it turns them into ludicrous theorists and adventurous mountebanks, what kind of vile poison will it give to drink to the vulgar herd, to the *many* in contradistinction to the *few?* Here we are not so much struck by the ludicrous as by the mournful aspect it assumes. It fills the heart of the poor with envy, with hatred toward those who have reached a higher round of the social ladder; it violently excites their desires for whatever is unapproachable to them; it leaves them forever disconsolate and unhappy, and not unfrequently it leads them to despair. Can there be for them a passion more baneful than pride? The subject could be indefinitely enlarged; our limits prevent us from developing it further.

Against such a terrible evil as this the Christian religion has taught us to press to our bosom a virtue which the world cannot appreciate, but whose name must be constantly dinned into its ears. It is humility; the precious jewel which Christ brought us from heaven, when He annihilated Himself according to St. Paul. And in order that man could put this virtue more easily into practice, the third evangelical counsel, called "religious obedience," intervenes and effectually roots out pride, one of the vices most opposed to perfection. A previous short explanation of the Sermon on the Mount has shown that humility is the essence of Christianity. It inculcates all the lowly virtues: meekness, forgiveness of injury, mercy, compunction of heart, unconquerable patience and peacefulness. All this is resumed in the comprehensive word *obedience*. Nothing subdues in man the spirit of pride to such a degree as the voluntary practice of it. To surrender one's will in the sense explained above is the first step to take in order to become truly humble, and when continued for a long time that practice necessarily conduces to the highest perfection of it.

But so far the described process has been confined to the act of removing the chief obstacles we meet in our way to holiness. Attention must now be given to the farther advance necessitated by the perfectibility of the soul. For if it is indefinitely perfectible, the first step such as it has been described, is not sufficient. It was only given as the first term of a series which supposes a large number of subsequent terms or steps. Here the virtues to be acquired must be considered in themselves, and not precisely as opposed to the contrary vices. Chastity is to be offered to the eyes of the reader in its inward beauty and not as the counterpart of a very ugly sin. And it must be, moreover, set forth in the various degrees of its course following a constantly ascending scale.

Look, then, at that sublime prerogative by which men are enabled to emulate the purity of the angels. To win it, that is to acquire it, in any remarkable degree is the greatest moral conquest of which man can be proud. For it supposes that the body is obedient to the soul, which is the main object proposed by what is called morality; and the subjugation of a whole empire is not to be compared to it, as being of an inferior nature. All our spiritual faculties are enhanced by it and partake of its loveliness. The *mind* grown stronger through it soars far above sense, and can dwell at ease on lofty contemplations without any interference from the vapors of a low, sensuous atmosphere; the *will* acquires all its vigor and, besides enjoying the entire strength of its determination, seems clothed with the angelic cleanness of innocence and the buoyancy of perpetual youth; the *memory*, free at last from all foul imaginations, revels in the warmth of guileless feelings, reflecting the purity of heaven, where she thenceforth habitually dwells. Oh, happy those who after long struggles are finally wedded to holy chastity! They find in her an anticipation of eternal happiness, since the great blessing of the hereafter promised us by religion consists in the ecstasy of divine love unmixed with the slightest annoyance from sense unsubdued. St. John Chrysostom tells us that this virtue raises man *above* the angels, since, dragged down as he is by the burden of his bodily organs, he has obtained such mastery over them that he can be compared to those blessed spirits whom God has not subjected to a union with matter.

But to better judge of it, let us see how tedious is the process, how arduous is the task. The great obstacle, it is supposed, has been removed. Whatever improper habit existed previously has been conquered, and the progress toward true virtue must immediately commence. It is not sufficient not to surrender any longer to the enemy as soon as he appears; the permanence of good purpose must be maintained. Habits of purity, in consequence, must be acquired. Do we sufficiently reflect on the labor required for the permanent acquisition of any habit whatever? We can easily know it by remembering what it has cost us for the possession of those which are almost purely of a physical nature and require very little mental exertion. What care, attention, and length of time is not necessary for walking straight, reading fast, writing rapidly, playing correctly on any instrument, even for managing a horse, using a sword skilfully, shooting a bird on the wing; in general, for any swift and effective command of our muscles, limbs, weapons, and utensils! Each of these exercises of the body begins with ludicrous attempts; and it is only after months and years of constant practice that we are at last masters of our movements and sure of the intended effects. The same is the case for the operations of the mind, for the application of our principles of logic in conversation or written composition, for the instant perception of all the consequences derived from one single principle, for every quick manifestation of intellect and judgment. It must be true likewise of our moral nature. Loose manners are not immediately replaced by strict and correct ones. After the first have been mended, the second must be slowly introduced by a process similar to the one just described for physical and mental habits. If men in general attached as much importance to the improvement of their morals as to the development of the body or the mind, they would soon find that the process required in the first case is still more difficult than in the two others. But unfortunately a strict morality is so burdensome and so uncongenial to the great majority of men that they too often close their eyes to its importance, refuse to listen to the voice of their conscience, and, because its reward is more to be expected in another world than in this, they wait for reformation until the latter part of their life, in case they are so lucky as not to forget it altogether.

This is the main reason why so little is done by many for the improvement of their moral nature. But those few who have a keener sense of their responsibility to God, and of the strict account they will have one day to render Him, can testify how difficult a task it is to acquire habits of virtue particularly with regard to chastity. The world and its maxims, the devil and his suggestions, the evil inclinations of our nature and their alluring seductions, are all banded together to oppose the slightest projects of reform. It is a regular fight that is to be carried on at every moment of life against the flesh, the world, and the devil. To speak of the flesh alone, is it not true that a constant watch must be kept over all our senses at once, and each one of them in particular? A number of habits, consequently, must be acquired by which our eyes, our tongue, and ears, and hands are placed under a constant restraint. All that mass of corruption must be purified and consecrated to God by holy chastity. In order that our minds and hearts should be chaste, all our senses have to be first chastened. Do we not begin to perceive how long a time it will take, and how slow our pace must first be before we can hope of running in the road of perfection? Yet all this is absolutely necessary for giving a practical turn to the perfectibility of our soul. We cannot say otherwise that we are "aiming at perfection."

In that warfare no account has been taken of the interior world, so superior in seduction to our senses themselves; namely, of our memory, imagination, natural instincts. These enter, however, as a powerful factor in the difficulties of the problem. And to make a complete enumeration of those difficulties, the temptations of the devil and the allurements of a licentious world would have to come under consideration. This is a very incomplete sketch of the tedious work which man must undertake if he seriously wishes to "perfect" his own soul, as the majority of people feel the importance of doing for the improvement of their bodily advantages and mental endowments. To render the view of it more adequate, and place it more vividly before the mind, a word must be said on the chief instrument which requires to be used for obtaining the intended effect. This is nothing else than a persevering effort at keeping the eyes of our conscience open, at placing on paper, as it were, a daily, nay, hourly account of what passes at every moment within the inmost recesses of our soul. It is called by all Catholics the examen of conscience; all undoubtedly practise it, more or less however, according to the degree of attention they bestow upon it.

To repeat, and repeat again the series of operations demanded by the process which has been just mentioned, is far from being pleasant to nature. Yet it is absolutely necessary to do so in order to acquire solid habits of virtue, particularly in the matter of chastity. It is as indispensable as the slow operation of the novice flute-player, when with his fingers ready, his eyes bent on the instrument, his mouth pressed on the aperture, he so ludicrously tries to charm our ears with the melody of a simple tune. To work on the harmony of the soul, to draw from her songs of joy and purity when she has lost even the memory of these sweet sounds, necessitates operations as painfully elaborate as those of a juvenile pianist. Let the operator, however, keep up his courage and not mind the titters of his audience. The time will surely come when he will be a skilful artist, provided he shows perseverance and industry.

But the question may be put: Can the soul, an immortal and immaterial spirit, be perfected by a process of this sort, only fit in appearance for the lowest beings in the scale of intellect? If the human soul had remained what it was at its creation, nothing of this would be needed and such a laborious course of action would never have been put in practice among men, since they would not have lost any part of their original integrity. But after the Fall the soul found itself rigidly wedded to matter; and to start again on the way to a far-distant perfection, material help was wanted, material means were to be taken; and even with these it was but the plodding along on a hard road by a being less than half spirit and more than half matter. In these considerations, it is true, no account has been taken of the grace of God, without which, however, nothing at all could have been accomplished. The reason of it has been previously assigned. But it must be remembered by the Catholic reader that the grace of God is not the pretended help invented by Luther and Calvin by which God does everything and man absolutely nothing. As the Church does not believe that human nature was totally depraved by the Fall, so likewise she teaches that man must co-operate with the grace of God for his own rehabilitation. We must not, therefore, be surprised that the perfectibility of the soul must be worked out more than half materially, and that "aiming at perfection" consists at first in dabbling in little measures of moral safety, such as they have just been detailed.

But how could be described the last stage of this progress, so different from the slow initial movement? When the Christian has earnestly labored in plodding along—to repeat the word that has been just used—the time comes at last when not only the enemies are conquered and the obstacles overcome, but the habit of virtue is solidly established, and the permanent love of holy purity triumphant. This must be examined a moment to understand how the soul is in truth indefinitely perfectible. Look at a musician who has become a perfect master in his art. He has acquired two wonderful habits which have cost him years of toil, but which he considers as sufficient for his reward. He can read at sight, as they say, the most difficult composition, and his instrument is perfectly under his control. With what a pure delight is not his soul entranced whenever he renders with precision and feeling the masterpieces of the kings of song! He makes his own the productions of the greatest composers that have ever lived, and feels that the noble' blood which coursed through the veins of a Mozart or a Beethoven warms up his own breast and circulates through all his frame. How gladly now he rejoices that he has spent so much time and employed so much labor in the arduous task in which he has consumed his youth! Had he been deterred by sloth at the beginning of his career, he would at this moment neither see the multitude of his listeners enraptured by the flood of harmony which he pours forth with the ease of a warbling nightingale, nor hear the thunder of their applause at the end of one of his mightiest efforts to please.

Far greater is the delight experienced by the noble athlete who has manfully fought and gloriously conquers. Helped by the grace of God he is the happy possessor of two habits likewise, but far more marvellous than those of the best musical performer. He has subdued by years of labor the interior world of his own imagination, memory, and instincts; and his exterior senses, now perfectly subject to his control, are reduced to be only the instruments of a pure mind and a clean heart. If he does not, on this account, receive the applause of men, he knows at least that he is rich of the approval of God and of the admiration of the angels.

Let not any cynic philosopher pretend that this is all a dream unrealizable in this life, and at best the dishonest boast of mere pretence. We know that in the Holy Church of Christ there are thousands, nay, millions—of pure souls such as have been just described; and they mainly owe their happy state to the strict daily examination of their conscience under the inspiration of God's grace. No one, at least, can deny that there is an immense number of people in all countries under the sun who have consecrated their virginity to God, and cannot be called hypocrites by men who are altogether unable to read into their souls. What motive could they have to feign purity without having it? If they are rational beings, would it not be better for them, in every respect, to live chastely in marriage than labor under such an imputation out of it? But besides those who have most willingly placed themselves under the restraint of the first of the "evangelical counsels," it is certain that there are still a far greater number of holy souls in the Church who live among men as if they were in the cloister, who have so perfectly subdued their senses that they lead in truth an angelical life, although they are surrounded with all the dangers of the world.

Would not this alone prove that the soul of man is perfectible, nay, indefinitely perfectible in this mortal life, and that the possibility or rather the duty of "aiming at perfection" is the highest prerogative she has obtained from God during her pilgrimage, and while remaining under the necessity of a personal union with a corruptible body? For the process which has been studied so far affects the soul herself in her highest moral qualifications, and under it the best part of man is undoubtedly "perfected;" that is, amended, raised on a higher level, intimately ennobled, and brought nearer to God. The reader begins to see how the Christian religion by the principles it inculcates deeply lays the foundation of true morality and holiness, and no other institution in the world can compete with it for the reformation of man and the establishment of God's kingdom on earth.

Similar considerations could be laid down and developed in the same manner with regard to the two other "evangelical counsels," and it would be as easy to prove that voluntary poverty and willing obedience contribute to the same result after they both have removed the obstacles opposed to perfection by covetousness and pride. What could not be said of the life-long effect produced by the disinterestedness incident to a total renouncement of worldly advantages? Is not the soul far more free and "perfect" when all motives of acquiring what is called property are removed? Look at the loveliness of St. Francis' character. Can there be found in the whole range of man's history a purer mind, a nobler heart, a higher soul in every respect? But it was undoubtedly the exuberant feelings created in him by his love for holy poverty that inspired his whole life. Let any one feel as he did in that regard, and the same result will be obtained; and it would be so for the majority of men if they were impressed with the same sentiment. Then, how radically would the world be changed! merely because the souls of men would be far more perfect than they are, and human society would be governed by far higher principles of morality. Voluntary obedience added to the two other evangelical counsels would complete the process, and change in fact the whole face of the moral world.

CHAPTER V.

THE ETERNAL DESTINY OF MAN, CONTRASTED WITH TEMPORAL THINGS, GIVES TO THE FOREGOING PRINCIPLES THEIR MAIN STRENGTH AND EFFICACY WITH REGARD TO THE PURSUIT OF HOLINESS ON EARTH.

1. *The Irremediable Defect of all Moral Codes which are not Founded on Christian Principles comes from their Want of a Sanction in the Absence of a Hereafter.*

THERE is a strange inconsistency in the writings of nearly all modern philosophers when they treat of morality. They often criticise Christian ethics, find fault with them in many points, openly accuse the obedient children of the Church of following in their actions a moral code which cannot be reconciled with the principles inculcated by reason and human conscience. Some of them even go so far as to pretend that history does not justify the claim of the Church when she declares herself to be the great teacher of sanctity; and the main object of this volume is to disprove this strange accusation. But their inconsistency chiefly consists in this, that finding fault with the Church's ethics, they replace them by a code deprived of any effective sanction, because they never dare to mention the retributions of a future life.

They seem to imagine that in order to establish holiness among men it is sufficient to enumerate the various pronouncements of intuitive reason with regard to morality. If it were so all men would be holy, because all know, or at least can easily know, what each one has to do to be virtuous. They do not seem to perceive that with this knowledge nearly all men do precisely the contrary, and that consequently the mere voice of reason or of conscience is insufficient. What does, in fact, their boasted teaching amount to? It is effectually reduced to the vain resounding of an echo in the wilderness; it is a voice that comes and goes; and they pretend to be better teachers than He who exclaimed: "Now the axe is laid to the root of the tree. Every tree, therefore, that does not yield good fruit shall be cut down and cast into the fire"! They pretend to be better preachers of morality than the Church, and they forget the most important part of the preaching! Let them at least adopt the measure best calculated to insure success, and there will be more consistency in their proceedings, particularly when the proofs of a hereafter are so plain.

But their reason for remaining mute on such an important point must be carefully examined, because we may find in it the best way of judging on which side is the true, the trustworthy teacher. When religion is altogether discarded and philosophy steps in its place, Heaven's commands cannot be intimated with confidence, and the moralist is reduced to inculcate the simple precepts of reason. Is this sufficient as a solid basis of simple ethics? It would be irrational to speak in this case of the spread of "holiness." This word, in fact, must be altogether struck off from the vocabulary of philosophers. They themselves understand that it would be almost ludicrous to use it in their teaching. But confining the inquiry to ordinary morality only, not of a high order of sanctity, it is proper to consider how far a human teacher can solidly establish it. There is no question here of a mere statement of principles. All agree that this is possible, because those principles are all based in reason, and reason is competent to write a full catalogue of them. But the attempt made in earnest by those philosophical teachers goes much farther. Either they undertake to *establish* morality among men, or all their books are perfectly useless. Now no one can pretend that a written catalogue of virtues suffices for this establishment. By printing a few pages in the form of the celebrated Epictetus' Table, and giving a copy to every living man, woman, and child, the process would be completed and morality triumphant. Something more than this must be required, as every one perceives, and philosophical clubs on the plan of those of Pythagoras must be set on foot and practically introduced among men. That this can be done by philosophers, to a slight extent, is not denied; but that it can comprise large classes of mankind is absolutely untenable.

The reason of it is chiefly derived from the infinite variety of interests that would oppose this project if it were seriously entertained. *Monsieur Jourdain*, in the celebrated comedy of Molière, has given, after all, the best cause of the universal opposition it would meet, by exclaiming: "Hang your moral philosophy that teaches me how to keep down my temper! I want for one to get mad when I choose; and you, reverend professor of morals, get out of my sight right away, or I may fall upon you and drive you off."

To speak seriously, the very idea of morality independent of religion cannot enter into the head of a sane man, unless he wishes to ruin both. True religion can no more be separated from the pursuit of the "good" than the "good" can exist unless it comes from God, the source of true religion. And this is the ultimate reason why there must be a religious sanction to any good code of ethics, and without it morality is a sham. At least no one can deny that the actual practice of true virtue by a great number of men, the formation of a large class in mankind known by their strict moral principles and applying them habitually in their daily life, absolutely requires that religion should intervene by pointing out to them as their goal the heavenly and eternal reward that God alone can promise.

A word has just been said of the "variety of interests" which always oppose the projects invented by philosophers for the "foundation of virtue." All the passions of the human heart, all the maxims of a specious but corrupt world, most of the social axioms current among mankind, form a web of well-connected hindrances firmly set against all those projects; and because the motives for virtue suggested by the most earnest reformers, even the strongest and most effective which they propose, are invariably taken from advantages which are more or less connected with earthly and transitory happiness, the opposing motives for self-indulgence, being likewise earthly and ending with this life, cannot be effectually resisted and overcome. This must be so particularly because in the constant conflict which naturally exists between virtue and vice, vice is always more alluring, and invariably assumes in moments of hesitation the brighest shape to entice the human heart, at the very moment that a veil is thrown over the conscience. Human motives of each kind put in both scales of the balance cannot keep it level; much less can the virtuous side prevail and conquer. It is very remarkable though very strange, in our opinion, that the philosophers of the "intuitive school," as it is called, take always for granted that human nature will assume on all occasions the shape and direction indicated by their moral systems, and that if a conflict is possible it will always be short and of a weak character. This only proves that they are poorly acquainted with human nature. Christian moralists, on the contrary, insist particularly on the terrible aspect which the contest often assumes, and on the ominous consequences which depend on the result. These last guides are more to be believed than the first, not only because they derive the doctrine they endeavor to inculcate from the teachings of theology, which is far preferable to philosophy in that respect, but chiefly because, being the acknowledged confidants of a great part of mankind, they can dive deeper into the human soul and know far better its most secret mysteries. They will all tell you that if a man hesitating between good and evil is told that by following his evil inclinations he ruins his *health*, destroys his *prospects in life*, alienates his best *friends*, etc., he may listen with some attention, appear even to have profited by the advice; but his amendment will be very slight and not endure long, because *pleasure* for him is more enticing than health, *enjoyment* is after all the best prospect in life, *boon companions* are in his eyes the best friends he could find, and so of the other strong motives of virtue you might propose. But if he has yet some principles of religion and you tell him that he openly disobeys God, cannot escape from the future judgment, is sure, if he continues, of an impending and eternal doom—in case the man has still some of his reason left, and he has not by previous crimes entirely stifled the voice of his conscience and excluded himself from all the influence of grace, he surely will retrace his steps and walk again along the path of virtue.

It appears incredible that there are men who cannot appreciate the strength of these reasons; yet there are, and many. The heading of this section has told us that "the irremediable defect of all moral codes which are not founded on Christian principles comes from their want of a sanction in the absence of a hereafter." This is to be discussed with some care, since it is the main question with us here. First, therefore, these philosophers may say that they do not exclude the "hereafter;" only they do not speak of it, being entirely limited to considerations derived from human *reason*. They must mean that they are in truth incompetent, because the existence of a future life with the necessary accompaniment of punishments and rewards belongs as much to the province of *reason* as the existence of our soul, nay, as the actual existence of the universe itself. Christian philosophers have proved it before this time; and to deny it would require that their proofs should be at least answered. The philosophers with whom the present discussion is mainly carried on must certainly admit it, if they remain consistent with their own principles. We have no doubt that most of them are fully persuaded that there is a future life, and that man's position in it will depend on his conduct during this one. Yet in their books on morals they never speak of it, and the only reason that can be seen for this strange reticence is that they feel their own *incompetency*. They are not religious teachers, and they can scarcely enter into the conscience of their fellow-men. This doctrine, besides, appertains as much to revelation as to reason, and they are in dread of the supernatural, which they constantly oppose. They shrink from placing themselves even on the borders of it, and feel the necessity of leaving in the shade whatever belongs to the departments of both religion and pure reason. But in doing so, they must acknowledge their incompetency not only for preaching openly a hereafter, but even for teaching morality at all. This is the second reason why there is an "irremediable defect in all their moral codes." The *supernatural* cannot be excluded from those codes; and some reflections are required to render it evident and satisfy the most incredulous that it is so.

Why is it that sin is sin, if not because it is opposed to the will of God? The prescriptions of the *divine* law alone can convince man that he has prevaricated when he has acted against them. Tear away the golden cord which unites earth with heaven, and there cannot be any more mention of sin or of virtue. It is not sufficient to say that every one is convinced that reason comes from God, and that whatever reason prescribes in point of morality is prescribed in fact by the great Author of reason. It is not sufficient to affirm that every one is interiorly convinced of it, and yet never acknowledge it in so many terms. It must be openly stated as the necessary foundation of morality. The principles of ethics must be proclaimed as expressing "God's Commandments," and nothing else. But this includes the true basis of a *supernatural* doctrine. The whole moral edifice raised upon it is nothing but the efflorescence of the tree which has thus been planted in the firm ground. If God has given "commandments," He has revealed Himself to man, and the details of that revelation must necessarily come afterwards. It is not logical to say that this revelation needs not have been exterior, and that the inward consciousness of the soul of man contains the only revelation he has ever received. For in this case the revelation would amount to nothing, on account of the well-known hesitations of human reason when left to itself, and of the absolute impossibility for the greatest part of mankind to frame an irreproachable and invariable moral code, unless man relies on a supernatural teacher.

Are all the philosophers agreed upon the ethical principles which go to form the "foundation of virtue"? Mr. Lecky proves most clearly, without wishing it, that they are not, by the very enumeration of the great number of systems elaborated on the subject by the chief upholders of the doctrine. If the masters of the science cannot agree, how will the mass of unintelligent people fare in the result? They will surely be altogether unable to make a single step in the path of virtue, whose "foundation" they cannot know. And the mass of unintelligent people is the mass of mankind. There are many millions of them to a single one of the bright luminaries who are their self-appointed guides. Who of them will dare say that there is no other revelation in point of ethics than the inner consciousness of reason? It would be not only proud and bold on their part, but most cruel and inhuman, since it would amount to the acknowledgment that man has really been left without the light he craves and the guide he absolutely needs, which cannot be confined to their own individuality. What did I say—bold and cruel? It would be worse still in some sense for the philosophers. It would convince them of having entirely stultified themselves by undertaking a task which they must feel is completely above human competency. They cannot exactly know what morality is as long as they reject the supernatural; they grope their way in the dark, and they stumble at every step. Still they pretend to teach mankind what it is to be virtuous, and they often go so far as to impeach and call in question the noble principles which the Church gives to men in order to practise virtue and walk securely on the road to perfection.

The plain doctrine of a hereafter is for the Christian absolutely unassailable as coming from the mouth of Christ, and thus his moral principles have a most firm foundation. The more so that many supernatural agencies are involved in Christian doctrine, and the basis of ethics, as was just seen, to be solid must rest mainly on the supernatural. But the peculiar aspect it takes with respect to the Founder of the Christian religion makes it still more appropriate to the moral needs of man; and this particular advantage is altogether denied to the mere philosopher. This must be seen somewhat more in detail in order to appreciate the advantage of the eternal over the temporal.

One of the most abundant sources of holiness in the Church is undoubtedly the example of Christ and the love which His divine character inspires to His disciples. An eloquent passage of Mr. Lecky himself on the subject is quoted in the "Church and Gentile World," (ch. iii.), but its effect on the soul of the true Christian can scarcely be apprehended by any one who does not believe. The inward agency of practical religion alone enables a man to fully understand how life itself can be sacrificed for an object of love which cannot be seen, and which is known only by report, as Jesus Christ is undoubtedly. But independently of such an act of heroism as this, required only of a few, and not usually entertained as a possible contingency, nearly all the actions of the Christian during an ordinary life are more or less influenced by the example of the Saviour and animated by the love which all the children of His Church naturally feel for Him. There is scarcely a single human concern on which some passage of the Gospel does not bear. The pious young man and woman, the enlightened Christian of any sex or condition, knows this practically if he has had any religious training of importance. The views of life generally taken by people of this class are more or less grounded on gospel truth. From the crib of Bethlehem to the cross of Calvary, the thirty-three years which went to compose the mortal career of the Redeemer are full of incidents which can be taken as moral examples of the highest and purest order.

Not only is this all connected with the supernatural, but we maintain that all this has more or less some reference to a hereafter, and that mainly on this account it is most powerful to promote morality, or rather to lead man surely, nay, infallibly on the road toward holiness and perfection. This is what was meant when in a previous page it was said that questions of the simplest moral doctrine must always be connected with the supernatural.

Is it not true that owing to the divine character of the Saviour He has indeed transferred heaven on earth, and we cannot think of Him and of His human actions without having before our eyes the spectacle of a hereafter turned into the present time? The expression may be bold, but it is exact, and the most simple reflection will show its truth to any one who pays the least attention to it. It is in fact the only meaning which can be attached to the pregnant phrase of our Lord so frequent in the Gospel, when He speaks of having come to establish the "kingdom of God on earth." Can the philosophers of the intuitive school be so little aware of the true position of the Christian as to imagine that he thinks of a future life only when he meditates on death and judgment? This may be true of the philosophers, if they ever consent to occupy their mind with such gloomy subjects as these. The Christian has a thousand occasions to reflect on the same subjects with an exuberance of joy. Or rather, though death and judgment are often set aside by him, he is always keenly alive to the truth that through Christ his soul is in constant communication with heaven. Can any one be blind enough not to perceive that this must have at all times a powerful effect on morality, or rather on holiness?

This truth will be rendered more forcible still—the subject is of so paramount an importance that even excess in this case must be pardoned by the reader—by a fact of almost daily occurrence, but to which people generally do not pay sufficient attention. No book can produce so powerful an effect on young people when they are somewhat seriously inclined as the "History of the Bible" when it is related with simplicity and accuracy. It is on many occasions sufficient to settle their religious and moral convictions for life, and it invariably improves their manners wonderfully. We have experienced it many times, and every one who will take the trouble of making the trial will be altogether satisfied of it. Now, what is the cause of it if not that the history of the Bible is in substance the narrative of the incessant action of God on the affairs of men, and particularly His inner dealings with the soul of each of us? It teaches us that we cannot for a moment remain out of His sight; that He is always intent on doing us good, as the most tender of friends, the most indulgent of fathers; it transports us at once into a world altogether different from this and accustoms us to consider ourselves as citizens of a holier commonwealth, the coheirs of Christ, the brothers of saints and angels, the happy companions of the blessed in heaven. Can anything be equal to this in training men up to well-doing? Do they not thus imbibe pure morality with life? In this commingling of earth with heaven, the hereafter becomes the present time, as was said before; the kingdom of God *has* come; the holiness of heaven must be that of earth. This may be called a dream by philosophers of the intuitive school; but we tell them that this dream is realized at this very moment by millions of the Church's children; and as there is yet, thank God, some innocence, guilelessness, purity, love of God and of Christ on earth, it is there that it can be found. Of course the mere philosophers must consent to admit that there is nothing of the kind on their side; and in their earnest efforts to spread pure morality by their dissertations on European and other morals, they cannot avail themselves of this *childish* means, as they pretend, which they must leave to the Catholic Church. But the strict consequence of it is that there is no hereafter for them, and their disciples must be left to the cold comfort that in practising virtue they attend to a concern of this life only, they cannot expect any other reward than the testimony of their conscience; they meanwhile are often in doubt as to what their conscience teaches, they chiefly are left alone in their solitary grandeur unsupported by heaven and yet merged into the endless troubles of the present life.

2. *Can there be a Solid Objection made Against the Christian Code of Morals?*

It is not intended here to advert to any of those objections in detail, and to answer them on the model of a scholastic dispute. They are often reduced to trifling points, when they are not altogether evident sophisms. The time and space consumed in such a task as this could not be repaid by any advantage that would accrue. The chief one of those difficulties even, which consists in affirming that among Christian nations morality has never been on a higher level than among pagans, does not deserve to be treated apart, because the Second Book of this volume will abundantly prove that it cannot be entertained by any man possessing the least degree of historical lore. The only measure that can be adopted on the present occasion consists in a general survey of the question at issue; and by grouping together all the conditions required for a high degree of moral goodness, it will directly become evident that they are all found in the Catholic Church and in no other institution on earth.

In order that a high degree of morality may be found anywhere, the precepts imposed by the code must be *clear*, so that the path to be followed may be well known; the same precepts must form a *complete* system of moral law, so as not to leave out any principle of virtue or any check against vice in matters of importance; the same must be imposed on man by an *authority* which cannot be repudiated or set aside. With regard to man himself, his conscience must be kept in a high degree of *keenness* by the very principles he has adopted; he must have *rules* to find out if the dictates of his conscience can be altogether trusted; and in no case must it be allowed to *remain grossly in error* for any length of time. Finally, there must be a powerful *sanction* to enforce this code, and at all times this sanction must remain *present* before the eyes of the doer. This last condition is the most important at this particular point of our investigations.

Can all those conditions be found together in any institution on earth, except it be a divine one? Does it not require the action of God Himself to have prepared for the moral guidance of man such a simple and at the same time perfect concordance between his interior faculties, his manifold duties, and the eternal object of his creation? It could be absolutely demonstrated that all this is found nowhere on earth except in the Catholic Church; but within its precincts the whole of it is admirably kept in its integrity. The philosophers of the intuitive school would undoubtedly be at a loss to find in their system all the particulars of this enumeration. We have had lately occasion to speak of their absolute silence on the belief in a *hereafter* as a necessary moral sanction. A *complete list* of moral precepts will never be found in their pages; and after they have insisted on a few moral axioms of the natural law, they think they have fulfilled the responsible duty they had assumed of guiding men in the path of virtue; and these axioms refer only to some of our duties toward our fellow-men. As to *conscience* and the *fear of error* in following its voice, they too often speak of it only for the purpose of finding fault with the Church, which is nevertheless the only institution which has ever undertaken the arduous task of purifying and enlightening the conscience of men, and done it, too, in all ages, and in millions upon millions of cases, for the great benefit of mankind. But, in general, because they remain in total ignorance of her earnestness, and zeal in promoting virtue, this action upon men's conscience is for them only a contemptible piece of casuistry, if it is not a veil thrown over moral corruption, and a snare to deceive souls. But whatever may be said to the contrary, the Church is in possession of that high trust, and has been for the last nineteen hundred years; and if her duty in that regard had been as poorly fulfilled as her adversaries are pleased to say, she would have lost it long ago; and the indignation of mankind against her for assuming unduly such a tremendous power would long before this have been raised against a truly sacrilegious presumption. On the contrary, among the ever-increasing number of her children during this age of real prosperity for her, the confidence, nay, the childlike reliance of the great majority of them seems to be as strong as ever, and in their eyes she is always the *judge* of morals, the *upholder* of virtue, the *opposer* of wrong-doing, the *oracle* of God in dictating what is to be done as well as what is to be believed.

We regret that space does not allow us to fully develop the previous paragraph, in which the conditions for a high degree of morality are enumerated and can be proved to exist in the Catholic Church. It would form by itself a full vindication of her claim as a guide to holiness. But we feel compelled to leave this subject to the consideration of the reader. Any one sufficiently well acquainted with Catholic moral theology can easily complete the task. It is in fact altogether elementary with us; but it often happens that the most simple facts with us become wonderful objects for outsiders. In this case it is so to a remarkable degree, and we sincerely wish we could at this moment enter into all the required details. But if we feel obliged to omit them, there is a line of general reflections which will not require such a long array of particulars derived from moral theology, and yet suffice for reaching the same conclusion. The question is about the Christian moral code and the objections which can be raised against it. Those who do so are always careful to speak only of the Catholic Church, not of Christ, as if both could be separated. We have just intimated that the solution of this question cannot remain in doubt even in the false supposition of such a separation. Moral theology, however, would become in this case the battle-field; and a long discussion would have to be undertaken to thoroughly vindicate it. We prefer to say that the Christian code is the code of Christ; and on this assertion we say that the whole case rests. The Church's adversaries openly deny it. They are used, on many occasions, to praise the doctrine of our Lord in His Sermon on the Mount. It is proper to examine if they can be altogether sincere in finding a great discrepancy between that doctrine of the Saviour and the main moral prescriptions of the Catholic Church. To an impartial man it is clear at first sight that the Beatitudes contain the very moral points against which our opponents object. The whole is comprised in few words, but full of meaning: humility, lowliness, the surrendering of rights, the forgiveness of injury, the neglect of earthly advantages, the choosing of the narrow and hard road, an ardent hankering after everything painful to nature. In fact, all the details set forth in a previous chapter when speaking of the "evangelical counsels," are embodied in this Sermon of our Lord as the main substance of Christianity. The Church in her application of the doctrine to the needs of weak mortals has softened it whenever it is susceptible of mitigation; but she could not repudiate its spirit and tendency, which consists in renouncement and self-sacrifice. For this she has been abused as if by doing so she had changed the religion brought down by Christ from heaven, and given a repulsive look to the Bride of the Saviour. This crime on her part has been ascribed to her casuistry, to her harsh feeling toward humanity, to a denial of Christian meekness. Hence the *morose* austerity of her monks, the *unnatural* enforcement of celibacy, the *degradation* of the human will by voluntary obedience, have been harshly descanted upon. Still any one who listens to the clear utterances of Christ in the Gospel must admit that the only fault of the Church—an irremissible one in the eyes of the world—is her too strict faithfulness in following the injunctions of Christ. Christ, therefore, is attacked through the Church, and the question recurs, Is Christ's code liable to any objection?

The man who believes in the authority of the Gospel as an inspired book, in the divinity of the Saviour as the Eternal Son of Almighty God, and in the strict communication of all His power to the Church as His representative on earth, cannot experience a moment of doubt as to the purity of morals which the Gospel, the Redeemer, and the Church herself uphold. He is firmly persuaded that there have never been on earth—nay, that there cannot be in the world—better teachers of good manners than all three, whose complete agreement is always assured. He even goes so far as to be convinced that all other teachers are only "wolves under the garb of sheep," such as the Saviour called them when He proclaimed Himself the only true Shepherd of souls. To confirm him in his belief he has the teaching of history itself, which tells him that whenever mankind has been left to its own guidance— that is, to that of philosophers and self-appointed teachers—the invariable result has been a gradual decline in morals, ending at last in degradation. On the other side, Christianity produced, suddenly at first, such a change for the better in the moral world that only a blind man cannot see it as a universal fact in history. Moreover, Christ's religion keeps in its bosom such a well-spring of purity and holiness that whenever the fickleness and evil inclinations of men have brought on corruption in the Church there has always been at hand a remedy to bring on the needed regeneration.

Again, that multitude of men who in our day seem to have lost their faith, and on whom the voice of the Church, of the Gospel, of Christ Himself, can scarcely make any impression, have an easy means to ascertain if, as they mostly pretend, the Christian is or is not far above the pagan in morality. Let them look at the world as it is, and they may change their opinion; for there are still pagans in the world. To make the comparison they must not be satisfied with considering only the exterior or public aspect presented by the so-called Christian nations as a whole. It is generally the view taken of it when this point is discussed; and there are unfortunately powerful elements of corruption introduced by unbelief in modern Christian society. These defective points come uppermost in considerations of this nature, and Christianity is made responsible for the moral deformity which in fact belongs to modern paganism. To properly compare the influence of Christianity in promoting good morals with that of pagan principles, we must select in modern society that part of it which is really influenced by Christian teaching; and there can be no doubt that this golden portion of the modern world is far above what is best in the paganism of our day. The two classes, Christian and pagan, are now to be seen at work side by side in all large European cities; and the simple view of it brings directly to the mind the powerful description of both such as they existed in the Roman world, fifteen hundred years ago, and have been described by St. Augustine in his great work *De Civitate Dei*.

This will become more forcible still from another series of considerations having the same object in view. At this moment the Christian nations have the hegemony of the world. They rule it, and loom up above the rest of mankind, as if they were of a superior nature. This does not date of yesterday, but has been acquired by several centuries of intercourse, trade, colonization, and political connections. It has been, undoubtedly, often the source of great evils, of untold abuses, of awful crimes. But the undeniable facts of oppression, invasion of rights, greed, and rapacity of some Christian nations in their colonies do not impair and weaken the truth that the present hegemony of the world by Europe was mainly the fruit of her superiority. And this superiority must be admitted as well in morals as in civilization, art, and military discipline. This last phase of European power was the main factor in the acquisition of social and political ascendency among the innumerable races which Europe undertook to subdue. But any one may see that military discipline in the modern sense supposes Christian principles. Fortunately for mankind it is still the Christian moral code which invariably directs modern warfare. Owing to this the countries where war is carried on are spared the former horrors of pagan times; and even on battle fields, on the only places where blood is shed, there are humane rules to follow which could not exist for pagans. It is sufficient to mention the care taken of the wounded belonging to the enemy, and the immediate friendly intercourse which directly follows the fiercest encounters.

This is extremely remarkable; but the same view of the subject must be taken on a much larger scale when speaking of the superiority at this moment under consideration. If the whole question is examined more closely, it is easily seen that Europeans have acquired their present proud position in the world by their whole system of morals, still more than by their theoretical knowledge and universal culture. They brought to foreign nations principles of right, of justice, of humanity, of real benevolence, which were not known among them before, and which Europeans themselves owed only to Christianity. Their missionaries preached the Gospel; they themselves built hospitals, asylums, houses of education. They changed at once the face of the moral world all over those benighted countries. Those various institutions of charity, enlightenment, and peace cannot exist except among nations blessed by a moral code worthy of the name and productive of an immense amount of good. The picture could be easily enlarged, and include the priceless advantages each of us derived from the institutions founded by those who preceded us in the various regions where we all had the happiness to be born. It was a blessing which we do not sufficiently appreciate unless we reflect seriously upon it. And it must be remarked that if the religion of Christ was to disappear at once from all places where it sheds still its holy influence, all these proofs of a superior morality would also vanish at once. It would be an unreasonable presumption to imagine that the exterior benefits of our holy religion would continue if its interior spirit had altogether ceased to exist, and if its name was completely disowned.

But there is still a further step to take, and a word of admonition to be addressed to the teachers of a rationalistic morality, should they be disposed kindly to listen for a moment. They consider the doctrine they preach as far above any other, and occasionally find fault with that of the Church. If it is not presumptuous on our part, we will ask them if they think they have derived it from any other source than from Christianity. They will surely answer that they found it in their own mind, as they do not admit any principles except those contained in human reason. There seems to be a great force in this remark, and we cannot but acknowledge it, because we also proclaim the rights of reason, and even its infallibility within its own range. But must it be conceded as a thing above contradiction, that if Christianity had never existed, human reason would be as enlightened as it is? Have not philosophers been benefited by it as well as other men? and are not many of their principles mere axioms openly proclaimed by Christian teachers long before the philosophy of the intuitive school was born? This is a fact easily ascertained by merely looking into the philosophical and theological treatises of Fathers and schoolmen.

A simple observation, finally, may not be without force. The philosophy of the intuitive school is not accepted by all philosophers. There are many men of other schools; for instance, the utilitarians. Why is it that the mind of the first has easily admitted the purer doctrine they follow, whilst the second reject it and are satisfied with a system far inferior in all respects? There can be no other answer to this question than to say the first have better kept the Christian principles they imbibed in their infancy than the second did. For both were Christian at first, as was universally the case not much more than a hundred years ago. With this we may conclude this partial discussion.

3. *The Contrast of Temporal with Eternal Things is Promotive of Good Morals and Holiness.*

The main object of our Lord's preaching being to conquer sin and establish virtue on earth, He constantly insisted on the necessity of despising this world and looking up to heaven: "Lay not up to yourselves treasures on earth, where the rust and moth consume, and where thieves break through and steal. But lay up to yourselves treasures in heaven, where neither the rust nor moth consume, and where thieves do not break through and steal."* And farther on, describing the future judgment at the end of the world: "Then shall the King say to them that shall be on his right hand: Come, ye blessed of my Father, possess the kingdom prepared for you from the foundation of the world. . . . And He shall say to them also that shall be on His left hand: Depart from me, ye cursed, into everlasting fire, which was prepared for the devil and his angels." †

All the moral precepts Christ inculcated were supported by this consideration of eternal rewards and punishments. He wished his disciples to keep constantly before their eyes the transitory and perishable character of all earthly blessings contrasted with the solidity and permanence of whatever is promised us in the eternal city. This must be the whole philosophy of the Christian; with the understanding, however, that during his pilgrimage he is not forbidden to use the things needful for this life, but he must not be "over-solicitous" in their pursuit, and if he have faith he is directed to think that his heavenly Father will not let him be deprived of them.

The Church as the representative of Christ cannot have another doctrine, and this she inculcates and urges on the mind of her children on all possible occasions. Let us see a moment if there can be a more powerful incentive toward holiness. Reason alone tells us that if kept constantly in view it abundantly suffices to preserve a man from moral delinquency, and to induce him to practise the highest virtue. Faith, it is true, requires, besides, that the grace of God should help us; but in the present inquiry no account is taken of it, and man is supposed to be left to his own

---

* Matt. vi 19, 20. † Ib. xxv.

natural ability, which, however, is never left unaided, since God has promised to *help* those who *help* themselves. The advantages resulting in general from any line of action are the springs which always act upon human nature to urge it on in the pursuit. See the vigor displayed by the worshippers of money, the votaries of pleasure, the candidates for political honors, the aspirants to fame. Is there any exertion which they are not ready to make at every possible sacrifice? And the stronger is the incentive the mightier will be the effort. This is invariably the case in the world; and it results from the very nature of man. What moral strength will not inspire the Christian who sees before him life eternal such as the Gospel discloses it? True, it is an unseen reward; but St. Paul tells us that faith is "the substance of the unseen." If one has faith, the guerdon promised him, though invisible, has a great deal more reality for him than anything earthly. It is said, also, that it is a far-distant reward both in space and time. Heaven, they pretend, is far removed from this earth, and eternity will begin only at the end of this world. The Christian thinks, on the contrary, that heaven is near and that eternity has already begun. Heaven is near, since Christ not only has made us heirs of it, but has placed it in our very possession whenever we keep His grace within our hearts. Is it not true that the practice of virtue on earth is what the Saviour often called "the kingdom of *heaven*"? Did He not say that His faithful disciples actually had it, since He brought it down with His divine person? We know and believe that in the state of grace the soul is in communion with God and His saints. Hence is derived the efficacy of prayer which is for earthly beings nothing else than the means of communicating with God. Heaven consequently exists wherever there are immortal spirits who have preserved their purity or recovered it. It is this conviction which fills the Christian soul with rapture and renders it so strong against temptation. His only fear is to lose his rights by falling away from grace. He is not yet in heaven, merely because he may after all be declared unworthy of it, and also because there is in the present life a veil which conceals from his eyes the unseen world, of which, however, according to St. Paul, he possesses "the substance" by faith. All this is Catholic theology which thus places heaven very near us. But it has been said, moreover, that eternity has already begun. Nothing is more easy to believe for any one who reflects seriously. The soul is essentially eternal: from the first moment of its creation its eternity has become a fact. Its temporal union with the body cannot change anything essential to it. That body even is to be resumed on the day of resurrection. Who does not see, consequently, that man on the day of his birth has begun a career which is to last forever? The eternity of the triumphant Church in heaven is not different from ours, except that the destiny of those we call the Blessed or the Saints is assured and ours is still hanging in the balance. But we are all citizens of a *permanent* city, as Scripture says.

All these considerations give an immense power to the Christian in his pursuit of holiness. Nothing can promote morality with more efficacy than the guerdon placed before his eyes and which he, as it were, obtains in the very act of practising virtue. But in all this not a word has been said of the co-operation of Christ Himself in these supernatural agencies; and yet it cannot be set aside. He promised His disciples two great blessings which must be considered a moment; namely, to abide with us and to come personally and visibly at the end of time—what is called His second advent. We envy with justice the happiness of the first apostles, who lived several years in the company of the Saviour. But to console them at the moment of parting, He said that "He would abide with them forever." This was said of us as well as of them. The invisible presence and sure protection of Christ is as certain for each of us as it was for those who heard the promise. And this is a new way of realizing heaven in the present time. If we believe that we are in His company and, as it were, under His wings, the earth is not what it often seems to be, a lonely cell in a gloomy prison. It is rather the most brilliant part of creation, since St. John tells us that *lucerna ejus est Agnus*—"the Lamb is the lamp of heaven" and on that account "the glory of God hath enlightened it." Though He is not perceptible to our mortal eyes, He can be seen by those of faith; and He has, moreover, promised that His visible presence would not be forever denied, but He would come again and appear full of mercy to His friends, amidst the terrors of the last day. This firm belief is for the Christian the source of a powerful incentive to virtue.

This is, moreover, perfectly independent from a gross millenarianism, and is undoubtedly contained in the Apocalypse of St. John (xx. 4–6). Hence the first Christians were all ardently looking for the second advent of Christ; and if we were as firmly convinced as they were, our feelings in that regard would be the same as theirs. It is true those who regard the Gospels as ordinary books take advantage of this, and imagine they have found in that fact a sure proof that gospel teaching is often a delusion. It is proper to consider this a moment, and show the fallacy of those pretensions. Christ had openly said that no one knew when the last judgment would happen, except His Father.*.

The Apostles, who had set it down in the records they wrote, could not but remember it and teach it to their disciples. The Saviour, however, had not stated even in a general way if His second coming would take place soon or not. Every one was free to think on the subject as he thought more probable; and from the fierce persecutions which began almost immediately after presenting to many of them all the characters which had been announced as the forerunners of the last days, a great number of disciples thought the moment was *near*. They were therefore ready to rejoice, because the Saviour had encouraged His disciples to do so as soon as they would perceive the signs of His advent: "When these things begin to come to pass, look up and lift up your heads, because your redemption is at hand."† Many did so and were deceived; but there is not a single passage of the New Testament going to prove that any of the Apostles shared in the delusion. The Apocalypse of St. John cannot be quoted in support of it, as it is well known that this grand Revelation, unveiled to the disciple of love, is still a sealed book for us, and that in announcing the last days with great clearness and power, not only not a word is said of the time, but everything on the subject of that future epoch is so obscure that nearly all the interpreters widely differ from each other. It is in our opinion a proof that St. John kept before his eyes all the time he wrote the assertion of St. Matthew, "Of that day and hour no one knoweth, no, not the angels of heaven, but the Father alone." Still in the face of all these circumstances, perfectly well ascertained and incontrovertible, many rationalists have persuaded themselves that the common teaching of the apostles was in favor of an almost immediate end of the world; and if they were deceived on that occasion, they must have been deceived on many others. The only text they can bring to bear on their pre-

---

* Matt. xxiv. 36. † Luke xxi. 28.

conceived opinion is the single phrase of the Saviour recorded by St. Matthew and copied afterwards by St. Mark: "This generation shall not pass till all these things be done." They understand the word *generation* as meaning (according to Webster) the people of the same period, or living at the same time. It is generally supposed to include a short period of thirty-three years. But it is unwarrantable to rely only on such a meaning, when there are several others very different. The Jews at the time of the Saviour could scarcely have understood it in that sense; a *generation* meant for them, what it does for us too, a family, a race —here the human race (see again Webster). In Greek, the language of the New Testament, it was certainly the principal meaning of the word γενεά. Homer knew no other. If later Greek authors, like Thucydides, attribute occasionally to it the sense of "the present age," it has then always a vague meaning answering to the phrase "the men of our age," never the precise sense contained in the words, "three generations make a century."

But our Lord could not possibly attribute to the word γενεα this last meaning, because He would have contradicted Himself, and assigned in fact the almost exact epoch of His second coming, after He had a moment before solemnly asserted that this was known to the Father alone. But this is amply sufficient on a trifling controversy which is but incident here. For the present object is to insist on the feeling of confidence and trust experienced by the primitive Christians, and resting on the certainty they had that the Saviour was not lost to them forever. He would come again and appear on earth in the midst of them. And this sweet conviction is also a blessing we enjoy in this age as well as our forefathers of the first century. To this we must return for a moment longer.

The whole of it is most clearly expressed in a passage of the discourse of our Lord to His apostles at the end of His last supper, and recorded by St. John:* "A little while, and you shall not see me; and again a little while, and you shall see me, because I go to the Father. . . . Amen, amen, I say to you that you shall lament and weep [during my absence,] but the world shall rejoice; and you shall be made sorrowful, but your sorrow shall be turned into joy. A woman when she is in labor hath sorrow because her hour is come; but when she has brought forth the child, she

---

* Chap. xvi. 16, *seq.*

remembereth no more the anguish, for joy that a man is born into the world. So also you now indeed have sorrow, but I will see you again, and your heart shall rejoice; and your joy no man shall take from you. . . . These things I have spoken to you that in me you may have peace. In the world you shall have distress: but have confidence; I have overcome the world."

This was evidently said not for the encouragement of the apostles alone, but for that of all His faithful disciples till the end of time. The entire history of the Church is, we may say, epitomized in these few words of Christ. If He "abides" with us as He promised He would, it is in an invisible manner, because, as He said, He has gone to the Father. He often leaves the Church, in appearance, to the mercy of her enemies. He seems, at times, to have forgotten her, and she dwindles away in number, power, influence, everything that can attract towards her the respect of the world. Then the heart of the Christian grieves at the sight of the constant increase of iniquity, and he shudders when he remembers the words of Christ, pronounced on another occasion: "But yet the Son of man, when He cometh, shall He find, think you, faith on earth?"* Then the only hope, the great desire excited in the heart of the true Christian, is to see Him come again, appear visibly, this time with majesty and power, so as to triumph at once over all the hostile forces that have combined against His Church. And this is not an illusion, a dream destined to vanish like smoke. Of all the prophecies ever uttered by our Lord there is not a single one which He has repeated so often as this, and in clearer terms. It must happen one day, if the world has been created by God and redeemed by Christ. This firm hope is occasionally almost the only link which unites the earth with heaven, but it is a link that cannot break. Otherwise both would have parted from each other long, long ago.

Thus the perpetual contrast existing for the Christian between temporal and eternal things (so that the future world is always present to his mind) cannot but secure forever his morality from swerving; or if ever it gives way, it is only for a moment. Those reflections prove the solidity of the moral structure which Christianity has raised on earth, and the futility of all systems which discard in moral science the consideration of a hereafter.

---

* Luke xviii. 8.

So far, however, this has been established only *a priori*, because the object of this First Book was merely to prove the strength of the *principles* on which the Church's holiness has rested from the first day of her existence, and continues to rest through all ages. The question must be now examined *a posteriori*, by looking at the *facts* of history, in order to discover if she has been in reality what she has all along professed to be. There is no need of mentioning that this is the most important part of the present work. Only time and space will scarcely allow the writer to develop it to the full extent it deserves.

SECOND BOOK.

FACTS.

CHAPTER I.

MORAL CHANGE EFFECTED BY THE APOSTLES OF CHRIST IN JERUSALEM AND IN THE JEWISH RACE.

1. *What is to be Understood by the " Kingdom of God" which Our Lord came to Establish?*

THE "kingdom of God" which the Saviour so often announced was nothing else than that of virtue, or rather of holiness. To be convinced of it, it suffices to go through the various passages of the New Testament in which this "kingdom" is openly proclaimed. Before Christ appeared, John the Baptist had announced that it was "at hand."* But when the Saviour sent his seventy-two disciples to preach His Gospel, He commanded them to openly publish that "the kingdom of God *is* come nigh unto you."† Should any one ask in what it precisely consists, the Saviour answers that it is opposed to that of Satan, which, every one knows, is sin. "If I by the Spirit of God cast out devils, then is the kingdom of God come upon you."‡ The same meaning is also expressed in the various similes used by St. Matthew in his thirteenth chapter (v. 47–50). But the strongest proof of it is furnished by St. Luke (xvii. 21) on the occasion of the same question being addressed by the Pharisees to our Lord; namely, "when the kingdom of God should come." He answered: "The kingdom of God cometh not with observation. .... For lo, it is within you."

---

* Matt. iii. 2.   † Ib. x. 19.   ‡ Ib. xii. 28.

A few words of comment are required on two at least of these last quotations. There is, first, the one contained in the verses 47-50 of the thirteenth chapter of St. Matthew: "The kingdom of heaven is like to a net cast into the sea, and gathering together all kind of fishes, which, when it was filled, they drew out, and sitting by the shore, they chose out the good into vessels, but the bad they cast forth: so shall it be at the end of the world. The angels shall go out, and shall separate the wicked from among the just."

The "wicked," cannot belong in the "hereafter" to the kingdom of heaven, no more than they could on earth when acting "wickedly." The just, on the contrary, by their virtues belong to it in both cases; and it is in view of the proposed reward that they encounter and overcome the world's temptations. Thus the termination of all earthly things was proposed to the Christian by the Saviour as the great sanction of morality. No philosophy as such can offer this supernatural motive as being naturally contained in the foundation of virtue; and no ancient religion, including even the Jewish, did it to the same extent as that of Christ. It is thus seen at once that the reign of holiness on earth preparing for happiness in heaven is repeatedly called in the New Testament the "kingdom of God;" and the Saviour had announced its actual appearance on earth as the consequence of His coming. In case Christianity had failed to bring it on, the Saviour's promise would have remained unrealized; and this no one can pretend, considering Christ's character.

But the other short text of St. Luke must be examined at a still greater length, because it places more vividly still before the eyes the great fact we are considering at this moment.

Some of the Pharisees inquired of our Lord when "the kingdom of God" should come; and He answered: "Lo, it is within you." The Saviour could read into those inquirers' heart. Whilst we cannot do it, still it is possible for us to guess at the meaning of those Pharisees without great fear of error. It is well known that at that precise moment when Christ spoke, and for a long time previous, the question of the arrival of God's kingdom thoroughly engrossed the Jewish mind. All knew that the fulfilment of the ancient prophecies was at hand, and they all expected that *Israel's kingdom should be restored.* This was understood, no doubt, in various ways; and some went so far as to predict, even among the pagans, that "a people coming from the east"—that is to say, the Jews—"would acquire universal dominion." This is at least the meaning of a well-known phrase of Suetonius. Many Hebrews found in this fond hope the source of that fanaticism which caused the destruction of so many thousands of them at the siege and capture of Jerusalem by Titus. But even the Israelites who were not under the influence of these powerful and deceiving emotions were nevertheless "waiting for the consolation of Israel," as St. Luke relates of Holy Simeon when Mary went to the temple for her purification. And in the same chapter* Anna, the prophetess, "spoke of Him (Jesus) to all that looked for the redemption of Israel." It is, moreover, to be remarked that even among Jesus' disciples, during His public career, wrong notions on the same subject were current, as we know from St. Matthew's gospel.† The mother of the sons of Zebedee asks of the Saviour that her two children should sit at his right and left hands in His "kingdom."

All these false interpretations of old prophecies were set aside by the Saviour's answer to the Pharisees: "Lo, the Kingdom of God is within you." There could be no question of Israel's restoration here. No stronger assertion could be made that the "kingdom" He came to establish was simply that of virtue or holiness. For expressed in these words it comprises the whole extent of the interior moral world in man, which, St. John says, receiveth enlightenment from the true light; namely, the Eternal Word. This cannot but apply to the light of conscience illumined from above. There are, however, apparently two meanings of this short phrase of Jesus, and they must be briefly discussed, to choose the only one which is truly acceptable.

The first meaning would limit this "enlightenment" (mentioned by St. John in the first chapter of his gospel) to the universal action of the Eternal Word when "He enlighteneth every man that cometh into the world." This cannot be the "kingdom of God" in Christ's intention, for reasons which will be presently given. For it means only that the principles of morality and holiness have been originally impressed on man's soul by the divine light coming from the Eternal Word. It is what Mr. Lecky calls the principles of the "intuitive school" of morality, which we would prefer to say are the immutable rules of action

---

* Luke ii.   Ch. xx. 21. *seq.*

forming the basis of our moral nature, as the eternal truths form that of our intellect. All truly great philosophers, even in pagan times, have recognized this immutability of moral principles, and placed its origin in heaven. This is also the "law" which St. Paul says is "written in the heart of all."* On this account it cannot be the "kingdom" which Christ brought us, since man, according to St. John and St. Paul, always had the first in his possession, and the one of which Christ repeatedly spoke depended evidently on his coming, and was a new boon conferred on mankind.

The first and universal privilege, dating from man's creation, was undoubtedly an inappreciable benefit which alone would show how far God has loved our race; since not only He at first conferred it generously on us all, but He did not take it away from fallen man, and left it to him in his forlorn condition as a persevering mark of his truly divine origin. By it, more than by any other characteristic, we are distinguished from animals in which moral nature is altogether absent; and by it also man could rise after his fall.

In this age of universal denial, it is true, many *scientists* relegate it among fables, do not believe in immutable principles of right, and would wish to deprive us of this last proof of our primitive dignity. On this account we cannot but honor those men who, like the author of the "History of European Morals," profess to believe in it, and ardently defend it on all occasions. They acknowledge in man immutable principles of moral goodness, and Mr. Lecky in particular speaks approvingly of St. Paul's "law of nature," meaning no doubt the text of the Epistle to the Romans mentioned above.

But we must repeat again that this is not the "kingdom of God" that Christ brought on earth, and which nevertheless He said *is within us*. If the Saviour had meant nothing more, the new *revelation* He came down from heaven to bestow upon us would have been useless in point of morals at least; and no superiority of any kind could be perceived in the Christian religion over gentilism and Judaism. Christ in this case would not have spoken, as He often did, of the "kingdom of God," destined to form a new dispensation; and in His moral teaching He would

---

* Rom. ii. 15.

have entirely confined Himself to *the law and the prophets.* It must be proved, therefore, that He went much farther, and that besides the immutable principles of right which are in the hearts of all, we have received a peculiar light from His doctrine, which has, by the help of grace, opened in us a new moral sense ; and this is truly *God's kingdom within us.* This deserves a most serious consideration in treating of Christian holiness.

Firstly, it must be at once admitted that the pure ethical code written primitively in man's conscience, and the development given to it in the Decalogue and the Mosaic Law, have not been superseded by the new lawgiver, except as to the ceremonial part of the Jewish Pentateuch. All the chief moral prescriptions in the gentile and Hebrew worlds were founded on man's nature and written by God's finger, either in their hearts or on the tables of stone. On this account Christ Himself said in his Sermon on the Mount that He did not come to destroy the law, but to fulfil it.* But if He had taken away nothing essential from it, He must have added considerably to it; otherwise the modern rationalists would justly pretend that a new revelation was not needed, since our moral nature was sufficiently enlightened and helped by the previous benevolent designs of God's providence. Secondly, a strong proof must be furnished that the Saviour's mission has bestowed on us a new code, far superior to the first, though supposing it, and easily distinguished from it by any one who chooses to look at the Gospel. This is manifestly found in the Sermon on the Mount, and particularly in the Beatitudes which form its introduction. Any one who is but slightly acquainted with the true character of Christ's religion must admit that His whole moral code is based on the Beatitudes and on the explanation He gave of them; and consequently that the spirit if not the letter of the new law is altogether different from that of gentilism and Judaism. A close consideration of this difference will presently enable the reader to understand that the virtues fostered by Christianity are placed on the ethical scale far above those of the natural order. Thirdly and finally, these virtues, which we call supernatural, must be shown to have all been eminently practised by Christ Himself, who according to St. Luke, *cœpit facere et docere*, leaving us in His life and words the true mean-

---

* Matt. v. 17.

ing of the one by the other. This must be seen somewhat in detail.

The inquirer, after merely looking over the fifth chapter of St. Matthew's gospel, will do well to ask himself if a moral law based on such principles of *blessedness* as those had ever been proclaimed to mankind, and can be said to be contained in the immutable principles of right and wrong, or even in the divine voice heard by Moses on the summit of Mount Sinai: "Blessed are the poor in spirit. . . . Blessed are the meek . . . . Blessed are they that mourn . . . . Blessed are they that hunger and thirst after justice. . . . . Blessed are the merciful . . . . Blessed are the clean of heart . . . . Blessed are the peacemakers . . . . Blessed are they that suffer persecution for justice' sake . . . Blessed are ye when they shall revile you and persecute you," etc.

The general spirit of this code consists in deriving blessedness or happiness—that is, the end of human life in the estimation of all—from what the most virtuous man, if reduced to the immutable principles of morality, would be at best obliged to consider as a most painful obligation. To esteem one's self happy when poor, when humble and lowly (which is the meaning of meek here), when mourning or suffering, when hungering after justice (without having it meted out to himself), when reviled and persecuted, etc. etc., is undoubtedly a doctrine which had never before been preached to men. Still no one can deny that this is the spirit of Christianity, and the true foundation of virtue for all sincere Christians. That it could not be contained in the best philosophers' codes, even in the slightest degree, is clear from the fact that it is evidently opposed to some of the most lawful natural appetites of man. That it was altogether foreign to the Mosaic law is well known to any one who has read the Old Testament, in whose records the holiest men complain often bitterly of the burden of poverty, of the acute pain of suffering, of the bitterness of persecution, etc., and on the contrary thank God with joy in times of worldly prosperity and abundance. Any enlightened Christian will, no doubt, recognize that the doctrine of the Beatitudes teaches indeed the moral perfection to which our *redeemed* nature is called; and he will never complain that it is unnatural and incomprehensible; but if he does not, it is because he is *redeemed*, and he has received the new moral sense required for a willing adherence to the Gospel's prescriptions. A philosopher of the purest type, on the contrary, a Jew bent on the most strict observance of the Mosaic law, will never be able to come to the same conclusion; and either of them will refuse to say that they can feel happy when they are poor, or in a lowly condition, or persecuted and reviled, etc. Therefore there is a great deal of difference between Christian and natural morality, though both come from God. That Christ intended His disciples should as strictly follow this moral code as redeemed human nature is able to practise it is clear from this, that He Himself gave the perfect example of it in His divine person. Go through the list of Beatitudes, and directly after revolve in your mind the chief circumstances of Christ's life : you will directly perceive the beautiful harmony of both ; and it is chiefly this correspondence of the one with the other which renders the reading of the first eleven verses of St. Matthew's fifth chapter so inexpressibly sweet to the true Christian. Who has not in his youth, if he were pious, shed tears in going over these harmonious lines reading like an entrancing poem with the constantly recurring rhythm: " Blessed are the poor. . . . Blessed are the meek. . . . Blessed are the clean of heart ". . . ? And this chiefly because these lines placed before his eyes the perfect image of the Redeemer.

What effect would this doctrine produce on mankind if it were universally adopted has been often made a question. And after what has been just said of its difference from the philosophical principles of the highest order, there is nothing surprising in the fact that some rationalists have thought that it would be impossible to found a human commonwealth on such a basis. They must certainly think it is a pure Utopia, unrealizable among ordinary mortals. But they are mistaken. It has been realized at all times in all the faithful members of the Catholic Church, since she has always placed these lines of Christ at the head of her code; and I tell worldly people, though they may not believe it, that there are at this moment millions of simple souls who have no other rule of conduct, and who consider it a sin whenever they in the least deviate from it.

That it was so chiefly at the beginning, and particularly in the churches of Jerusalem and Rome, is one of the questions we will soon discuss. But, what is very remarkable, some mere philosophers of the "intuitive school" have perceived the truth of it and admirably expressed it. We allude here to Mr. Lecky in his

"History of European Morals." It is true he does not make any direct allusion to the doctrine of the Beatitudes in the passage we are going to quote; but the reader will easily recognize that it was an oversight on his part, and it would have given much more point to his remarks.

"It is not surprising," he says, "that a religious system which made it a main object to inculcate moral excellence, and which by its doctrine of future retribution, by its organization, and by its capacity of producing a disinterested enthusiasm, acquired an unexampled supremacy over the human mind, should have raised its disciples to a very high condition of sanctity. There can, indeed, be little doubt that, for nearly two hundred years" (why not three hundred?) "after its establishment in Europe, the Christian community exhibited a moral purity which, if it has been equalled, has never for any long period been surpassed." When and where was it ever surpassed or equalled? "Completely separated from the Roman world that was around them, abstaining alike from political life, from appeals to the tribunals, and from military occupations; looking forward continually to the immediate advent of their Master, and the destruction of the empire in which they dwelt, and animated by the fervor of a young religion, the Christians found within themselves a whole order of ideas and feelings sufficiently powerful to guard them from the contamination of their age." *

Had the author alluded in this passage to the Beatitudes, which the Christians kept constantly before their eyes and tried to copy in their lives, his description might have been still more pointed. Some details would have been dropped and others added, and the whole would have been more satisfactory and true. The last period, in which he says that "the Christians found within themselves a whole order of ideas and feelings sufficiently powerful to guard them against the contamination of their age," would not have been limited to this last result, however important it may be. The fact was that "the whole order of ideas and feelings" which the Christians found within themselves, or rather in the help furnished by their religion, raised them completely above the *natural order*, as is proved by the text of the Beatitudes, and made of them holy beings, "partakers of the divine nature," according

---

* Hist. of Europ. Morals, vol. ii. p. 11 (New York, edit. 1877).

to the text of St. **Peter**. It was the proclamation of a true supernatural life.

This "new order of ideas and feelings" was the infallible result of the new moral code given them by Christ, which is not only succinctly expressed in the eleven verses of the Beatitudes, but in many other passages of the Sermon on the Mount. The Saviour, in saying that His disciples should not neglect to keep the prescriptions of the law and the prophets, insisted at the same time on the remark that the injunctions made to the " men of old " do not suffice for His disciples. All his new precepts suppose the doctrine inculcated in the fifth chapter of St. Matthew on poverty, meekness, mourning, mercy, thirst for justice, and love of enemies; and this had never been so far required of men. Still, the first Christians, *even before the gospels were written*, knew that this was imposed upon them as a duty; and it was the literal fulfilment of these new laws which gave to the primitive Church the charming character it directly assumed.

2. *First Establishment of God's Kingdom on Earth.—Origin of the Church at Jerusalem.*

Among all cities in the world Jerusalem has always been distinguished by its sanctity. In patriarchal times it was called Salem, and Melchisedec ruled in it over his tribe as high-priest and king. St. Paul did not hesitate to write of him that he was " first indeed by interpretation king of justice, and then also . . . king of peace; without father, without mother, without genealogy, having neither beginning of days nor end of life, but likened to the Son of God, he continueth a priest forever."* Melchisedec was, therefore, a prototype of Christ, and his city was already the City of God.

David made it his capital, and, alluding to the offering of bread and wine by its ancient ruler and high-priest, he addressed the future Messias by the solemn words: " Thou art a priest forever, according to the order of Melchisedec." This secured for it a high and everlasting destiny. In its precincts, near Mount Sion, David also appointed a place for the future Temple which Solomon built. During more than nine hundred years it was the

---

* Heb. vii. 2, 3.

only spot on earth where the true God was publicly worshipped. Jerusalem was then called emphatically the Holy City, the City of God; and it has ever since continued to bear that name, to our very day, in spite of its desecration by Mohammedanism. Isaias and Tobias particularly, among the prophets of the old law, have given it that title in the highest burst of their enthusiasm. Nay, more; even after its destruction by the Romans the disciple of love has forever consecrated this glorious epithet by transferring it to the Church in heaven, which he called "the New Jerusalem, the City of God."

Our Saviour, it is true, in shedding tears over its future fate complained of this city as having put the prophets to death: *Jerusalem, Jerusalem, quæ occidis prophetas.* He knew that after having persecuted God's messengers, it would at last slay God's Incarnate Son. But of all its crimes this would be the only one inexpiable. Until that last moment, Jerusalem was always punished for its iniquities as a child is chastised by his father, with a view to reformation; and being brought back by severe discipline to a sense of its sinfulness, it was again received into favor, and never ceased to be the "City of God." Placed in the centre of the ancient world, with Europe to the west, Asia to the east and north, and Africa to the south, it continued during long ages proclaiming God's unity in the midst of idolatrous nations, and preparing the future union of the human race in the same belief, hope, and love. Oh, how ardently Christ loved it! chiefly when He shed tears and announced its fall; which was not nevertheless to be final, since it is destined to rise again from its ashes and to be brought back to more than its former splendor: *Calcabitur a gentibus donec impleantur tempora nationum.**

Our Lord, however, wished at that last hour to make Jerusalem the centre of His religion; and it is proper to see a moment how He prepared everything for that great object. When He entered the city in triumph, and was received by the whole people with loud hosannahs, there seemed to be a prospect of it. The Jews proclaimed Him the Son of David, and by giving Him this title they seemed to acknowledge Him as the Messias. He directly made the Temple His residence and that of His disciples during several days, retiring for the nights to the Mount of Olives.

---

* Luke xxi. 24.

It is the positive statement of St. Luke;* and He had never before in His life taken such a bold step.

His previous progress from Galilee is minutely described by the evangelist from the 31st verse of the eighteenth chapter to the end of the nineteenth. Whilst walking from Jericho to Jerusalem, a circumstance is given in detail † which makes it certain that the Saviour still intended to make of this last city the *capital of His kingdom*, though He foretold at the same time the Jews' obduracy.

It is also remarkable that on entering into the Temple directly after His arrival, "He began to cast out them that sold therein and them that bought." He was evidently taking possession of *His house*, for so He called it: "My house is the house of prayer, and you have made it a den of thieves." His wish, therefore, of saving Jerusalem persevered still in spite of His foreknowledge that His benevolent designs would be frustrated. Nothing proves better than these passages of the Gospel that man remains always free to reject the grace of God even of the most affective and enduring nature. The Jansenistic efficacious grace is thus most evidently disproved.

But there is another fact more extraordinary yet in the same line of thought, which must be examined, because it goes still farther and proves that Jerusalem and the Temple should not have been forsaken even after Christ's death, if the Jews had at last opened their eyes at the preaching of the apostles. This can be concluded from the whole course of action of the Saviour during these five or six days employed by Him in preaching to the multitude.

He had taken possession of the Temple, as was seen; and He evidently wished to make of it the first Christian Temple, not only in point of time, but likewise in point of splendor and glory. This gorgeous edifice had never before heard such a powerful voice as resounded in it to the admiration of thousands of hearers. Several passages of our Lord's sermons at that time, such as St. Luke sets them forth in his chapters twentieth and twenty-first, can be considered by themselves as a proof of Christ's divinity. No one but a God could speak thus. What a magnificent opening it was of the new Law with such a preacher! How true it was that, as had been foretold long before, this last temple was at that moment far more glorious than that of Solomon! For it had been said : ‡ " The Angel of

---

* Ib. xxi. 37, 38. † Ib xix. 11–23. ‡ Mal. lii

the Testament, whom you desire, shall come to His temple, . . . and the sacrifice of Juda and of Jerusalem shall please the Lord," etc." Oh, the blindness of the Jews who did not perceive the accomplishment of the promise they had heard!

But stranger still. When, "by killing the author of life," as St. Peter said in his second sermon, the Jews had finally forfeited all their claims to the title of God's people, another attempt was made to win them over; and had they listened at this last hour, Jerusalem would still have been the centre of the new religion, and the Jewish Temple the true seat of God's glory. The apostles did not yet think of going to the gentiles, and for many days after Pentecost the Temple was their place of meeting, praying, and preaching, undoubtedly from the injunction of Christ Himself.

After the apostles had remained ten days in retirement, and received the Holy Ghost on the day of Pentecost, Peter converted almost instantaneously by his preaching eight thousand of his countrymen, and a congregation or church was formed which must now attract all our attention. The first circumstance most worthy of it is the custom which was directly established among the old disciples and the new converts of meeting in the Temple every day. This is expressly stated after the first sermon of Peter, when already three thousand had declared their belief in Christ: "*They continued daily with one accord in the Temple.*"* The apostles were with them, and at the very beginning of the third chapter it is said that "when Peter and John went up into the Temple at the ninth hour of prayer, a certain man, who was lame from his mother's womb, was carried," etc. This is the first miracle recorded in the new dispensation after that of Pentecost. And from the expressions used by the sacred writer it appears that the apostles with their followers began directly to follow the custom of going to the holy place every time there was in it a public meeting for devotion.

A second sermon of Peter brought on a new flock of five thousand converts, and we still perceive that the increased multitude continued "to come with one accord in Solomon's Porch."

There was not, evidently, on the part of the *new* believers in Jesus, no more than on that of the *first* disciples, any wish to conceal their belief; and their manifest intention was to use the

---

* Acts ii. 46.

Temple altogether as the place of their ordinary meetings, until, having embraced in their fold the great majority of the nation, the old Temple of Jerusalem would have become the first Church of the Christians, and even their most secret assemblies would meet in it. This is the natural conclusion of several texts.

But from the beginning of this movement the "priests and the officers of the Temple" had made up their minds to oppose a further increase of the new religion; and the measures of coercion they began to adopt soon spread terror among those who were in great number thinking of following the first converts' example. St. Luke remarks on the subject that "of the rest no man durst join themselves unto them;" that is, there was a sudden check given to open conversions. It was simply the effect of cowardice. They listened with pleasure to the apostles, they admired those who had the boldness to declare openly their conviction; they were themselves convinced of the truth; but they were afraid. That the people's conversion was becoming universal as early as the miraculous cure performed by St. Peter and St. John on the lame man is clear from the 21st and 22d verses of the fourth chapter: "All men glorified what had been done in that wonder which had come to pass. For the man was above forty years old in whom that miraculous cure had been wrought." But as soon as the persecution of the apostles and their disciples by the priests and officers of the Temple began in earnest, we read in the fifth chapter (v. 13): "Of the rest no man durst join himself unto them; but the people magnified them." It was, therefore, pure cowardice that prevented the bulk of the nation from acknowledging Christ. Had they been courageous men; had they stood up for the right they had of embracing the truth, the only thing required before long for making Jerusalem a Christian city would have been the substitution of the priests of the new law—that is, the apostles—in place of those appointed by the old dispensation, who then had only a shadow of authority, dependent almost altogether on the people's will. We see nowhere that the Roman power contrived to confer the high priesthood on its tools against the nation's wish. It merely in general sanctioned the majority's choice; and Pilate on Christ's trial had reminded the Jews that "they had their law." The decision, in fact, remained in the hands of the Jews.

There was a moment, consequently, when the total conversion of

Jerusalem to Christianity was not only possible but easy. Partly for this reason, probably, the apostles not only did not openly reject the Mosaic law, but continued to practise it. In their daily meetings in the Temple together with their disciples, they, no doubt, followed strictly all the prescriptions even of the ceremonial law, except when it contained mere types of a future Christ, which it was now necessary to forego, since Christ had come. All the prayers of the ritual, therefore, except those of a sacrificial character typical of a future victim; all the ceremonies attendant on public devotion, as standing up, raising the hands, bending of the body, prostrations, festivals and fasts, etc., were strictly attended to. A stranger, a Greek, for instance, looking up from the gentiles' court, and contemplating that multitude which every day surrounded the apostles in the vast precincts of Solomon's Porch, would have sworn that they were Jews and most faithful observers of the Jewish rites. It has been said that the Hebrew converts to Christianity were allowed to continue to practise the Mosaic law only for the sake of "burying the synagogue with honor." There might have been at first a better reason, and this is the one which has just been mentioned. They were waiting for the Temple and its adjuncts to fall into their hands. Nevertheless we give these considerations only for what they are worth, and consequently with some diffidence.

Several passages of the Acts of the Apostles, which it would be useless to quote, show that besides the eight thousand converts numerically mentioned as the fruits of St. Peter's two days' preaching, many more joined the Christian Church on the following days. We would refer chiefly to the fourteenth verse of the fifth chapter. It seems even that a "multitude" of the inhabitants of all the cities in the neighborhood of Jerusalem were constantly bringing in the sick and those possessed by the evil spirit, in order that the apostles should restore them to health; and it is not rash to infer that in their gratitude many of them embraced the new religion. It is not possible, it is true, to say how many additional thousands must be comprised in those various classes of people. It can, however, be maintained that the Christian Church at Jerusalem, after a few days, or perhaps weeks, of existence, formed a very respectable body of people, even in the immense throng which crowded the city at the time of Pentecost. It is proper now to consider them apart from those Jews who "durst not join them." We must begin to speak of the Christian Church of Jerusalem as such. The Temple was not their only place of meeting, and it is important to consider this peculiarity with attention.

Although they met in it several times a day, they had also public assemblies among themselves in private houses, and St. Luke relates in his second chapter of the Acts the chief object of these reunions. The distinction between both religious meetings is clearly indicated in verse 46: "And continuing daily with one accord *in the Temple*, and breaking bread *from house to house*, they took their meat with gladness and simplicity of heart." He had already said in verse 42: "They were persevering in the doctrine of the apostles, and in the communication of the *breaking of bread*, and in prayers " All Protestant as well as Catholic interpreters agree that mention is made here of the Eucharist; and that the reception from " house to house" of the sacrament by the faithful followed a meal called henceforth *agapæ*. Most Protestant writers, however, in our day imagine that it is more conformable to the text to understand even the participation in this sacrament as a simple receiving of bread and wine. They say that it was much later, in the second century only, that Christians believed it to be the body and blood of Christ. It is important to examine this question directly, though very briefly, because, in our firm belief, it was the worthy daily reception of the Saviour Himself, under the species or appearance of the elements, which was the chief source of sanctity in the first Christians.

On this subject it is somewhat remarkable that St. Luke, who wrote the Acts of the Apostles, and calls there the Sacrament, *the breaking of bread*, uses exactly the same expressions in his gospel when he speaks of the institution of the holy Eucharist by our Saviour: "And taking bread, He gave thanks, and brake." The same terms also are used by St. Matthew and St. Mark on the same occasion. But all of them immediately add that our Lord, in giving the Sacrament to His apostles, said : " This *is my body* which is given for you . . . . In like manner the chalice also . . . saying: This is the chalice; the new testament *in my blood*." These are the very expressions of St. Luke ; St. Matthew and St. Mark speak equivalently. The words used in the Acts, consequently, must have meant not only the breaking of bread in general, but the same as containing the body and blood of Christ; and in that sense the first Christians must have understood this passage. There cannot be any necessity of going down to the second century for finding this belief in the real presence as current in the Church. It was undoubtedly propagated by the apostles themselves. And this is sufficient for our purpose here; for this is not the place to discuss further the figurative sense invented by the Sacramentarians in Luther's time. The literal sense is certainly the obvious one contained in the gospels; and the *figurists*, if we may use this expression, must prove that it is not the true one, and that their own is the only one admissible. It is certain that the whole Church understood the eucharistic dogma as Catholics do until Berengarius proposed the figurative meaning in the twelfth century. But his opinion was directly anathematized by all the churches; so that the archdeacon of Angers had absolutely no following until Zuingli and the other *reformers* of the sixteenth century came to teach religion as their fancy dictated, and raised the ire of Luther himself. It is well known what became of it altogether under the Sacramentarians' successors.

We perceive, therefore, in Jerusalem, directly after Pentecost, the new Christians meeting daily in the Temple for prayer, thanksgiving, and other religious exercises, *except sacrifice*. This chief rite of every religion worthy of the name was performed in *private houses*, because they had not as yet any building devoted to their own religious offices, and perhaps also because, as already mentioned, they had reason to hope that the Temple would soon be devoted entirely to Christian worship. It remains only to remark that the great sacrifice of the new law announced by Malachi, the last of the prophets, was thus first of all offered up in Jerusalem, and very near the consecrated spot where the blood of Christ had gushed forth on the Cross in atonement for sin. This was undoubtedly the great source of holiness in the Church at its origin.

3. *Extraordinary Characteristics of the Judeo-Christian Congregations.*

Nothing will be better calculated than these characteristics to impress the reader as to the height of sanctity to which the Hebrew race was at once raised. Firstly, their *faith*,—that is, their supernatural belief in the old and new dispensations,—must have directly acquired a strength sufficient to bring them up to the heroism of martyrdom, such as Stephen had already given them the example. They all had known Christ, and what they had seen of Him when He was in their midst, what they had heard and witnessed from the apostles since Pentecost day, filled them with a firmness of belief scarcely to be comprehended in our day. They clearly saw the accomplishment of the prophecies which they had read with delight all their lifetime. They soon had to bear persecution together with the apostles; and *it is seen nowhere*, such was the ardor of their faith, that a single one of them faltered at the moment of temptation. There were certainly cowards in Jerusalem—thus have they been called—but none amongst those who had openly joined the Church. It was only of the multitude which *durst not join it*, though convinced of the truth, that the Acts of the Apostles mention this want of determination.

It is true that in the eyes of philosophers faith is not a virtue, and is too often only a delusion leading to fanaticism. We beg to differ from them. Faith is in fact the firmest foundation of true morality, and is called by the Church the first of the theological virtues. On this account it depends on grace as all virtues do, and is a gift from God, who alone can infuse it into the mind and heart of man. But independently of this, every one can easily perceive that the *source*, the *active principle*, and the *sanction* of morality rest on faith. Its *source* is God Himself, from whom all virtues originate; so that the immutable principles of right and wrong imprinted in the heart and mind of man are eternal only because they are first and foremost in God. But faith alone can fully apprehend this sublime origin of our moral ideas, not the reason of man. If reason also can be convinced of it to some extent, the utilitarian doctrine so common among men in our day proves that it often falters in the pursuit of this principle, and faith alone can secure it with stability to the human mind. Man, therefore, will be virtuous when he believes in God as the source of virtue.

In a second place, faith is the *active principle* of morality; because the passions arrayed in the heart of man on the side of wrong and against right are always so insidious, and often so overwhelming, that man on many occasions surrenders even the conviction of his reason in order to follow the fascination of his appetites. Faith alone becomes then the active, daily, nay, hourly principle which can secure for us the victory over our senses and passions. Any one who has studied himself and tried to establish the reign of virtue in his heart knows it without fear of being mistaken. Thirdly and lastly, faith is after all the best, often the only, *sanction* of morality; because human motives confined to this world and irrespective of another life cannot in the majority of cases overcome the obstacles always opposed to the practice of virtue. There must be in us a conviction that there is a judge in heaven, and a dispensation of rewards and punishments after death, in order to become effectually superior to temptation. Much more could be said on this interesting subject. This must suffice. But it is not difficult to understand the solid basis of the purest morality which the new faith of the Jewish converts placed and laid down firmly under their feet, for them to stand upon in the eyes of God and man, as the supporters of justice and the followers of Jesus, the great moral model proposed to mankind. This new pattern was far above that of the Mosaic law, and the belief which introduced it was far holier than their old faith.

The second characteristic of the new Christian congregation was *charity*, without which faith remains inoperative. It is forcibly expressed in the 32d verse of the fourth chapter of the Acts: *Multitudinis autem credentium erat cor unum et anima una.* "The multitude of believers had but one heart and one soul." This was for them, at the same time, the source and the proof of a high sanctity. For Christ has said that all His moral law is contained in the love of God and of the neighbor. The text of the Acts is remarkable; and it is doubtful if it could be possible to express in stronger terms the close bond of a holy brotherhood such as united together the first Christians of Jerusalem. The love of one's country,—true patriotism,—it is said, makes of all the citizens a band of brothers. But when has it happened that an historian of ancient Rome,—for instance, at the time of the republic, when patriotism was most exalted and ardent,—could say that all Romans had but one heart and one soul? There may have been some particular occasion, like the coming of the Carthaginian enemy under the lead of Hannibal in front of the very walls of the city, when all the ordinary feuds and contentions between patricians and plebeians were merged into one grand purpose; namely, the firm resolve of dying rather than of being conquered. But the terms used by St. Luke do not refer to some particular occasion or other; they are general, and indicate the habitual state of feeling among the Christians. It will soon be proper to come back to this comparison between the religious feeling mentioned here and the *virtue* of patriotism among the ancients; because the pretended want of that virtue among the Jewish Christians frequently becomes with Mr. Lecky a ground of accusation against Christianity itself, and in particular against the first converts at Jerusalem. But for the moment we must consider their close union alone. This was so intimate that they had but "one heart and one soul." It is known that it was the intention of Christ, when He established "the kingdom of God" on earth, to inspire all His followers with that strong principle of concord, with that undying affection for each other; and we see here that His benevolent design was carried out in perfection at the very first preaching of the apostles to their countrymen.

The law of Moses, undoubtedly, upheld as a duty among Jews the same harmony and union; and many texts of the Pentateuch and of the Prophets could be brought forward to prove it. But how was this Mosaic precept obeyed generally among them? There is no question of private or individual cases; many could be cited to show that the precept was well known and heroically acted upon. Nothing brighter could be brought forward, even in Christian annals, than the Book of Tobias. But take the whole nation together or some large portion of it, and try to ascertain if there was ever among them "one heart and one soul." And to come to a more practical example, compare the new Church at Jerusalem with the mass of those Israelites who refused to become Christians. All the circumstances preceding, accompanying, and following the siege of Jerusalem, which happened so soon afterwards, are perfectly well known, and have been recounted in detail by Flavius Josephus. How different appear the Judeo-Christians on one side and the *patriotic* Jews on the other, during the whole period which intervened between Pentecost and the capture of the city by Titus! Among the first there is concord, harmony, a holy charity ready at all times not only to support but to help practically each other. Among the second, strife, discord, the most inveterate hatred, the bitter division of parties until the whole nation is dissolved and utterly destroyed. It has been said, however, that the first picture, so enticing and bright, is known only from a few words of St. Luke. But independently of this writer's inspiration, which Catholics are unfortunately almost the only ones to admit, St. Luke suffices as an historian, because he had been an eye-witness, spoke to the purpose, and was contradicted by nobody. There will soon be an occasion to speak more in detail of that spirit of pure charity when we examine the holy and free community of goods which soon became the most marked feature of the Church at Jerusalem, at a time when it already contained so many thousand members. For it must not be forgotten that this bright picture was not confined to a few families, but comprised a not inconsiderable part of the population of the city and its neighborhood.

Before this is done, however, it is proper to state and discuss what has been said lately of the want of patriotism among the first Judeo-

Christians, so as to suppose in their heart not only indifference for, but a real hatred of, their countrymen. It is a violent accusation which in a noted passage of the "History of European Morals" is brought against them, and in various other parts of the same work is directed against Christianity in general. This accusation, if supported, would fearfully detract from the virtue of charity, which would cease to be the characteristic of the first Christians in spite of what St. Luke may say in their favor. It is proper to discuss this at some length.

4. Did the first Judeo-Christians hate those of their Countrymen who had not Embraced the Faith?

These are Mr. Lecky's words in his first volume (page 416, Appleton's edition) : " The Jew, who deemed the abandonment of the law the most heinous of crimes, and whose patriotism only shone with a fiercer flame amid the calamities of his nation, regarded the Christian with an implacable hostility. Scorned and hated by those around him, his temple levelled to the dust, and the last vestige of his independence destroyed, he clung with a desperate tenacity to the hopes and privileges of his ancient creed. In his eyes the Christians were at once apostates and traitors. He could not forget that in the last hour of his country's agony, when the armies of the gentiles encompassed Jerusalem and when the hosts of the faithful flocked to its defence, *the Christian Jews had abandoned the fortunes of their race, and refused to bear any part in the heroism and suffering of the closing scene.* They had proclaimed that the promised Messiah, who was to restore the faded glories of Israel, had already come; that the privileges which were so long the monopoly of a single people had passed to the gentile world; that the race which was once supremely blessed was for all future time to be accursed among mankind."

It seems clear that the writer adopts here the well-known opinion of the Jews with regard to the Christians' want of patriotism. The passage I have taken the liberty to *underline* would alone justify this supposition. More still, the whole paragraph was evidently penned with the intention of producing the same impression on the reader's mind. Moreover, what is said in Mr. Lecky's second volume of the want of civic virtues or patriotism among the primitive Christians of the whole Roman Empire (to which we will presently allude) is a proof that this is with the gifted author a standing objection applicable to the whole of Christianity, at least in the primitive ages; and thus the tender union of all the new converts among themselves, a union remarked by the pagans themselves, who could not but exclaim, "See how those Christians love each other," is made to appear as a kind of positive selfishness. It looks as if the followers of Christ despised, or rather hated, the whole of mankind, particularly their own countrymen, owing to their *fanatical* attachment to the new religion. This is altogether untrue, and it must be proved that it is. The case of the Judeo-Christians must be first considered.

Patriotism is a great civic virtue, commanded by religion as well as by the principles of the "intuitive school" of philosophy. The precept of the Saviour is well known: the Christian must love his neighbor—that is, all mankind—as much as himself. But those Catholic theologians who have speculated on the details of charity (Fénelon among them, if I remember well) say that he must love his country more than the generality of mankind, and that he must love those bound to him by blood-relationship more still than his country *in abstracto*. There are certainly cases when he must sacrifice everything, including himself, to the just demands of his fatherland. But if his countrymen are evidently wrong, he must sorrowfully stand aside without, however, taking part against them. This, I think, is true patriotism as understood by Catholic theologians. The ultraist ideas of Greek and Roman pagans on the subject are not the standard by which the Christian must regulate his conduct. What rule did the Judeo-Christians follow on this subject from the day of Pentecost to the downfall of Jerusalem? This is the question which must be discussed with attention and exactness.

It can be proved that they followed the path of good citizens, though not that of fanatical Stoics. As Jews, they must have evidently shared in the feelings of the good Israelites of the period, such as the Gospel represents them to us. Many Judeo-Christians must have known by reputation at least both Simeon, who before he died had so long waited "for the consolation of Israel," * and Anna, Phanuel's daughter, who spoke with joy to all those who were "expecting Israel's redemption." † All those former Jews had loved their country; it must have been the same with the new Christians who followed in their footsteps. And

---

* Luke ii. 25. † Ib. 38.

let not any one say that, in point of fact, at the downfall of Jerusalem they hated it and refused to contribute to its defense. This "hatred" is not proved; and they had good reasons for "standing aside," which is the only thing they did. They had the positive precept of Christ, which they followed implicitly. He had predicted all the details of that terrible day, and had forewarned His followers to leave the city at the approach of the Romans. Can it be pretended that Christ did not love His country, when the Gospel says so positively that He "shed tears" over its fate? What reason has Mr. Lecky to think that the heart of all Judeo-Christians of that epoch who had listened to Christ did not also bleed, when they contemplated from afar the frightful calamity?

But were they not "apostates and traitors"? They may have been so called by those madmen who disgraced their race and religion, particularly during the siege of Jerusalem; they were not in truth in the just appreciation of impartial observers. Not only had they not apostatized from Judaism, but whilst, according to the teachings of the apostles, the law had been fulfilled by Christ and replaced by a better one, they continued to keep all its precepts. With James, their bishop, they regularly worshipped in the temple; James himself was allowed to enter the *holy of holies*. Let Mr. Lecky listen to the gentlemen of the Tübingen school, and they will tell him (which is, however, going too far) that they all were strong partisans of the *Petrine theology;* and this doctrine pretended to impose circumcision and all the Mosaic rites even on the Gentiles. On the contrary, they all were bitterly opposed to the *Pauline* doctrine, which considered the law as worthy of no respect. If this is an exaggeration of the Tübingen theologians, at least it cannot be denied that all Judeo-Christians kept the Mosaic law; some say in order to bury the synagogue with honor, we say perhaps in order to keep Jerusalem as the centre of the new religion. Apostates from Judaism! Who can say so, whilst they are seen everywhere during the apostleship of St. Paul, keeping their synagogues open on the Sabbath, even most probably after their conversion, although at the same time they celebrated every other day of the week the new Pasch of the Christians? Did not St. Paul often worship with them in the synagogues when he preached to them before going to the Gentiles?

That they were no more "traitors" to their country than "apostates" from their religion must be clear to every one who pays attention to the teachings of Christ when He spoke to them as a Jew to

Jews. Had He not commanded them, during His passion, to weep over the fate of their country, and not over His own fate? "Daughters of Jerusalem, weep not over me, but weep for yourselves and for your children. For behold, the days shall come wherein they will say: Blessed are the barren, and the wombs that have not borne, and the paps that have not given suck." Following the open teachings of Christ as explained by St. Paul in several chapters of his Epistle to the Romans, they must have believed that Israel had *not* been rejected by Almighty God. For after having declared in chapter x. (v. 12) that "there was no distinction between the Jew and the Greek, but that God was the Lord of all, rich in blessings for all those who invoke Him," he said in conclusion (ch. xi. 25, 26) that "the blindness of Israel was only temporary until the fulness of the gentiles should have entered the fold. Then the whole of Israel would be saved." They would have openly transgressed the precepts of their new teachers had they been traitors to their country. It is certain, on the contrary, that they all expected Jerusalem would rise from her ashes; the same as all Christians must believe that the day of her glory shall infallibly come—a glory far greater than the first.

Consequently, the expressions of Mr. Lecky at the end of the paragraph previously quoted—namely, "that the race which was once supremely blessed *was for all future time to be accursed among mankind*"—are positively untrue. The first Judeo-Christians entertained no idea of this kind with regard to their own race; and those of their countrymen who refused to acknowledge Christ could not have imagined that in order to become Christians this persuasion would be first required of them. Their refusal to join the Church could not have been grounded on this supposition.

We might rest here; but in order not to come back to the question relative to the want of patriotism and civic virtues among the first Christians in general, it is preferable to speak of it in this place. It will give more point still to what has just been said of the accusation brought forward against the first Judeo-Christians of Jerusalem.

The author of "European Morals" treats of it in his second volume; and in the Table of Contents it is headed, "Decline of the Civic Virtues." Many details contained in this part of the work are as true as they are interesting; but the conclusions drawn by the author from this Decline are either unwarranted or at least exaggerated, and to attribute to it, as he does, "one cause of the downfall of the Roman Empire" is completely erroneous. This must be the main object of this brief discussion.

In the first place, it is principally to the spirit of asceticism that Mr. Lecky attributes this declension of patriotism; and the monks are made to appear truly haters of the world and of their country. A few words have been written on this subject in the first volume of "The Church and the Gentile World" to prove that they "hated" nobody and no institutions. But a very important remark on this subject could not find place in that previous work. Among the various facts brought forward by Mr. Lecky against Christianity to prove his point, the most striking are generally ascribed with justice to heretics, such as the Donatists, the Monophysites, etc. In Mr. Lecky's opinion they were all Christians, and thus the burden falls on Christianity itself. But we will take the liberty to remark that the Church cannot be made responsible for the excesses of her most ardent enemies; and to bring as a proof that the Christians did not care for their country, or hated it, the indisputed fact, for instance, that "the conquest of Egypt by the Mohammedans was in a great measure due to an invitation from the persecuted Monophysites," cannot have any weight in the opinion of impartial men who are aware that this "invitation" could not have been prompted by the spirit of Christianity, or rather was totally opposed to it. The Monophysites had openly renounced the Church's teaching.

But independently of this observation, it must be firmly maintained that the decline of patriotism in the Roman Empire originated long before asceticism began, and consequently it could not be one of the causes of it, as Mr. Lecky pretends. That the primitive Christians were compelled by their religion to refuse altogether to bear arms and enlist as soldiers, is well known to have been the opinion of Tertullian; but Tertullian was at that time a Montanist, and this was one of the tenets of that sect. Many facts on the other side could be brought to prove the contrary with regard to the orthodox Christians, and Mr. Lecky himself admits several examples of it. In general it can be affirmed that whenever Christian soldiers, during the first three hundred years, threw down their arms and their military belt, it was because they were commanded to do as soldiers things which God's law forbade: such as to offer incense to idols or to the image of the god-Cæsar. There are in ecclesiastical history pathetic examples of that nature; and on those occasions the true patriotism of the Christian soldier is often depicted in glowing terms.

As a confirmation of this it must be admitted by all impartial writers that after Constantine's conversion the majority of fighting men in the empire was composed of Christians. Yet at that time monachism had already spread all over the world; and if occasionally soldiers were allowed to leave the ranks in order to enter a monastery, there was no fear that this should become general and deprive the empire of armies. Then as now, men preferred the license of the camp to the strict and obscure life of a convent.

These considerations, however, are mere trifles in the present discussion. The decline of patriotism had begun long before St. Anthony withdrew into the wilderness. The great cause of it must be found in the corruption and degradation of the Romans under the first emperors. Christianity would, in fact, have brought back the civic virtues if the western races in Italy and Greece had not been profoundly tainted by a notoriously luxurious life. Mr. Lecky is fair when he declares somewhere in the same part of his work that the luxurious living of even many ecclesiastics and prelates in the fourth and fifth centuries cannot be attributed to any of the principles of Christianity, but to the immoral atmosphere in which they were born and brought up. These are not his expressions, but his thoughts. All things considered, it looks as if the idea of the Abbé Darras in his "History of the Church" was true; namely, that western and southern Europe, on account of its excessive corruption, could not be altogether reformed by Christianity itself; and that the destruction of the Roman Empire by the barbarians was necessary, previous to a perfect penetration of pure morals throughout a renovated society.

Be this as it may, it is certain that the "civic virtues" suffered nothing, or very little, from asceticism or Christianity in the primitive ages, and that the causes of the decline in the Roman Empire must be looked for in a quite different direction.

5. *Characteristics of the Community of Goods among the First Christians in Jerusalem.*

This has been called communism by several Christian writers. The word itself is rather objectionable, owing to the modern association of ideas with which it is connected. But, these aberrations of new theorists being severely set aside, it expresses energetically the truth, and a better one could scarcely be found.

The subject is twice mentioned in the Book of St. Luke, and both texts must be first quoted. We read in the Acts (ch. ii. v. 44, 45) : " All they that believed were together, and had all things common. Their possessions and goods they sold, and divided them to all, according as every one had need." And a little farther on (ch. iv. v. 32) : " The multitude of believers had but one heart and one soul. Neither did any one say that aught of the things which he possessed was his own, but all things were common unto them."

It must be first understood that this was not imposed by the apostles as an obligation. The story of Ananias and Sapphira, which is recounted in the fifth chapter, proves it (v. 4). It was suggested only as an advice which they could follow or not, as they chose. But after giving their consent they were bound to perform their promise. All, meanwhile, gave their willing consent, as the second chapter (v. 44) proves ; and this was the first brilliant example of charity given to the world by Christ's followers. It did not this time come from the heart of those impulsive Celts of Galatia, who subsequently would have willingly " plucked out their eyes" and offered them to St. Paul. It was willingly adopted by that harsh, calculating, and selfish race of Abraham, which from the time of Jacob and Esau has always known so well how to strike hard bargains and require their fulfilment. At the time of our Lord the Jews were in general more selfish than ever. Yet we see that "a multitude of believers" among them not only had together but " one heart and one soul," and consequently were full of interior feelings of love ; but they at once go much further : " *All*," without exception, " *had all things common.*" None of them wished any more to say that " *aught of the things which he possessed was his own. All things were common unto them.*"

The fact of *dispossessing* one's self altogether of personal property so as to effectually confer its advantages to the whole community, is one of the hardest practical acts of charity as a virtue. We call with justice those men charitable who, keeping their property in their hands and under their entire control, distribute a good part of their revenue to the poor; we praise them as giving the best practical proof that they love their neighbor. But the first Christian Jews of Jerusalem were not satisfied with this. The rich among them became in reality poor in order that the poor should receive their portion as their *due*. Almsgiving was not destined any more either to engender pride in the heart of the giver or to create a blush on the cheeks of the receiver. All were to be on the same footing as brothers, and the humane feeling was to assume a new form which had not yet appeared on this earth.

This was the simple way brotherly charity was introduced among men; and a Jewish Christian Church gave the first example of it. But it soon became common among Christ's followers, and from that time down to this it has become the distinguishing characteristic of the Catholic Church. In our cold age it is still as bright as ever. Wherever you go through Catholic lands you see thousands of establishments devoted to its practice; and the first care of the Catholic missionary in heathen countries is to call the people to him by the attraction of his abundant gifts. Those who were not born in the Church, who even often oppose her and find fault with her, are bound, if they are not altogether blinded by prejudice, to acknowledge this most remarkable social fact: that the Catholic Church has always been, and is still, most active and zealous in charitable deeds and in tenderness for the poor. Mr. Lecky on this subject never professes two opinions. To his honor it must be said that he never ceases to repeat that the social virtues, and particularly deeds of the most ardent charity, have always adorned the Catholic Church; that as it was inexhaustible in the first ages, it has continued ever since to be at least extremely remarkable; and in the worst time (which was for him the mediæval period!) it went rather too far by freeing the poor from the need of almost any exertion, and depriving them consequently of self-reliance and personal activity. Much could be said in answer to this; but we prefer to feel satisfied with this acknowledgment by the author of "European Morals" of the inexhaustible treasure of love which has always flowed from the Church's heart.

She has converted the world more by the constant and universal practice of this virtue than, perhaps, by her teaching, miracles, and exhibition of power. In our age even, if she still brings constantly back to her bosom many erring children from heresy or schism, it is particularly the spectacle of her charitable exertions for the poor of every age and condition that brings conviction to those who were farthest from her on account of the prejudices of their birth. And this is true of this new world of America, as it has always been of the old continent.

This priceless virtue originated in Jerusalem; and it is seen there at once carried to perfection. The community of goods among the first Christians was established chiefly to help the poor, and the apostles themselves undertook to preside at the daily or weekly distributions. In spite of their high dignity complaints soon arose, and the difficulty of conciliating their priestly functions with this charitable office being soon made evident, seven deacons were chosen and ordained for the purpose of introducing perfect order and efficiency in the just apportionment of charity. A new order was thus introduced into the Church's hierarchy merely for the sake of *charity*. There must have been a second motive for it which is not mentioned in the Acts, but is derived from the new Christian spirit. As it affected the entire body of believers, if the poor were benefited the rich became acquainted with a new virtue, *self-renouncement*. This, which is called voluntary poverty, is the first of the "evangelical counsels" in the Saviour's teaching. It brought to this earth the first appearance of what has been justly called the "religious life." It was not as yet in Judea a complete scheme, because celibacy was not openly proclaimed; but from the practice of voluntary poverty the Christians not in Judea alone, but everywhere, would be henceforth invited to follow Christ in chastity and obedience as well as in His total disregard for worldly possessions.

These two motives, charity and self-renouncement, which brightly shine in the communism of the first disciples at Jerusalem place it at once at an incomparable height above all other earthly projects of philosophers and theorists. As a French author in the *Encyclopédie Catholique* (Paris, 1854) has justly remarked: "The social form of communism (abstractedly from religious communities) is the worst of all political institutions, and the most pregnant of baneful consequences for humanity. Sympathies and repugnances are violently opposed; society falls into atony; personal rights are bound up with iron manacles; injustice becomes permanent.... The members of this kind of state have no property; but the *community* enjoys the whole; and what is the community itself? It is personified in the rulers of this strange association. Either in case these rulers receive their right from their birth, as in the ancient sacerdotal castes, or when their authority is the result of elections, they are in fact complete masters. Labor is exacted; passive obedience is rigorously prescribed. Human activity, talent, and life is the state's property; every other private corporation, the family among others, is proscribed. The state is a huge machine which cannot bear any competition."

These are generally the offensive features of communism as proposed in modern theories; but the spirit of charity and self-renouncement could not subsist with them in Jerusalem. The picture presented by the Christian community was precisely the reverse. The rulers instead of being harsh and despotic masters were the servants of all. We do not see that labor was organized as in a modern manufactory. If obedience was the rule, it was sweet as rendered to God and not to man. The stern axiom that the activity, talent, and life of the individual is the state's property was never invoked as the Church's rule. Self-sacrifice was left to the initiative of every one, and if it was in its effects as thorough as in any communistic association, it was the offspring of the heart and expected its reward from Heaven. This has been the model copied in all religious communities in after-time.

States as individuals can be judged from their fruits: *a fructibus eorum cognoscetis eos*. Communistic organizations, even simple attempts at them, have before this excited the dislike of mankind. The Jerusalem community, on the contrary, has furnished to all subsequent ages of the Church a theme of admiration and a model for imitation. For it is a mistake to imagine that this sublime example has never been reproduced. At the first establishment of Christianity in all countries something of the same nature has been perceptible at least in the precincts of particular houses devoted to a life of perfection. It was only in Jerusalem that *all* the Christians embraced this life, and it lasted but a short time in all its splendor; but everywhere the same ardor was displayed by multitudes of men and women who felt irresistibly impelled to follow their Saviour and Master. As long as the Catholic Church shall exist the example of the first Christians will be followed by hundreds and thousands. The heart of Christ throbs in her bosom because she is His Bride and can never be unfaithful to Him.

6. *Was ever the Virtue of Charity Practised in any other Religion or Institution as well as in the Catholic Church?*

In the opinion of many men charity is practised in all religions, is encouraged by all philosophies, is the natural fruit of all civilizations, and the Catholic Church cannot claim the monopoly of it. In a certain sense that holy virtue is fostered by the natural feelings of the human heart; and it would be absolutely erroneous to deny its existence outside of the visible pale of the Church. It must be maintained, however, that the true motive of charity, as it was first displayed at Jerusalem—namely, the love of others and the renouncement of self—can scarcely be supposed entirely free from selfishness, unless it is prompted by the love of Christ as its source. The love of God among men cannot properly have any other origin; and that of the neighbor is but the corollary of the first.

A great number of modern writers on morality, however, pretend that the stream of pure charity is nearly, if not quite, as broad and deep anywhere on earth as in the Church's bosom. They speak of the Buddhists in the eastern part of Asia, of some Roman emperors of the Antonine dynasty, of the Mussulmans even (those eternal readers of the Koran), of the constant and active display of charity among Protestant nations, as if the Church of Christ had nothing better to boast of. It is unavoidable to allude to these various facts to which many authors of our day give a great prominence. Unfortunately the discussion must be brief on a subject which would require volumes. For the sake of order we will follow chronology, begin by the Antonines in Rome, and end by the followers of Gautama in our age.

In speaking of the Antonines, we first advisedly exclude the emperors who preceded them; though Mr. Lecky, in his second volume, gives a great importance to the distribution of corn and salt and land to poor citizens, from the prosperous days of the republic down to Christian times long after Constantine. He thus includes in the scheme several centuries before the Antonines. The author of the "History of European Morals," who enumerates those "various measures" as being eminent among the brightest pagan acts of beneficence, shows, nevertheless, his usual fairness by adding that "neither in practice nor in theory, neither in the institutions that were founded nor in the place that was assigned to it in the scale of duties, did charity in antiquity occupy a position at all comparable to that which it has obtained by Christianity. Nearly all relief was a state measure, dictated much more by policy than by benevolence; and the habit of selling young children, the innumerable expositions, the readiness of the poor to enroll themselves as gladiators, and the frequent famines, show how large was the measure of unrelieved distress." *

This is sufficient for the present purpose, and, in Mr. Lecky's book, applies to the Antonines as well as to the previous or subsequent emperors. Still a broad distinction must be made in favor of the Antonine dynasty, because it seems indubitable that several of those princes were truly animated by a benevolent spirit, altogether superior to that which had previously prompted the periodical distribution of " corn and salt and land;" and, moreover, the majority of authors who oppose pagan charity to that of the Church confine themselves to the period included between Nerva and Septimius Severus. This is in fact the only period of the pagan empire in which there can be question of charity. Before that epoch every measure of relief for the poor was mere policy; after it, if some emperor like Alexander Severus was still animated with a spark at least of the Antonine spirit, it was, as it were, a spasmodic effort which does not deserve to be taken into consideration.

In spite of the remarkable enumeration of charitable deeds performed by emperors of that dynasty, such as Mr. Lecky gives it in his first volume, † although he must have taken a great deal of pains to gather examples from all possible authors, from monuments, and from medals, in order to place the whole under the eyes of his readers (he cannot be blamed for it), still it must be confessed by the author himself that it is rather a meagre exhibit during a period of a full century, at the time of the greatest prosperity of the empire. It cannot be doubted that there is, at this moment in Paris alone, in France, ten times more active benevolence and charity displayed by the government and private individuals than there was then in the whole Roman

---

* Hist. of Europ. Morals, vol. ii. p. 78. † Page 76, foll.

Empire. Still Paris has lately passed through several bloody revolutions, the first of which entirely destroyed, at a fell blow, all the institutions which the charity of ten centuries had accumulated. But without coming to so late and recent an example, it can be maintained that when this new benevolent spirit of the Antonines gave these proofs of its active existence, the seven deacons in Rome, helped in their researches by the seven notaries, did more to assuage the misery of the Roman poor than Nerva and Trajan and Hadrian and Antoninus the Philosopher, and Antoninus the Pious, and the great Marcus Aurelius himself, ever could do for the same object. And, moreover, none of those princes would probably have thought of it had it not been for the side view they already had of the Church, although their policy confined her to the Catacombs.

And the same difference between the pagan and the Christian spirit continued ever after. So that when Julian the apostate came on the field of the great struggle between the old and the new, as he could judge better of the state of affairs, because he had himself been baptized, what did he see? and what did he say? He saw that the Church had triumphed, owing to her all-embracing charity, and that paganism was nearly dead, owing to its inborn selfishness ; and he said to his priests and hierophants, and to the mystic philosophers of Alexandria: "Follow the example of the Christians, and establish everywhere houses of relief both for the soul and the body." But it was too late. What he saw only irritated him; and what he said did not produce any effect whatever. Enough of Roman pagan charity.

Must I come, in a second place, to the spirit of Moslem and Turkish benevolence? I blush at the very idea of discussing such a subject as this. But a thousand voices all around compel me to answer them. For to our shame there is no denying that in this age many pretended Christians are lost in their admiration of a few verses of the Koran, and entirely shut their eyes to the world-wide effects of the strange charity which that book pretends to preach. It must seem to every one that Mohammedanism has had a fair field for proving the true spirit which animates it. It has subjected to its sway the fairest countries of this earth. After having subdued them by the sword, centuries have been given it to mould them at its will. Having entirely destroyed the ancient institutions that had ruled over those populations, it has imposed everywhere its own inborn despotism. What benefit has accrued to mankind from the indubitable and immense changes it has introduced into the world? If it has "inculcated, on the whole, an extremely high and noble system of morals," as Mr. Lecky pretends,* it must have had a very beneficent influence over those nations which have been subject to its control during so many centuries. For nothing is calculated to make men happy and prosperous like the establishment among them of "God's kingdom," which is virtue itself; that is, "a high and noble system of morals." But is it not demonstrated by this time that every country in Africa, Asia, or Europe which has been for a long period under the sway of Mohammedanism is now reduced almost to the lowest stage of degradation? Look at Egypt, Asia Minor, Greece, Persia, Armenia, Arabia, Hindostan, and contemplate the baneful effects of Moslem or Turkish rule. The fairest part of the globe has been made the ugliest; the richest has become the poorest. What was active and progressive is now torpid or dead. Whatever the Mussulman has touched falls to the ground and lies prostrate, altogether unable to rise again. The description could be indefinitely prolonged; we leave it to the reader's imagination.

What are, after all, the remarkable advantages which have resulted for the world from the doctrines of the Koran and the practical application of them by Turk or Saracen? The majority of those writers who seem to believe that there are many are satisfied with generalities, and never condescend to give us particulars. The author of "European Morals," knowing that this cannot suffice, has done his best to offer us a list of them in his second volume.† Firstly, therefore, "it has preached the purest monotheism among ignorant and barbarous men." To qualify this pretension, which is the strongest in point of fact, it must be said, also, that it has barbarously destroyed in Persia, together with Christian monotheism, that of Zoroaster's religion, which was the noblest in Asia, at least in ancient times. It has driven to apostasy many Christian nations in Europe, although a Catholic Review in England, relying on some verses of the Koran has maintained, not long ago, that the Mussulmans have everywhere tolerated, or perhaps favored, the religion of Christ. This is altogether false. As to the pagan nations which it has subdued, it must be said that in Africa, at

---

* Vol. ii. p. 251. † Page 251, foll.

least, it has *not* given many proofs of zeal for the destruction of fetichism, most probably with a view to keeping on the Dark Continent a large supply of men eminently fitted for slavery, to which the Koran forbids to reduce "the believers."

Secondly, it is maintained that "it has inculcated, on the whole, an extremely high and noble system of morals." A word has just been said on the subject, and it seems sufficient on account of the glaring result of this "system of morals" over the whole world. We will only add that whenever the Koran teaches a high morality (which it does here and there) it always copies from the Gospel, to which the honor of it must be referred.

Thirdly, Mr. Lecky praises it again for "having borrowed from Christianity that doctrine of salvation by belief which is perhaps the most powerful impulse that can be applied to the characters of men." If Mr. Lecky understands by this the Protestant "doctrine of salvation by faith," he is mistaken in placing it among the moral advantages of Mussulmanism, because the Koran does not teach it, and the Mohammedans do not practise it; they have fatalism in its place. Besides, the doctrine of salvation by faith, understood in the sense of Luther and Calvin, instead of being "the most powerful impulse applied to the characters of men," is one of the most baneful dogmas invented by heretics of ancient and modern times; is, in fact, destructive of all morals when it is strictly understood. This is not the place to prove it. Every one can judge of it by looking over Moeller's "Symbolism."

Fourthly, according to Mr. Lecky, "Mohammed's religion possessed a book which, however inferior to that of the opposing religion, has nevertheless been the consolation and the support of millions in many ages." If the Koran has been the source of such a blessing "to many millions," it is only owing to the ignorance and besotting stupidity of those deluded peoples; for there is scarcely anything in that book which the reason of man can approve, his conscience sanction, and his good taste avow, excepting always what it has "borrowed from Christianity." As to calling it only "inferior" to the Bible, Mr. Lecky evidently did not sufficiently reflect on the impropriety of comparing it in any sense to it. A perfect farrago of nonsense (which the Koran certainly is when it does not "borrow from Christianity") cannot be mentioned in the same phrase with the Bible, the greatest boon that was ever conferred on man, after the living teaching of the Church.

Finally, the author of "European Morals" says a word of praise on *fatalism* itself. As to this question it seems to us altogether useless, nay, absurd to discuss it. Whilst Christianity has made, with such an earnest zeal, of the great duty of confidence in God, of resignation to His will, of a complete reliance on His fatherly care, a true foundation of virtue, to find any moral beauty in fatalism, such as the Koran teaches it, implies an obliquity of vision which we are surprised to see in so eminent a writer and so acute a reasoner. This is all that can be said in favor of Mohammedanism. Yet the question of charity is scarcely touched in those considerations. The sum total of it consists in building fountains for the thirsty traveller, and caravanseries for the pilgrim, besides some hospitals for the insane.

We experience as great a repugnance to speak, in a third place, of Buddhistic charity as we felt in discussing the moral beauties of Mussulmanism. Still a word is absolutely required here, on account of the great number of men who, following the lead of Mr. Max Müller, find in the moral doctrines of Gautama almost the exact counterpart of those of Christ. It is one of the most remarkable aberrations of our age that whilst Christianity offers the spectacle of all the virtues, in a form which is acceptable at the same time to the most refined and enlightened and to the rudest and most ignorant men, many learned and clever writers try their best to find fault with it; and being scarcely able to bring against it any reasonable accusations, they use their truly extensive knowledge to discover on the face of the globe spots unknown before them where some travellers pretend that there are moral wonders which can be brought into comparison with it. And forthwith descriptions are written which throw almost into the shade whatever any one of us can see in our Christian surroundings of moral beauty and perfection. It is precisely the reverse of the evolutionists' process, who, having everywhere under their eyes the spectacle of a dignified humanity worthy of coming from the hands of God, gather from every side whatever they find in travellers' books of monstrous samples of degradation and barbarism, which they instantly give as the faithful portraiture of our species, and the proof that we came originally from some ape or ascidian!

It is said, therefore, that the Buddhists of eastern Asia have in their books the solemn injunction of the highest moral precepts, which they exactly follow in their lives; that Gautama's doctrine gives to his code of ethics as strong a sanction in its promise of Nirvanà's blessings as can be that of Christianity; and finally that if the Christians have the example and the love of Christ to urge them on to the practice of holiness, the same is true of Buddhism with regard to what is reported of Gautama's life, and of the ardent devotion which all true Buddhists experience for him. This is the objection in all its strength, and we do not remember to have seen it presented in so vivid a shape in whatever Mr. Max Müller has said in favor of it.

First, therefore, we beg leave to say that it would be too long to wade through the fourteen Buddhistic folio volumes—this we think is the number of them—of nonsense and puerilities, in the midst of which a few moral maxims, derived from antique Hindoo wisdom, are thrown at random. It seems, however, that there are in those books many beautiful precepts which (according to some travellers of the stamp of the Abbé Huc) the poor, unsophisticated Tartars of the Gobi desert repeat constantly and try to follow the best way they can. But this is not a precise code like that of Christianity; and there is nowhere in the immense compilation of *Sakya-mouni* anything like the Decalogue and the Sermon on the Mount. Those Buddhistic precepts are mere traditional sayings which pass from mouth to mouth, and are interpreted by every one to the best of his ability. Any one who is acquainted with Gautama's biography must be persuaded that he received them from the Brahmans of his day, who themselves had inherited them from their ancestors or read them in the Vedas or the Zends. The true character of these sacred books of Hindostan and central Asia is well known; and it is now almost demonstrated that they contain at least a part of the primitive revelation communicated by God Himself to the first patriarchs. They are consequently part and parcel of Christianity which began in fact on the day of creation, and will last till the day of judgment. This, however, does not give to Buddhism a semi-divine character; because in itself it was a heresy from Brahmanism, and a very evident corruption of primitive doctrine. This, in few words, is the answer to the first branch of the objection.

With regard to the sanction which Gautama gave to his moral code in the promise of Nirvanà, it is a great subject of wonder that any one should compare it with the sanction of the Christian code which consists in the promise of eternal life. It is well known that in the idea of *Sakya-mouni* Nirvanà was a positive annihilation, in order to escape from the endless transmigrations of Brahmanism; and that the knaves who are even at this time at the head of this pretended religion are well aware of it, and share in the same delusion with their founder. Mr. Max Müller acknowledged it in a short lecture he delivered in praise of Buddhism; and his excuse for insisting on what he thinks to be the *admirable* sanction of this code is that the ignorant people do not think that by Nirvanà they will ever be annihilated, but on the contrary transferred at once to a heavenly paradise as enticing as that of Mohammed. This is sufficient, in our opinion; and it would be only a loss of time to discuss any longer the supposed resemblance or equality of sanction both in Lamaism and Christianity. In the first it is imposture and hypocrisy; in the other, the asseveration of a God-man.

A word also must suffice for the third branch of the objection. A Christian must consider it a disgrace to be reduced to examine if there is any resemblance—setting entirely aside the equality—between the example of Christ and that of Gautama; and also between the love we feel for our Lord and that which the Buddhists experience for their living Buddhas. The inward consciousness we have that Christ is true God, coupled with the wonderful knowledge we possess of the divine attributes themselves, constitute a motive for virtue so far above any other consideration, and particularly so eminently superior to the gross ideas the Buddhists have of the Deity, that it is positively incomprehensible any one should assume that there is any resemblance between both systems of religion, with regard to the love of a divine founder. The more is it so that Buddhism professedly rejects the existence of God, as Mr. Max Müller admits.* In Gautama's well-declared opinion, the world is the result of "a concatenation of causes and effects;" as to God there is none other. So he was, after all, so early as his time, a learned evolutionist, and could no more by his concatenation of causes and effects give a real sanction to his

---

* This gentleman acknowledges that there is a passage in Gautama's books in which the founder of the sect gives as a reason of his rejection of Brahmanism that the creation of the world is attributed in the Vedas to Brahma or God, which is, he pretends, an *imposture.*

moral code than the partisans of the system of evolution can do it at the present day.

There remains to consider charity in Protestantism, to complete the circle prescribed to the present inquiry. At a first glance it looks indeed as if there was among Protestants a powerful stream of benevolence, entirely *distinct* from the priceless treasure constantly gathered in and generously lavished from the bosom of the true Church. At least in this happy country how many non-Catholic families endeavor to rival in this respect what is most generous in Christendom! We could quote from our own experience admirable examples of it which might bring sweet tears of sympathy from the eyes of many readers. We prefer to bring others' testimony rather than our own. This is the emphatic acknowledgment of the Little Sisters of the Poor, who do not hesitate to say—at least I have heard it from their own lips—that they are helped in their ministrations to old and infirm people as much if not more, by most respectable persons who unfortunately do not belong to our Holy Church than by the Catholics themselves. There can be no doubt of this; and the extent of those charities is much greater than many people imagine, and they are very often as generous as they are unostentatious. But we are bound to say that this is not to be attributed to the Protestant spirit, but to that of genuine Christianity. Whatever view may be taken of the Reformation, even in the supposition of those who think falsely that there was in the primitive reformers a sincere religious zeal, it is impossible to deny that the result was most fatal to the previous working of true charity. All that had been done so abundantly, magnificently, and universally to assuage human misery was at once destroyed, or at least modified so as to entirely change its character. William Cobbett has proved it in his "History of the Reformation," and there is no need of enlarging on the subject. As this strange phenomenon was not true only of England, where alone Cobbett examined it, but became as worthy of note in Germany and Scandinavia as in Great Britain itself, it must be pronounced to be essential to the new system of religion originating in the north of Europe during the sixteenth century. Protestantism expunged at once brotherly charity from the list of Christian virtues, if not expressly and by issuing a new command against it, at least *de facto* and by the natural influence of the new principles.

If, therefore, genuine charity has continued to be practised by many excellent men born in Protestantism, it must not be attributed to their religion, but to the "testimony of a Christian soul" which remains in them. And that it is so in truth is proved by the fact that at least a great number of those benevolent people who are not, and probably never will be, Catholics cannot likewise be called Protestants, because they do not make profession of belonging to any one of the sects. Most of them declare emphatically that they are Christians and nothing else ; and we must believe them when they say so. It is the misfortune of their birth that has been the reason why they do not profess any creed ; and the feeling which must be in our hearts preferably to any other toward them is the sincere desire and prayer that their charity for the poor should be at last rewarded by the knowledge of the truth which has not yet reached their mind. We maintain that their deeds are altogether independent of their Protestantism, if there is in them any remnant of it ; and the source of their benevolence is not *distinct* from that of the Catholic Church.

This digression will have been most useful if it brings on the conviction that from the bosom of the true Church alone the source of true charity has ever gushed forth ; and it is time at last to bring back the reader's mind to the consideration of the first Christians in Jerusalem, from which we first started. In our day socialism and communism are endeavoring to ape that primitive organization as it was shaped by Christ's apostles. But in vain do they pretend to bring the same blessings to the poor ; in vain do they proclaim the brotherhood of mankind, and the necessity of reforming abuses and restoring to the people their rights. Their godless system is only calculated to increase the evil, and destroy human society without the hope of rebuilding it ; precisely because they discard at once all ideas of religion and morality. Without these, however, it is as impossible to establish happiness and virtue on earth as to build an Egyptian pyramid without foundation, or to construct a material city in the clouds.

7. *Holiness was Fostered among the First Judeo-Christians, by the Observance of the Mosaic Law.—A Word on the Essenes.*

The Jews, who were destined to realize in the church of Jerusalem a moral commonwealth recalling to the mind the still-remembered felicity of the golden age, had possessed in the Mosaic Law the strictest precepts ever given to a nation. Their code was essentially adapted to the whole of mankind, because the Decalogue was in itself an open and exterior promulgation of the moral principles which God has deposited in the human conscience.

The priests, to whom was assigned the duty of explaining the moral law, and the prophets, who, besides foretelling the future, had also received the mission of correcting abuses when they arose, had during long ages maintained the pure doctrine among the people. Their morality was essentially the same with ours, as has been proved; and owing to the help they obtained through training and instruction, they could easily form to themselves an enlightened conscience; whilst the pagans, uninstructed and untrained, could with the greatest difficulty unravel the entangled web of the natural law hidden in the inmost recesses of their souls.

In the course of ages, it is true, Sophists had also appeared among the Jews, and unsafe teachers had obscured by their comments the purity of the original text. The Saviour had come to apply a remedy to those aberrations; and without destroying the former law, He had announced a more perfect one based on His example as well as on His teaching. This was the plain and at the same time sublime ground-work on which the apostles built; and the first edifice raised according to the Saviour's plan was the particular church of Jerusalem, which would probably have become the head of the universal future Church had it not been for the stubbornness and blindness of the great majority of the nation.

Let us, therefore, contemplate a moment what would most likely have been the pattern of all Christian congregations throughout the universe in case the headship of the new religion had remained in the hands of the Hebrews. For it is very probable that if Jerusalem had continued to be the Church's centre, as it certainly was during the first ten years of the apostolic preaching, it would likewise have continued to be the pattern for all other churches; so that instead of Linus and Clement, both from the gentile world, the first successors of Peter would have belonged also to the Jewish race.

In the first place, the general rule would most probably have been that of equality in point of wealth among the Christians. There would have been no poor people and very few rich men among them. The great majority of wealthy converts would have continued to bring the total value of their property to the spiritual rulers' feet, and the portion of the poorest would have been proportionately increased. It is impossible now to judge accurately what would have been the total result. It is clear, however, that universal comfort would have been the rule among Christian nations.

In a second place, if the apostles did not take upon themselves to dictate to the new converts what part of their goods they should keep and what part they should give in charity, they insisted, nevertheless, on the clear precept of the Saviour that "His disciples must not be attached to this world," and that "they must do to others what they would wish others should do to them." They inculcated likewise the great truths that "God blesses the poor," and that "the rich can but with difficulty enter heaven." These are principles of human or rather heavenly management far preferable to those which go to form what is now called the science of political economy. There can be scarcely any doubt that in case the Jewish capital had not been destroyed, and had become the head city of Christianity, the same model being copied everywhere, a comfort and happiness would have been established among mankind such as the world has never seen and shall never see. It would have been the complete realization of St. Paul's saying, "Godliness is profitable to all things, having promise of the life that now is and of that which is to come."* But even in that supposition no one must imagine that this "comfort and happiness" would have been the great, most important, and supreme object of religion. If modern socialists could by their systems procure the same amount of well-being to humanity, they would consider themselves as the great benefactors of mankind, and they never would suppose that anything more could be done for man, though nevertheless the highest aspirations of his nature would still remain unfulfilled. But Christianity could not remain

---

* 1 Tim. iv. 8.

satisfied with such a paltry boon; and since the whole doctrine of the Gospel preaches the renouncement of the world and the impossibility of man ever reaching true happiness in it, it is evident that in the beautiful picture the Acts of the Apostles give us of the first Christian congregation there must have been something far superior to its exterior outlook. It was indeed at the same time *Tabernaculum Dei cum hominibus,* and this immense privilege of being "the dwelling-place of God among men" was the true and unfailing source of that charity which procured even so many worldly blessings. We must, therefore, briefly see, in a third place, the part there was in it for "God and the soul," as coming both from the Mosaic and the Christian precepts. God was, in fact, everything to them. For Him they were at this moment turning their backs on the worldly promises of the Law, though they continued to practise it. For, if it is not true that under its dispensation eternal life was unknown, and that it never was promised to them, still it is sure that there was in the Mosaic Law more mention made of this world's happiness than of the other's. The new doctrine, on the contrary, told them that, even for this life, they must rely on God and on Him alone. They must not accumulate treasures which "the moth consumes and the robber steals away;" they must rely on Providence for the necessaries of life, and be satisfied with them.

Their ancestors had been "God's people," but their countrymen were no more so. The new gathering among them, originating with Christ, was to form a new race, and they were to be forever "a people acceptable to God, a pursuer of good works."* They must on that account entirely belong to Him. God was never to be out of their aims—out of their thoughts. They were to sacrifice to Him everything they had, everything they hoped, and to be persuaded that in giving all they had to the poor they gave it to God. This was to be the great principle of the "Christian economy." For the sake of God alone they must throw far behind them all selfish considerations; and self-interest, which always lies at the base of all systems of human benevolence, must be discarded as below the dignity of a Christian.

The simple words of the Acts of the Apostles, on which we now comment, will necessarily give to any one who reads them atten-

---

* Tit. ii. 14.

tively the idea that this was in truth the groundwork of the picture by which the church of Jerusalem was represented by St. Luke in those glowing and attractive colors. It was because God had come to establish " His tabernacle among men," that the inhabitants of the new city had but " one heart and one soul," and brought to the feet of the apostles all they possessed, in order to distribute it among all. The new kingdom of God, in fact, visible in the "exterior" peace and harmony, was nevertheless altogether "interior"—*Regnum Dei intra vos est.* And as it has been proved by several texts of the New Testament that God's kingdom consisted essentially in holiness, which is thus inseparable from the Church, it was the sublime though simple practice of the highest conceivable virtue which was the real source of the universal well-being. Not only, therefore, God ever present was at the base of the system, but the soul was the actual field on which this system was entirely carried out; and for this reason particularly "God's kingdom" was said to be " interior"—*intra vos est.*

It was proper to enter into these details, because the holiness of the Church is our theme, and nothing can more effectually strike the reader than to see sanctity itself enthroned at Jerusalem on the very first day of the Church's existence. The life of St. James, the first Christian bishop of the city, is one of the most precious examples of that sanctity; and we may with fairness assume that the moral conduct of the people was to a great extent a copy of that of their pastor. The details of it have been preserved by Eusebius of Cæsarea from a most precious fragment of Hegesippus, which all the Catholic histories of the Church invariably reproduce.

The Christians of Jerusalem, not satisfied with the new obligations imposed upon them by the Gospel, practised at the same time most strictly all the injunctions of the Mosaic law. St. Paul himself called this a heavy burden, and would not allow it to be imposed on the gentiles. He went so far as to call the Galatians foolish, *insensati*, because by submitting to the rite of circumcision they had contracted the obligation of bearing that burden. It is known to theologians that the Mosaic precepts, rites, and ceremonies did not contain *ex se* the source of grace, nor, consequently, of sanctity. Still, as it was a constant restraint on human freedom of action, it cut off at least a great number of occasions of sin, which are generally held out to man, when he allows his inclinations to follow their free bent, even in matters otherwise allowable. The church at Jerusalem, on that account, must have presented a spectacle never seen in our Christian congregations, except on the part of the small number who devote themselves to a monastic life. The rules of a monastery, in fact, are alone a near reproduction of the burdensome prescriptions of the Pentateuch; and the first chapters of St. Luke's book, which vividly describe the daily life of the apostles and their new brethren, either in the Temple or in private houses, complete the picture of holiness which the portraiture of charity and mutual help and love had so exquisitely begun.

It is easy to understand the whole of it, if one remembers what Philo and Josephus have written of the Essenes, who precisely flourished at the time of our Saviour. These were only Jews, and they had for their guidance only the precepts of the Mosaic law. They never became Christians; and because they lived east of the Jordan river, at a good distance from either Jerusalem or Galilee, they never could have any intimate relation with incipient Christianity. In course of time they became fanatical Jews, like those who fought against the Romans; and as they disappeared from history shortly after the destruction of Jerusalem by Titus, it can be therefrom inferred that this was a fatal blow to their organization. If Pliny speaks later of them it is only as of a sect perishing in his time, when it is known that it was then reduced to a few individuals. Consequently the effort made by some modern writers to identify them with the Christians of Jerusalem, and even to represent our divine Lord as an Essene at the beginning of His career, is altogether futile, and disproved by the whole of their history, and particularly by their dogmatic tenets.

But is it not wonderful to contemplate the nobleness of their ethical code and the purity of their lives, whilst it is certain that their only moral guide was the Pentateuch of Moses, modified by some Alexandrine tenets? The high character of their strict monotheism; their firm belief in the immortality of the soul; their rejection of bloody sacrifices as being inferior to the practice of self-renouncement; their morals, in fine, which could be resolved into three short prescriptions—namely, love of God, love of virtue, love of men; all this is calculated to prove that the Mosaic law, when practised strictly and intelligently, could bring its adherents to a high round of the moral ladder, and that it truly fostered holiness among the Judeo-Christians.

What is most surprising in the Essenes is first their strict observance of continency, refusing even to enter the bonds of marriage; and secondly, their absolute renouncement of personal property, so as to have everything in common ($\varkappa o\iota\nu\omega\nu\acute{\iota}\alpha$), exactly the same as we have admired it in the first Christians of the Holy City. The picture of both, Christians and Essenes, is so perfectly alike that one can scarcely imagine they could have coexisted at the same time and near each other without coalescing. Nevertheless it is altogether certain that they never belonged to the same organization, and that the Essenes never professed any of the Christian tenets, such as original sin, redemption by Christ, the necessity of a sacramental system, of baptism in particular, etc. etc. The sameness of both bodies with regard to the points mentioned above came only from the fact that both were adherents to the Mosaic law, which the Christians practised in perfection together with the great St. James, their apostle and bishop.

But besides the law of Moses the new Christians had the Gospel, which raised them morally far above the Essenes. If any one wished to know how this could be, how there could be a moral teaching superior to Philo's doctrine, a holiness more striking and complete, he has only to inquire more particularly from Philo himself in what consisted that "love of men" which formed the third or last of their moral prescriptions. He will soon learn that this "love" was restricted to the "brethren of the order," and even only as long as they remained brethren. Yes, none of those beautiful details of a common life ($\varkappa o\iota\nu\omega\nu\acute{\iota}\alpha$), by which they renounced personal property, extended farther than an organization which at the time of its greatest prosperity did not embrace more than four thousand souls. And as was just seen, in case a member of this community fell into a heavy sin he was immediately cut off from it and refused all help and assistance in his greatest need. According to Josephus,* the case had happened, and the unfortunate brother had died of hunger because his former friends would not grant him a crust of bread. The Judeo-Christians of Jerusalem could not be guilty of such

---

* Antiq., viii. § 8.

an enormity as this, because Christ and St. Paul had extended the meaning of the word "brother" to the human race.

Did they not all, Jews and Hellenes, partake of the same Eucharist; that is, of the body and blood of Christ, who being the head of the body, made of all the members the partakers of the same privileges, the partakers, in fact, of what St. Peter called the "divine nature"? This was the source of the holiness to which the Jews of Jerusalem had been raised, and before which the sanctity of any other community of men must pale and dwindle away.

CHAPTER II.

CHRISTIAN HOLINESS IN THE EAST—THE THERAPEUTÆ IN EGYPT, AND THEIR RELATIONS WITH THE CHURCH AT JERUSALEM—FIRST DEVELOPMENTS OF MONASTICISM.

1. *Who were the Therapeutæ? Their connection with Jerusalem.*

THAT the Therapeutæ in Egypt had been for several centuries intimately connected with the Essenes in Palestine is now admitted by all critics. Both were branches growing on the same stem, and that stem can be called Hebrew pietism, to use a modern expression. The Essenes, as was just seen, never became Christian; and though their moral code was very superior to that of pagans, they were left far behind by the converts made by the apostles in Jerusalem. The Therapeutæ, differing in this from the Essenes, became the first disciples of St. Mark in Alexandria, and their total conversion to Christ induced the belief, universal formerly, that they mainly composed the primitive church of that city; that they had not existed before the arrival of St. Mark; and that the disciples merely took the name of Therapeutæ on the banks of the Nile, as they were called Christians at Antioch.

This opinion is now disproved. They flourished in the country during a couple of centuries before Christianity was preached; and originally they were only pious Jews, leading the holy life described by Philo in his book *De Vita Contemplativa*. But their name disappeared afterwards, because, having all become Christian, there was no need for them of a distinct appellation.

Many Judeo-Christians in Palestine were inoculated with Ebionism after the death of St. James. That baneful heresy never made any proselytes in Egypt, though there must have been a constant intercourse between the Therapeutæ and the church at Jerusalem; and it is proper first to convince ourselves of this, on account of the great influence it had in shaping the moral ideas of the Egyptian Christians and making them, as it were, a branch of the Palestine church.

It is known that during a long time before and after the apostolic age, the Hebrew schools of Alexandria were more celebrated even than those of Jerusalem; and many Jews must have constantly travelled from the banks of the Jordan to those of the Nile. We know likewise from the Acts of the Apostles (vi. 9) that there were at that time in the Holy City synagogues of Jews belonging to Cyrenaika and to Alexandria. Thus on one side the African Israelites had their particular places of worship and religious instruction in Jerusalem, whilst on the other Hebrews from Palestine went to Africa to study in the peculiar schools of the Alexandrine Museum alloted to them.

We are not reduced, however, to these general considerations in order to conclude from them the intimate relations which must have existed between the primitive church on Mount Sion and that of Egypt. This might, no doubt, amply suffice when we consider the sameness of both institutions and the peculiar holiness which prevailed in both, evincing evidently an identity of origin. But there are, besides, positive testimonies of great weight to confirm those views and to make them absolutely certain; so that the primitive Alexandrine church can be considered as a faithful copy of that of Jerusalem, and the same holiness must have obtained in both.

These testimonies are those of Eusebius, St. Jerome, and Cassian. But as they are mainly grounded on Philo's writings, it is proper to briefly discuss a couple of points which have been strongly controverted with regard to this last writer. Was Philo ever a Christian? Did he intend to describe the first Christians of Alexandria when he spoke of the Therapeutæ? These two questions deserve a moment's consideration. Both Eusebius and St. Jerome believed that Philo embraced Christianity *very late* in his life. St. Augustine was of a contrary opinion. Whatever side may be adopted, the evident conclusion is that he was not a Christian when he wrote his books. But the question of his religion has absolutely nothing to do with the intimate relation existing between the Egyptian Therapeutæ and the Jerusalem Christians. Yet this remark was necessary, because some modern critics speak on this subject almost as if no Therapeutæ were Christians in case Philo was not. This is altogether unallowable. Philo's case does not decide that of the Churches. It remains for us to consider a moment if the Jewish writer intended to describe the first Alexandrine Christians when he spoke of the Therapeutæ in his book *De Vita Contemplativa.*

St. Jerome was emphatically of that opinion.* At the beginning of the eighteenth century there was in France a lively controversy on the subject, and undoubtedly those who sided with St. Jerome (Montfaucon particularly) had in our belief the best of the controversy. But even independently of this, supposing that Philo did not intend to describe actual Christians when he portrayed the Therapeutæ, what does it matter if in point of fact it must be admitted that they were? The Jewish author's intention cannot be known, and it is idle to put even the question, since he has not himself revealed it to mankind. But let us examine the testimonies of Eusebius, of St. Jerome, and of Cassian on the subject, the last chiefly, who lived so long in Egypt and must have reflected the Egyptian tradition. Do not those testimonies stand by themselves independently of the private opinion of any writer on Philo's religion or intention? They must be quoted to be appreciated.

In the time of Eusebius it is extremely probable, if not absolutely certain, that all the Therapeutæ had been converted and were actually Christians. From the eremitical life which was at first universal among them they had gradually passed to the cenobitical phase of monachism. This last institution had spread before this all over Egypt, and was then flourishing and still daily progressing. The bishop of Cæsarea gave a short description of those monasteries in the fifteenth and sixteenth chapters of the second book of his "Ecclesiastical History." His main object was to prove the perfect identity of the monastic life practised in his time with that of the previous Therapeutæ; and in this second part of his discussion he simply uses Philo's book as an authoritative exposition of that ancient Jewish asceticism. He does not, consequently, rely on Philo's religion or intention, but only on his faithful delineation as that of an eye-witness; and from the life of the monks well known in Eusebius' age he concludes as to the perfect identity of both. "Those ancient men," he says, "were called $\theta \varepsilon \rho \alpha \pi \varepsilon \nu \tau \alpha \iota$ and $\iota \kappa \varepsilon \tau \alpha \iota$ by Philo. The first word ($\theta \varepsilon \rho \alpha \pi \varepsilon \nu \tau \alpha \iota$) indicated that their great object was both to *worship* and *care for*" (Eusebius derives both meanings from this single Greek word); "namely, to *worship* God with the greatest diligence, and to *care for* their own souls by curing them from all moral

---

* In Catalogo.

distempers. They were called likewise ικεται—that is, suppliant—because their principal office was to beseech and supplicate God."

There can be no doubt that in the opinion of Eusebius the Therapeutæ, personally known to Philo more than two hundred years before his time, had led the life of monks, a life agreeing in the main points with that of the first Jerusalem Christians; consisting particularly in having but "one heart and one soul," and in being detached from this world in which they could possess nothing. For his object all along was to prove the identity of both. Living himself so near Egypt, and being in constant intercourse with some old bishops of his own neighborhood, who had been personally acquainted with Origen (as was remarked in the "Church and Gentile World"), he must have been perfectly well informed as to the origin of Christianity in Alexandria. He knew that in his time the Therapeutæ had all embraced the new religion, or nearly so, and this alone would prove that Montfaucon was right in his controversy with President Bouhier at the beginning of the eighteenth century. This last gentleman brought forward a great amount of erudition to prove that the Therapeutæ of Egypt had been only Jewish philosophers and ascetics, and he concluded there had never been Christians among them. He did not perceive that if they had been only Jewish ascetics before the apostolic age (which nobody denies), the case was very different with them since the time when St. Mark appeared on the banks of the Nile; and the fact of their being all Christians in the age of Eusebius precisely demonstrates what Bouhier pretended to disprove.

But St. Jerome's testimony will place the truth in a still clearer light. He lived, it is true, much later than the celebrated bishop of Cæsarea; but he had thoroughly studied Christian antiquity, and in his time Christian antiquity was a recent affair. He not only spent many years in Palestine, on the confines of the Egyptian desert, but he had frequent intercourse with many Egyptian monks, visited their monasteries, and must have been familiar with all their traditions.

This he writes of the primitive church in Alexandria:* "Mark went to Egypt, carrying with him the Gospel he had written, and being the first to announce Christ in Alexandria he founded the Church there, with such a height of doctrine and holiness of life that he brought up all the followers of Christ to his own pattern

---

* Lib. de Script. Eccl.—de Sto. Marco.

of excellence. So that Philo, the most learned and eloquent of the Jews, taking notice that the first Alexandrine church followed still Jewish rites (*adhuc judaizantem*), wrote a book on their way of life, as a matter of praise for his own nation." And in the same work, in his biography of Philo himself, Jerome speaks more pointedly still and to the purpose : " Philo the Jew, born in Alexandria, of a sacerdotal race, is placed by me among the ecclesiastical writers, because, when he wrote on the church founded in Alexandria by the evangelist Mark, he openly praised the Christians. . . . From his words it appears that those first followers of Christ led a life exactly similar to that of our monks. None of them possessed any property; there were neither poor nor rich among them; they distributed their goods among the needy; they spent much time in psalmody and prayer; they applied to their own advancement in sacred learning and purity of life, exactly as St. Luke relates was the case with the first Christians in Jerusalem."

St. Jerome, in this last passage, may have been mistaken as to Philo's intention. It is very probable that the Jewish writer knew not that what he saw and described was a new efflorescence of piety coming from Christ, with whom he was not, perhaps, thoroughly acquainted. He knew that the Essenes in Palestine and the Therapeutæ in Egypt had flourished for a couple of centuries; and it is very likely that he *intended* to speak only of Jewish ascetics, not of Christians. But in point of fact many of those pious men had already, in Philo's time, embraced Christianity, at least in Egypt; and they were all gradually destined to take the same step; and St. Jerome was perfectly right in saying that the life of those primitive Egyptian disciples was exactly similar to that of the monks living in his age, and also to that of the first disciples in Jerusalem, as described by St. Luke. This is all that is pretended before coming to an exact description of the peculiar holiness then prevailing in Egypt.

A word remains to be said of Cassian's testimony. He does not speak of the Jewish author of *De Vita Contemplativa*, and confines himself to the cenobites living in his time. But there is a short passage in his second book, *De Cœnobiorum Institutis*, which precisely falls in with our actual purpose, and proves that the life of the first Christians in Egypt was precisely like that of the first disciples in Jerusalem; and moreover that, in his opinion, it had continued to his very time, and was reproduced in his day by the monks among whom he remained for about ten years of his own life. This is important, because the details of that peculiar holiness are perfectly well ascertained by this work of Cassian, and by his still more copious *Collationes;* so that we can form a correct idea of it such as it was practised by the first Christians of Palestine and Egypt. This is his exact meaning translated from the original Latin:

"When the Christian faith was propagated (in Egypt) there were already in the country some holy men, truly worthy of bearing the name of monks, who received from the evangelist Mark of blessed memory, the first Alexandrine bishop, a rule of life which expressed to the letter the eminent character of the primitive church in Jerusalem as we find it in the Acts of the Apostles. That is to say, 'The multitude of believers had but one heart and one soul ; neither did any one say that aught of the things which he possessed was his own ; but all things were common unto them; etc. Nay, they went much farther than this ;" and Cassian directly begins to give copious details of the cenobites' daily life which the first Jerusalem Christians did not altogether practise, since they continued to live with their wives and did not withdraw into solitude; still the life of both was otherwise alike.

It is evident from the whole passage that in Cassian's time the Christians in Egypt firmly believed that at the very cradle of Christianity in their country the holiness of the first Jerusalem congregation prevailed also in Alexandria. It had been brought by Mark, who had himself witnessed the first outburst of that piety in Jerusalem, and did his best to bring up his Egyptian converts to the same height of sanctity. The author of the work *De Cœnobiorum Institutis* does not say a word of the former Therapeutæ, probably because in his time they were all Christians and had lost their former name. But he must have believed like Eusebius and St. Jerome that they had formed the nucleus of that primitive Alexandrine congregation of which he speaks so highly. It must be, therefore, considered as proved that what has been said a few pages back of the Judeo-Christians in Jerusalem is true also of the Egyptian primitive church ; and if there was need of it, other witnesses could be found in Epiphanius, Palladius, and many other ecclesiastical writers.

2. Description of the Primitive Christian Life in Egypt.

At first convents were unknown, and it is much later that Pachomius opened the first *monastery*. But in Egypt more than in Palestine ascetics lived apart from each other, though they did not go as yet into the wilderness, but they built their *cells* in the neighborhood of cities and towns. It was the fury of the persecutions, particularly those of Decius and Diocletian, which obliged those holy men to withdraw into the desert; and the Egyptian Paul was, for this reason, called the first hermit. Before him, however, and from the dawn of Christianity in Alexandria, there were already hermits, anchorites, ascetæ, by whatever name you wish to call them, who devoted themselves to a life of prayer and manual labor such as the world had never witnessed before.

Some very interesting details of it are given by Cassian in his second book, *De Institutis* which are precisely those we need, because he describes there not what took place in his time, but what was customary when "the primitive church's perfection"—*Ecclesiæ illius primitivæ perfectio*—" was in full vigor." *

"They withdrew," he says, "into the most hidden and retired places they could find in the suburbs of towns—*Suburbiorum loca*; and there practised abstemiousness to such a degree that it was a matter of wonder particularly to those who were not yet Christians. They spent whole days and nights in reading the Holy Scriptures, in prayer, and manual labor; the appetence of food, even the memory of it, appeared to be forgotten, and it was only after two or three days of an absolute fast that they consented to take the necessary food and drink, in which, however, they never indulged before sunset. They thought that the entire day must always be spent in the soul's care, and the body allowed its refreshment only at night."

According to the same author the memory of those ancient monastic customs all over Lower Egypt must have continued for a long time to be known in all its details by tradition, since it was only after true monasteries began to flourish—that is, after Pachomius, that it was thought necessary to write down rules of the most exact precision, in order to prevent divisions and schisms.

---

* Lib. ii. cap. v.

During nearly three centuries, therefore, custom alone ruled, a custom well known, as he says, *indigenarum relatione*—"from the constant report of the inhabitants." It can be concluded from this passage of Cassian that the conventual rules in vigor in after-times were merely the written expression of a former state going up to the very cradle of the Christian religion.

These rules are given out at length in both the Institutes and Conferences of Cassian. It does not enter into our scope to translate or copy them even compendiously. But St. Jerome has written an admirable and graphic abridgment of them, in his twenty-second letter *Ad Eustochium, de custodia Virginitatis*. A few passages of it on the cenobites cannot be omitted:

"The first rule among them is to obey the superiors and do whatever is commanded. They are divided into bands of *ten* and of a *hundred;* so that nine of them recognize an officer in the tenth man, and the ten officers in their turn are under the authority of the hundredth one. As to the order of the day, it is as follows: All remain in solitude in their cells until the ninth hour"—three o'clock in the afternoon. "The only persons who can then enter the cells are the officers of the decades, whose chief function is to bring consolation and comfort to whomsoever is agitated and in grief. At the ninth hour all meet in a common hall. Psalms are sung, Holy Scripture is read, and when the prayers are over all sit down to listen to the one whom they call Father, who begins to address them. . In the midst of the most profound silence no one either looks on another or is heard even to breathe. The copious tears of the audience are the only praise of the speaker; and mourning never breaks forth into groans. When the Father dwells upon the kingdom of Christ and the future beatitude in glory, you might see their lips moving and, with their eyes turned toward heaven, saying softly with the Psalmist: 'Who will give me wings like a dove, and I will fly and be at rest.'

"After this, the meeting being over, they go to their meal, at which all in turn help and serve the others. At table no noise is ever heard, and no one speaks even with his neighbor. Their fare consists of bread, of herbs and roots, with no other condiment than salt. Wine is drank only by the old men, and in small quantity by the children, in order that the advanced age of the first may be supported, and the tottering steps of childhood may be strengthened. . . . The daily labor of each one is supervised by the officer of each decade, and the total produce of the whole is faithfully reported every month to the superior of the house. To him devolves the charge of tasting the food before it is placed on the table, and of procuring for each member of the community the clothing and linen he needs. For no one can take the liberty of asking a new tunic or cloak, or a new set of mats for reclining at night. If any one gets sick he is immediately taken to a larger and well-ventilated apartment, where some old brothers take such care of him that he cannot long for the comforts of any city, or even the affection of a mother.

"On Sundays the whole time is spent in prayer and reading, which is also the case during the week, after they have completed their daily task. Every day some chapter of the Scriptures is studied. They all follow the same rule of fasting the year round; that is, till the ninth hour. But during Lent each one can follow his own inclination for holy austerity, and prolong his fast according to his devotion. From Easter to Pentecost the meal is anticipated; so that fast is broken by an early dinner and not by supper only; but though their life is thus made less austere, agreeably to ecclesiastical tradition, they never load their stomachs by taking two meals a day."

This passage of St. Jerome suffices to give an idea of the abstemious and holy life of the first Christians in Egypt. If modern moralists complain that, with the practice of some virtues, many others are not mentioned which must go to compose a complete course of ethics, an answer can be given comprehensive enough for the purpose. This short sketch is far from being even an adequate abridgment of Cassian's book. As was stated, this could not enter into the present scheme; but by a simple reference to both the Institutes and Conferences, it will be easily seen that the practice of all the Christian virtues was strictly taught and enforced in those holy houses. And not only positive holiness was the rule according to David's precept, *Fac bonum;* but the contrary vices were strongly checked in obedience to the first part of the Psalmist's verse, *Declina a malo.* It is sufficient to go cursorily through the various chapters of Cassian's works, to be persuaded of the thoroughness of the method.

But is it necessary in this age to come down to a vindication of this kind of life? In the sketch of it that has just been drawn, none of the shocking features objected by Mr. Lecky against Egyptian monasticism in his "European Morals" can be perceived. The simple reason of it is that this unobjectionable rule was the usual tenor of life in those houses; and the extraordinary facts brought together by the author of "European Morals" were only anomalies which the accompanying text often explains and renders more acceptable to reason. It cannot be denied, however, that this sublimity of virtue is little in keeping with the fastidious habits of our modern civilization. Must we condescend again to apologize for it? A slight attempt at it has been made in the "Church and Gentile World," and, as we expressly speak in this volume of Christian holiness, we would consider it derogatory to our very object to renew the attempt. The thing cannot be supposed to be subject to controversy. Both in Palestine and Egypt the origin of those holy rules and customs went up to the Apostles, and consequently to Christ Himself. Every Christian must be persuaded, for that reason, that they expressed the purest evangelical doctrine. To find fault with some details because they differ a great deal from our way of life is unworthy of a moralist, not to say of a Christian. It is not only in this age that this captious spirit has been manifested, but at all times there have been many instances of it, and St. Jerome had already to rebuke Vigilantius for his violent attacks on the monks of his day. But in spite of these bitter vituperations there have been in all ages multitudes of men and women ready to embrace and practise whatever was most particularly impugned; and a greater multitude still of ordinary Christians who did not indeed feel the courage to walk in the same road of perfection, yet admired it and encouraged it to the best of their ability.

The intimate relation existing between the primitive church in Palestine and that of Egypt would give rise to very important considerations. Had the majority of the Jews been converted and Jerusalem been spared, it is very probable that the same extraordinary kind of holiness would have prevailed at the origin of Christianity all over the earth, and that what seems now to us an idyllic and graceful story, belonging only to the Judeo-Christians of the Holy City in Palestine, would have been repeated in all countries visited by the primitive apostles. We will see in the next chapter that the same was likewise very probably true of the church at Edessa, which originated simultaneously with that of Jerusalem.

It is interesting, therefore, to look a moment at the moral prospect which would have been offered to the eye by those immense Oriental regions, in case the Jewish race, sanctified at once by the practice of these extraordinary virtues, had continued in possession of the leadership in the great social revolution which Christianity was to effect. The Jews were at this epoch dispersed through the whole world, but particularly in the East. Any one who reads the second chapter of the Acts of the Apostles, in which St. Luke speaks of those who had come to Jerusalem for the feast of Pentecost, will be struck by this remark, and conclude that the whole Orient was full of them. The Christian converts among them who would have been the Church's rulers in the present supposition could not but have copied exactly the proceedings of the first apostles in the Holy City. What has just been called the intimate relation of the Alexandrine primitive congregation with that of Jerusalem would have become a universal fact in the whole Orient at least, for a longer or shorter period, according as the primeval fervor would have lasted a longer or shorter time. The apostleship of St. Paul shows that even after the Jews had repeatedly refused to listen, he continued to address them everywhere preferably to the gentiles. Before St. Peter went to Rome he considered himself as the apostle of the Jews. It was only at Cæsarea that, in consequence of a vision, he received into the church the family of the Roman Cornelius; and at Antioch, as an exception, he preached to the Greeks as well as to his countrymen. Everywhere else he devoted all his energy to the formation of the Judeo-Christian congregations. Had there been a sufficient response from those whom he addressed, the Church would have undoubtedly presented at least in the whole Orient the spectacle offered primitively in the limited field assigned to St. James in the Holy City.

But a question remains to be briefly examined, before passing on to the next chapter. So far Egyptian holiness has been considered only among the Therapeutæ, who were the first disciples of St. Mark in Alexandria. Can the same be equally attributed to the whole Egyptian nation after the conversion of this extraordinary people? Would the descriptions of St. Jerome and of Cassian be as appropriate for the inhabitants of Upper Egypt as for those at the mouth of the Nile? The answer to these questions must be affirmative without possibility of contradiction.

The whole Coptic church originally was eminently monastic; and it extended as far south as Nubia, and farther. The same holiness of life so remarkable on the shores of the Mediterranean Sea, at Nitria for instance, prevailed likewise at Tabennæ, near the tropics. The copious details furnished by ecclesiastical history cannot leave any doubt on the subject. And moreover, in the fourth and fifth centuries, at the time of Palladius and of Cassian it continued in its primitive fervor. Athanasius witnessed it everywhere in his travels when Constantius forced him to flee from his see. Along the Nile as far as the first cataract, in the wilderness east of the river nearly to the shores of the Arabian Gulf, it was the same heavenly life that flourished in those arid solitudes. Virtue had prevailed over the depravity of paganism. The idols lay prostrate all over the country, and the only divinity that was universally worshipped was the Triune God, the great source of holiness and life.

CHAPTER III.

HOLINESS IN UPPER SYRIA AND NORTHERN MESOPOTAMIA—EDESSA THE CENTRE OF THE MOVEMENT.

1. *Christianity was Preached at Edessa in the Apostolic Age.*

THOUGH the number of Jews in the first century of our era was very considerable in Southern Mesopotamia, particularly at Babylon and its neighborhood, there is no positive proof that the same was true either of the northern part of this celebrated country or of the adjoining state of Edessa under the Abgar dynasty. The Syriac civilization and literature, moreover, which then began to throw an extraordinary splendor over the East, would seem to indicate that the elements of this high culture were native to the land, and did not receive any important increase from Hebrew proselytes. It does not appear, consequently, that there could be any intimate communication between the Jews of Palestine and the Christians of Edessa. It is, on the contrary, certain that neither Essenes nor Therapeutæ ever flourished on the banks of the Upper Euphrates; and there is not, in this case, the strong conjecture which has afforded a first test of the close connection between the primitive churches of Palestine and Egypt.

Still, the perfect sameness of the primitive Christian institutions in both countries, particularly the complete identity in both of the same kind of monasticism, naturally bring on the conviction that the Church began in Edessa as in Jerusalem by exhibiting to the world the spectacle described in the Acts of the Apostles. Details must be furnished more abundant still than have yet been brought forward; and they may produce a strong persuasion that the holiness of the primitive congregation at Edessa bore a great resemblance to that of Jerusalem and Alexandria. It was the same sanctity of the same universal church. In a first place, it has been proved in "The Church and the Gentile World" that Christianity was preached in Lesser Armenia almost as early as at Jerusalem;

and, we must add here, by some of the same apostles and disciples, who must have done their best to kindle in the hearts of those new neophytes the identical fire of faith and charity their preaching had produced in the city of David. According to a universal tradition, preserved all over the Orient, but particularly prevalent in Edessa itself, Thaddæus, one of the seventy-two disciples of Jesus, was sent, soon after Pentecost, by St. Thomas the apostle to King Abgar, who then ruled over this country. The process of conversion was already going on with the friendly help of Abgar, when Thomas himself arrived, and remained so long in the city and its neighborhood that many have thought he never went to India, but confined his mission to Western Armenia and the adjacent territories. This opinion is disproved; and it must be now admitted that after several years of labor on the Upper Euphrates, Thomas went East through the vast regions of Central Asia, which he was the first to evangelize. But according to the best-authenticated opinion, after his departure St. Jude, called also Thaddæus, coming himself to Edessa from Palestine, became the apostle of all Mesopotamia, north and south. Christianity was, therefore, preached on the Euphrates by two at least of the apostles who had established the Church at Jerusalem.

The city of Abgar was thus evangelized just at the time when Jerusalem was beginning to offer to the world the spectacle of holiness previously described, and several years at least before Mark had begun his ministry in Upper and Lower Egypt. All this is not only upheld by tradition, but Eusebius of Cæsarea thought he possessed proofs enough of it to consider it historical, and has given it a place in his "Ecclesiastical History."

Edessa soon became a thoroughly Christian city, and was most probably the first in the whole world which deserved the name. Hence, according to Assemani,* it was eminently called *the holy* and *the blessed*. As early as Trajan's reign, that part of Armenia being already annexed to the Roman Empire, numerous martyrs honored it by their constancy, and shed their blood for Christ. Barsimæus, its bishop, was one of them; and several of its citizens are known by name as having perished in the same persecution.

The strongest reason, however, that can be given of the very

---

* Bibl. Orient., i. 201, 278, 417.

early establishment of Christianity in Lesser Armenia is the fact mentioned in a previous work, that the total translation of the New Testament in Syriac, the language of Edessa, cannot be supposed to have been completed later than the middle of the second century; that is, about 150, fifty years only after the death of St. John. The Greek and Latin Scriptures, in Greece and Italy, cannot be traced to so high an epoch; and although it is absolutely certain that they were then known all over the western world, still there are not of their existence the same strong proofs which we now have of that of the *Peshito* or Syriac version. It required a great Christian vitality to possess so early as this the whole New Testament.

But what reasons have we to think that the heroic virtues practised by the Christians of Jerusalem and Alexandria flourished likewise at the same time on the Upper Euphrates? This is to be considered attentively.

2. *Monasticism and Theology, Two Sources of Holiness at Edessa.*

It must be held as certain that monasticism existed very early at Edessa and in its neighborhood, as well as at Nisibis, and in the whole of Northern Mesopotamia. We have not, it is true, any precise account of its origin there as there is for Egypt. But it appears in full vigor in the third and fourth centuries; and it seems that it began also by the hermit's cell, as it did along the Nile. Nearly all the great men who became celebrated in the Church by their labors for the faith, in that country, prepared themselves for their ministry by a longer or shorter period of total retirement from the world. They usually removed from the towns into some remote and desert places, and lived mostly in caves, spending their time in prayer, the study of Holy Scriptures, and the practice of austerities, preparatory to an apostolic life in the world. It was a repetition of what was taking place at the same time in Egypt. Often men who belonged to the noblest families adopted this severe kind of life as a preparation for preaching or teaching. St. James of Nisibis, whose mother became the wife of an Armenian king, spent several years in a desert before he began to preach the word of God. This peculiarity gave to Syrian asceticism an aspect somewhat different from that of Egypt, where the anchorites continued all their life in retirement. Still the austerities practised in both countries were nearly the same; and since Mr. Lecky calls the monks along the Nile maniacs, and almost brutes, on account of their mortified life, he might have applied the same epithets to those of Syria, if another Rosweide had published their *Vitæ Patrum*. We shall presently see what to think of it.

We do not possess, unfortunately, the same abundance of details for the beginnings of monasticism in and around Edessa that Rosweide's celebrated work gives us for the Egyptian monasteries. But the multitude of holy houses of that kind along the Upper Euphrates in the third and fourth centuries is an irrefragable proof that those institutions must have begun at the very origin of Christianity in that country.

Did they spring up from the native soil or were they imported from outside? No positive answer can be given to this question. Still, the remarkable differences which can be perceived between both kinds of establishments would justify the opinion that those of Edessa did not come from any other country, but must have originated there; and in this case it must have been the fruit of the first preaching of the apostles Thomas and Jude in that city. This point is of such an importance that it must be examined more closely.

Though essentially the same with that of Egypt, the monasticism flourishing on the Upper Euphrates in the third and fourth centuries presents such a peculiar aspect that it is difficult to believe it came either from Palestine or Egypt. There are chiefly two particulars which impress the mind as deciding the case without almost any fear of error. These are first the high intellectual range of the Syrian schools, and secondly their ardor for the propagation of the faith in foreign parts. This gave rise to two features which can be seen nowhere else to the same extent; namely, schools of the highest excellence inside of their monasteries, and missionary work of the most extensive character outside of them.

Neither of these two features appear in the least in the Egyptian convents, and very little in those of Palestine. In all of them, it is true, the monks read and studied; but the schools of Edessa and Nisibis present a totally different character from those of the two other countries. Study in these last was all directed to the individual and strictly ascetic improvement of the monks; in the first, on the contrary—namely, those of Syria—it soared directly up into the highest regions of poetry and theology, as a preparation for proselytism.

Nearly everything which has come down to us from the monasteries of Egypt in a literary form consists of what is called *Verba Patrum*—the Words of the Fathers. In these there are often profound views of human nature, and a high and accurate appreciation of this and the next world. The most attentive critic will not find in all the sayings of the seven wise men of Greece anything to compare with what often issued from the mouths of those austere monks who had the folly, according to Mr. Lecky, of making their habitual dwelling in the sepulchres of the dead. But as was said, everything was directed among them toward the spiritual improvement of the monks alone, and all their studies were confined within those limits. The same was also the case in Palestine. Nay, there was no great difference in this regard, later on, in the monasteries of western Europe, at the beginning at least, under the rule of Benedict, of Bernard, of Francis.

It was not so on the Upper Euphrates. Every monastery, so far as we can trace their history, contained a *school* of the highest order of intellect. It is true the various branches of learning which now engross the entire attention of modern Europeans were perfectly unknown in those holy establishments, although profane learning was not altogether excluded. But the Christian religion in its highest development offered an inexhaustible field of culture to those gifted Asiatic minds. The most sublime and at the same time exact theology transported them into a world very different from ours, but far more entrancing and profitable to the soul. Not of those men could Mr. Lecky say that they *had a grovelling mind*, though the phrase is certainly misapplied by him in the case of the Egyptian cenobites. The reader will soon have an occasion to listen to some strains of that divine harmony coming from Edessa, and our only regret will be that it could not be possible to make quotations as numerous as we would wish.

But theology, under the pen of those great writers, soared aloft on the wings of a truly inspired poetry; and the spectacle has, perhaps, never been seen anywhere else on earth, of truth, absolute truth, presented to the gaze of men under the brilliant garb of the most alluring fancy. These schools, being as numerous as the monasteries themselves, were found everywhere in the country, and many of them had been in the fifth century so long in existence that the epoch of their foundation was absolutely unknown. Edessa and Nisibis contained many; but no city of importance was altogether deprived of them.

The second feature which distinguished the Syrian monasteries from all others was the missionary work they undertook, sometimes to a great distance from their habitual place of dwelling. In the monastery of the Acœmetes, at Edessa, the monks were divided into squads of one hundred and fifty men, and each squad was composed of missionaries speaking one at least of four languages—namely, Latin, Greek, Syriac, and Persian—so that they might "evangelize the whole world." They went as far as Palmyra, Antioch, Jerusalem, and Constantinople. All these countries being civilized, they had prepared themselves for their gigantic intellectual work by long studies all derived from Holy Scripture and the tradition of the Fathers; and we may suppose that their way of propagating the Gospel was somewhat different from the one subsequently adopted by the Irish monks who in the eighth century left likewise their island to convert the barbarians of Gaul and Germany. The Syrian ascetics had to evangelize refined people.

These two most remarkable features of the old Syrian monasteries seem to furnish a sufficient proof that they were of native growth, and consequently can be traced back, at least in their incipient stage, to the very apostles who first evangelized the country; namely, Thomas and Jude. The schools, which were all pure monastic establishments, could certainly be traced to a high antiquity, since Bardesanes, who flourished about 150 of our era and must have been born a very few years after the death of St. John, had been educated in one of those schools of his native city, his parents being at the same time already Christian. Let the reader ponder on this and judge of the antiquity of monasticism at Edessa.

But what of holiness, which is all along the important consideration for us? It will be directly seen that the question is already decided, though it has not been treated in a direct manner. It naturally follows from all the circumstances which have been just narrated. If monastic life in Northern Mesopotamia differed considerably in two particular points from that of other countries, it remained essentially the same in every other respect. Consequently the supernatural virtues which made of the primitive church in Palestine and Egypt a paragon of holiness and a paradise of bliss were likewise practised on the Upper Euphrates, so as to be an exact reproduction of them. If we are altogether deprived of details in this last case, with regard to the incipient stage of this happy state, as soon as authentic documents are furnished in the third and fourth centuries the reader becomes convinced of a perfect identity in all those primeval shoots of the Christian tree. The eighteen opuscules of St. James, bishop of Nisibis, which have fortunately come down to us, would suffice to furnish a demonstration of it. The spirit of faith, charity, chastity, obedience, and true humility, which he describes as being the holy obligations imposed on the Christian ascetic, is precisely the same mainspring by which the neophytes of Jerusalem and Alexandria were moved. The whole of it was evidently derived from the doctrine of the Beatitudes, from the Sermon of Christ on the Mount.

And that this is the faithful picture representing the life followed at Edessa by the majority of its inhabitants, even out of the monasteries, is proved by the title of "the holy," "the blessed," which Assemani tells us the city itself had early acquired throughout the whole eastern world. But besides the general description left us by the learned Maronite, we happily possess a much better means of being convinced of it. This consists in the numerous songs of Ephrem, which in the best editions of his works bear the name of *necrosima*, or *cantus funebres*. It seems that this most learned and pious deacon was invariably chosen to speak at the grave of all those who died in his time within the precincts of Edessa. That he would have considered it a sacrilege to utter a lie on any of those solemn occasions must be admitted by all who are acquainted with his character and sanctity. That everything he said of the dead was true to the letter cannot be doubted by any one who has perused those funeral discourses even in the poorest translations. Go through the whole collection; it is long; it contains nearly a hundred of those compositions; but no one will ever find the task tedious. If the translation is accurate and sufficiently well done, it will be one of the most attractive books that can be found in the literature of any nation. Still, it is the simple description of what was then the ordinary life of this Christian people. Many of them were monks, and the reader will soon find it by some casual expressions of the speaker. But there were also common folks, following the various avocations of an ordinary life; there were children brought to the grave almost before they had tasted the sweetness of it. There are many mournful expressions addressed to the relations and friends of the dead, speaking of their loss, of their just grief; but always opening before their eyes the prospect of heaven as the just reward of the most eminent virtue.

It must be confessed that in our age the same praise is often addressed to the dead, whose rich coffins are brought to the foot of the altar profusely covered with flowers and handled with the deepest veneration and respect. Still, no one can conclude that our age is a reproduction of the first days of the Christian Church; and should society become still much worse than it is at present, the same fulsome panegyrics would probably be heard around the grave of our modern Christians. But the same cannot be supposed when the speaker was Ephrem, and those of whom he spoke were his dead countrymen, who had been known to all those present. People had not yet reached in the process of civilization the period of insincerity which distinguishes our own. They would not have tolerated it.

No! the deacon of Edessa could not utter untruths when he had before him the cold remains of a Christian who was at that time already judged by his Maker, and beginning the endless existence in which there could not be any more deceit and fraud. In these circumstances the *cantus funebres* of the Syrian monk afford the proof that the holiness of the Christian Church in Palestine and Egypt was also that of Edessa and the country around.

There was in it, however, a peculiar character derived from the two extraordinary features mentioned above. It was essentially the same as that of other countries, since it sprung from the spirit of self-sacrifice which undoubtedly characterized all of them. Still there appeared to be in Palestine and Egypt more simplicity; in Edessa more sublimity. Pure holiness embraces both expressions. There can be nothing more simple than virtue itself, which is always without guile; there can be also nothing more sublime, because it raises man to God. And what is most remarkable, true sublimity is always most simple. Pagans even knew it, as appears from Longinus.

The extraordinary elevation of thought so remarkable in the Christians of Edessa deserves to be closely studied, in order to rightly judge of their true holiness. For their subjects of meditation were all concerned about God and a higher life; and there was nothing earthly in their contemplation. This is always for man one of the greatest sources of sanctity. Consequently their literature sprung up entirely from Christianity, without any profane admixture; and it has just been said that it was confined to the deepest theology and the highest poetry; the first always exact, the second always brilliant. No offspring of a sensuous imagination could go hand in hand with these two virgin daughters of Heaven.

It has been remarked also that there was no Syriac literature before the Christian era. There was no fear of the previous mythology being mixed up with revealed truth, as in Rome and Greece. Thus it became at once the highest expression of the true holiness which Christianity alone can give; and all know that the literature of any people is invariably the exact expression of its character. Let us see this more in detail.

Depth and exactitude in theology have been supposed to be derived from the peculiar aptitudes of the Greek and the Latin minds, setting aside from view the action of the Holy Spirit on the Church, by which alone the purity of doctrine is secured. This conception of the development of theology is true in the main; and, undoubtedly, if God had not given us the Latin and Greek doctors, much of what we know of the supernatural world would not have yet come within the domain of our intellect. But in the benevolent designs of Providence, the whole Oriental world was not to depend entirely on the European (Greek or Latin) interpretation of Scripture and Tradition, which is, as everybody knows, the source of theology. The Orientals could also study Scripture, and they had their own traditions; and if the spirit of holiness animated them, they could also find out the meaning of Holy Writ, provided they remained humbly dependent on the last word of the true Interpreter—the Church.

It was evidently with this intention that God determined there should be a text for the eastern mind, as there were two for the western; and the *Peshito* of the New Testament appeared at least as early at Nisibis and Edessa as the Greek complete Testament at Alexandria and the *Vetus Itala* at Rome. Anteriorly to Christianity the Old Testament was known in Europe; but its Peshito or Syriac version was, according to the common opinion, only contemporaneous with that of the New. The Christians of Edessa, and with them the whole East, had, therefore, as early as the West the written word of God, old and new, in their possession; and doctors could speculate on those great subjects, on the banks of the Euphrates, at the very time that other doctors began to do it along the Nile and the Tiber. Let the reader keep in his mind this first fact: that nearly all the Latin and Greek Fathers of the Church published in the course of their life commentaries on all the books of the Old and the New Testament; and by the open discussion in councils of the opinions contained in those commentaries the science of theology began its course, which is not yet ended, but of which the Council of the Vatican is destined to give us the highest expression ever yet produced. Now let every one be persuaded that the same took place in northern Mesopotamia, taking the *Peshito* as a basis; and Ephrem, and James of Sarug, and many other Syrian doctors wrote commentaries, most of which have unfortunately perished or have never been translated into our modern languages. These are the precise theological speculations which are to be briefly studied in order that we should become somewhat acquainted with the science, and chiefly with the holiness that those men of the Orient derived from the Christian doctrine they had embraced. The object to be reached is now plain; the execution will leave many things in an unsatisfactory state, on account of the small number of quotations our space will permit. The reader, however, must start from the thought that if one of the greatest motives we have for thinking the Church holy is derived from the expression of that holiness contained in the writings of the Latin and Greek Fathers, he will have at least some slight idea that the same is true likewise of the Syrian doctors in theology.

But after this simple word on theology, and before coming to quotations, a word more must be added of Syriac poetry. It was said a moment ago that if the theology at Edessa was exact, the poetry was brilliant, and that nowhere else, perhaps, were the sublimest thoughts on God and the soul clothed with the most alluring garb of fancy. And even this last aspect of the case is not disconnected from the question of holiness, which must remain paramount in all these considerations. For the imaginative faculty in man has unfortunately been seldom devoted to the furtherance of virtue. In the fine arts, in poetry, in eloquence, it has often become a great source of corruption. But it was proper that when "the kingdom of God" would be established on earth this faculty should be purified of its dross, and altogether consecrated to the exaltation of true beauty. The Latin and Greek Doctors of the Church undoubtedly did it to a great extent in the West; and their pages are full of the most brilliant and alluring images that human fancy has ever conceived. This poetical gift, however, often reaches among the Orientals a far higher degree of excellence. They seem to be unable to express their thoughts unless under the veil of transcendent metaphors, which emit sparks of fire and rays of light, so as to dazzle the beholder and transport the listener with rapture. This can be called *the consecration of fancy to holiness.* After resurrection it will be one of the most delightful emotions of beatified man in heaven, and it is certainly one of the sweetest feelings of the purified heart of man on earth. It is in our eyes one of the *evidences* of Christianity; for the religion of Christ alone has restored to us this gift which must have been most prominent in our first parents in paradise, but which they nearly lost by their fall; a fall which turned, in fact, its beauty into lewdness and changed the heavenly aspirations of fancy into earthly and grovelling sensations.

It has been maintained by some German critic, whose name I forget, that the fancy of Ephrem and of James of Sarug soars often toward the highest regions of poetry, but occasionally falls flat into *diffusion* and *unmeaningness.* This is the thought: the expression need not be absolutely required. It is very likely that in case this German author had been born of native parents on the banks of the Upper Euphrates or of the Ganges, he would have been more able to appreciate the *meaning* of those great men, and he would not have called *diffusion* what was with them only a natural development of their deep thoughts. Any European endowed with some imagination cannot possibly find anything unmeaning or diffuse in whatever fell from the pen either of the deacon of Edessa or of the great bishop of Sarug.

3. *The Theology and Poetry at Edessa were eminently Conducive to Holiness.*

St. Ephrem often delivered discourses on Faith. Eighty-seven of them have come down to us; and they always are a mine of deep divinity. The chief dogmas of the Christian religion are passed in review, and often explained with the splendor of the most exalted fancy. Hear how he finds the image of the Trinity in the sun—(the translation of the Rev. J. B. Morris of Oxford is mainly used:)

"The sun is our luminary, and none is able to know it; how much less to know man, and still less God! The light of the sun is not subsequent to it; neither was he at any time without it. The sun itself being the first, the light is the second, and the warmth the third; these two last depart not from it, nor are they identical with it. Look at the sun in his altitude, which is thought to be one; descend, and look, and behold his light, a second; try and feel and search his heat, a third. They are like, and yet not like, one to another. The second is blended with him, though well distinguished from him; and the third is mingled with him, distinguished, blended, and mingled." It would be difficult to find a more forcible image of the divine Trinity, with the chief mysteries it contains. But let us go on:

"Light, and heat, and the sun are individual subsistences; there are in them three kinds mingled in a three-fold way: himself, and also the light, and the heat the third, dwelling one in the other, and agreeing without stint. Mingled, yet not confused; blended, yet not bounden; assembled, yet not compelled; free, yet not divergent. Let then the disputers ponder the things which are seen; for lo, one are these three, and the three are one; blended, yet not compounded; distinct, yet not several! There is a marvel in all these things which putteth us to silence."

All metaphors are of course defective; and a captious man could object that the personalities of the Son and of the Holy Spirit are not sufficiently brought forward by this splendid image of the sun. St. Ephrem knew it as well as any caviller; and in the next discourse—the forty-first—he comes back again to this figure of the Trinity. Fully aware that the heretics often support their erroneous opinions by material comparisons which can be distorted to any purpose, he exclaimed: "As to the Lord of natures, His Nature is hidden from all. Grant me, O Lord—and this would be preferable—to form no shape of Thy Nature by the creatures. But if any one shapes it out so, with the evident intention to lead the daring astray, the Gospel is the faultless mirror, and in it the Three-fold are seen without possible contradiction, since in them the apostles went forth and baptized (in the name of the Trinity) without wrangling." The meaning of the holy deacon is evidently here that if metaphors are used to express mysteries, their sense must be explained by the simple words of the Gospel, not that of the Gospel by the metaphors. Here we perceive the accuracy of the dialectician associated with the imagery of the poet.

Who will not recognize both of them in the following passages on the Incarnation, taken from the fifty-first discourse on Faith?

"Who is able to requite Thee for having humbled thy Majesty unto our own littleness, for having brought thy Highness down to the limits of the lowliest condition, and brought Thine own Life down to the rank of mortality? Thine inexhaustible Richness came down and dwelt in indigence; and Thou hast subjected Thy Lordship to the yoke of dependence. Praises be to Thy goodness! Who, Lord, can gaze upon and understand how Thy invisibleness came down to a visible state, Thy mysterious concealment came to the light and to an unclose manifestation, and Thy eternal seclusion came forth to boundless openness? These things happened to Thee, Lord, because Thou wert Son of Man. Praises to Him that sent Thee!

"Who would not be afraid at the sight of it? since though Thy rising and Thy Human Birth were so manifest, still so incomprehensible is Thy Generation that it hath baffled the proudest investigators. For there are that preacheth that it was a body only that Thou tookest; and there are that teacheth that it was a soul and a body; others have erred in thinking it was a heavenly frame. Praises to Thy Generation! Lord, seal our mouth: for, if Thy revealed estate has baffled the wise (since they have not been able to grasp Thy Birth of Mary), if also men comprehended not Thy Humanity, who ever shall be equal to Thy Divine Generation? Praises be to Him that begot Thee!

"Whatsoever may be allowed, let us sing, O Lord, upon our harp: let us utter nothing thereon which is not permitted, seeing it is the harp of frail creatures. Neither are our sounds of it equal to the probing of Thy Generation, nor even on the harps high and spiritual of the highest angels can It be comprehended. Praises to Thy mysterious secretness! Lord, let my tongue be a pen for Thy glory, and let the Finger of Thy grace mark out and write therewith words of edification. The pen, Lord, cannot, without one to hold it, write at its own will. Let not my tongue slide off into speaking, without Thee, aught which edifieth not. It would be audacity in us to call Thee by a name different from what Thy Father called Thee, who called Thee 'My Son' alone on the river Jordan. When Thou, even Thou, wert baptized, the mystery of the Trinity baptized Thy Humanity; the Father by His voice, and the Son by His power, and the Spirit by His overshadowing. . . . True is it that by the names wherewith Thy body was baptized our bodies also are baptized; and though there be very many Names of the Lord of all, He hath baptized us in the Father and the Son and the Spirit distinctly. Praises to Thy majesty!

"Who hath seen in the subtle air a way akin to the way which a fowl wendeth, or a man walking as upon the back of the wind? The breeze is spread out, and makes a path for that which walketh there, and admonisheth not to go outside of it at all, for outside of it is death. Praises be to Thy admonishing! Lord, make me also to be fully instructed by that danger, and to be afraid of going beyond the boundary of my faith. The Truth is easy and straight: to them that believe it is easy; and to them that are perverse it is difficult. The simple disentangle themselves, and escape; the learned err and fall into the pit of disputatiousness. Oh, that the Lord may lift them out! Praises to Him who findeth all!"

Beauties of this kind can be met with in almost every page written by the Fathers of the Syrian Church, or rather by the Syrian monks; since all those holy men were monks; and the reader may begin to perceive how the monasticism of Syria promoted also holiness, though in a different manner from that of Egypt. Unable to go on indefinitely in the same path, and unwillingly compelled to prescribe ourselves narrow limits in these translations, we will conclude by a last quotation on "the mystery of the Cross," in which Ephrem found with justice the essence of Christianity and the most attractive views of Christian theology. The whole is taken from the seventeenth and eighteenth discourses on Faith.

"God, seeing that He was never at any time sufficiently searched out by man, clothed Himself with a body which can easily be searched out. We might thus cease from searching into His Divine Nature, and rest ourselves in the Generation of His Human Nature. He thus gently induced us to ask how the divine nature came down, and in the womb was for nine months silent. Thirty years also He remained on earth, that by His long stay we might become used to Him. He left those above, and became a companion unto those below. He even on earth left those that were found, and sought for those that were lost. He left those that were wise; He chose those that were simple; and by them He spread His simple preaching unto every man. He left the chariot of the four living creatures in heaven (Ezechiel), and came down; and of the Cross He made Himself a chariot unto the four quarters of the world.

" Thou art the Son of the Living One, and Thou art the Son of a mortal. Thou art the Son of our Creator, O Lord, who in Thee established all things, and also the Son of Joseph,* that workman who learnt by Thee. By Thee it was that the Maker without teaching established all things! with Thy Finger the Creator fashioned all the creatures! by Thee it was that Joseph fashioned his carpenter's work, since he saw that Thou wert his Teacher! Hail! Son of the Creator. Hail to the Son of the carpenter! who, when creating, created everything in the mystery of the Cross. And haply even in the house of Joseph, that carpenter, with the Cross he was busied all day.

" The young of a bird, unless it be matured, is not able to break through its covering (the egg's shell), owing to its imperfect state, and faith which is under silence is also imperfect. Oh, perfect it, Thou that perfectest all things! The race of birds is brought up by a three-fold advance, from the belly to the egg; from hence to the nest, and when it is perfected it flieth in the air; it spreadeth its wings in the mystery of the Cross. And faith, too, is perfected by a three-fold advance. For since in the Father, and in the Son, and in the Holy Ghost the apostles believed, thus the faith flew unto the four quarters of the world in the mystery of the Cross. The three-fold names are sown in a three-fold way: in the spirit, and in the soul, and in the body, as in the mystery of the Cross. When our Trinity was perfected by the Three-fold One, it reigned unto the ends of the earth.

" If the little bird drew in its wings, and refused to receive the silly mystery of the Cross, the air would then refuse her, and not bear her up; but her wings praise the Rood. And if a ship spreadeth her sails on the sea, in the mystery of the Rood and from the yoke of the wood, she maketh a bosom for the wind; when she hath spread forth the Rood, then is the course spread clearly out for her voyage. If the ship was that of the Jew, the Cross rebuked him by his deed, since, though not intending it, in the ship himself with his own hands hath spread and displayed the mystery of the Rood. Thus the sea by the Rood was subjected to the unbelievers: for unless the crucifiers had made wood into the form of a cross, and upon it had hung the sail as a Body, the voyage would have halted.

---

* At the end of these quotations the meaning of this expression will be sufficiently explained. It is several times repeated in this paragraph; a single word at the end of this long passage will show in what sense Ephrem believed that Jesus was the son of Joseph.

"Neither again does the land yield itself to the crucifiers, without the fair mystery of the shining Rood. It is the sign of a Rood (the plough) which worketh it and softeneth it, and scattereth the seed therein. . . . If the crucifier buyeth a lamb and killeth it, upon wood he hangs it, Lord, that he may shadow forth the slaughter of Thee. And again when he hideth wheat in the earth, the living seed preacheth thy resurrection. . . . And in his vineyard is the cluster full of the type of Thy blood; and when upon his tree the fruit hangeth, it is the type of Thy Cross and of the Fruit of Thy Body.

"Lo! in the house of unbelievers the preacher of Thee crieth aloud : Ye that sleep, arise, be watchful ! since it is plain what he signifies by hanging and clapping his wings there (on the cross). Lo! he proclaimeth the resurrection of the dead to that buried living man (the Jew). And if in her nest, by mere touch, a bird conceiveth holily in her womb by the warmth of the cherishing wings, and hath her issue without other intercourse, then lo! in his own house *he hath a mirror of Mary.*"

St. Ephrem was mistaken in thinking that this could happen to any bird; but it was universally believed in his time of some kinds of fowls. At least this last phrase expresses the sense in which the holy deacon had called Jesus the Son of Joseph and the Son of the Carpenter. Pity that more of this cannot be transcribed. For nothing could be better calculated to give us a thorough knowledge of the Christians of Edessa than their theology and their poetry combined into one grand whole, and bearing the truthful expression of their minds and hearts. It was Christianity alone that had produced this magnificent efflorescence of beauty; and in this splendid literature there was absolutely nothing which was not thoroughly Christian and promotive of the highest morality.

The social and moral state of that noble country before the preaching of the Gospel is well known. After the brilliant period of the Assyrian Empire it had sunk down into the immoralities of pagan Semitism, and of its literature at that time nothing is known, because there was none. Suddenly one of the grandest outbursts of eloquence and poetry begins by Bardesanes in 150, to last several centuries, and end, unfortunately, by the bastard Christianity of Nestorius in the sixth age. During more than four hundred years, consequently, it produced a number of powerful writers fully equal to the greatest doctors of the Greek church at the same epoch. But it must be insisted upon here: In the Syrian church it was altogether the product of monasticism. And this monasticism was exactly alike to that of Egypt and Palestine in its interior spirit, though somewhat different as to its exterior manifestation. And the reason of the difference was that on the Upper Euphrates the monastic institutions embraced a course of higher studies in theology and oratory, of which those of Egypt and Palestine were almost wholly deprived. But read the private lives of James of Nisibis, of James of Sarug, of Ephrem, and many others—in fact, of all those Syrian Fathers whose biographies have come down to us—and their austere life is fully equal to that of Anthony, of Pachomius, of Paul the hermit, of Hilarion, and scarcely inferior to that of Simeon Stylites.

The Christian virtues of humility, of the love of lowliness, of abstemiousness and chastity, of disinterestedness and separation from the world, were as remarkable and heroic in Nisibis and Edessa as they were in the Thebais, in Tabennæ, in Nitria, and in the wilderness around the stern Mount Sinai. To the primitive Christianity of Jerusalem and Alexandria, which have already been recognized as identical, was to be added that of Northern Mesopotamia, as ancient as the others. It exhibited to the world the same spectacle of simplicity and greatness, of stern austerity and sweet charity; namely, the perfect realization of the doctrine of Christ in His Sermon on the Mount.

4. *Some Objections are Answered, and Conclusions Drawn.*

The *facts* which have been thus far enumerated are calculated to strike powerfully only when they are accompanied with sufficient details. This was scarcely possible within the limits naturally prescribed to this volume. A captious reader may complain that the subject was not fully elaborated; and he may say that history until the present age was written in this unsatisfactory manner; but more is now required by criticism. There is some truth in this remark. Still, it can be insisted on that the description of a peculiar sanctity so far given out with respect to the primitive ages of Christianity in Palestine, Egypt, and Syria is strictly sufficient for all purposes. And this is true for the following reasons:

In a first place the previous work, "The Church and the Gentile World," is intimately connected with this one, and forms the first link of a series which is not yet ended. As its object was to describe not only the early propagation of Christianity, but likewise the immediate moral change it effected in the world, many details strictly appertaining to the object of the present work were given which it is not necessary to repeat. With respect to Palestine and Egypt, particularly, the description of the purity of manners and of the sublimity of virtue, as contrasted with the previous corruption of paganism, cannot have been so soon forgotten by the reader. All this must be taken in connection with the facts and reflections to which we have so far confined ourselves here.

This has been even remarked in the short preface to the present work. But it is must be said, besides, that this apparent shortcoming owing to paucity of details is sufficiently redeemed by the general considerations contained in the First Book, which have naturally a bearing on the whole volume. When they are kept in mind the most unsatisfactory narration of facts acquires a great strength; and what would be in other cases a weak basis of certitude often turns out so strong as to raise the subject to the height of demonstration.

However few are the details brought forward to prove the sanctity of any community or nation, as soon as it is known that the sources of that sanctity were then of such a character as has been described in the First Book it is impossible to resist the conviction that it was of the highest order, and transcended at once the limits of natural ethics. The knowledge possessed by this community that their first ancestor had been a godlike being at his creation, and that even in his fallen state man is destined to be not only restored to his former privileges, but even raised higher so as to partake, as it were, of the divine nature, is sufficient to show at once the goal toward which he is constantly advancing. As soon as this is firmly believed by any people the motive of a powerful exertion becomes pre-eminent, and must act on the whole scheme of morals. Chiefly is it so when this belief is not unwarranted, but is contained in a primitive revelation fully known formerly to all mankind, and even later on kept still under the veil of myths in its traditions. Particularly when this truth is proclaimed after centuries of obscuration by the infallible voice of a God-man and His Church, this becomes a most powerful incentive to the practice of the highest virtue. The original dignity of man, and his restoration through redemption by Christ, was as strongly maintained by the early Fathers as it has been ever since, and this took place in the West as well as in the East. But the most numerous and splendid texts on the subject were penned by *Eastern* Doctors. Even among the few examples we could furnish they were far more numerous than the Latin Fathers.

But the peculiar sanctity of those primitive Christian nations was still much more powerfully affected by the other sources of a high virtue which have been sufficiently developed in our First Book. The Decalogue which Christ had reaffirmed and explained, becoming henceforth the heirloom of the whole human race, was to be forever a constant well-spring of the holiest morality. In its new state of development through Christ's teaching, it took, as was seen, deeper roots in the Hebrew mind and heart; and from them it was directly conveyed to the neigboring nations. Egypt and Syria must have been the first to receive it from the apostles; and it is easy to conceive how the conscience of these highly cultivated peoples must have been suddenly enlightened and strongly confirmed in virtue by its clear enunciation and strict precepts. The Decalogue, it has been proved, has been instrumental in giving to modern nations a high moral superiority over the ancients. But as we imbibe its precepts, as it were, with the milk of our mothers, it does not produce upon us the powerful effect which followed its first introduction among mankind. The reader must remember what has been said of the advantages possessed by a written and exterior code over the simple averment of our "inner consciousness." The clear knowledge of God's will and the resounding of His voice, as it were, became for the Egyptians and Syrians the most powerful incentive for practising virtue in the highest degree, chiefly as they were the first among pagan nations to enjoy that privilege. Thus it is seen at once that, however scanty are the materials used for a general description, the portraiture is all-sufficient to give a correct idea of the substantial holiness which is all along the subject of our theme.

This becomes more clear still when, in a third place, the life of those races of men is known to have been altogether influenced by the *example* and *grace* of the Redeemer. What is it that chiefly impressed on the character of those new-born nations a type of excellence such as had never been seen before? It was undoubtedly the divine pattern which their new religion had placed constantly under their eyes. None of the Egyptians and Syrians, it is true, had seen the Saviour during His mortal career; and they could not, like the Jews of Palestine, remember the acts of sublime virtue and of unbounded benevolence which attested His divinity, chiefly owing to His absolute power over nature. But they knew them from those who had been their happy witnesses; namely, the apostles who had accompanied Jesus during the last three years of His life. The apostles preached only Jesus and "Him crucified." There were no other means taken by them for propagating the new religion. During several years, no doubt, the gospels had not yet been written; but did not the preachers know the gospels—namely, the life of Christ—by heart, particularly since the Saviour had foretold that the Paraclete would come over them and "bring all things to their mind, whatsoever he should have said to them"? The Paraclete had come down on the day of Pentecost, to remain with them forever. Under His constant inspiration they could not preach a false Christ; the one they announced, of whom they constantly spoke, whose actions and discourses they were enabled to relate with the most minute circumstances, was the true "One which was from the beginning, which they had heard, which they had seen with their eyes, which they had looked upon, and their hands had handled (namely), the word of life." Thus St. John spoke at the beginning of his first Epistle; and all the apostles could and did repeat the same.

The Egyptians, instructed by St. Mark, and the Syrians, by St. Thomas and St. Jude, were therefore far more privileged with regard to the knowledge of Christ than we can be at this distance of time; since the gospels which we possess contain a very small part of the Redeemer's life, and the apostles knew it in its entirety. Still, we are aware that in our age the Christians find in the example of the Saviour, whom they are bound to imitate, one of the greatest incentives to virtue. What must it have been for those who received that knowledge from unimpeachable eyewitnesses, whose narratives were naturally impressed with the warmth of a true apostolic faith and the ardor of a true apostolic zeal?

But, as has been seen, it was not only Christ's example, as an exterior model for imitation, which became for those new nations a powerful source of sanctity. It was chiefly Christ's influence as head of a new human race, from whom holiness flowed in a copious stream through all the members of the mystic body—the Church. The process has been described from numerous passages of St. Paul's Epistles. It briefly explains the supernatural, nay, divine character of Christianity, and carries with it an essential holiness as a necessary consequence. It consists not only in the presence and influence of Christ, who, as He promised, "abides with us," but also in the "indwelling of the Holy Ghost" who resides in the Christian's heart as in a temple, according to St. Paul's expressions.*

If this sublime truth is destined to be, to the end of time, the firm ground on which our belief in the Church's sanctity rests, it must have appeared with a greater degree of excellence at the beginning of Christianity, when we know from the Acts of the Apostles and from the apostolic Epistles that there was then a superabundant effusion of the Holy Spirit's gifts, far superior to whatever we can witness in our day. Still, every Christian knows and firmly believes that if there is at this moment an ever-flowing source of sanctity in the Church, it is mainly owing to the divine influence of the Head over the members, and to the perpetual immanence of the Paraclete.

The few *facts*, therefore, to whose recital the writer was naturally confined, and to which many more might have been added if time and space had allowed, receive a powerfully-increased strength when those *a priori* considerations, as they have been called, are kept in the mind with respect to those eastern races which were the first conquests of Christianity after Palestine. It has been seen, moreover, that in Egypt at least all the features of the first Jerusalem congregation were reproduced, so as to make of both a single picture of the most entrancing moral beauty. All historians have admitted that the Church founded by the apostles in Palestine was a paragon of purity and holiness; and when remarks from our First Book, drawn from history and revelation, are attentively examined, the same must be said of the first Christian congregations on the banks of the Nile.

Finally, the considerations derived from the practice of the evangelical counsels, and the firm belief in a hereafter, complete the intended demonstration. It has been strictly proved that both in

---

* 1 Cor. iii. 16.

Egypt and in Syria "the way of perfection" was followed by a large number of the new disciples; and this from the very beginning of the Christian religion. The few facts which have been mentioned on this subject could have been indefinitely supplemented by the numerous details given out in the writings of St. Jerome and of Cassian. In the impossibility of doing it, recourse can again be had to our lengthened *a priori* reflections on this never-failing source of sanctity in the Catholic Church. By this simple process, warranted by all the rules of logic, the primitive churches of Egypt and Syria again become the exact reproduction of the sublime picture first drawn by Christ Himself in the simple sketch of the Beatitudes. The new moral sense imparted thereby by the Saviour to His disciples, so superior, as was seen, to the simple light of reason, and even to the precepts of the Decalogue, became a new guide leading the Christian neophytes to the practice of numerous virtues until that time perfectly unknown to mankind, and placing them at once on the high road toward moral *perfection*. The Beatitudes contain the essence of Christianity; and even those who are satisfied with the common way of "precepts" must do their best to submit to their holy influence, and to become animated with their sublime spirit. But those disciples who feel themselves impelled by a superior calling to a higher life, and propose themselves to follow the extraordinary way of the "evangelical counsels," find in the doctrine of the Beatitudes a clearer light to guide them, and a far more sublime scheme of virtue. They alone follow strictly the advice of St. Paul "to put off the old man whom the desires of error have corrupted . . . and put on the new man;" namely, Christ Jesus. For, as was seen, Christ in His human life has followed in perfection the road of the "evangelical counsels," and only those who endeavor to strictly walk in His footsteps can hope to reach the summit of sanctity.

This the first Christians of Egypt and Syria did with an ardent zeal, to the great scandal of modern rationalists, who openly express their antipathy, because they completely ignore, nay, they absolutely refuse to study, the true scheme of redemption. Having made up their minds to exclude the supernatural from whatever concerns our humanity, it is not surprising that the Christian scheme seems to them superstitious, even when it is evident that it is absolutely derived from the doctrine of Christ and His apostles.

The disciples of St. Mark in Egypt and of the saints Thomas and

Jude in Syria reasoned differently, and, seeing that the new revelation came evidently from heaven, they strove with a holy ardor to reach as far in virtue as the new doctrine impelled them and the example of Christ showed them the way. Thus, even should we have given a smaller amount of details than we did, the evident conclusion would still be that their virtue was most eminent, and that the preaching of Christianity among them produced a moral change altogether unexpected, and began among them an era of holiness such as the world had never yet witnessed.

It is sufficient, in conclusion, to add that the plain doctrine of a hereafter, henceforth introduced among them with all the strictness that the voice of God Himself could give it, gave to their new moral sense, as it has been called, a sanction as firm as the new edifice of holiness was extensive and magnificent.

Many consequences could be drawn from the narrative contained in these three initial chapters of our Second Book. The first would be the extraordinary character of the "new creation," so different from what had ever appeared before in the moral world among men. The precepts given, the virtues encouraged, the counsels insinuated, were all of a new pattern. An immense number of men threw themselves at once with the most extraordinary ardor in the path just open before them. This proved that Christianity was congenial to the highest human aspirations. Nothing appeared impossible to the neophytes, because they looked only to heaven above their head, and they despised a world which cannot satisfy the infinite ambition of the human soul.

Others shrank from such an arduous enterprise, and either were satisfied with a half effort toward moral goodness, remaining far behind the great Leader, Christ, and His most enthusiastic followers; or, worse still, some turned their back on a religion which proposed to man a goal elevated out of view in the clouds, and preferred to remain grovelling on this earth. These men remained pagans, and were the ancestors of our modern rationalists or positivists. Still, the new religion went on increasing in power until it covered the earth with sublime institutions of charity, intellectual progress, and, last not least, lowly and altogether hidden self-sacrifice. Thus began the modern epoch in history.

A second consequence worthy of being studied would be the

astonishing literature which walked in the footsteps of the new religion, and became so remarkable in Lower Egypt and Syria. Only a word of it could be said in these pages.

A third and last conclusion would result from the consideration of all the social, political, and individual ameliorations which the new virtues preached by Christianity brought on in their train. All this must be left to the reader's consideration, in order to see the change effected in the West after this inadequate description of it in the East.

CHAPTER IV.

CHRISTIAN HOLINESS IN THE WEST—MORAL CHANGE EFFECTED IN THE ROMAN EMPIRE AT THE FIRST PREACHING OF CHRISTIANITY.

1. *This Moral Change Began very Early.*

WE will not attempt to minutely describe the depth of corruption into which Rome had sunk when the first apostles, Peter and Paul, came to regenerate it. The modern researches, which have completely unveiled the moral degradation of the Romans, would make it easy to go through the chief details of the shocking picture. But besides the painful character of the task both for the writer and the reader, it is doubtful if the most accurate pencil could adequately represent the monstrous figure in all its deformity, and give a sufficient idea of it. Mr. Lecky in his "History of European Morals"* has justly said: "The mass of the Roman people were plunged in a condition of depravity which no mere ethical teaching could adequately correct. The moral condition of the empire is indeed in some respects one of the most appalling pictures on record, and writers have much more frequently undertaken to paint or even to exaggerate its enormity than to investigate the circumstances by which it may be explained."

These "circumstances" he details in the next pages of his book, and he thinks they were "the imperial system, the institution of slavery, and the gladiatorial shows; each of these," he says, "exercised an influence of the widest and most pernicious character on the morals of the people." These three sources of corruption Mr. Lecky examines at length, and he chiefly develops, with great justice, the deleterious effects of the gladiatorial shows. But though the celebrated writer attaches a great importance to this investigation of *causes*, because he always tries to explain

---

* Vol. i. p. 255.

every fact naturally, we may be allowed the liberty of thinking that there were other "circumstances" as powerful as these to produce the excessively low moral state of Rome. One of these was undoubtedly the enormous wealth unjustly acquired by the patricians during the two previous centuries, when the riches of the whole world were concentrated in the capital and made of it, according to the expression of Sallust, "the sink of the universe." A Christian might find another cause, more powerful still, but the expression of which might bring a smile on many lips in this age. This was nothing else than the one expressed by all the Fathers, and based on the Apocalypse of St. John; namely, that "pagan Rome was the seat of Satan's empire." We entirely share in that conviction, whatever others may think; and in the midst of the broad denial so emphatic in our day with regard to the devil's existence, we persist in maintaining that this "existence" gives the best explanation of the dark side of history.

Be this as it may, the sources of Roman corruption may be discussed; but people will continue to disagree about them. The only important point is that it was a dreadful fact and remains, as Mr. Lecky said, "one of the most appalling pictures on record;" and, moreover, it was such, according to the same writer, that "no mere ethical teaching could adequately correct it;" which means, we suppose, that even the Stoic's doctrine, so much admired by Mr. Lecky, was incompetent in the matter. This agrees perfectly with our own opinion, and it will be abundantly proved in the following discussions.

The present view of the subject must be confined to describing, as accurately as possible, the change effected in Rome among the patricians as well as among the plebs in a remarkably short space of time; and this is also fully admitted by the author of "European Morals" when he says: * " There can be little doubt that, for nearly two hundred years after its establishment in Europe, the Christian community exhibited a moral purity which, if it has been equalled, has never for a long period been surpassed." We may rest satisfied with this admission, though the facts which will be passed in review must carry the reader much farther, and convince him that the "moral purity" of the Roman Christians "sur-

---

* Vol. ii. p. 11.

passed" indeed everything that the world has seen before or since, except from Christians elsewhere.

First, there is the remarkable fact of the "great multitude" of those who, according to Tacitus, suffered martyrdom under Nero St. Peter had been in the city about twenty-five years, and St. Paul a little more than two, when this astonishing proof of a mighty change in Rome was afforded. To judge of it the chief circumstances of the fact, well known from Tacitus, will amply suffice. A short discussion is required here.

Nero had set on fire a great part of Rome, and was soon frightened by the feeling of horror it excited against him among the citizens. Out of fourteen "regions" into which the city was divided, four only remained entire; three had been totally destroyed; in the seven others a few houses were left standing, most of them tottering and half-burnt. Thousands of people had perished, objects of art without number had disappeared, and the private wealth of many had been devoured by the flames. All accused Nero of the crime; "therefore," says Tacitus, "Nero threw the blame on those whom the vulgar called Christians, and who were the object of public hatred, being accused of enormities."

The great Roman historian did not trouble himself much as to the truth of these "enormities"—*flagitia*. He thought, however, that the Christians were less truly convicted of incendiarism than of the "hatred of the human race"—*odium generis humani*. This is rather an ambiguous phrase, as is often the case in Latin. It may mean that they "hated the human race," or that "the human race hated them." Both meanings will be presently examined; but a preliminary remark must be first made, of some importance in the present case. There is no ambiguity in Tacitus with regard to the name of the new "superstition." Those who are *infected* with it are called *Christians* even by the vulgar. They are no more confounded with the Jews. This alone would go a great way to prove that a large majority of them were Romans, not Israelites, and that there were already a very great number of Christians in Rome.

But what were those "enormities" charged to them? They could not be the calumnies spread later on against them, which became universally believed by the pagans only under the Antonines. People had scarcely heard yet of these pretended orgies. Dom

Guéranger thinks it was simply a fulfilment of Christ's prophecy: "You will be an object of hatred to all, *on account of my name.*"* But something special must have been brought forward against the Christians, in order to explain that hatred naturally. It may have been only the secrecy of their meetings which induced the vulgar to attribute to them what was known to be the fact for many impure oriental sects then prevailing in Rome. Tacitus not having given any details, we are reduced to conjectures. But as it is sure that many pretended crimes were objected to them, the mere name of Christians, derived from that of the Saviour, became odious to the rabble.

This is probably what Tacitus meant when he wrote that they were "convicted of mankind's hatred." This may signify, as was said, either that the Christians hated mankind or that mankind hated the Christians. Many modern non-Catholic writers adopt the first meaning, although if we look at the whole passage it is not the most natural. The best commentators on this phrase of Tacitus admit the other. If the first interpretation is preferred, it was of course a calumny, since every one must recognize that Christianity has always preached the brotherhood of mankind and the precept of charity towards all men, and has particularly done so at its first establishment. The second meaning of that phrase is, on that account, much to be preferred to the first. Yes! mankind, chiefly at that time, hated the Christians, and consequently the name of Christ.

Was there a motive for it? One might be found in the fierce opposition which the moral principles of this "superstition," as it was called, must have raised among the Romans of that period. For was it not shocking, in the pagan's ideas, that a set of men should place another world above this, above the glorious Roman Empire particularly; should renounce every pleasure that this brilliant society afforded; should distribute their property to the poor, and proclaim that voluntary poverty was a holy object of ambition? Did not also the Roman vulgar already know that the Christians openly denounced *sin* in any shape, and avowed on their part the purpose of radically changing, in this respect, the notions of mankind, and establishing the reign of conscience over that of a polished depravity? This was sufficient motive for war. Tacitus himself, who like other Stoics, pretended to uphold the most strict principles of virtue, must have

---

* Matt. x. 22.

imagined that the virtue of the Christians was degrading, slavish, worthy of detestation or at least contempt. This superstition, consequently, was to be crushed.

But there was still a stronger motive at the bottom of that deep hatred. The proselytism of the new "sect" was so active that no class of Roman society could escape its approaches. It had already penetrated into the "household of Cæsar;" outside of it, patricians had before this entered its ranks; and a much greater number of the poor and the slaves had become the open disciples of Peter and Paul. Each new member, filled with a holy ardor for the *salvation* of others, did their best to communicate what they called their happiness to their former friends and acquaintances. So far there had not been any open persecution against them; and they already "persecuted mankind" by their entreaties and perhaps threats; yes, threats of the wrath of God, of the coming days of dishonor for the state and their own individual ruin. Was not this intolerable? The Jews were likewise proselytizing in Rome, though Mr. Lecky unaccountably thinks they were not. The proofs of it are too well known for denial, and the discoveries of M. De Rossi in Jewish cemeteries have placed it beyond contradiction. But the Jews did not speak so much of *sin* as the Christians did; and the glory of their Messias' kingdom was to burst forth on earth and not in heaven. Thus the Jews might have been despised by many; they were deeply hated by very few. They were allowed to proselytize quietly, as it was easy for those whom they approached on the subject to laugh at them and have done with them simply by a witty word or two. The Christian proselytism was very different, and if anybody laughed at it, it was a laughter of the kind called sardonic, which is not precisely promotive of kind feelings.

These short preliminary remarks were necessary to properly understand what took place when Nero took advantage of the popular hatred against the Christians, in order to turn away from himself the public suspicion of incendiarism. All the circumstances described by Tacitus will tend to prove what kind of men were those whom Peter and Paul had converted in Rome, and it will be easy to judge what immense moral change the apostles had already effected among a great number of Romans. The glowing words of St. Peter in his first Epistle will finally render the text of the great Roman historian luminous in its atrocity;

for St. Peter in his first Epistle most probably spoke of that persecution, as well and better than Tacitus.

In a first place, though Nero accuse the Christians of having set Rome on fire, few, if any, according to the Roman historian, believed it; but the great crime of which they were *convicted* was only their name. "The author of that name"—*auctor nominis*—says the historian, "was Christ, who, during Tiberius' reign, had been condemned to death by the procurator Pontius Pilate. The execrable superstition repressed at first by this public execution was again spreading, not only throughout Judea, but in the city itself—Rome—whither all possible evils come to converge."

The first who were arrested by the Roman police or by the pretorians—Tigellinus, their infamous prefect seems to have been very active during this persecution—confessed, it seems, their guilt of incendiarism, and denounced a "great multitude," "who were less guilty," says Tacitus, "of arson than of mankind's hatred." This very guarded narrative evidently implies that the first who were arrested, and who denounced a "large multitude" of others, were simply Tigellinus' tools. That nefarious man's plot succeeded but too well; but it evidently supposed that there was no other accusation brought against the "great multitude" of others than their name of Christians; and the Epistle of St. Peter will soon give us the positive proof of it. At that moment, to be a Christian was the same as having been guilty of burning Rome. If those who were "first arrested" confessed that they had individually participated in a plot of incendiarism, in "denouncing," as they did, a great multitude of others they could not bring individual proofs against so many; and there cannot be any reasonable doubt in the mind of an impartial reader that the only thing that was done consisted in "denouncing" them as Christians; and this was sufficient for their "conviction."

It is not read anywhere that what invariably was the case in all subsequent persecutions, happened likewise in this one; namely, that the denial of being a Christian was a sufficient justification, or, what is better still, that the act of professing repentance and renouncing his religion made a man directly free from all pursuits. This would not have suited Nero, who wanted victims. Neither Tacitus nor any other Roman historian tells us that the Christians protested in any way against these atrocious proceedings; and what is worse for the writer of the *Annales*, he himself never protests in his narrative against such a flagrant injustice. On the contrary, he describes with the greatest coolness, in all its horrible details, that immolation of several thousand persons in the gardens of Nero, without saying a word to excite compassion for their fate. He states, it is true, that the spectators at last began to feel pity at the fearful sight—*miseratio oriebatur*—but it cannot be known from his story what he himself felt. He was too great a Stoic to let it appear.

No attempt can be made here at any description of these horrors. But it is very important to briefly examine the astonishing heroism of these Roman Christians. They seem to have submitted uncomplainingly to tortures which the human imagination can scarcely conceive. Dom Guéranger, in his *Sainte Cécile*, thinks that the words of Seneca to his friend Lucilius, in his 78th letter, refer to them. Seneca must certainly have been a personal witness of that awful drama; and the details he gives in that letter can scarcely have reference to any other scene enacted at that epoch, except to the execution of these Christian martyrs. "No human suffering can be compared," he says, "to the action of fire on living limbs, to the rack, to burning blades, to instruments of steel opening again half-closed wounds and penetrating deeper into the flesh. Still, men have suffered all this without uttering a groan! Nay, more: they have not asked any respite! What do I say? The judge could not extort from them a word of answer. They have been seen smiling in the midst of these tortures; and the smile came from the heart." Tacitus' narrative in its coolness and dryness does not contain a word which would in the least weaken this passage of Seneca.

What could have been the source of the strength which supported these heroes of religion? They all were converts; they had been pagans a great part of their lives; and many of them may have led a life of sin before their conversion. On the other side they were not mere Stoics. Pride did not enable them to make a show of courage and heroism. They were the humble followers of an humble Saviour. If we wish to explain their wonderful behavior we have only to open the First Epistle of St. Peter. It was not written for them, it is true; but the Galilean Fisherman could not speak to the Jews of Pontus and Galatia to whom that letter was sent in one way, and in another to his Roman disciples. He must have often repeated, during his long apostolate in Rome, the very words he had penned carefully in that epistle; words which he knew would be treasured up by the whole Church in all ages. This text of the prince of the apostles will have besides this advantage, that it will throw a flood of light on this sublime tragedy enacted in the valley of the Vatican, where Nero had his pleasure-gardens. The doctrine Peter had preached to the Romans was the ground of their strength, and had already raised them to the highest pitch of holiness.

The wonderful state of sanctity to which *all* Christians are called, and of which the Romans were to give very early many examples, is particularly described in the second chapter of this Epistle—the first one having chiefly reference to converted *Jews*. "Laying aside," says St. Peter, "all malice, and all guile, and dissimulations, and envies, and all detractions; as new-born babes, desire ye to be fed with the rational milk of guilelessness, that thereby you may grow into salvation: if so, you have tasted that the Lord is sweet." It is impossible to describe with more simplicity and accuracy, at the same time, a new society totally unknown in Rome a few years previous, and which can now be appreciated in many of its details, from the acts of martyrs, the inscriptions in the catacombs, and the lives of many of its young saints, as Agnes, Petronilla, Emerentiana, Cœcilia, etc. All these, with many others, must have often read this short passage written by St. Peter in their city, since they have expressed it so well in their lives: "Laying aside all malice, and all guile; . . . as new-born babes, desire ye to be fed with the milk of guilelessness: . . . if so, you have tasted that the Lord is sweet."

A few lines farther on the apostle himself declares that this holy society was the result of a mighty change which all could witness. "You are a chosen generation, a kingly priesthood, a holy nation, a purchased people, that you may declare by your conduct the virtues of Him—Christ—who hath called you out of darkness into His marvellous light. You who in time past were not a people, but are now the people of God; who had not obtained mercy, but now have obtained mercy." A short sentence of the Second Epistle of the same apostle comes here so appropriately and naturally that it may as well be added to what precedes:*
"Through Christ God hath given you most great and precious

---

* Chap. i. v. 4.

promises; that by these you may be made partakers of the *Divine Nature;* flying the corruption of that concupiscence which is in the world."

Could the prince of the apostles have written such a description of the Judeo-Christian church in Pontus (which was reproduced in perfection and on a far larger scale in Rome) without having at the same time under his eyes the blessed reality of it? Are not passages of this kind—and there are many in the canonical Epistles—a sure voucher of the Church's holiness at her birth? But what must chiefly attract the attention of the reader is the reference made in it to the Neronian persecution as described by Tacitus. It is only a conjecture, but a strong one. These are the main grounds of it:

Peter in his first chapter (v. xi.) lays down the true foundation of the Christian's hope that "by suffering he will acquire eternal glory;" namely, the words of the ancient prophets, "who had foretold those sufferings that are in Christ, and the glories that should follow." Christ is the great pattern; and after His example martyrdom is to be expected by His disciples as a stepping stone to beatitude. This thought comes up everywhere in this Epistle.

On the model of Christ, therefore, he insinuates in the second chapter (v. 12): "Let your conversation be good among the gentiles; in order that, whereas they speak against you as evil doers, they may in future time, by the good works which they shall behold in you, glorify God in spite of themselves, on the day of His visitation."

A new step in advance is made from verse 19 to the end of the chapter: "This deserves a reward, if for conscience's sake toward God a man endure sorrow, suffering wrongfully. For what glory is it to commit sin and be buffeted for it? But if doing well you suffer patiently, this is worthy of reward before God. Indeed, unto this you are called; because Christ also suffered for us, leaving you an example that you should follow His steps; who did no sin, neither was guile found in His mouth; who when He was reviled did not revile, when He suffered He threatened not; but delivered Himself to him that judged Him unjustly."

Did not this doctrine of Peter—for it was, and has ever since been, a Christian doctrine—thoroughly explain the fortitude of the Roman Christians under Nero? And in the fourth chapter a positive allusion is made to the title of Christian mentioned by Tacitus: "Let none of you suffer as a murderer, or a thief, or a railer, or a coveter of other men's goods. But if *as a Christian*, let him not be ashamed, but let him glorify God in this name. For the time has come that judgment should begin at the house of God. And if first at us, what shall be the end of them that believe not the gospel of God? And if the just man shall scarcely be saved, where shall the ungodly and the sinner appear? Wherefore, let them that suffer according to the will of God, commend their souls in good deeds to the faithful Creator." *

This may be called a splendid commentary on the passage of the Roman annalist. Tacitus was the first profane writer who called the new believers by their true name, *Christians*. Until his day they had been confounded with the Jews; from that time forth they began to form a body apart. Peter was the first inspired writer who used the same expression on the eve of a great persecution in the Roman world. It is true that, according to the Acts of the Apostles, it was at Antioch the followers of Jesus received that title; but this book does not mention who gave it to them. It may have been still unauthorized, and may have become frequent only from the time Peter let it escape from his pen. It is difficult not to see here a connection of some kind between both the profane and the ecclesiastical writers. Peter must have often used that expression when addressing his flock in the senator Pudens' house; and as we know from Tacitus that this name became the innocent cause of the death of a great number of people under Nero, the apostle, enlightened from above, must have referred to this in addressing his people on the eve of their own martyrdom. Thus the name given to the followers of Christ by both Peter and Tacitus; the mention suggested by both of them that the Christians died for that name and not for any crime punishable by human laws; the heroism displayed by the victims, which Peter fully explains by the example of Christ, whilst Tacitus cannot; all the chief circumstances of that fearful tragedy allow us to conclude that Peter truly spoke of it in this Epistle; and the holiness of the sufferers is the strict conclusion of the whole story. For can there be a higher holiness than that

---

* Chap. iv. v. 15, *seq.*

of Christ, which Peter proposed to his Roman flock as their pattern, and which they copied so faithfully chiefly in their death? This is a first indication of a great moral change in Rome.

2. *Can this Moral Change be Explained by Natural Causes?*

Nothing was so much opposed to the humility and *guilelessness* of the Saviour as the stern pride of the Roman people, chiefly of the patricians. It is, however, customary to many writers in our day to represent them as having been prepared, even by their universal dominion, for the feeling of meekness which the Christian religion was destined to spread everywhere. M. Mommsen has pretended that "the polity of the Cæsarian state was really nothing but a citizenship of the world, and its nationality nothing but humanity" (quoted by Fisher, " Beginnings of Christianity," p. 69). This has been equivalently repeated by many modern authors whose chief object is to prove that Christianity was only the explosion of the philosophical and humanitarian doctrines which Stoicism and the liberal views of the period had originated among pagans. But in spite of so many assertions apparently supported by texts and facts, it remains certain that if it had not been for the mission of Christ and His apostles, the whole world probably would have fallen under the crushing weight of despotism which the "Cæsarian state" had undoubtedly brought into existence. What would, in this case, have become of the "citizenship of the world" brought on, according to M. Mommsen, by "the Cæsarian state"? It could not have been anything else than "the citizenship" of slavery. That is, the very fact of being a Roman citizen would have imposed on the wearer of that title the heavy burden of submission to the most despotic laws. To understand it it is sufficient to look at the reigns of Tiberius, Caligula, Nero, and Domitian. Can any one believe that it would have been a pleasant yoke to carry, and that the happy citizens of this universal empire would have enjoyed all the sweetness of social intercourse which the Christian religion afterwards knew how to impart?

The Antonine dynasty in Rome has brought into this discussion a confusion of ideas which it is proper briefly to clear up. Because the imperial despotism has been administered during about seventy years by a few princes of a mild disposition; and because under their sway the laws did not bear too heavily on the citizens, people conclude directly that the comparative mildness of their administration was due to the Cæsarian state; and M. Mommsen was emboldened to maintain that this most despotic form of administration was nothing but "a citizenship of the world," and that it became the real source of the mild social maxims which have been since attributed to Christianity.

But was it possible that the Roman Empire should continue forever to be ruled by princes of the type of Nerva, Antoninus, Alexander Severus, etc.? Think of Commodus, of Elagabalus, of Caracalla, and others, and inquire if the Cæsarian state under their sway was nothing but the citizenship of the world, and if the Roman nationality was then equivalent to humanity. There is an evident sophism in that brilliant sentence of the great German writer.

Mr. Lecky likewise in his "History of European Morals" props up the same ideas by a number of facts and texts, of which it is proper to discuss a few of the most important. He does not, however, attribute the citizenship of the world to the Cæsarian state; and the short answer just given to Mommsen cannot be addressed to him. He ascribes it first to the process of amalgamation in the Roman world which had begun from the very days of the republic, and gave to many Roman writers new and large views on "the duty of charity to the human race." He takes this last phrase from Cicero,* and gives many other texts of the same author.† He thinks that "the same principles were reiterated with increasing emphasis by the later Stoics," and speaks on the subject as strongly as any other modern writer. The intention is evidently to make it appear that the ideas of "the human brotherhood," of "charity for all," etc., did not originate from Christianity, but from Greek and Latin philosophy; and on that subject he *proves* that the Greek social disposition was far more tender than the Roman spirit, which was always remarkable for its sternness and austerity. Plutarch is the author whom he chiefly admires for that gentleness of soul, and of him he makes almost a Christian.

The Stoics, who, he believes, contributed powerfully to spread the ideas of universal brotherhood, were not, in his opinion, ani-

---

* De finibus.   † De off., De Legibus, etc.

mated with the same moderation and sweetness of temper as Plutarch was; and he confesses that their doctrine had nothing to do with the gentle virtues of humility, charity, and tenderness for the poor which has constantly distinguished the religion of Christ. In this he is perfectly right, and the little he says on the subject affords already a proof that Zeno's tenets could not have brought about the conversion of Rome. This conversion, however, he thinks to have been perfectly natural; and being ourself fully convinced that he is in error, we must discuss the question at some length.

As a preliminary remark it is not to be denied that the writings of Cicero, Seneca, Plutarch, Pliny, and the Neoplatonists contain many things which can be called, to a certain extent, a preparation for Christianity; there is something looking like Gospel precepts here and there inculcated in those philosophical treatises. Many texts and facts quoted by Mr. Lecky cannot be set aside and scornfully rejected. But the question remains, Could all this have brought on among mankind the practice of the "milder virtues" as they are enforced in the Sermon on the Mount, of which the Roman Church in the first three centuries has left such heroic and delightful examples? If the modern theories on the conversion of Rome must be admitted as naturally explaining the wonderful change which then took place, there must have been a real and easily perceived coincidence between the social and moral ideas current among the pagans of that epoch and the state of things which struck the eyes of all, for instance, when the catacombs were freely opened under Constantine. This view indeed revealed to the world the lowly but priceless virtues which had been practised there by millions of human beings during two hundred and fifty years. Was there anything like it in the previous Greek and Roman philosophy?

This is to be examined and discussed briefly, but as exactly as the importance of the subject requires.

Mr. Lecky himself tells us equivalently that this was not to be expected from Stoicism itself, which " was quite capable of representing the widening movement, but not equally capable of representing the softening movement, of civilization." * That is to say, in his opinion Stoicism prepared mankind for Christianity, through

---

* Page 247.

the progress of civilization, by its doctrine of universal brotherhood; but "its condemnation of the affections, and its stern, tense ideal . . . were unsuited for the mild manners. . . . of the age of the Antonines. . . . . A class of writers began to arise who, like the Stoics, believed virtue rather than enjoyment to be the supreme good, . . . but who at the same time (unlike the Stoics) gave free scope to the benevolent affections, and a more religious and mystical tone to the whole scheme of morals." These writers were, according to him, the eclectics, peripatetics, and Platonists, among whom he mentions particularly Pliny the younger and Plutarch, chiefly the last.

This seems, therefore, to be the theory of Mr. Lecky on the conversion of Rome: Christianity, as the explosion of civilization, was not the result of the Stoics' doctrines alone; but many other writers flourishing at the same time or shortly after actually introduced the spirit of the "mild virtues" which the Christians were to practise in perfection during two centuries, and *no longer*. In all sincerity I believe this to be the candid opinion of the author of "European Morals," and the essence of his most interesting book. And as he has persuaded of it a great number of people in our day, and to my personal knowledge some educated Catholics are inclined to adopt his conclusions, it is important to prove that this cannot explain the conversion of Rome. We have, fortunately for this demonstration, most clear historical data on the holiness of the Roman Christians of that primitive epoch; and it will be neither difficult nor long and tedious to prove that the whole mass of eclectic and peripatetic and Platonist philosophers had absolutely nothing to do with that wonderful result which we call: *the establishment of the religion of Christ in the capital of the world*. The great and unique causes of this astonishing fact were the grace of God, the preaching of the apostles, and the practical acceptance by an immense number of Romans of the doctrine of the "Beatitudes." Plutarch, no more than Epictetus, could not predispose the Romans for it. The only thing that might be said is that it was not perhaps so difficult, or rather impossible, for a Roman to feel a kind of attraction towards the Gospel morality as it had been when Stoicism ruled alone. Had Mr. Lecky confined himself to this, there would have been no need of entering into any discussion on the subject.

In the first place, the doctrine of Plutarch, on which Mr. Lecky relies a great deal to prove his thesis, has been discussed at some length in our book on "The Church and the Gentile World;" and it is difficult to see how it could have any influence in bringing the Greek and Roman worlds to a due appreciation of the Christian virtues. The author of "European Morals" scarcely brings forth any fact which could invalidate the opinion advocated in that volume; namely, that the writer of the "Parallel Lives" had no perceptible influence in preparing mankind for higher aspirations than those of his dear polytheism. The strongest remark of Mr. Lecky* is simply this: "Plutarch, in a beautiful treatise on 'The Signs of Moral Progress,' treated the culture of the feelings with delicate skill. The duty of serving the Divinity with a pure mind rather than by formal rites became a commonplace of literature, and self-examination one of the most recognized of duties." This is something, but it is far from being adequate to the introduction of the Christian "Beatitudes." Christianity, besides, had formal rites, and its self-examination was far different from that of the Stoics.

From Plutarch Mr. Lecky passes on to Marcus Aurelius, in whose life he finds almost all the Christian virtues practised in perfection. But as all he could say of him as a philosopher is derived from his "Meditations," which he himself acknowledges "consist of rude fragmentary notes ... written for the most part in hasty, broken, and sometimes almost unintelligible sentences amid the turmoil of a camp," † Mr. Lecky cannot give him a prominent place among those who prepared the coming of Christianity. The more so that the same Marcus Aurelius became a fierce persecutor of the Christians, and the God he adores in his "Meditations" is either a harsh *Fatum* or a Universal Soul, to whom no man will ever have to give an account, even after having examined daily his conscience during life. Mr. Lecky does not say a word of this. Still, it is generally admitted at this time by all sincere critics and Greek scholars; and he himself confesses that "on the subject of a future world his—Marcus Aurelius'—mind floated in a desponding doubt."‡

In a second place, after this hasty sketch of "Stoic, eclectic and Platonic" philosophers who are supposed to have predisposed the Romans to the sublime moral ideal of Christianity, it is necessary to

---

* Vol. i. p. 249.   † Page 250.   ‡ Page 253.

look at this ideal, to understand its true purport, to know by whom it was preached, and how it was accepted by an immense number of the inhabitants of Rome. This must come entirely from ourselves, because the historian of "European Morals" never says a word of it, and seems to be satisfied that everybody knows perfectly well what Christianity is, and was at its first establishment. Unfortunately, however, Mr. Lecky poorly understands it; at least had he given us his ideas on the subject, they would most probably have widely differed from the truth, since he scarcely admits the supernatural in any shape. In his opinion the religion of Christ is a religion like any other, which he thinks resulted from *civilization*, and must have, consequently, been naturally evolved by an indefinite rising of the human scale in point of morality, owing to what is called *progress*. This may be said to constitute the essence of his book, and to this we must demur.

The moral purport of Christianity was to establish holiness on earth. Christ came to preach the kingdom of God; that is, virtue; and He announced that He was the only pastor of souls, all others being hirelings. The character of that holiness is described particularly in the Sermon on the Mount, and it is summed up in the eight Beatitudes. This is well known, and scarcely deserved to be repeated. But it is proper to insist here that this could not have been the result of a natural development of morality, such as Mr. Lecky and the men of his school understand it. That Christ was a heavenly teacher and brought us a heavenly doctrine must be admitted by all those who believe in the supernatural characters of His religion; and none of these will be inclined to admit that it was simply a natural development of human progress. But here we do not write for the true Christian; we must for a moment address ourselves to those who have not yet discarded that title and nevertheless give it a completely different meaning. The question which is to be briefly discussed is simply this: Can the Evangelical Beatitudes be the result of human thought and direct men to a purely human destiny? If Christianity is only a form of human civilization, it must be altogether included within the limits of this world, and it can neither have a *divine* origin nor lead to a *divine* hereafter. The philosophers of the intuitive school refuse to admit either of these. Would the Beatitudes proclaimed by Christ be of any value, morally speaking, if they were thus understood? And another question can be added: Did Christ Himself understand it so? The answer to this last question being the most simple and easy, it is proper to begin by it.

Why is it that our Lord requires of His disciples to be "poor in spirit"? He gives the reason of it directly: "For theirs is the kingdom of heaven." Why must they be meek? Because "they shall possess the land." This cannot be an *earthly* land, which is never procured by "meekness." Why are they "blessed when they mourn"? Because "they shall be comforted." In another world certainly, since this "beatitude" of mourning must continue as long as they remain in this. Why is it that those who suffer persecution are "blessed"? "Theirs is the kingdom of heaven," is the answer. Go through all these "beatitudes," and you see the same.

Christ, therefore, declared that the civilization which He was bringing us was not to be confined to this world; that it supposed "heaven" both as its origin and its end; that human progress was not His main object, but an eternal hereafter. If we speak of the Christian religion, we must suppose that Christ knew it; and the ideas of Mr. Lecky and of his school are not the only ones suited to determine what must be the Christian "virtues." This is already a great deal, and we might stop here.

But there is to examine also the first of the two questions which have been just proposed. Would the Beatitudes proclaimed by Christ be of any value, morally speaking, if they were circumscribed by the limits of this world? In other words, would they bring on the moral progress of which Mr. Lecky speaks? This is an important point for those who do not raise their moral ideas above the human compass, and refuse to admit anything supernatural even in the moral world.

There is in this age a greater depth of anti-Christian ideas on this subject of moral development than is contained in the theory of Mr. Lecky. He at least acknowledges that man did not begin his career as a brute, and he admits in the lowest tribes of mankind a full possession of the natural law. He explains to the best of his ability the apparent anomalies as to the moral code which have been found among savages; but he does not pretend that in rising in the scale of civilization they gradually elaborate principles of virtue which they had not at first. These principles, he justly thinks, are the heirloom of the human race. In this he fully agrees with St. Paul.

The contrary absurdity, which does not deserve a refutation, and of which enough has been said in the First Book of this volume, is totally repudiated by the historian of "European Morals." But he often reiterates in his first volume his firm belief that, the principles of the natural law common to all being presupposed, there is everywhere among mankind a constant rising in the moral scale by their own agency. This he does at length in his first chapter on the "Natural History of Morals." When, later on, he comes to the consideration of the pagan empire, and chiefly to the conversion of Rome, he applies evidently to the matter in hand, the principles of this system which he has elaborately laid down; and his main object is to prove that the history of morals is a *natural* one—such being the word used in his first chapter—and even Christianity cannot be excluded from the system. Its moral precepts have been, according to him, naturally developed from previous philosophical tenets. Only, it is no more a simple philosophy as were the "ethics of paganism." "Those of Christianity were part of a religion." Unfortunately, however, the author does not examine if that religion was divine. It was evidently, in his appreciation, an efflorescence of the previous religions, or of the enthusiasm of its Founder. Its moral system was only a new link in the continuous chain of development which had taken place among men from the beginning, and which particularly obtained a great extension in Rome under the Antonines. We maintain that there was in point of fact no link between the moral doctrines of the most advanced pagan writers of that period and the principles of the Sermon on the Mount summed up in the Beatitudes. It can even be said that there is no possibility of a link between both, for the simple reason that the highest moral doctrine of the pagans considered only this life as its object, and the Beatitudes looked chiefly to the next. The first was from the earth, earthly; the second from heaven, heavenly. The first was undoubtedly well adapted to advance civilization as usually understood; the second left this civilization in the background, though it secured it in the end. Morally speaking, therefore, if we adhere only to Mr. Lecky's ideas, the Beatitudes would have had no value, would have produced scarcely any effect; because they were not intended directly to increase the happiness of man on earth. This is to be discussed at some length.

This celebrated writer never, to our knowledge, speaks of the Sermon of Christ on the Mount, and never mentions the Beatitudes. He thinks, no doubt, that Christianity is sufficiently well known and appreciated when it is said that "it preached the milder virtues;" that "it carried benevolence and charity much farther than Seneca or Plutarch;" that "for nearly two hundred years after its establishment in Europe, the Christian community exhibited a moral purity which, if it has been equalled, has never for any long period been surpassed." This, however, is not sufficient, and does not give a true idea of the primitive Church, whose extraordinary condition of sanctity was based on the "Beatitudes" and on nothing else; and these solemn "blessings" of Christ could not stop there, nay, they surely did not stop there. Their realization in Rome, particularly, proved that the new Christian morality did not only carry the principles of the natural law farther than the pagan philosophers had done, but was of a peculiar kind which the first did not even suggest, and could not be, consequently, a further link in their development. Christianity indeed left the principles of the natural law intact; nay, supposed them, and required first and foremost from its adherents a thorough fulfilment of them. But its ideal was far above those principles, aud to pretend that this ideal was altogether realized by the practice of the "milder virtues," etc., is to show a profound ignorance of the Christian religion as to its moral object. We are sorry to use such an expression in the present case, but it is unfortunately true that any one who limits the divine mission of Christ to a mere natural standard is profoundly ignorant of its purport.

That purport was to establish on earth the reign of supernatural virtue—what is called Christian holiness This belongs absolutely to the "order of grace," and cannot be included in the "order of nature." Not only its origin must be divine; and faith, hope, and charity, the fundamental basis of the whole moral system, must be gifts of God, and obtained by prayer like all other supernatural "graces;" but all the virtues which flow from these first belong to the same order, or they would not be *Christian.* The strict consequence is that if all the acts of virtue performed by the pagans were not so many sins, as Luther pretended, still those natural acts could not introduce the soul into heaven, and could be connected but very remotely with the scheme of redemption. For Christianity is the scheme of redemption, and nothing else.

This is Catholic theology, Mr. Lecky will say; and he could not as a philosophical writer bring it into discussion. This may appear a perfect excuse in his eyes. We must, therefore, endeavor to prove that he is bound to accept this "Catholic theology" or renounce his reason; because it is the only way to fully explain the scheme of Christ, and to understand the conduct of the first Christians in Rome, who did not certainly think that their religion was the efflorescence of any philosophy.

Not only the Beatitudes proposed openly heaven as the great objective of morality, and thus placed the whole system altogether outside of the previous pagan moral scheme; but their acceptance by the Roman Christians proved that they relied wholly on "grace" for the practice of virtue, such as Peter and Paul had preached it to them. It is here a question of facts, and not positively of "Catholic theology." Mr. Lecky himself will admit that the moral doctrine inculcated by the first apostles in Rome must have been that of Christ. But nothing is so clear in the Gospel as the insistance of the Saviour on the necessity of prayer, more still to obtain spiritual blessings than temporal ones. *Oportet orare et numquam deficere*—The Christian "must always pray, and never faint." * "The Christian cannot do anything for his salvation except with the help of heaven through Christ."† There is no need of a greater number of texts. The simple reading of the Gospel proves that this was the doctrine preached by the apostles and practised by the Christians, chiefly at the beginning. Go into the Roman catacombs, and see how they understood the duty of constant prayer and always expected miraculous effects from it. The virtues, consequently, which it was their duty to perform they considered as heavenly, as gifts of God. It was not on their lips that could be found the well-known pagan prayer: "Give me, O ye gods, long life and wealth; as to virtue, I will know how to practise it."

The truth is that Catholic theology alone explains fully to our reason the misery of man and his greatness; and all its teaching is but the faithful expression of our moral condition. We would fail in duty every day and hour of our life if we had not God to help us; for nature is weak, and divine grace alone lifts us up to the highest regions of what is called holiness. If any men on earth ever understood this, the first Roman Christians were prominent among them. They knew that the religion which they had just embraced placed them far above the moral level of their ancestors. They themselves expressed it by words very common

---

* Luke xviii. 1. † John xv. 5.

among them: "Their eyes had been opened by the divine mysteries, and they could see the realms of bliss unknown to them before. Their ears had been opened likewise, and the heavenly harmony had now a meaning for them. A new flavor had perfumed their palate, and they could taste how the Lord is sweet. They were in fact new creatures, and from sons of men they had become sons of God." Let not Mr. Lecky say that this is only Catholic theology. Knowing so well as he does Christian antiquity, he will himself acknowledge that all this and much more was included in the new Roman moral code. How can it be said that this was only a further link of the former ethical teaching of Stoic, eclectic, and Platonic philosophers?

3. *This Truth is Confirmed by the New Moral Doctrine, which could not be Derived from any Previous Religion or Philosophy.*

The doctrine of the Beatitudes must have been the main ground of the apostolic teaching, and the whole life of the first disciples in Rome gives a thorough illustration of it. The apostles must have preached "poverty;" and though we do not hear of a community of goods among them, as was the case in Jerusalem, still many well-ascertained facts prove that practically it amounted nearly to the same. The alms of the first Roman Christians were not only profusely scattered among the poor of the great city, as the genuine acts of St. Lawrence's martyrdom evidently suppose; but they were soon sent abroad in abundance, and spread generously through the whole world, wherever Christian churches had already been founded. The primitive history of the Church, even with the scanty materials we possess, furnishes a great number of examples of it; yet undoubtedly many facts of a similar character have never come down to our knowledge, and are now buried in oblivion.

This must have taken place from the very first years of St. Peter's pontificate in Rome; and it is believed by many that St. Paul positively alludes to it in his Epistle to the Romans, when he says of them: "Your faith is spoken of in the whole world." Their faith was known by their deeds of charity. This meaning can very well be admitted here, since the best way to announce to the world that there were believers in Rome as well as in Jerusalem consisted in the universal distribution of their bounty. It is not probable that so early as this an epistolary correspondence between all the churches had been established; charity must have been the first to spread the news of faith.

This resulted in Rome as well as anywhere else from the first beatitude, "Blessed are the poor in spirit." This had never been preached to men as the foundation of happiness; that is, of virtue. To be so totally detached from this world as to give up personal property and bestow it on others goes far beyond any moral prescription addressed heretofore to mankind. Even on Mount Sinai God Himself, giving His law to the Jewish people, had not so much as alluded to it. Alms-giving was undoubtedly a virtue in Israel, and the admirable exhortation of Tobias to his son speaks apparently as a prophetic echo of the Gospel. Still, there is an immense difference between both. The elder Tobias did not induce his son to become poor himself in order to relieve more effectually the poor. The voluntary poverty which has always been advocated and practised in the Christian Church could not enter into the ideas of the most faithful Israelite. But at the very head of the eight Beatitudes of Christ it is proclaimed as the foundation-stone of the new moral system. How could it naturally spring from any former one?

If it could not, it can, on the other side, explain perfectly this unbounded effusion of charity which has ever since been the distinguishing mark of the Catholic Church. Whatever accusations her enemies may bring against her, they are obliged to confess that nothing has ever equalled her profound commiseration for all the misfortunes of mankind. And this has been the case in all ages and all countries. At this moment the fact is as striking as it has ever been; and in the age of Claudius and Nero it was already pre-eminent. If any one wishes to know the true reason of it, he has only to reflect on this fact: that the Catholic Church is the only one which preaches "voluntary poverty" in the thorough sense inculcated by Christ at the very opening of His first sermon to the multitude. The divine Redeemer has conferred His first blessing on that holy virtue; and this has been the true foundation of the Christian moral system which originates, proceeds, and culminates in charity.

An apparently serious difficulty, however, requires here a short discussion. "Voluntary poverty," which is proved for Jerusalem, does not seem equally proved in the case of the primitive Christians of Rome. St. Peter does not seem to have enforced it in this last city, as he did in the persons of Ananias and Sapphira in Jerusalem; and no text can be adduced to show that the Roman Christians had everything in common. It is undoubtedly true that this doctrine, as far as it supposes a common life, did not pass immediately into the institution of monasteries, in which "vows" are taken by which the religious state is constituted. This seems to have been done in Rome at a comparatively late epoch. Still, the individual and voluntary renouncement of personal property to a very great extent must have been practised from the very beginning.

It is proved beyond question that there were persons practising asceticism in some of the noblest Roman families. The "vow" of virginity was strictly pronounced by many disciples of Christ who aspired to perfection. Agnes and Cæcilia are two remarkable examples of it. It is certain, likewise, that the charity of the new Christians was unbounded; and St. Denys of Corinth, writing to the Roman Church under Soter, who was raised to the Papacy in 161, could not only praise that holy Pontiff for the abundance of his alms, but he used in his letter these very words preserved by Eusebius of Cæsarea: "In your present liberality you only imitate, O Romans, the example which has been given to the world, *from the very beginning*, by your ancestors, the Christians of Rome." This was but repeating that their generosity had always been proverbial.

To show how poverty was practised, though there were no convents, the example of Lucina can be quoted. The identity of this lady with the Pomponia Græcina of Tacitus has been all but demonstrated by De Rossi, whose proofs have been admirably condensed by Dom Guéranger in his *Ste. Cécile*. She was accused, according to Tacitus, of having renounced the national religion and embraced a "foreign superstition." This was as early as A.D. 57, under Nero. She was tried by the domestic tribunal; that is, by her husband Plautius and nearest relatives. They declared her not guilty—*insons*—which means, probably, that the proofs brought against her did not carry conviction. The Roman annalist remarks* that Pomponia lived a long time after this, since she died "forty years" after the execution of Julia, Drusus' daughter,

---

* Lib. xiii.

which happened under Claudius. Thenceforth " she always wore a mourning dress, and appeared in public sad and dejected. As long as Claudius lived she did it silently and with impunity; after him it was for her a matter of glory." These words of Tacitus have exercised the critics. Justus Lipsius thought that instead of forty years it must have been fourteen. She could not, he thought, remain so long in mourning for Julia. Frenschemius answered that Tacitus' text ought to be respected, all the MSS. mention *forty years*, etc. But De Rossi, in proving the identity of Pomponia with the Christian matron Lucina, has rendered easy of comprehension this passage of the celebrated historian. The lady, he said, had found an easy means of practising her religion unmolested. Her pretended mourning exempted her from being present at pagan pomps; and her sadness allowed her to carry on without suspicion the digging of her Christian cemetery, which has been proved to have been one of the most ancient in Rome.

Henceforth her life was entirely devoted to works of charity. Probably her husband died long before her, and she could use her immense wealth for any object she chose. She thus became the great model in Rome of Christian "widows," as described by St. Paul.* But what is most remarkable is that the name she took, Lucina, was likewise adopted by several other Roman ladies who followed her example. In the Church's annals during the first three centuries we meet with the charitable doings of other Lucinas, and all of them are represented as entirely devoting themselves to alms-giving and works of mercy. This evidently supposes "voluntary poverty" in those who undertake to lead such a life. Thus, although there were not yet monasteries in Rome, the first of Christ's "Beatitudes" became the groundwork of the new Christian morality, without the formality of a "vow."

It is time to speak of the second: " Blessed are the meek; for they shall possess the land." Though the Saviour's lips uttered this sentence in Judea, and in the midst of a multitude "from Galilee, the Decapolis, Jerusalem, and the country beyond the Jordan,"† it can be maintained that He had, even at that time, the Romans before His eyes, and He intended that His apostles should, at the proper moment, din this doctrine into the ears of the proud inhabitants of that powerful capital of the world. It was not certainly

---

* 1 Tim. v. 5, *seq.* † Matt. iv. 25.

through "meekness" that Rome had "possessed the land." Her stern policy of conquest is well known; and at that epoch, more than ever before, she held the civilized world in her firm grasp. It is easy for a modern philosopher to speak of her "polished manners" and of the "milder virtues" of the "Antonines." But it is hard to believe that this philosophical humanity could have been the introducer of the Gospel's "meekness," which is of a very different type. How can both be compared together? Marcus Aurelius himself, in spite of the tender strains of his Meditations, which Mr. Lecky says " breathe a spirit, if not of Christian humility, at least of the gentlest and most touching modesty," was, after all, a gloomy and desponding more than a meek man.

"We," says the historian of "European Morals," "who have before us the records of his inner life, can have no difficulty in detecting the deep melancholy that overshadowed his mind; and his closing years were darkened by many and various sorrows. His wife . . . was not worthy of his affection. . . . His only surviving son had already displayed the vicious tendencies that afterwards made him one of the worst of rulers. . . ." And after several other circumstances of the same character, the writer concludes a long paragraph by saying: "Shortly before his death he dismissed his attendants and, after one last interview, his son; and he died *as he long had lived*, alone." The Italics are ours. Gloom and misanthropy would be the proper words for such a kind of meekness as this.

And what was the result of all his philosophical teachings? Mr. Lecky says it directly after: "The mass of the Roman people were plunged in a condition of depravity which no mere ethical teachings could adequately correct."

The principles of the apostles on "meekness" were already at that time succeeding far better than the doctrine of those professors of the "milder virtues" so highly praised by the same writer. There is not, certainly, in "the whole range of literature," to use a phrase almost common with Mr. Lecky, anything like the new language and the new manners the Church had introduced in so short a time among all classes of the Roman people. For De Rossi and Dom Guéranger have proved that in nearly all the great patrician families the Church had made converts even *before* the celebrated epoch of the "Antonines," as early as the domination of the *Flavia Gens;* namely, under Vespasian and Domitian, or, if you like better, at the very end of Nero's reign. We refer here to the noble work of the Abbé de Solesmes, *La Société Romaine aux deux premiers siècles.* The proofs are there offered that in the proudest Roman families there were most *meek* Christians, whose gentleness of disposition has never been surpassed if it has been equalled in any age or country. Read the Pastor of Hermas, the Epistles of St. Ignatius and St. Clement, which, together with St. Mark's gospel, formed the daily food of their minds. See the paintings still preserved in the catacombs of Domitilla, of Lucina, of Pretextatus, etc., all of them belonging to the apostolic age, and say if ever before the world had witnessed such a purity, simplicity, gentleness; to which the Saviour had invited all His followers by the heavenly expression, *Blessed are the meek!*

How can any thoughtful man believe that this transformation of the Roman character was effected by the reading of the Meditations of Marcus Aurelius, who was a fierce persecutor of the Christians, or by the mild philosophy of Plutarch, who did not suspect that there were thousands of people around him, all of them meek disciples of a meek Saviour, although he must have seen them? To suppose it requires a strange aberration of mind, or rather an incredible thoughtlessness. For those who invent these theories to explain naturally the sudden appearance of new virtues perfectly unknown until then, persuade themselves that it was so before endeavoring to persuade others of it. They evidently do not reflect on the complete dissimilarity of two moral systems such as were those of Greek and Roman theorists and those of Jesus' followers, who had received their belief and way of life from the simple teaching of Jewish apostles. Should they examine the facts with more care they would undoubtedly perceive that the word *meekness* may mean very different things. New theories might have been introduced able to modify the former sternness, or rather harshness, of the Roman nation, so as to render them less barbarous than they were formerly; so as to produce some little change in the way of dealing with slaves, of treating women and children, of organizing government among conquered tribes, etc. But the meekness which has received the Saviour's blessing, which He practised first and afterwards preached through Himself or His apostles to all nations, was a virtue which not even the best pagan moralists could appreciate, which they even despised when they saw it at work, which increased, in fact, their hatred of the Christians, as frequently happened at the time. Had any one told Marcus Aurelius, or Pliny, or Plutarch, or any other promulgator of the "milder virtues" that their fine sentences would culminate in the introduction of that Christian spirit which they all considered as the basest and most contemptible in existence, they would have laughed him to scorn, and denied with energy that the doctrine they announced had the least resemblance with "that low and grovelling superstition," as they called it. And it is proper to conclude these reflections by the remark that if, on one side, the pagan philosophers would have refused to admit any point of coincidence between their theories and the new religious spirit, the Christians themselves, on the other, would have protested with more energy still against a supposition which appears so natural to many persons in our day.

The following beatitude is, if possible, a greater proof of the same truth : "Blessed are they that mourn, for they shall be comforted." Here the absolute impossibility of deriving this heavenly doctrine from any previous teaching whatever is too apparent to require any discussion. Yet this was one of the first axioms of the new moral code which the Roman Christians hastened to adopt with a visible eagerness. Their life during nearly three hundred years was a life of "mourning" indeed; and they thanked God in the midst of persecution, because they knew the most easy way to heaven is through suffering. With this new moral doctrine martyrdom became a boon, and luxurious life a curse. There is no possibility of denying this; and every one must admit that this is the very substance of Christianity, since St. Paul himself said that the only thing he preached was "Christ crucified," and that he himself was nailed to the cross with Christ—*Christo confixus sum cruci.* *

Mr. Lecky, who does not say a word of this "beatitude," no more than of any other, speaks nevertheless of the persecutions; and his main object is to *disprove* the opinion of those authors who maintain "that the triumph of Christianity in Rome is naturally inexplicable, and who reply (to the observation that a religious transformation was then inevitable) by pointing to the

---

* Gal. ii. 19.

persecutions which Christianity had to encounter." He had already endeavored to do the same with regard to miracles, in which he does not believe, and which, he thinks, are a completely unsatisfactory *evidence* of religion. But he is much more profuse on the subject of persecutions, which he imagines could not prevent the Christian religion from triumphing, independently even of the slightest supernatural cause. The heroism of the Christians, which he fully admits, was, in his opinion, as natural an effect as is the stubbornness of any man who upholds a great cause; and he thinks he has thus removed from his path the greatest obstacle to the establishment of his system, by which everything becomes easy without the intervention of God.

It would not be very difficult to prove that Christian heroism was inspired by heaven, and had nothing to do, for instance, with the stubbornness of atheists, some of whom have actually died by fire in support of their absurd denial of God's existence. But we will take the liberty of remarking that the question is not there. It lays in the "beatitudes" preached by Christ, and in nothing else; and our simple means of conviction is to show that these "beatitudes" could not come but from heaven. That of "mourning" particularly is absolutely inexplicable by reason alone. It could not come from the previous doctrine of philosophers preaching "the milder virtues;" it was opposed to all the natural inclinations of man; it declared that man was not created for the mere enjoyments of this life; and if the simple promise of being "comforted" in an eternal hereafter was sufficient to make it acceptable to man, this was the most irrefragable proof that man is a supernatural being coming from God, and returning thither by the "royal way of the cross"—*Regia via sanctæ crucis*, as the author of the "Following of Christ" says.

This was the main support of the martyrs in the terrible ordeal they had to go through. They despised this world and aimed at another. They accepted unhesitatingly the word of Christ, *Blessed are those that mourn;* it was altogether a new virtue never preached as yet by any philosopher. They called it the great virtue of *patience;* but they gave to this word its original Latin sense, *pati,* namely, *to suffer;* yes, to suffer every kind of tortures, and to consider themselves happy when their flesh was torn by the executioners' hook and their bones were crushed by the teeth of the wild beasts. St. Ignatius of Antioch said it was the only way to become the *wheat* of Christ. No atheist, no supporter of heresy, could ever find in this doctrine the ground of his fortitude. Mr. Lecky will be bound to confess that this was altogether superhuman; for it is not from his pen that the accusation of fanaticism would fall, in writing on the persecutions; and the last paragraph of this long chapter of his book is an admirable picture of the sublime courage of our Christian ancestors.

The reader will feel, I hope, the strength of this demonstration. It lies in this: Powerful writers of our age bring all the fascination of their style, all the copiousness of their erudition, all the subtlety of their minds to prove that Christianity was established without the intervention of God; that consequently the virtues which it preached were only natural virtues, and the holiness which it spread on earth was earthly, apt to be dimmed, obscured, nay, liable to corruption, and infallibly tending to looseness of morals and social evil, as they pretend has been the case in Christianity. The great means taken by those writers to produce that impression on mankind consists in deriving all the gradual improvement of morals among men from our inner consciousness, and from no other source. *A natural history* of European morals is gradually, copiously, and magnificently, in some respects, elaborated, so that the series of its development looks as if we had before our eyes the simple monograph of any animal *genus* in natural history. The thirty or forty *species* included within that *genus* are there described, showing the gradual change naturally effected in each of them, and their natural generic correlation. If God has at all acted in this last case of the Christian virtues, to produce thirty or forty special new ones, it is evidently only through man alone as a secondary cause. He has, meanwhile, remained in the solemn grandeur of His rest; and what falls under our eyes is all natural, and can be explained naturally from our inward consciousness.

If we can prove that there is not in fact such a correlation as is here supposed; that one system of morals cannot possibly come from the other; that in their origin, progress, and ultimate object those virtues or truths betray constantly a diversity which can neither be gainsaid nor explained naturally, it is clear that the great diagram is a delusion as applied to morality, and that a totally different picture is to be made of it as to its true origin and progress. This, I think, has just been done.

The simple exposition of three or four "beatitudes" or blessings of Christ have sufficed to prove that this is the case for the Christian system of morals; and it would be altogether useless to go through the others. The reader can easily do so himself without our help; he has only to read the fifth chapter of St. Matthew and follow our rules of interpretation. The most simple mind, provided it is sincere, can easily perceive that between the philosophy of the Stoics, eclectics, and Platonists on the one side and that of Christ on the other there is such a doctrinal and impassable abyss that it is sheer folly to derive one from the other. To attempt it even is a useless task; and the greatest talent in the world cannot succeed in deceiving others for a long time; and here our limits prescribe that we should rest.

It would be, however, unpardonable to be satisfied with the scanty details which have been so far furnished of the holiness of the first Christians in Rome. A somewhat more extended picture of it must be drawn, and to this we now proceed.

4. *Some Further Proofs of the Church's Holiness in Rome.*

A word has been said of asceticism in the Eternal City, and the names of Agnes and Cæcilia have been mentioned. But we are not reduced to this simple statement. There is a work of St. Clement of Rome which has been the subject of some controversy, though everything goes to prove its genuineness. It gives a remarkable insight into the purity which began to flourish from the days of St. Peter in the most corrupt city of the whole universe, in that infamous Babylon which was anathematized by the mildest of the apostles, St. John himself. There is good reason to consider this little book as an authentic expression of the exquisite purity of life among the Roman Christians.

True, it is said in general that the first epistle of St. Clement is the only genuine piece of writing we have from him, and that the second and third are considered spurious by all critics. It would be, however, preferable only to maintain that there is no possibility of taking the least exception to that first epistle. But at the beginning of last century the learned John James Wetstein, from Basle, for a long time professor of theology at Amsterdam, a Protestant consequently, found at the end of a Syriac manuscript which he had received from Aleppo two letters attributed to the same Pope Clement, addressed to *virgins*. He translated them into Greek and Latin, and soon became persuaded of their authenticity. The immense amount of erudition he brought to bear on the question would have convinced all minds, had it not been for the opposition of Venema, divinity professor at Franeker, who attacked the opinion of Wetstein and found a large following among many Protestants.

Still, the proofs afforded by the Amsterdam professor were far from being invalidated; and the objections of Venema, whatever may be their critical value, possess in fact very little strength, particularly for one reason which must always have a great weight in the opinion of Catholics. The doctrine on virginity contained in these two letters is perfectly in accordance with Roman early traditions, and bears consequently a great probability of internal evidence. For it must be carefully remembered that what is well known of the Roman church in the second and third centuries is a sure voucher that the same existed already in germ in the first, whenever there is no positive proof of the contrary. But in the second and third centuries the picture was in the main the same as described in these two epistles of St. Clement, from which the subsequent holiness must have been derived.

A short passage of these letters will be sufficient for the present purpose: "Whoever aspires to a higher life must live as do the angels, in a divine and heavenly atmosphere. The virgin shrinks from sensual longings. Not only she gives up her right to satisfy them in whatever is otherwise lawful; but she clings only to that hope of which God, who cannot deceive, gives us the sure warrant. That hope is far above the one to which men only look when they wish to be surrounded by children of their own. As a reward for her generous self-sacrifice she will have a share in the felicity of the angels themselves."

To understand well the strength of these few words, we must transcribe the reflections which Dom Guéranger has made on them in his *Société Romaine:* "Such was the language of St. Peter's disciple, whom the prince of the apostles had chosen to bring about the renovation of the Roman Babylon. Nothing less than this strong language could oppose a sufficient flood-gate to the devastating stream of corruption which then overspread the empire. Had Christianity only proposed to men the practice of what was then called *honestum*, as the philosophers did, its efforts would have been fruitless. Stoicism could, by inspiring pride, give strength enough to despise death; it was above its power to give the death-blow to those sensual doctrines which were at that time the strongest prop of the Cæsars' tyranny. The ideal of chastity presented to the eyes of all in that corrupt world could alone stem the torrent of depravity which had well-nigh overwhelmed the dignity of man. For the good of mankind Christian morality began to shine in the universal gloom, and, many bright examples of it in the upper ranks of society coming in aid to its open maxims of true virtue, the exterior world had to take an account of it. Roman corruption was struck with awe in hearing that virginity was an open object of veneration for a large number of the new religionists, whilst the highest social privileges and the most terrible punishment could scarcely keep in the line of their duty the six vestal virgins on whom rested the honor and safeguard of the Eternal City."

Soon after St. Clement, Justin Martyr gave to the pagan Romans the simple details of the most holy life which was already led by a great many of their countrymen. "There are among us," he said, "in this city men and women in great number who have reached the age of sixty or seventy, and, having from their infancy lived under Christ's law, they have persevered to this day in the holy state of virginity." Athenagoras a little later on could say the same equivalently in his Apology to Marcus Aurelius.

We are not, therefore, reduced to a few authorities with regard to this austere asceticism so remarkable from the origin of Christianity in the city of Rome, and were we to quote the numerous facts preserved by the Roman traditions and ascertained in this age by recent discoveries in the catacombs, a much greater number of examples, belonging to the first century and to the following epoch of the Flavian dynasty, would give to this truth the strength of a demonstration. But there is after all no need of it, since the author of the "History of European Morals" himself admits willingly that Christian purity in Rome during the two first centuries has never been surpassed for any long period in any part of the world.

This transformation of Rome was so striking, and took immediately such large proportions, that even in the apostolic age the Church of Christ was already personified on the seven hills as the

City of God, the society of the saints, the reproduction, in a finer form, of the first earthly paradise. Hermas began doing it in his First Book of Visions, when the Church appeared to him as a woman at the same time old and venerable, young and beautiful, etc. The whole Christian literature of that primitive epoch is redolent of the perfume of holiness and clothed in the garb of a holy simplicity, such as no one could have expected to see in the midst of a depravity unheard of as yet in the annals of the world.

Any one, however, aware that the Gospel had just been written, and that the fifth chapter of St. Matthew had already proclaimed the ideal of the new religion, could not wonder at the sight of the sublime virtues practised by the new disciples. They were but the realization of the promises of Christ when He had pronounced his "blessings" on the head of His future followers: "Blessed are the poor," "blessed are the meek," "blessed are they that mourn," "blessed are the clean of heart," "blessed are the peacemakers," "blessed are ye when they shall revile you."

This conveys the best idea that could be given of the moral change effected in Rome by the simple preaching of St. Peter and St. Paul. By comparing the pagan city such as it is now known from the labors of recent archæologists with the new Christian community formed on the pattern laid down in the Sermon on the Mount, the conviction is irresistible that from the foulest corruption a great number of its inhabitants had reached at once the highest sanctity.

A short passage from "The Church and the Gentile World"[*] will be, I hope, most appropriate to the present occasion. The Roman on becoming a Christian "fell prostrate before the 'power and wisdom' of God, surrendered himself to the impulse of divine grace, and, closing his eyes to all earthly things, he was guilty of the greatest *folly—stultitiam*—a man, as man, could commit. But in this act of madness he directly experienced an immense moral change, and became a new man, a unit among many, destined to form a heavenly community, such as the world had never seen before. Who could be able to describe it with the scanty materials we have at hand? The gloomy corridors of the catacombs . . begin to unfold under our eyes the spectacle of that city of God so different from the city of the world which at the time

---

[*] Vol. II. p. 430.

gloried in its name—Rome, strength—and in its eternal destiny. De Rossi has already extended his discoveries far enough to embalm forever the sweet memory of primitive Christianity in the City of the Seven Hills; and when his task shall be accomplished then we will completely know the new and holy generation to which Peter and Paul gave birth. Petronilla, Pudens, and Pudentiana . . . will then be familiar names to every Christian," etc.

We must simply refer to that work for the ampler details it contains on the subject.

5. *The Moral Change Effected in Rome during the Apostolic Age was Permanent.*

A strong objection is brought forth that "after the first two centuries the purity of the Christian Church in Rome did not remain what it first was, and a great decline took place. Holiness seemed to have departed, and corruption crept in under a civil legislation better certainly than that of paganism, but very far from fulfilling the Christian ideal of morality. This was chiefly remarkable in Constantinople, which was called the New Rome, and had been founded by Constantine with the view of making it a Christian city, from which, for this reason, every vestige of an idolatrous worship had been strictly excluded."

This is said equivalently, and with many details, by the author of the "History of European Morals." The intention is evidently to ·insinuate that the new religion of the Romans was mainly responsible for that corruption which has become proverbial whenever mention is made of that dark period of Roman history, the Lower Empire.

Instead of shrinking from giving the objection its whole strength, we consider it a duty to quote verbatim by and by the most striking details furnished by the celebrated author, so that the reader may be able to judge, when he hears the answer, if at that epoch the Church had really lost her ideal of sanctity.

I. In these strictures on Christian morals, very little is said of the Western Empire; that is, of Rome itself. There was a more promising field of objections in the East, and this is immediately taken advantage of. But the primary question concerns Rome and the West; and before coming down to the Byzantine period, it is important to examine if, after Constantine had left Rome for

Byzantium, there was, in truth, a decline in the morals of the Roman Christians. The emperor had embraced the new religion; but a considerable number of his subjects in the West were still pagans; and whatever might be his wish, he had to legislate according to the actual moral state of the empire. His desires were repeatedly expressed in public proclamations, in which he earnestly exhorted all the Romans to follow his own example. Seeing the impossibility of obtaining it, he acted prudently in enacting laws which were not a pure expression of the Christian ideal. Mr. Lecky admits that they were better than those of paganism; and if time and space allowed, it could be easily proved that many of them went a great step in advance of former human legislation. But they did not, and could not, go beyond that scope. It would be a pure sophism to make the Church responsible for these legal deficiencies. The Church had no dealing whatever in their enactment. She had her own laws; and to prove a decline on her part, it would be necessary to point out any change that had taken place, at least, in her discipline. This cannot be done, and the author of "European Morals" has not attempted it.

After the emperor had left, the popes remained in the old city, which was soon to become the capital of Christendom. They were the true and sole legislators of the Christians. It was only a long time after that they became masters in civil and religious matters. Did they meanwhile allow morality to perish, or even to decline, in the mass of their increasing flock? If they did, it would be proper to prove it; and no proof whatever of it is afforded. There are, on the other side, strong reasons for believing that the popes performed their duty.

First, there was an unbroken succession among them which makes it difficult to suppose, on their part, a change of conduct in their spiritual administration, unless facts show it. Miltiades and Sylvester, who witnessed the end of persecutions, were the immediate successors of those heroic pontiffs who sustained the shock of the whole Roman power under Diocletian and Galerius. No mention is made by any contemporary author of a relaxation in the strict discipline which had prevailed during the era of martyrdom. The only feature which strikes any one who studies attentively that transition period is the care taken by Sylvester and the popes who followed him to organize most strictly the whole material framework of the Church; and this must have highly contributed to the correctness of Christian life. A great number of decrees were passed to establish with more precision and vigor the various degrees of the hierarchy, from the patriarchs and metropolitans down to the lowest grades of the clergy. The lay people were not forgotten; and a further attempt was particularly made to check the progress of slavery and to secure the sanctity of marriage. Julius I. chiefly, whose election dates from 337, fixed the degrees of consanguinity which made marriage unlawful, and proclaimed the natural right the slaves possessed to contract it. He made a special decree to render valid the union of a master with his female slave. The Christian policy which was destined to entirely abolish the ancient laws on servitude was so early as this inaugurated.

In a second place, in the conflict which immediately began between orthodoxy and heresy the popes displayed an extraordinary activity, not only in order to secure the dogma, but also to strengthen the bonds of discipline. They were mainly instrumental in promoting the reunion of bishops in councils. Thus the Arian troubles brought on a great number of those assemblies in the east and west, precisely as the previous Donatist controversy had done in Africa and Rome. But the custom was soon introduced to enact in all councils decrees of discipline as well as decrees of faith. The loose conduct of heretics, besides, becoming better known in spite of great distances, spurred on the zeal of the popes to prevent the introduction of bad manners and even of slight abuses. The modern authors who descant on early Christianity know in general very little of the activity of the Roman pontiffs at that epoch; and owing to this want of knowledge they cannot judge of their influence over the morals of their age. Should they consult the large Latin collection of Migne, they would cease to pretend that there was then a moral decline in the Church. The great cause of their error is probably their habitual want of discrimination between the pagans and the Christians in the fourth and fifth centuries. Polytheism and its concomitant, immorality, had not lost its hold on a large number of men; and though the Church was free, it did not embrace the universality of citizens. The Christians, owing to their newly acquired liberty, were mixed up with the pagan part of the population in a degree which had not been equalled during the previous centuries. The depravity which was still prevalent appeared to affect the Christians themselves, and whoever judges of them only from the common reports of contemporary writers on the morality of the age will form of them an estimate far below their true worth. It must be insisted again that the popes were their only legislators; and from the action of the popes we must conclude what the disciples were in the main.

Thirdly and lastly, the consideration of the personal merit of the Roman pontiffs in the fourth and fifth centuries is a most striking proof that there could not have been any moral declension in the Church at that time. Who can detect in Miltiades, Sylvester, Julius I., Liberius, Damasus, Siricius, and Anastasius I. less holiness, zeal, and energy than in the best popes of the second and third age? They all belonged to the fourth, and are better known than their predecessors, owing to the universal peace proclaimed by Constantine. The only question raised against any of them concerned Liberius, who was said to have given way to the threats of Constantius. This reproach of the Gallicans has been proved to be an error founded chiefly on some interpolations by heretics in the text of St. Athanasius. The admirable letter of this pope to the Arian emperor would be sufficient to prove him incapable of giving way to even a moment of weakness. And not only this letter vouches for his energy, but more still for his truly apostolic spirit and pure virtue. The third paragraph of it must absolutely be quoted : " Your sagacity," he tells Constantius, "must suggest to you that no feeling can enter my soul which should be unworthy of a servant of God. The Almighty is my witness, and the whole Church will confirm the testimony, that I have always trampled under my feet all worldly aspirations, and looked with faith and fear before God only to motives approved by the Gospel and apostolic tradition. When I was still in a subordinate ecclesiastical office I followed as my rule not the impulsiveness of passion, but the divine law always prescribed to and observed by Christians ; and I tried to repress self-importance and the love of glory in my observance of the divine precepts. With regard to the position I now hold, God is my witness that I was placed in it in spite of myself. I hope to remain in it without God's offence as long as I live. The line of conduct I now follow is not of my own choice, but it is prescribed to me by apostolic rule, which must always remain firm and in force. Following constantly the traditions of our forefathers in the faith, I have never tried to add anything to the prerogatives of a Roman bishop; but I have never allowed their curtailment. Attached to the faith which has been transmitted to us by the succession of so many great bishops, many of whom have been martyrs, I wish to preserve it forever inviolate."

Of all the pontiffs whose names have been mentioned above it is doubtful if a single one would have felt his inner life unworthy of such a testimony to himself. At least, in all the documents that have been preserved as coming from them the same conscientious spirit of devotedness to duty is visible. And those of the following century were not inferior to them. Nay, it would not be rash to maintain that during the first nine centuries of the Christian religion the Roman bishops were mainly actuated by the same noble sentiments. If there was, therefore, a decline in the morals of the people, it came from external circumstances over which the Church and her rulers had no control. Such were the barbarian invasions and the spread of heresy. But the Bride of Christ remained pure; nay, immaculate, without wrinkle and deformity, as the apostle said.

There has certainly never been in the world's history any dynasty of rulers so worthy of the gratitude of mankind, and of public veneration for their virtues, as the popes have been during many ages. At the same time that they appeared on the world's stage as powerful men in State concerns, they offered to the eyes of men the spectacle of holy pontiffs, true vicars and representatives of Christ, preservers and propagators of Gospel truth, and the highest promoters that the world has ever seen of morality and true virtue. Was there ever a public crime they did not condemn? an incentive to holiness they did not foster? Did ever the poor, the weak, the defenceless find better advocates and protectors against their oppressors? All this belongs now to elementary history. The author we take the liberty of criticising is not, certainly, the man to din in our ears the absurd tales of anti-papal ranters. He respects himself and his readers too much to endorse senseless accusations which he well knows are altogether groundless.

Still, he occasionally makes mistakes. In the passage previously alluded to he attributes to the popes of the fourth century a legislation which was not their own, as was seen, but belonged to Constantine, and was not intended purely for Christians but for a still pagan empire. Mr. Lecky, however, as was said, is very sparing of objections concerning Rome when he wishes to prove that there was a moral decline in the Church. He falls, consequently, on some of the Fathers, and, I am sorry to say, he speaks of things which he did not know sufficiently. Thus he finds that "a fertile source of degrading superstition" was already contained in the teaching of St. Augustine, "which together with the progress of asceticism gradually introduced the doctrine of the utter depravity of man."* Yea, he firmly believes in "the Christian notion of the enormity of little sins, . . . the belief that weaknesses of character and petty infractions of duty . . . may be made the ground of eternal condemnation beyond the grave, though this was altogether unknown to the ancients." This is attributed, perhaps, to the popes, certainly to the Fathers of the Church in the fourth and following centuries, and would undoubtedly have been a decline in sound morals.

But Mr. Lecky may rest assured that the teaching of St. Augustine, in particular, never introduced the doctrine of the utter depravity of man; and that the enormity of little sins, the belief that weaknesses of character may be made the ground of eternal condemnation, has never been a "Christian notion" at least in the Catholic Church. These were altogether Protestant aberrations in the sixteenth century, of which Christianity cannot be made responsible. It is Calvin who first proclaimed the "utter depravity of man." As to the other strange doctrine about "little sins," etc., it is but the consequence of the denial of purgatory by all the Protestant sects. This has been already hinted at before.

The Calvinistic dogma of Adam's fall may have been propped up by heterodox theologians with the help of some scraps of phrases found in St. Augustine's works. But these few sentences could not convey the sense given to them, because the great doctor of Hippo never believed in the "utter depravity of man." The best proof of it is contained in the well-known passage of the "City of God" where he speaks of the "virtues" of the pagan Romans, to whom, he thought, God had given an almost universal empire as a reward for their sobriety and purity of character. Mr. Lecky is,

---

* Vol. ii. pp. 5, 6.

however, excusable on this point, because, not knowing sufficiently Catholic theology, he could not understand the purport of the "Pelagian controversy," of which he has attempted in this place to say a word which could not be but a blunder.

To admit such radical changes in moral teaching as Mr. Lecky openly proclaims supposes that the Church is not an infallible teacher in such matters as these; and naturally this is the starting-point of modern rationalistic theories. These theories are consequently propped up by every semblance of alteration in doctrine. But Catholic writers can demur to this supposition and prove that the alteration did not take place, and could not have become "the source of a degrading superstition," as has just been done. This first stepping-stone of the gifted author furnished him, however, with the opportunity of launching forth, later on, into many details on the Catholic doctrine concerning "hell and purgatory during the middle ages," which he evidently meant, so early as the fourth century, to have been "the source of a degrading superstition." But there cannot be as yet question of the middle ages. It suffices here to maintain that the doctrine on hell and purgatory has never varied in the Church. The first—that on hell—is clearly the doctrine of the Saviour Himself in the Gospel; the second—on purgatory—independently of Scripture, is so clearly an outcome of reason that all those who in our age believe still in future rewards and punishments, without being children of the true Church, confine them to a sort of purgatory, by refusing to admit an eternal retribution even for the greatest crimes.

Still, it is insisted upon that there was an immense change in that regard. During the three first centuries, it is said, "Christianity was regarded rather as a redemption from error than from sin."* But later on the doctrine of the "utter depravity of man" became so prominent that a most terrific legislation was enacted in the Church for the punishment of sin. Excommunication was the last and highest of these; and "the excommunicated man must live hated and alone in this world, and be prepared for damnation in the next."† And in several passages of Mr. Lecky's book excommunication is represented as altogether inexpiable, and leaving man without the faintest prospect of pardon in this world and the next. Had there been such an alteration in the moral teaching of the Church,

---

* Page 5. † Page 7.

she would not undoubtedly have remained the same Church; and primitive Christianity, as it was called, would have in reality disappeared very early. But all this is altogether untrue.

In a first place, it cannot be proved that during the first three centuries Christianity was regarded rather as a redemption from error than from sin. M. de Pressensé in his *Histoire des Trois premiers Siècles* may say so; but he cannot prove it. For, in this case, the Christian doctrine would have already been altogether different from that of the apostles and of Christ Himself.

No man who has read the Gospel and remembers something of it can maintain this. Christ came to preach against *sin*, and bring back the sinner to the path of virtue. All the apostles without exception reproved men for their *sins*, and exhorted them to repentance and reformation. All the Fathers of the earliest ages preached the same doctrine, and denounced the most terrible punishments against *sinners*. It can even be maintained that if at the same time Christianity was also "regarded as a redemption from error," these errors of which Christianity redeemed man were represented as most heinous crimes. The greatest of these was idolatry, which was from the beginning denounced as the head and front of all other *sins*, etc. etc.

But to pretend that "excommunication" took the form it obtained in the tenth century owing to a radical change in the polity and the morals of the Church, is both to ignore entirely the apostolic teaching and to attribute to the mediæval Church a doctrine altogether inconsistent with her practice. It was St. Paul who "excommunicated" the incestuous man in Corinth; and it was St. John himself who in his second Epistle (v. 10), speaking of any apostate, commanded the faithful "not to receive him into the house nor say to him, God speed you. For he that saith to him, God speed you communicateth with his wicked works." The mediæval Church never said anything stronger than St. Paul and St. John against excommunicated persons, and the mediæval Church always received back the repentant sinner to communion even if he had been excommunicated, though the period of reconciliation was sometimes removed to the time of death.

There never was, consequently, in the Church any change of the kind attributed to her. She always taught the same principles of holiness, and enforced them in the same spirit, though her discipline was not always the same; because there must always be in a living organization a development conformable to the successive needs of an advancing or receding civilization. This suffices for the West; since nothing more of importance is found in the objections of Mr. Lecky with regard to that part of the empire.

II. It is in Constantinople and the East that the author of "European Morals" finds the strongest proofs of a complete alteration in the morals of Christianity. There is undoubtedly a great deal of strength in the difficulties proposed by the gifted writer. It can be proved, however, that if many facts seem to support his opinion, they all took place after the total separation of the East from the West, of the Patriarchs of Constantinople from the Roman Pontiffs. The popes cannot be made responsible for the moral and social aberrations of the eastern schismatics. This must be as clearly explained as space and time will permit.

"The history of the (Eastern) Empire," says Mr. Lecky,[*] "is a monotonous story of the intrigues of priests, eunuchs, and women; of poisonings, of conspiracies, of uniform ingratitude, of perpetual fratricides. After the conversion of Constantine there was no prince in any section of the empire altogether so depraved, or at least so shameless, as Nero or Heliogabalus; but the Byzantine Empire can show none bearing the faintest resemblance to Antonine or Marcus Aurelius. . . . . At last the Mohammedan invasion terminated the long decrepitude of the Eastern Empire. Constantinople sank beneath the Crescent, its inhabitants wrangling about theological differences to the very moment of their fall."

This picture may appear perfect to "the general reader," as the expression now has it; but it is far too much condensed to treat worthily of the question. It is not by a generalization of this kind that the Church can be fairly judged; and serious accusations grounded on it can have no strength in the eyes of any impartial man. A first remark that may suffice to disprove the whole paragraph is simply this: The deficiencies of the State are all along in this passage, and in several others, attributed to the Church, which seems to have fallen behind the former "pagan civilization," as it is somewhere else asserted. Still, nothing is so well known as the fact that the great fault of many of those Byzantine rulers was precisely their insistance on ruling despotically over the Church, to which had they been completely masters they would have given so early as this the form it has assumed in mod-

---

[*] Vol. II. p. 13.

ern Russia. The Church and the State must not be, therefore, confounded.

But the chief fault which can be found in this wholesale accusation is the length of time it embraces—a full thousand years. During that long period there were centuries when scarcely any objection of the kind could be raised. Even were it true that after Constantine there was not any ruler to be compared with Marcus Aurelius—we will not attempt to disprove this, though it might, perhaps, be easily done—still, a general remark of this kind does not even touch the question. The only subject to be discussed is simply this, was there not in the Byzantine Empire, directly after Constantine, whatever the State might be, a Church teaching men the most sublime doctrine, and fostering on all occasions the highest purity of morals? It is in fact directly after Constantine as well as in his own time, that we find in the East the highest development of both faith and sanctity. It is sufficient to mention the names of Gregory Nazianzen, Gregory of Nyssa, Basil, Cyril of Jerusalem, Cyril of Alexandria, without saying a word of John Chrysostom, a host in himself, who followed almost immediately after.

Is it of these men and of their epoch that Mr. Lecky says: *
"The Christian faith planted in the dissolute cities of Asia Minor had produced many fanatical ascetics and a *few* illustrious theologians, but it had no renovating effect upon the people at large." If this was really his intention, he has seldom written anything less commendable and worthy of acceptance. It cannot be doubted, on the contrary, that there never was, perhaps, in the history of the world a period more illustrious and more glorious morally and intellectually; and the renown of it accrues to the Church alone. The few names just mentioned could be surrounded by a brilliant galaxy of others, followed by a multitude of excellent Christians; but there is no need of it in the eyes of any one acquainted with the history of Asia Minor at that period, lasting very near two centuries.

It is at the same epoch, likewise, that were convened the General Councils of Constantinople, of Ephesus, of Chalcedon; and whatever may be said of some pretended councils of the same time, where the majority of bishops were Arian or Nestorian, no

---

* Page 14.

violence can be objected to those great assemblies in which the Christian dogmas were solidly explained and established, to govern henceforth the whole world and give to Europe that moral preponderance which she has not yet lost. When was it that Christianity was more majestic, more holy, more visibly the solemn organ of God Himself, than in those discussions, animated it is true sometimes, but always ending in the establishment of truth? Can any writer, chiefly if learned and impartial, pretend that there was a decline in the Church directly after Constantine either in faith or morals?

The author of the "History of European Morals" speaks of the councils only, we think, on one occasion and unfortunately he falls here into two blunders: the first in relying on Dean Milman, of whom he quotes in a note an outrageous passage; and the second in making religion responsible for the deplorable disorders which generally accompanied the councils of *heretical* prelates. He actually makes it a blot on the purity of Christ's Bride that, "in the 'Robber Council' of Ephesus, Flavianus, the bishop of Constantinople, was kicked and beaten by the bishop of Alexandria." Had he explained who that bishop of Alexandria was, the reader would not have been induced to believe that it was a crime chargeable to the account of the Church. It must be maintained again that the deeds of Arian or Nestorian bishops cannot be imputed to the Church by whom they had been condemned, nay, excommunicated.

A second period in the long duration of the Byzantine Empire could be made of the sixth century and the beginning of the seventh; and though the policy of many rulers of that age in Constantinople already prepared the era of decadency, which soon began rapidly to increase, still there were bright exceptions to this, and Catholic historians call attention to the fact that invariably periods of reform took place in the East whenever the emperors and the patriarchs of Constantinople came back to a thorough union with Rome. In fact, was there space and time, it could be proved that the dark picture drawn by Mr. Lecky of the moral degradation of Greek society in the Lower Empire was precisely the result of a schismatical tendency, more or less prevalent, by which the unity of the Church was loosened through the

---

* Page 197.

disregard of Roman authority: and this took place only after the seventh century.

The degradation for which the modern Greeks have often been justly upraided became total and final only after the complete separation of the East from the West. Thenceforth we entirely admit the truth of Mr. Lecky's strictures. It is consequently evident that his spirited generalization on the Byzantine Empire was far too much condensed, and could not be called a solution of the present question.

But for this last period even the actual case required some qualifications. If it must be admitted that "the Mohammedan invasion terminated the long decrepitude of the Eastern Empire, and Constantinople sank beneath the Crescent, its inhabitants wrangling about theological differences to the very moment of their fall," an impartial writer must also acknowledge the important *qualification* that this happened only after a struggle of six hundred years with the Moslems.

In less than half a century the Mohammedans had completely subjugated the whole Orient: Arabia, Egypt, Palestine, Persia, etc., to the very borders of India and Turkestan; but in order to destroy thoroughly the degraded Byzantine Empire, it took fully six centuries to complete the business. This alone would prove that there was still some energy left in those people "led by priests, eunuchs, women," etc. That energy they chiefly derived from their religion. This was no doubt a lame Christianity, deprived of much of its power by division and schism. Still, there were in it precious germs of recuperation, and owing to this the fleets of the Turks could not reach the Sea of Marmora and lay siege to Constantinople before the whole country around had been reduced to slavery by the enormous power of immense armies enriched by the plunder of the Eastern world.

It is doubtful if the modern writers who take a visible pleasure in heaping reproaches on the heads of "degraded" Christians will take notice of this remark. It is here made, however, in a spirit of fairness and impartiality toward the modern Greeks, a fairness of which many men boast in our age without being always consistent, and showing it whenever occasion requires.

It would not be difficult to bring forward an immense number of examples of heroism and holiness of which the Church can boast in those centuries of pretended decline, between Constantine and the end of the Roman Empire, both in the West and in the East. That she continued during the whole period to teach mankind, and to educate the new generations in the strict Gospel maxims established by Christ and His apostles, in spite of state deficiencies, would be easy of demonstration. But the limits prescribed to this work prevent it, and allow us only to conclude this part of it by a few considerations.

This long period of time was entirely devoted to the consolidation of the moral change effected everywhere by the apostles during their short lifetime. Had there not been a perseverance of the same principles, and a constant agency of the same causes; that is to say, had not God continued to act as He had done at the very beginning of Christianity, the heroic efforts so fruitful at first would soon have completely vanished. The subsequent Church organization coming only from men animated by a spirit of their own, naturally different from that of their predecessors, would have taken a shape differing widely, if not altogether, from the previous and primitive one.

We would soon have seen in the Christian Church a process of variations in morals such as the Protestant sects have constantly displayed in point of belief from the time of their origin. Who can perceive in the Lutherans, Presbyterians, Anglicans of our day the exact reproduction of their prototypes in the time of Luther, Calvin, and Henry VIII.? Bossuet, as early as the seventeenth century, proved the radical changes introduced into those human systems, so successful at first as to threaten the total destruction of Catholicity. But the immense power of that admirable work on "The Variations of Protestant Churches" cannot at this time produce anything like the impression it made at the beginning, when so many were converted by only reading it. It is seldom indeed, in our day, that any Protestant feels the force of that unanswerable demonstration. They all, or almost all, say that in the nature of the case *variations* were necessary; and the most radical of those that are now introduced please them instead of being distasteful. The visible consequence of it is at last the open denegation of every former Christian principle dogmatic or moral, and this cannot produce on them any impression of dread or awe, because they all have come to consider Christianity as simply an outcome of human reason, which is naturally always active and on the move, ready to admit to-day what was denied yesterday, and longing for new systems in the persuasion that the former ones have crumbled down into dust.

The same would undoubtedly have happened to Christianity itself, as early as the epoch of Constantine, if God had not directed and governed His Church as He had visibly established it. It would be now impossible to find any resemblance between the Christians of the age of Pope Sylvester and those of the time of Gregory I. The dissemblance would have increased much more as the distance would have been greater from the original starting-point. Yet it is now impossible to point out a remarkable diversity, particularly in the matter of virtue and holiness. Read the biographies of the saints belonging to both epochs, and you will be surprised to find how the feelings were the same and the belief identical. The extraordinary moral purity of the two first centuries, which extorted from Mr. Lecky the avowal that "it has never been surpassed," is as remarkable in many holy souls living in the fourth or fifth ages and later on. The only difference that can be perceived is this: In the apostolic period and directly after, the Christians were yet comparatively few and, the memory of the apostles being still fresh, *all* the faithful shone brilliantly by their virtues; and the contrast of the universal corruption in the whole pagan world rendered the phenomenon more striking and wonderful. Under the Christian emperors of the fifth and following centuries, the great majority of the Romans had embraced the faith; and there were among them many, no doubt, who did not live up to their profession. But all those who did so differed in nothing from the primitive disciples in Rome. In purity, charity, devotion to duty, and strength of faith they were not behind their former brethren, whose heroic examples they constantly kept under their eyes. The Christian religion appeared exteriorly to have declined owing to the lukewarmness of many; the Christian principles had not varied an iota, and were still professed and practised by a sufficient number to show that the source of holiness was still as warm and as copious as it had ever been. As an example in point, it is impossible not to see in all the Christian friends of Jerome and Augustine, in the bright examples of the most sublime virtues which they both relate in their letters and tracts, a perfect identity with those of an apparently purer age.

This general reflection can apply to the whole history of the Christian Church. Because she is always the same Teaching Body, and has received from her Founder and Spouse the care of souls for all time to come; because, also, the source of grace in her is constantly the same through the abiding of the Holy Spirit; it follows there can be no change in the morality she teaches, nay, in the holiness which is her great characteristic, and which she fosters with all possible care in her children. Hence we have constantly before our eyes the spectacle of the highest virtues, whose eminent practice must always be strictly proved in any one before he is admitted among "the saints." This is true of the tenth and following centuries as well as of the first; and in proper times and places the remark must be repeated, particularly for the mediæval period, which has always been more or less misrepresented.

Before this is reached, however, the spread of the highest Christian holiness among the northern barbarians when they came to destroy the Roman Empire must be briefly mentioned, and shall be the subject of the next chapter.

CHAPTER V.

THE BARBARIAN WORLD CONFRONTED BY THE CHURCH, AND BROUGHT TO THE PRACTICE OF THE HIGHEST CHRISTIAN VIRTUES.

1. *A Short Sketch of German and Scandinavian Tribes before their Conversion.*

EVERY Latin scholar is acquainted with the glowing description of German manners by Tacitus in his small book called *Germania.* Is it a reliable document? Nearly all modern writers accept it on trust; and they take occasion from it to attribute much of the subsequent civilization of Europe to the virtues of those northern tribes by whom the Roman Empire was destroyed. It is proper to examine this question with care.

In a first place, what means had the great Latin annalist to know for certain all the details he gives? He acknowledges himself that the Germans wrote no books.* He could not form any judgment of their thoughts, scarcely any of their institutions, which he knew only from hearsay. It may be pretended that he had received his information from Roman generals—chiefly Agricola—who had fought in Germany, and were often excellent observers of men and things. But every detail they could communicate had come to them only from some casual intercourse with German prisoners, or perhaps occasionally with German chieftains who came to the Roman camp for international negotiations.

The Romans at the time of Tacitus had never seen the working of German institutions in any German country. They in fact never conquered any extensive tract of that distant territory, as they had in Gaul. Yet it is known that in this last case the whole clan system of the Gauls had escaped the observation of so acute a man as Julius Cæsar. For it is evident from his Commentaries

---

* Cap. 19.

that he had not the least idea of that system after having resided ten years in the country and witnessed every day the social organization of those tribes. How could any Roman general form an exact judgment of German polity and manners, whilst they were always severely excluded from any insight into those social concerns? The Germans throughout their wars against Rome hated and despised the Romans; and they would never allow them to look into the privacy of their homes. What rendered the case still more hopeless was the fact, mentioned in particular by Tacitus, that the Germans had no cities, and they all lived apart from each other, each family constructing its dwelling wherever fancy dictated. How could their institutions be studied?

A great deal of importance, it is true, is given by some critics to the fact that Pliny the Elder, according to his nephew, had commanded a large division—*alam*—of a Roman army, and had afterwards extensively travelled through the country; some say he had visited it to its extreme eastern confines. He certainly wrote twenty *books de bellis Germanicis*, which have been lost, but which Tacitus undoubtedly perused. It was probably the best document the great Roman historian possessed. But as Pliny's object was to write of the *wars* between Rome and the northern tribes, it must have been only the narrative of a man speaking of cautious enemies, as the Germans were, who never showed the least confidence to the Romans, and never for certain allowed them to enjoy the freedom of intercourse which is always absolutely required to form a right judgment of a nation.

Pliny the Elder, besides, was not a close observer of human manners, no more than of natural productions or animals, of which he relates more fables than true and reliable facts. It is very likely that Tacitus has given us the substance of what was reasonable in the narrative of the naturalist, whose name he never mentions. But he must have added much of his own, or perhaps given to the facts a turn favorable to his object, which was to satirize the vices of his countrymen. That Pliny had travelled to the extreme eastern limits of Germany is not proved and cannot be believed. The only thing certain is that he had visited the western coast as far as the Elbe, and he had seen the source of the Danube, which every one knows is very near Switzerland.

But in a second place, every close reader of Tacitus' *Germania* soon becomes convinced that his chief purpose in writing this book was not so much to praise Germany as to put Rome to shame. The whole of it, in fact, is a violent satire against the corruption of the great Imperial City, or rather of the whole pretended republic. The learned critics who have written notes to the Delphin edition do not fail to remark it in many places; and when this fact is acknowledged by such men it is most surprising that serious authors should still draw from it proofs of German virtue, when the writer intended chiefly to speak of Roman vice.

For the purpose of estimating the true character of those northern barbarians, it seems far preferable to consult the writers who had occasion to see them at work for a sufficient time, after they had established themselves, with all their customs and institutions, either in Gaul or Italy. Such a writer is undoubtedly Salvian of Marseilles. Nay, in his celebrated book *De gubernatione Dei*, he may be considered to have leant too much in favor of the barbarians; because in his priestly heart he felt too acutely the vices of the pretended Romans of his day. It must be universally acknowledged that he knew those tribes much better than Tacitus, because he was for many years in the midst of them, and could see the working of their social organization, and the byplay of their virtues or their vices. When he wrote his book the northern hordes had already taken possession of the greatest part of Gaul and of a good portion of Italy and Spain. They were at the time carrying their devastations to Africa, where we shall have occasion to examine the *virtues* of the Vandals. Salvian fortunately wrote a great deal of them, as well as of several other Germanic nations.

It would be easy to find other writers giving to the picture darker colors still, as for instance the African historians, who describe the horrors of the persecutions of the Catholics by the Vandal Arians, or, in Great Britain, Gildas, speaking of the Anglo-Saxons. Salvian purposely, it seems, passed over the barbarian vices as lightly as he could, because his main object was to upraid the degenerate Christians of Gaul, Spain, or Italy, for the moral disorders by which they had called on themselves the wrath of God. On this account he is to be preferred, in order not to fall into the exaggeration of some Catholic writers who have given to the barbarian invasions a darker hue than the facts themselves warranted. Chateaubriand was one of them. In describing those calamitous times in his *Etudes historiques*, his expressions almost convey the idea that at the end of the scourge there was scarcely a human being of the former population remaining alive and able to resume the thread of history. This is absolutely untrue.

The presbyter of Marseilles in his powerfully written book speaks of a certain number of German tribes which Tacitus never mentioned; and of the many names of nations recorded in the Annals of the Roman historian not a word is said, apparently, in the eight books *De gubernatione Dei*. It is proper to say a preliminary word on this strange anomaly. Tacitus speaks of a great number of *nations* living along the Rhine and on the shore of the German Ocean as far as the Elbe, because this was always at that time the seat of war between Rome and Germany, together with the Lower Danube. This was the only part of Germany really known to Tacitus and his countrymen. Of the immense eastern and south-eastern territory it can scarcely be said they knew anything. Tacitus speaks particularly of the *Cauci* and *Suevi*, who were subdivided into many tribes. Then he passes to those living on the Danube, of whom the Romans could have some knowledge, since at the time of the great historian war was constantly going on along that river.

When Salvian wrote, the great invasion which the Romans had succeeded in beating back during more than three centuries had finally taken place, and the barbarians of the East as well as of the West were everywhere victorious. They already occupied a large part of western and southern Europe; and in their own internal complications new combinations of tribes had arisen, and new names had come uppermost in popular nomenclature. To give a single example of it, the Franks, unknown to Tacitus under that name, were in fact the coalition of several tribes which the Roman historian mentions, such as the *Bructeri* and *Angrivarii* or *Ampsivarii*, etc. The same is true of the Saxons, of whom Tacitus does not seem to speak; but the *Longobardi* and *Angli*, whom he mentions, belonged certainly to that race. The narrative of Salvian is preferable, because the names he gives to the Germans remained forever afterwards the same, and he had all possible opportunity of observing their manners and customs, as he lived in the midst of them.

To be more accurate in his descriptions he speaks first of those who were still pagans, intending to make us acquainted later on with those whom he calls heretics namely; Arians. For a good number of them had, so early as this, embraced a bastard Christianity which we will have occasion to know better afterwards, particularly in the case of the Vandals, who were ardent promoters of Arianism.

Of the pagan tribes he mentions first the Saxons, who, he says, were ferocious—*gens fera*. The word means in Latin that they were cruel like wild beasts—*feræ*—that is, ardent in shedding blood and inflicting on their victims the most excruciating tortures. He did not consider if, as Germans, they were more chaste than the Romans, and preferred liberty to death. This was what Tacitus looked to. Salvian was struck by the exterior characteristic of the nation, which was an inborn ferocity that in course of time became the peculiar distinction of all Scandinavian tribes. For the Saxons came primitively from the neck of the Cimbrian Chersonesus, what we now call the province of Holstein, and belonged, consequently, to Scandinavia. If there was anything remarkable in the numerous tribes which then inhabited the shores of the Baltic Sea and the vast peninsula of what we now call Norway and Sweden, it was their barbarous cruelty and their thirst for human blood. Thus Salvian was a better reader of character that Tacitus himself.

Of the Franks he says in the same place that they were untrustworthy—*gens Francorum infidelis*. If we look to the *Historia Francorum* of Gregory of Tours nothing is more striking, even after Chlovis, when they had embraced Christianity, than their treacherous disposition; and the whole history of the nation, under the Merovingian dynasty, is a succession of horrors perpetrated through the most horrible deception and hypocrisy. Salvian had thus anticipated the judgment of history, and given to the Franks the character they were to assume most prominently at their first settlement in Gaul. But the reader must at the same time remember that there was subsequently a total change in the nation; and nothing became more remarkable in them that their deep sense of honor and their invincible repugnance against deceit. It is in France chiefly that chivalry prevailed during the whole of the middle ages; and until the beginning of the Revolution of 1789, the French nobility continued to give to the world the example of the most chivalrous virtues. This was undoubtedly the result of the deep influence the Christian religion obtained at last over their naturally treacherous character. For even after they became Christians they continued for a couple of centuries, and perhaps more, to act in accordance with their native disposition, which Salvian pronounced to be *infidelis;* that is, untrustworthy, deceitful, in common language treacherous, and abominably cruel under the garb of friendship.

The reader, however, must not implicity believe what Mr. Lecky insinuates when he speaks of the Franks of the first dynasty. He pretends that Gregory of Tours, St. Gregory the Great, and many *holy* bishops approved of crimes committed with the most atrocious artifice by Chlovis, Clotaire, Fredegonde, Brunehaut, and others. This cannot be concluded from their words. Many of the expressions, in which they profess to admire the benevolent workings of Divine Providence, by whose instrumentality these horrible vices turned to the benefit of the nation, can be resumed into the simple truth that God knows how to draw good from evil. The justly admired popes, bishops, Christian historians of those times have given in their writings and throughout their lives sufficient proof of their deep acquaintance with Christian morality, and their unswerving faithfulness to its precepts. Every impartial writer is bound to give to their words a meaning consistent with their well-known principles. But the men who generally refuse to admit the interference of God in the affairs of this world think they must discard with a sort of horror the idea that whenever morality is transgressed God can be supposed to interfere in the act, either by turning it to a good account or even by punishing it. To preserve His own dignity, God must, in their notion, remain supremely indifferent to it and severely independent of it in His thought or action. A Christian cannot share in these views. This was the reason why Gregory of Tours wrote of it in the terms he used.

In speaking, however, of the treachery of the Franks, Salvian insists, as he often does elsewhere, on his firm persuasion that the sins of the barbarians were not of so heinous a nature as those of the Roman Christians; and the reason he gives of it is very remarkable as proving the unfitness of those barbarians for receiving the Gospel's doctrine. He says : "If the Frank forswears himself, what does it matter to him, since he thinks that his perjury is rather a simple way of speaking than a crime ?" And a little farther on he adds : "Is it wonderful that the barbarians are fond of deceiving others, when we know that they ignore the guilt of deception ? Their acts do not imply the contempt of the divine precepts, since they do not know that these are 'commandments of God.' The man who is ignorant of the law does not infringe the law by his act. But for us, Christians, the guilt is certain, because we are acquainted with the divine law ; and when we sin openly against *written* precepts we at the same time profess to know that they are from God, and yet we trample under our feet His orders and commandments." Let not Mr. Lecky say here that Salvian evidently did not know in speaking thus that there is a natural law of God inscribed in the hearts of all men. Salvian knew it perfectly well ; and on this account he ascribes the advantage of the Christian over the pagan to the peculiarity of his having a *written* law ; namely, the Decalogue. The natural law inscribed in the pagan's heart was, in Salvian's opinion, so much obscured by his passions and appetites that he could be said to be ignorant of it. How far he was guilty was the secret of God. The presbyter of Marseilles knew that the pagan sinned also when he perjured himself; all he maintained was that the Christian's guilt was still more grievous.

Many other passages in the book *De gubernatione Dei* go to prove that the barbarians did not any more listen to the voice of conscience. Practically it was dead ; and the first step to dispose them to accept Christianity was to awaken it from its deep lethargy, from a sleep which amounted to an almost complete extinction of moral life. How could it be done naturally?

From the Franks Salvian passes on to the Gepidæ and he says that this nation was *inhumana*, deprived of humane feelings. They did not go so far as the Saxons in their brutality. The first were like "wild beasts"—*feræ*—the second had simply lost the mild feelings natural to the heart of man as long as he remains man morally.

The Gepidæ having come originally from Scandinavia like the Saxons, there is nothing surprising in the fact that they were only inferior to these in brutality. It would, however, be difficult at this time to state in detail in what precisely consisted that insensibility to humane feelings. The Gepidæ never had, as a nation, so much importance in history as the Saxons and the Franks. They were compelled by Attila to serve under him against their will; and directly on recovering their independence after the death of "the Scourge of God," they were first shorn of their power by a severe defeat they experienced at the hand of Theodoric, and finally were totally destroyed by Alboin, king of the Lombards in

566. We must simply remark here the acuteness of Salvian, who, seeing clearly a shade of difference in inhumanity between them and the Saxons, called these last people *gens fera* and the Gepidæ *inhumana*.

The Huns appear directly after in the short catalogue of barbarian tribes given by Salvian. These were not properly Germans; but under their great leader Attila, who called himself "the Scourge of God," they had come from beyond the Danube. The general opinion about them now is that they belonged originally to a very distant country in central Asia, and were Turanians by race; consequently, very different from the other western tribes, who belonged undoubtedly to the great Japhetic stock. It is believed that the Hungarian Magyars are the outcome of the Huns. The presbyter of Marseilles did not take heed of what is now called ethnology. His object was to describe briefly the chief nations of the north who invaded and destroyed the Roman Empire in his own time; and the Huns were undoubtedly one of the fiercest and most important. It is the same object we have in view; and the origin and ethnical characters of those barbarians, not being a factor in the problem, can be excluded from the question. The only thing worth considering is the chief feature remarked by Salvian in the Huns. He says of them they were *gens impudica;* that is, renowned for their lewdness.

Tacitus has praised the chastity of the Germans; and though his object must have been particularly to reflect on the gross incontinence of the Romans of his time, his testimony in this case must be accepted purely and simply. We will soon have occasion to speak of what Salvian says of the Vandals, whose cruelty is so well known, but whose chastity was undeniable. The Huns, it is true, were eastern Turanians, not German; but this difference of race, as was said, cannot be taken into account, because the present scope is to inquire what prospect there was of converting those wild nations to Christianity, and this was evidently independent of their origin.

It must be, moreover, maintained that when Germany is praised for the native chastity of its inhabitants, it cannot be pretended that they practised this virtue in the same degree as the Christian ascetics, or even as married people in a well-behaved Christian community. The only real ground of this good opinion was that they were not so profligate as the Romans of the fifth century.

Of the Huns the same could not be said. Such was the extent of that loathsome vice among them that when they took possession, for instance, of a corrupt Roman city, their brutal lewdness exceeded all the bounds imposed by whatever remained of decency among the unfortunate and vicious inhabitants. Though the degraded Romans were every day witnesses, in time of peace, of private and public excesses among themselves, which were condemned alike by their religion and by the most ordinary moral sense, the horrors perpetrated in time of war by the barbarous Hunnic conqueror were of such a horrible nature that even their imagination could not have anticipated it.

It must be acknowledged, nevertheless, that the inconceivable devastations carried on by the Huns—who destroyed everything in the countries they invaded, so that it was the boast of Attila that grass could not grow any longer in the soil trampled upon by his troops—often drew away the attention of the victims from the bestial lust of the conquerors. In the universal ruin which overwhelmed those wretched populations, scarcely anything distinct could be perceived worthy of a particular notice. Consequently the few writers who have preserved the records of that calamitous epoch seldom make mention of this loathsome vice of the Huns. In those lamentable chronicles events are recounted without peculiar details. It is as in the sack of Troy under the pen of Virgil: *Fuit Ilium*, and enough has been said.

They do not, however, forget to mention that Attila, who had a large number of wives and concubines contrary to the custom of all German chieftains, wished to add to them Honoria, the grand daughter of Theodosius, merely to show his contempt for that great imperial family. It is known that the invasion of the West depended on this demand of the barbarian, and that on the refusal of Valentinian III., Gaul and the empire appeared doomed to destruction, and were saved only by the skill and valor of Aetius.

The testimony of Salvian alone, however, is amply sufficient to prove the lewdness of the Huns. He lived and wrote precisely at the time this frightful calamity took place. He had all possible opportunity of observing the Huns, who devastated Gaul and the north of Italy under his eyes. He always paid a great attention to the moral or immoral habits of the barbarians he described. What Tacitus had said in general of the Germans, that they were chaste, he confirmed with regard to several of those nations, some of whom were most barbarous and cruel, as for instance the Vandals. When, therefore, he says of the Huns that they were *gens impudica*, it must be true. And this must suffice for the present purpose.

It would be tedious to expatiate at length on the other pagan tribes mentioned in the book *De gubernatione Dei*. It will not be possible even to speak so profusely of those whom Salvian calls *heretics;* that is to say, Arians; and our remarks on this subject must be confined to the Vandals, who may be said to include in their characteristics those of all the other German nations belonging to the same category of Christians, but heretics.

Yes, Christianity had so early as this conquered some of those wild tribes, but unfortunately they were not the children of the true Mother, and on this account they had not been changed from wolves into lambs. The history of the invasion of Arianism among them has not yet been sufficiently elucidated. The subject would prove of great interest if undertaken with earnestness and discretion. For there was a moment when it appeared probable that all Europe, through the barbarians, would have embraced the doctrines of Arius. When Chlovis with his Franks submitted to the Catholic Church's authority, all the other German nations were Arians. The Goths in all their subdivisions, the Burgundians, the Vandals, the Alani, and many other tribes, not only did not acknowledge Rome's spiritual supremacy, but most of them were fierce haters and persecutors of the Catholics. How did this great evil originate? It seems it came from the Goths.

A good number among them—the Goths—had been formerly and very early converted by Greek captives from Asia Minor; and Theophilus, their bishop, had assisted at the Council of Nice and subscribed the Catholic Symbol. But Ulphilas, his successor, who translated the Bible for them into Gothic, embraced Arianism later on, for reasons scarcely known at this time; and his great reputation for learning and piety among his people induced the whole nation to adopt his heresy. It is probable that it was the example of the Goths which induced many other German tribes to embrace at the same time Christianity and Arianism. For in the whole of the fourth and fifth centuries the Goths, Visigoths, and Ostrogoths had obtained a great influence over the whole barbarian world.

It is probable likewise that those wild tribes preferred Arianism, because the bishops of that sect were invariably at that time more addicted to intemperance of language and action than became mild followers of an humble Saviour; and this possibly pleased the Germans more than a strict enforcement of the precepts of charity and forgiveness of injuries would have done. The whole history of Arianism in the fifth century proves that those sectarians, to whatever class they belonged, bishops, monks, magistrates, soldiers, simple laymen, thought they were rendering a service to God—*obsequium se præstare Deo*—when they pursued with the most violent hatred those who adhered to orthodoxy. It was congenial to the northern hordes to wreak their vengeance on those they thought God's enemies, and thus Arianism attracted them.

Of all the barbarians who were animated with such feelings as these, Salvian chose to speak first and foremost of the Vandals, and we most willingly follow him. The western churches had been preserved from the baneful doctrine of Arius by the popes and such men as Hilary of Poitiers and Ambrose of Milan; a fierce German people was going to show its zeal against them by following unreservedly its native ferocity. Religious hatred among them was ably seconding their natural thirst for human blood; and the atrocity of their devastations has to this day deeply remained engraved in the traditions of all Europe, and has been stereotyped in all European languages, in which the words Vandal and Vandalic mean simply destruction.

It just happens that a full narrative of their inhuman irruptions has been written by Dom Ruinart, the celebrated and most accurate author of *Acta sincera martyrum*; and a short sketch derived from his "Historical Commentary on the Vandalic Persecution" will give the reader a sufficient idea of the native ferocity of these barbarians. As it was, after all, a pure and simple expression of Teutonic leanings in the Vandals at that primitive epoch, it will be easy to judge what obstacles the Church had to overcome in order to inspire them all with the most common Christian feelings.

Whatever may have been their place of origin, the Vandals first became known to Europe at the very beginning of the fifth century, when Stilicon thought of using them to depose Honorius and treacherously place his own son Eucherius on the imperial throne. The Vandals, defeated at first by the Franks, succeeded afterwards in crossing the Rhine on the 31st of December, 407, according to the computation of the best authors. They were not alone; many other ferocious nations came along with them; but they were the standard-bearers of the invasion, and to them the worst excesses of barbarism can be attributed. The whole of Gaul, from the Belgian frontier to the Pyrenees, was at once entirely devastated, so that a contemporary writer could say in a short poem, *De Providentia divina:* "The ruin of Gaul would have been less complete and thorough if the whole ocean, breaking through its barriers, had overwhelmed the whole country."*

St. Jerome in a letter to *Agerruchia* summarily described the scourge: "Whatever is comprised between the Alps and the Pyrenees, between the ocean and the Rhine, has been completely laid waste by the Quades, the Vandals, etc. Mentz, such a noble city, has been taken and destroyed; thousands of its inhabitants have been slaughtered in the church. The capital of the Vangiones (Worms) has perished after a long siege. The inhabitants of the powerful cities of Reims, Amiens, Arras, Tournay, . . . Strasburg, have been sent as slaves to Germany. The provinces of Aquitania, Novempopulania, Lyons, and Narbon have been entirely ravaged, except a few towns reduced to an abject fear and to the extremity of famine. I cannot without tears speak of Toulouse, which the merits of Exsuperius, her bishop, have alone so far saved from destruction."

Salvian, an eye-witness, has described the same calamity in terms more forcible still than Jerome did, because he related what he had seen. "In all cities the same horrible spectacle struck the eye of the survivors. I have seen with my own eyes, and touched with my hands, the nude corpses of men and women left on the ground, bleeding and torn, a prey to dogs and to carnivorous birds."

The fury of the barbarian wars spread like the ocean over the whole territory; and finding in the Pyrenees an obstacle to its progress, the bloody stream recoiled, to finish the work of devastation in Gaul. During a full decade of years the Vandals, with and after the Visigoths, made of it a charnel-house, and of the proud monuments of the country a total wreck.

When this country had been turned into a wilderness, the treachery of some Roman general, who was still at the head of an army, in what we now call Languedoc (Novempopulania) allowed them to

---

* Si totus Gallos sese effudisset in agros
Oceanus, vastis plus superesset aquis.

cross over the mountains, and they rushed over Spain as they had done over Gaul, as they were destined to do afterwards over Africa. For it has been remarked by a contemporary author that those savage hordes might have established themselves in Gaul, had they simply wished for their dwelling a rich agricultural country, enjoying a mild climate. This purpose is the motive generally assigned by modern writers to the invasion of the south of Europe by the northern tribes. No object of this kind appears in the wild wanderings of the Vandals. They seemed to devastate the finest regions of the south for the mere pleasure of laying them waste; and the destruction of Spain as described by Salvian, in the work of Dom Ruinart, looked indeed as if they had no other object. The only foot-prints which remained after them were famine and pestilence. What has been related with horror by Josephus of a single mother who, in the siege of Jerusalem, fed on the flesh of her own children is attributed to many mothers in Spain by Idatius, a bishop of Gallæcia, who was an eye-witness to those horrors. This is a short passage of his lamentable description: "Famine raged to such a degree that human flesh became the food of human beings; nay, mothers went so far as to slaughter their own offspring, and prepare from their limbs a foul aliment. The beasts of prey, accustomed after a while to feed on those who had perished by the sword or through pestilence, became bold enough to attack strong and athletic living men, as if they were bent on destroying the human race."

The Vandals remained long enough in Spain to give their own name to the southern province of Andalusia, called from them Vandalousia. It is known they were finally induced to pass on to Africa by the Roman general Bonifacius, who, believing the false reports of Aetius, turned traitor to avert what he thought to be his own impending doom. The barbarians were led by Genseric, who began a fierce persecution of the Catholics as soon as he had firmly established his power in Mauritania and Numidia. This persecution has been described chiefly by Victor Vitensis, a contemporary bishop in the province of Byzacene. Sufficient details of it will be found in Rohrbacher's *Histoire de l'Eglise*, by any one curious to know them. It is doubtful if the pagan emperors Diocletian and Galerius ever carried barbarity against the Christians in the Roman Empire so far as the Arian kings Genseric and Hunneric did against the orthodox bishops and people of Africa.

This short sketch, however meagre and defective, cannot but

impress the reader with the fact that Tacitus had no adequate knowledge of the Germans when he wrote his short book *De Germania*. Had he even been sincere in the praises he bestowed upon them, he did not, he could not, know them sufficiently well. In his time the Germans had not penetrated far enough into the Roman Empire to furnish a true estimate of their characteristics; and they never had allowed the Romans to dwell among them, so as to study their manners, customs, or leanings. Salvian and Victor Vitensis are much safer guides for those who wish to form a correct idea of those ferocious hordes, when suddenly from the fifth century down to the tenth they confronted the Church of Christ in the whole extent of western Europe.

And since the question of fairness of description with regard to the Teutonic race has naturally come to be discussed here, it is proper to return a moment to the Anglo-Saxons, whom even Salvian knew imperfectly, because in his time they had not yet reached the south of Germany. He could only say that they were *gens fera*, and by this simple word he showed a better appreciation of them than Tacitus. At this time, however, much more is known; and precisely because there are still writers who openly bestow a fulsome admiration on them, even when they were pagans, it is proper to examine the subject more attentively. An historian must tell the truth, though he must severely avoid even the semblance of exaggeration. But to judge of the difficulty the Church must have met in her holy purpose when she first applied to the conversion of those tribes, it is just and proper to show what they were. And it precisely happens that Montalambert, in all good faith and simplicity, repeated for the Scandinavians the blunder of Tacitus for the Germans in general. For his narrative, when speaking of the Anglo-Saxons in his " Monks of the West," leaves the reader under the impression that among all nations of the world those bordering on the Baltic Sea were even *originally* composed of the moral stuff of which true, noble, persevering Christians are made. We firmly believe the contrary, and must show the reasons of our belief; protesting, however, of our profound respect for the author of the life of St. Elizabeth. He wrote what he thought was true; he wished to serve the Church in writing what he did of the Anglo-Saxons. But in our opinion he was mistaken; his always ardent admiration of England biassed his judgment; and he did not see clearly enough that there has probbly never been in the whole history of the Church so extraordinary and unexpected a conquest as that of the Baltic tribes. Montalembert had some idea of it; and a few phrases here and there prove that he was not totally blind on the subject, but he was firmly convinced of the original greatness and nobleness of the Scandinavian nations, and on account of that conviction he dictated several most beautifully written pages in the third volume of his "Monks of the West," to which we must give presently a word of reply.

"The Anglo-Saxons,"* he says, "brought with them to Great Britain a language, social institutions, and race characteristics of a powerful, or rather indestructible, originality. Language, institutions, characteristics, have triumphed in their essential traits over the vicissitudes of time and chance; they have survived all subsequent defeats, all foreign influences; and sending down their roots into the primitive soil of Celtic Britain, they subsist still as the indestructible basis of the social edifice of England."

A couple of pages farther on, he adds: "This race of pirates, of men given to prey over, to hunt after, and steal their fellow-men, possessed, nevertheless, the essential element of true social order.... They alone founded in Great Britain an inexpugnable society, whose solid base was already laid down when monastic missionaries came to bring them the light of faith and of Christian virtue." A great deal more is said of the same purport; and the reader feels inclined to conclude that if England is so powerful to-day she owes it more to her Anglo-Saxon origin than to her conversion to Christ; since many other nations, which have been converted likewise, do not show the same harmonious characters of solidity and endurance; and these characters are attributed to the Saxons before they became Christians.

The general objection which can be justly raised against such generalizations as these is that the difference between the social and moral orders existing in those tribes when they were pagan and what they became under the influence of Christianity is not sufficiently marked. It looks as if the change effected among them—a change admitted here and there by the gifted author—was but of a secondary character, leaving the primitive moral features of those tribes nearly the same as they were under the influence of paganism; and to that permanency of characteristics the main attributes of the English

---

* French edit., 1866, vol. iii. p. 336.

nation in modern times are ascribed. This impairs essentially the writer's judgment on the whole subject.

It becomes glaringly evident when mention is made, directly after, of the political institutions among those northern hordes. "The portion of Great Britain," says Montalembert, "which has since been called England, was composed (under the Heptarchy) of an agregation of tribes, and of independent communities, among whom the exigencies of war against their neighbors of the north and west were developing a gradual tendency toward unity. It formed an aristocratic federation in which families of a supposed divine origin presided over the social and military life of each tribe, whilst personal independence remained the foundation of the whole edifice. This independence always knew how to revindicate its rights when a prince more able or energetic than others had begun to weaken them. . . . Every right which freemen had not expressly given up and passed over to chiefs elected by themselves, or to constitutional bodies freely acknowledged by all, remained inviolably their own."

This is indeed a dream of the past; and few will be induced to admit that the fierce Anglo-Saxons of Hengist had already the germ of a constitution nearly as perfect as that of England in this age or the last. It is useless to bring forward any more quotations. The only thing we will allow ourselves in answer will be to give the opinion of Lingard on the moral and social state of those rude tribes. He at least establishes a broad distinction between the pagan Anglo-Saxons and their Christian posterity in the time of Bede; and we cannot be afraid of exaggerating in strictly following an author so judicious and moderate in everything he wrote. Every one must remember that he was the first Catholic author who compelled the Protestant English themselves to adopt in the main his historical statements, and in general submit to his well-laid-down judgments of men and things either for ancient times or modern transactions.

"By the ancient writers" * he says, " the Saxons are unanimously classed with the most barbarous of the nations which invaded and dismembered the Roman Empire. Their valor was disgraced by its brutality. To the services they generally preferred the blood of their captives; and the man whose life they condescended to spare was taught to consider perpetual servitude as a gratuitous favor. Among themselves *a rude and imperfect system of legislation entrusted to private*

---

* Antiquities of the Anglo-Saxon Church, vol. i. ch. i.

revenge the punishment of private injuries; and the ferocity of their passions continually multiplied these deadly and hereditary feuds. Avarice and the lust of sensual enjoyment had extinguished in their breasts some of the first feelings of nature. The savages of Africa may traffic with Europeans for the negroes whom they have seized by treachery or captured in open war. But the more savage Saxon conquerors of the Britons sold without scruple, to the merchants of the continent, their own countrymen and even their own children. Their religion was accommodated to their manners and their manners were perpetuated by their religion. In their theology they acknowledged no sin but cowardice, and revered no virtue but courage. Their gods they appeased with the blood of human victims. Of a future life their notions were faint and wavering; and if the soul were fated to survive the body, to quaff ale out of the skulls of their enemies was to be the great reward of the virtuous, and to lead a life of hunger and inactivity the endless punishment of the wicked.

"Such were the pagan Saxons. But their ferocity soon yielded to the exertions of the missionaries," etc.

This is the true verdict of history with regard to this question. Modern writers, it is true, pretend that the Eddas and the Sagas, better known to-day than in the time of Lingard, oblige the historian to modify this harsh judgment of the celebrated English writer. One thing is certain: that admitting all possible reversal of judgment, this cannot be carried to the extent alleged by Montalembert in his "Monks of the West." Lingard's judgment remains still much nearer to the truth; and to be convinced of it one has only to read what Cantù has written on the Scandinavian tribes in his "Universal History," and the copious extracts he gives from the very Eddas and Sagas which are invoked as a proof of nobleness of character and generosity of disposition in those ferocious savages of the North Sea. The great Italian historian quotes a very long list of books printed from Icelandic and Norwegian MSS.; and the substance he gives of their contents is assuredly an almost complete vindication of Lingard's opinion. It is particularly impossible to admit that their political and social organization resembled in the least the admirable balancing of checks and counterchecks which form the safety of the English constitution in our age. Especially the spirit of social compromise by which Great Britain has effectually escaped the revolutionary excesses so rife in all other European nations cannot even be thought of when there is question of the pagan Saxons. The description of their "rude and imperfect system of legislation" by Lingard is in complete accordance with the simple records of all ancient writers on the subject. It is perfectly true that "the ferocity of their passions continually multiplied among them deadly and hereditary feuds." As to the other statement that "avarice and the lust of sensual enjoyments had extinguished in their breasts some of the first feelings of nature," it is fully borne out by many texts quoted by Cantù, whose judgment could not be biassed on any English political or social question, because he was an Italian without any connection whatever with England.

2. *Remarkable Moral Change effected by Christianity in all Germanic and Scandinavian Nations.*

To proceed with order and lucidity in a subject which is naturally very intricate, those nations will be considered first who embraced the Christian religion outside of their own country during their invasion of southern Europe; and in a second place, those to whom Christianity was preached in Germany itself by English or Irish missionaries. The narrative must be very succinct and brief.

I. The first are mainly those just described in the preceding section. Except the Franks they all became Arians, and most of them persecuted the Catholic Church with a violence not inferior to that of former pagan princes. It is proper to examine at the outset what moral change, if any, their Arian Christianity brought among them.

It is difficult to perceive in the Visigoths and Suevi, in Spain, in the Vandals in Spain likewise, and afterwards in Africa, in the Lombards in northern Italy, any progress in morality, any perceptible mildness of manners, any attempt at Christian discipline, any germ of what has been so far called holiness, although they were Christian Arians. It is related with justice * that the Visigoths led by Alaric showed some humanity in the sack of Rome, as St. Augustine remarked at the very beginning of his great work *De Civitate Dei;* and this is attributed in the "Manual of

---

* Alzog, Am. ed.

Universal Church History" to the fact that the Visigoths were *Germans*. But on the very next page it is admitted by the same writer that this horde of barbarians, being afterwards led by Ataulf into Gaul, where they settled around Toulouse, "this first kingdom established in Europe by the *Germans* was, *even after it had assumed a distinctively Christian character*, conspicuous for deeds of barbaric violence, which were usually followed by the more terrible scourges of pestilence and famine."

Again, the same writer acknowledges that after the Vandals, Alani, and Suevi—all German tribes—had overspread Spain, "they began their work of pillage by sacking cities, pulling down churches, and putting to death Catholic bishops and priests," though they were Christians.

There is no need of repeating that the same is said of the Vandals under Genseric and Hunneric in Africa, though very few examples of it have been previously given by us. The reader having gone so far in the "Manual of Church History" comes back naturally to the beginning of the chapter, and wonders when he reads again "that the mildness and clemency exhibited by the barbarians on this occasion [the sack of Rome by Alaric] are evidence of that humane feeling so characteristic of the Germans." We must continue to be of the opinion previously expressed: Originally Germans were savages.

This time, however, it assumes a much stronger form, not only because the native ferocity of those nations had not evidently been touched by their conversion to Arian Christianity, but also because they had not even understood that their new religion, being that of Christ, obliged them to adopt a strict discipline both sacramental and ascetic, as invariably happened whenever any nation embraced Catholicity. No ecclesiastical writer has ever mentioned that in those Arian churches of the Visigoths in France and Spain, of the Vandals in Africa, of the Lombards in Italy, the least zeal was manifested by their clergy for the reformation of manners, the correction of abuses, and the extirpation of sin. No council of Arian bishops has ever been recorded for such purposes in Spain, whilst, on the contrary, as soon as Arianism disappeared under Reccared we hear of those numerous Catholic councils of Toledo which remain still to-day one of the greatest glories of old Spain.

Again, in Roman Africa the student of history sees with dismay all the previous moral organization of the Catholic Church demolished at once; all the former provisions of synods and councils discarded at a blow; all the strict rules of discipline disappearing, though so far they had been enforced more or less according as the zeal of ecclesiastical rulers grew more or less ardent; yea, all these precious means of reform and sanctification which sustained the spiritual life of Catholicity in Africa were blotted out at once, without being replaced by any effort of zeal on the part of the Arian bishops. So that when the Moslems arrived, a few years afterwards, Christianity disappeared entirely and suddenly in that part of the world. Not a vestige of it remained in Mauritania and Numidia, whilst there have remained Christians to our own day in Egypt, Syria, and Asia Minor, where Mohammedanism was so early triumphant and enjoyed such an immense power in the very centre of its empire. Was not this difference brought on by Arianism, which neglected everything except the persecution of Catholics?

Mr. Lecky might interpose here, and say that the Franks, though they were a Catholic nation, did not appear, under the Merovingian dynasty, to have improved much in point of morality from the time when they were pagans; and many facts related by St. Gregory of Tours show a rather slight alteration in their former barbarous customs. It is proper to touch this question, although few Catholics of the present day will admit a parity between them and the Arian Germans. It is only to the rationalists that we address ourselves here.

In a first place, it is remarkable that when Gregory of Tours relates the atrocious deeds of Chlovis and his posterity, the horrible narrative affects only the rulers of the nation, and they always act from some well-known political motive. They want to reach power by the destruction of their enemies, or, what is worse, by doing away with their own relatives in order to reign in their place. But in spite of some innuendoes of the author of "European Morals," they all knew that their religion did not approve of their deeds. If occasionally Gregory of Tours, himself a bishop, speaks of the Providence of God making use of those crimes for furthering the good of the Church or of the people, it can always be understood in the Christian sense of St. Paul himself, who teaches that God knows how to draw good from evil. But those Merovingian monsters knew very well that, according to the teaching of their religion, a proportionate atonement in this world or the next would be required of them. In their most atrocious deeds the Franks acted only like all Christians who blindly follow their passions. Nothing more can be concluded from that monstrous history. It cannot be pretended that even for the worst of them no moral change whatever had taken place when they had become Christians. For they had at least acquired some gleams of conscience which they had not before their conversion; they knew their crimes were crimes, which before they did not seem to suspect.

But in a second place, all those Frankish rulers were not of the class which alone Mr. Lecky has described. Gregory of Tours mentions some beautiful instances of pure virtue among them, of which nothing is said in the "History of European Morals." It is proper that a few examples of it should be given here, and these will be confined to the men, for the good deeds of holy women among the Franks would carry us too far. We will thus be able to see if they had gained nothing from Christianity.

There was during the reign of Chilperic a certain Duke Chrodin or Rodin, whom the author of the *Historia Francorum* calls "a man of excellent goodness and piety, much given to alms-deeds, a great purveyor of the poor in their necessities; always ready to enrich the Church and support the clergy. He was all the time founding new country villages, planting vineyards, building houses, opening wild districts to cultivation. When bishops had no great means to help the poor, he called them to his house, gave them a dinner, and at the end of it he distributed among them his newly built villages already occupied by husbandmen; and giving them money, utensils, servants, with cloth and linen, he told them with the greatest benignity and good nature: 'All this, mind ye, is given to the *Church*, that whilst the poor enjoy the benefit of it they may by their prayers obtain for me mercy from God.'" *

It is impossible to say more in these few words. This simple picture of true charity is perfect; and it must be allowed that those Frankish dukes, after all, were not all bad men. The reader learns besides from this short passage that when a rich man gave anything to the *Church*, it was not done in order to gratify the gluttony of a few prelates or monks, but to benefit the poor through the Church, which alone could then possess in security, and without the fear of plunderers, what was given, as they thought, for all time to come. To give to the Church was to give to the poor; and the bishops understood well, when they received presents of the kind mentioned

---

* Hist. Francorum, lib. vi. cap. 20.

here by Gregory of Tours, that they were merely trustees of a fund which belonged in fact to their wards, and of which they would have to give an account to God.

That the Franks in the worst times of the Merovingian dynasty enjoyed a fine appreciation of the highest Christian virtues is proved by many details contained in the *Historia Francorum* and in the *Liber de gloria Confessorum* of Gregory, who *wrote mainly for the Franks*. If they had been the brutal savages they are represented to be by some modern writers, the following rather long story would have been absolutely above their ken. They could not have appreciated any detail of it. Yet many other passages of the same books were written for them in the same spirit, and would have been, in the language of the Gospel, " pearls thrown before swine," if the Frankish nation had been the set of barbarians which is naturally supposed by the one-sided selections made from their history by Mr. Lecky. The books of Gregory, I repeat, were mainly written for them, and many of them knew Latin ; this is a well ascertained fact.

"About the same time"—namely, when Nepotianus was bishop of Clermont in Auvergne, the fifth on the list, towards the end of the fourth century—"Injuriosus, an Alvernian senator, asked in marriage a young lady of the same rank in life, and the day of nuptials was appointed. Both were the only children of their parents. At the end of the ceremony they were conducted to the bridal bed; but the bride, turning herself to the wall, began to shed a flood of tears, and appeared in the deepest affliction. 'What is the matter,' said the young man; 'please tell me, dearest.' And as she kept silent, 'I beseech thee,' he added, 'in the name of Jesus Christ the son of God, that thou tellest me the cause of thy grief.' Then the bride turning herself toward him, 'If I were,' she said, 'to shed tears all the days of my life, they could not allay my sorrow. I had determined to keep immaculate my virginity for Christ's sake; but alas! what I have kept so far unsullied I am at the moment of losing. Christ the Immortal had promised me paradise for my dowry, and He leaves me in the arms of a mortal man. . . . But why should I speak longer? Wretched is my fate; heaven was promised me, and I am plunged in an abyss of woes! Why was not my first day the last? Death would have been welcome rather than the milk which sustained my life. To the sweet embraces of my nurse I would have preferred the gloom of a funeral. The simple sight of earthly blessings terrify me when I look on the hands of my Redeemer pierced with nails for the world's salvation. What is to me a diadem brilliant with gems, when I see the crown of thorns around His head? I turn away from the thought of thy far-spreading estates to think only of paradise's beauty.' . . . In the midst of that heart-rending lamentation the young man, full of compassionate pity, said at last: 'Our noble parents, wishing to leave heirs after them, have thought of our union in order that after their demise their ancestral possessions should not go to a stranger.' At these words the bride exclaimed: 'What is the world? what is wealth? all is vanity. Life itself is a dream in comparison with that other life which knows no end. There alone is found eternal beatitude, and a light undimmed by a period of darkness. And what is more, the presence of God Himself fills the soul with the sweetness of an eternal contemplation, raising man to the condition of angels, the true source of an ineffable and undying joy.' 'Dearest,' exclaimed the young man, 'thy thrilling words have opened my eyes, and eternal life appears to me like a brilliant ray filling all space and reaching heaven. If thou wishest to remain pure in wedded life, I will bind myself to the same sublime effort.' To this she answered: 'It is hard for a man to grant this to a wife. If, however, thou succeedest in doing it, and we both remain pure in the midst of this life's trials, I will give thee a share in the dowry which the Lord Jesus Christ has promised me on the day when I swore to remain forever His servant and His spouse.' Arming himself with the sign of the cross, Injuriosus promised to do what his bride wished; and both, holding each other's hand, fell into a sweet repose. They continued many years faithful to their resolution. And it was only at their death that the world became aware of it.

"The bride was the first to die; and on the day of her funeral, when Injuriosus placed her in the sepulchre, he said: 'I give Thee thanks, O Eternal God, that as I received this treasure from Thee, the same I return immaculate to Thy hands.' The dead lady revived at these words, and, smiling, she said: 'Why dost thou reveal what nobody asked of thee?' Then the tomb was closed, and not long after he followed her."

This story is very different from those invariably chosen by the author of "European Morals" to amaze his readers. Still there are many others of the same style in the *Historia Francorum* of Gregory of Tours. Injuriosus was not probably a Frank but a Gallo-Roman. The book, however, was undoubtedly written for the *Franks*. Can any one suppose that a northern barbarian, able to appreciate such an exalted virtue and to relish the reading of this beautiful legend, had not received from his new religion a moral ideal far superior to whatever he knew of morality before? It was a complete change of thoughts and aspirations.

And the Franks soon learned to aspire personally to the same sublimity of virtue. Thus we read that " Friedeburga, the daughter of Duke Gonzo, though affianced to Sigebert, the son of Thierry II., withdrew to the church, and there, clinging to the altar and covered with a nun's veil, declared in presence of her betrothed her intention of dedicating her virginity to God. The prince generously waived his claim."* It is known, besides, that many noblemen and not a few princes and kings among the Anglo-Saxons embraced also the life of the cloister; and the story of Henry, Emperor of Germany, who lived with his wife Cunegunda as brother and sister, is not ignored even by those who have a very slight acquaintance with history.

But there are in Gregory of Tours' works many other facts which powerfully illustrate the holiness of many Franks under the Merovingian dynasty. No one must imagine that all the rulers and chieftains belonging to the nation were like Chlovis, Fredegonde, and Brunehaut. Several Merovingian kings and princes gave examples of virtue which could be attributed to the Christian religion alone, and particularly there was very soon in the whole nation a political, military, and social advance resulting from their Christianity, which placed them far above their previous level.

The modern historians who speak of Guntran do so in general as if he had been a weak prince, of a very irresolute character, and given over to superstitious practices rather than to genuine religion. This judgment is not borne out either by Gregory of Tours or by Fredegarius, the only reliable authors who have written on those times. His supposed irresolution was in fact Christian prudence, and his religious feelings were exactly those of Duke Chrodin briefly described a few pages back. Weiss and

---

* Alzog, vol. ii. p. 103.

Fiévée, the writers of the article *Gontran* in *Michaud's Biographie Universelle*, have given in detail the explanation of the apparent weakness of character of this excellent king, and showed that he could not act otherwise in the political circumstances in which he found himself involved. They have perfectly well understood the narratives of Gregory of Tours in his *History*, and of Fredegarius in his *Chronicon*.

As to his religious feelings, those authors who see everywhere superstition in the prodigalities bestowed on the Church by kings and rich men will do well to attend to the details previously given on the practical charity of Duke Chrodin. They will soon perceive that this is precisely the kind of religion inculcated by St. James in the celebrated passage which always bears repeating: "Religion clean and undefiled before God and the Father is this: to visit the fatherless and widows in their tribulations, and to keep one's self unspotted from this world."

This was the religion of Duke Chrodin and King Guntran among the Franks. The details given by Fredegarius particularly are convincing proofs of it. Guntran's character, in fact, takes almost the form of that of Louis IX. in France. Both are inscribed in the Calendar of Saints.

If Dagobert I. did not carry Christian holiness so high above human weakness, still he receives from Fredegarius such a testimony that few French monarchs at any time deserved it. "This king," he says, "was kind-hearted to his faithful subjects, but terrible to those guilty of perfidy; a lamb toward the well-intentioned, a lion toward the rebellious. . . . He filled the heart of the poor with joy by rendering them justice. And his justice was such a one as God Himself approves."

But it is proper to say a word in conclusion on the immense advantages acquired by the Christian Franks with regard to their influence over Europe through diplomacy and military organization. This, it is true, scarcely belongs to morals, yet it is strictly connected with them. During many ages the Franks had been hovering along the Rhine before Chlovis' conversion, almost unknown to Europe, and deprived even of the most simple chronicles; but a couple of hundred years later we see them in constant intercourse, either by war or diplomacy, with Spain, Italy, Germany, and even Constantinople. This contrast is a strong proof that the Christian religion had wrought among them a wonderful change. This appears chiefly in the reigns of Chlovis, Theodebert I., Guntran, and Dagobert; and as soon as the Merovingian line becomes unworthy of governing such a noble-spirited people as the Franks were, the Carlovingian dynasty steps on the stage of history, and furnishes directly in close succession such men as Charles Martel, Pepin the Short, and Charlemagne. Is not this a complete demonstration of the truth that whilst the Germanic nations who had embraced Arianism do not seem to have made any moral and social progress in renouncing their former idolatry, the Catholic nation of the Franks can be proudly pointed out as the irrefragable proof of the contrary.

As a last confirmation of the previous reflections it must be remarked that not only the worst Merovingian rulers had at least a conscience of which they were totally deprived when pagans; not only many Merovingian princes and kings gave proof of a genuine Christian spirit; but, in a third place, the bishops who then ruled the Church in the Frankish dominions were most of them men of the highest virtue and the most exalted character. A great number of instances of it might be brought out. The *Historia Francorum* and the *Liber de gloria Confessorum* (both celebrated works of Gregory of Tours) could furnish the materials of a large volume. Unfortunately time and space forbid it. The only thing possible is to maintain that the ecclesiastical history of the Merovingian period is one of the most glorious in the whole brilliant annals of the French church. Alzog condescends to say:*
" Dissension and debauchery were for many years after the death of Chlovis familiar to the house of the Merovingians; and those bishops who had the courage to rebuke the royal libertines were sent into exile." "These," he adds, "were frequently the ablest and most fearless defenders of the Church." It seems surprising that, writing as he did a "Manual of Church History," he has not at least given out some of their names. Nothing more was required for this than to go through the headings of many chapters in Gregory of Tours. This plain-speaking and forcible writer does not hesitate to call many of these bishops *saints;* for they were not only "able and fearless defenders of the Church," they were also holy men, and their names have been inscribed in the Roman Calendar. To supply this deficiency of Alzog it will

---

Christianity among the Franks, § 155.

be sufficient here to give a few words of Gregory quoted from a work of Paulinus now lost: "If you look at those holy Priests of the Lord—namely, Exsuperius of Toulouse, Simplicius of Vienna, Diogenianus of Albiga, Dynamius of Ecolisma, Venerandus of Auvergne, Alithius of Cahors, and at this time Pegasius of Petrocorium—you will find that wherever evil prevails there are directly most worthy prelates ready to guard the deposit of holiness, of faith, and of religion."

Turning from the Catholic nation of the Franks, it is proper to cast a last look on the other Arian tribes. The baneful heresy of Arius had invaded the whole barbarian world at the first epoch of their conversion. The Franks alone had adopted Catholicity. Soon it appeared, after the settlement of the Germans in southern Europe, that the whole of Spain, the whole of Mauritania and Numidia (which then belonged to Europe), a great part of northern Italy and of Switzerland, and finally what remained of the population of Germany after the emigration of so many tribes, were destined, in rejecting Christ's divinity, to remain rationalist philosophers rather than Christians. This was the aspect presented by the religious world in the fifth and a part of the sixth centuries.

Had there not been over those nations a powerful influence of divine grace, there would soon have been an end of Christianity; since if you take away the belief in the divinity of our Lord the whole supernatural character disappears from it, and there remains only a cold rationalism which cannot any more be called a religion. Moreover, in becoming Arians they had received nothing of the mild disposition inculcated by the doctrine of the Gospel. They had remained the bloodthirsty savages that they were when pagans, and it could not be said of them that Christianity had effected a complete moral change in the world.

But how strange! how unaccountable! A hundred and fifty years pass away, and Arianism has completely disappeared! France is not the only Catholic nation; Spain, Italy, Germany, enjoy that title with her; and Europe begins that long career of progress, civilization, and superiority over the whole world which must have come from her union with and subordination to Rome, since no other cause whatever can account for it.

How did it come about? How did Arianism perish in Europe? No one can say. The ecclesiastical history of Spain during the fifth and sixth centuries, ending in the seventeen celebrated Councils of Toledo, tells something of it for that noble country; but the recurrence of the same fact of conversion from Arianism among other nations is not explained by what took place in the Spanish peninsula. No historian has yet undertaken to unravel the mystery of that great providential event. It is a pregnant subject indeed for any Catholic writer who would have time and opportunities at his command. But in the midst of all this obscurity a great truth strikes the beholder: The barbarian world has been transfigured! Holiness is now possible, nay, easy; and that sweet Figure of the early Church in Jerusalem, in Alexandria, in Edessa, in Rome, will be again offered to the world in Great Britain, in the Frankish dominions, in the wilderness of the Asturias, in the forests of Saxony, nay, on the frozen shores of Scandinavia, Iceland, and Greenland.

3. *Holiness among the Anglo-Saxons in Great Britain—A Sufficient Test of the Previous Opinion.*

To describe the virtues practised among all the northern nations after their conversion to Christ would go far beyond our necessary limits. At this moment we are still occupied with those tribes which were Christianized after their migration from their native territory; and we will have, farther on, to speak, though briefly, of the settlement of Christianity in the whole territory of Germany itself and Scandinavia. On the outset of so long a task, it seems preferable to choose a single one of those races and examine to what degree of holiness they soon arrived, as a test for all of them; and it seems there are reasons for choosing the Anglo-Saxons in Great Britain preferably to all others. They were primitively, as Lingard says, "classed with the most barbarous of the nations which invaded and dismembered the Roman Empire." They for a long time opposed a sturdy resistance to the spread of Christianity among them, not only in Germany, but likewise in Great Britain after they had entirely devastated it, and established their coarse idolatry over the whole of it outside of Wales and Cornwall. With the exception of this last refuge of the Britons, there remained absolutely no Christians in the whole island when St. Austin arrived in Kent with his companions. After many years of labor the Roman missionaries sent by Pope Gregory had scarcely made any progress, when the holy work was undertaken in the north by the Irish monks of Lindisfarne led by St. Aidan. All the details of the difficulty peculiar to the conversion of the Saxon tribes can be read in the "Monks of the West," by Montalembert; and when studied with attention those details prove that it was a far more arduous task for the Church to subdue these barbarians, and inspire them with the mild manners of the Gospel, than the conversion of Greece or Rome had ever been. On this account, probably, rationalist writers have never pretended that these northern savages were naturally prepared to accept Christianity. It has been often insisted upon, though preposterously, that the Greek and Roman polytheists had been led by philosophy to embrace the doctrines of Christ. No one has maintained this opinion likewise for the Germans and Scandinavians. All admit that they could not feel any attraction for the maxims inculcated in the Sermon on the Mount; and the resistance of the Anglo-Saxons during so many years after their migration into Great Britain is perfectly in accordance with the well-known propensities of these wild tribes.

Had it not been the work of divine grace, and had they only consented for some natural reason or other to turn their back on the worship of Thor, Woden, and Freya, and to substitute Christ in their place, the aspect Christianity would have assumed among them would have been completely different from what has been seen of it in Jerusalem, Alexandria, Edessa, and Rome. Supposing only the natural order, the difference would have been absolute; and particularly the high purity of morals, so conspicuous in those celebrated Christian centres of Asia and Europe, would have been altogether impossible in the island of Great Britain, in the midst of the single Anglo-Saxon element. Still, it is easy to demonstrate that the same practices of the highest sanctity obtained at last universally among the posterity of the wildest among the Scandinavian nations in Great Britain. There is, fortunately in proof the unexceptionable testimony of Bede, himself an Anglo-Saxon, a man full of a just admiration for his own race after it had become Christian, whose declarations are as unanswerable as they are clear.

To feel the absolute strength of the demonstration the reader has first to imagine all the labor required of the first missionaries, and see how reluctantly all the various states of the Heptarchy had become Christian. Then he has to examine what was the real character of the religion they had successively embraced and they were at the time practising. A simple look given at the short statement of the previous labor and difficulty, such as it was, found in Alzog's "Manual of Church History," * will render the subsequent sketch of the result drawn by Bede very striking, and enable the modern mind to wonder at the height of virtue to which those uncouth barbarians had been at last raised. I merely refer the reader to the historical narrative of Alzog ; an abridgment of it would not suffice, and the whole narrative cannot be copied here.

As to Bede, to render more easy the present writer's labor, it just happens that the good Anglo-Saxon monk, at the end of his "Ecclesiastical History," gives a bird's-eye view of the whole Anglo-Saxon church on the very year he completed his great work ; that is, two hundred and eighty years after the first landing of the Angles on the island. It is proper to copy this, in order, as it were, to locate the details, full of the perfume of holiness, which must be forthcoming afterwards.

"At the present moment, Tatuini and Adulf preside as bishops over the churches of the Cantuarians [Canterbury]. Inguald is the bishop of the eastern Saxons [London and Westminster]. Aldbert and Hadalac are the bishops of East Anglia. Danihel and Forheri rule over the western Saxons. In the province of the Mercians Alduini is bishop ; and Walchstod in that part of Mercia which is beyond the Sabrina [Severn] toward the west. Wilfrid (not the great Wilfrid of York, who comes soon after) rules over the Huiccians; Cyniberet over Lindisfarne. The bishopric of the island of Vecta [probably Wight] is in the hands of Danihel. The southern Saxons [Sussex], having been already several years without a bishop, are under the administration of the prelate who rules over the western Saxons [Wessex]. All those southern provinces, as far as the Humber, are governed in temporal matters by their own kings, who are, however, subject to Ædibald, king of the Mercians. In the province of Northumbria, which is under the power of King Ceolwulf, there are four bishops, namely: Wilfrid, in the city of York ; Ediluald, in Lindisfarne; Acca, in Hagulstad ; Pecthelm, in the city called Casa Candida, which, owing to the large increase in the number of the

---

* Vol. ii. p. 50, *seq.*

faithful, has been lately made a bishop's see. The Pict nation, at peace now with the Angles, has received the truth, and now enjoys it in union with the universal Church. The Scots [Irish] who live in Britain are satisfied with the territory they occupy [Scotland], and have ceased to quarrel and plot." (Bede was never fond of them.) " Among the Angles, owing to the peaceful and serene time in which we live, a great number of the Northumbrians, both gentle and simple, prefer to consecrate themselves and their children to the monastic vows, and, having laid down their arms and subdued their warlike feelings, they consent to have their heads shaven, and thus humbly wear the monk's tonsure. What will be the end of all this the following centuries will show. This is the present state of the whole of Britain in this year, the two hundred and eighty-fifth since the advent of the Angles into it, and the seven hundred and thirty-first since the Incarnation of our Lord. In Whose name and eternal kingdom let the whole earth rejoice; and let Britain congratulate herself that she has received His faith ; and let the islands of the sea be glad above measure, and by their deeds bear testimony to His holiness."

Could there be found a more appropriate text to introduce the picture of Anglo-Saxon sanctity ? The only drawback is that the few examples we will be reduced to choose among so many contained in Bede's writings can scarcely give to the reader a satisfactory idea of it.

He has just told us that in Northumbria the Angles (a tribe of Anglo-Saxons) had at last embraced Christianity, and from ferocious warriors, such as they were, many of them had become humble monks. A remarkable instance of the various steps required to produce this extraordinary change of disposition is narrated at some length in the *Historia Ecclesiastica Gentis Anglorum:** Peada, the son and heir of the ferocious Penda, ruled over the Middle Angles. His father, king of Mercia, had been undoubtedly the most cruel and unrelenting enemy of the Northumbrians, chiefly of those who were Christians among them. He perished subsequently in a battle against Oswy, their king. Peada, however, his son, sues for the hand of Alchfleda, the daughter of Oswy. It was said that she had vowed her virginity to God. The king of the Northumbrians, nevertheless,

---

* Lib. iii. cap. 21.

does not refuse, under that pretext, to give his daughter to the young chieftain of the Middle Angles. He only protests that Alchfleda shall not marry him unless he becomes a Christian with all his nation. Perhaps he thought that Peada would not accept such a proposition as this. But the young king consents to be instructed; and when he hears that all Christians have received the promise of a heavenly kingdom, that all enjoy the hope of resurrection after death, and of a future immortality, he declares that he will embrace this doctrine though the king's daughter should not be given him in marriage; and instantly his nation is ready to receive baptism with him. Finan, an Irish bishop from Lindisfarne, administers the holy rite to Peada, to his nobles and his soldiers, and to all their servants, in a place called now Vaubottle (some say Walton).

This is a strange story which no rationalist will willingly admit, at least so far as the grounds and sincerity of the faith are concerned. But when several details of this extraordinary tale are known the doubts of the rationalists themselves may be somewhat shaken. Before this is done, however, the remainder of the story must be given out. Four priests are sent with Peada and his wife to administer the rites of religion to the new Christians of Middle Anglia. These four priests were Cedd or Cedda, Adda, Berti, and Diuma. The three first were Angles, the last an Hibernian. Their ministration was so successful that Diuma was consecrated their first bishop by Finan; and at his death Ceollach, another Irishman, succeeded him.

This first peculiarity of the story is a strong reason why this remarkable conversion should be thought real and sincere; and this must be seen somewhat in detail.

In reading Bede, not only on this occasion, but all along his "Ecclesiastical History," it is manifest that the great instrument used by the providence of God for bringing those wild tribes to the practice of genuine Christianity was the Irish race; namely, the monks from Lindisfarne or from Iona. Sometimes the missionaries came from Ireland itself, chiefly from the great bee-hive of Bangor. Bede, putting aside for a moment his Anglo-Saxon prejudices, admits ungrudgingly the Christian spirit of the Irish, who, in their island opening freely their schools to all strangers, cherished particularly the Anglo-Saxon youths, to whom they gave not only free education and free board in their houses, but furnished them wtih books and everything required for pursuing their studies. And he does not fail to often mention that if a large number of converts among the Anglo-Saxons entered also with spirit into the arduous labor of converting their countrymen, many of these had been educated in Ireland or in the Irish establishments of Iona and Lindisfarne. But all those who are acquainted with Montalembert's "Monks of the West" are fully aware of all these details.

If they are briefly copied here, it is not so much to refresh the reader's memory as to call his attention to the strong basis it gives to the opinion of those who firmly believe in the sincerity of the moral change effected among the savage conquerors of the Britons. The Irish are now acknowledged to have been the best missionaries of the eighth century. If so far we have not placed them in the glorious category of those nations who have honored the primitive Church by their holiness, it is simply for the reason that nobody can refuse them that precious prerogative. Our own ideas have never varied from those expressed in the *Irish Race*. They were from the beginning Christians of Christians, and have remained so to our very day. Ardent believers in the supernatural, they practised first what they preached; and they preached what they knew to be true. It was not an idle and unfounded superstition that they spread over the earth. In their primitive universities, which were merely convent schools, they made a deep study of the true foundations on which Christ's religion rests; and before they admitted any individual or nation to the rites of baptism, they first ascertained that' the catechumens were aware of all the dogmatic and moral obligations they contracted in becoming Christians. Because Bede, in briefly relating the chief events which illustrated the primitive history of the Anglo-Saxon church, is satisfied with the meagre sketch we have copied, the reader must not conclude that in the space of two or three days Bishop Finan had merely mumbled over them some prayers and recited some biblical stories to them, and then taking the Saxons by the hand had plunged them in the stream and forthwith declared them to be Christians.

Who was that Irish bishop Finan ? It is proper to look a little more closely to this. Bede has haply given in full his description and the high character of his practices and proceedings. It is important to quote the passage exactly: "Whatever I have so far written of this great man [*viri*] and of his works (never praising his wrong notions about the Pasch, nay, detesting them as I have done in the book which I have composed, *De Temporibus*) I have explained with the veracity of an historian. I have exactly described what he did, and praised all his acts which were worthy of praise, and which deserved to be recorded as likely to be useful to the reader, namely: the deep attention he paid to peace, charity, continence, and humility; his soul raised above anger and avarice, pride and vain-glory; the care he took to practise the divine precepts before teaching them to others; the long time he gave to reading and holy vigils; the authority worthy of a priest with which on one side he rebuked the proud and the powerful, and on the other the sweetness with which he consoled the afflicted and gave support and defence to the poor. This man—to embrace many things in a few words—took the greatest care not to neglect anything prescribed in the *gospels*, or in the books of the prophets or *apostles*, but, on the contrary, to fulfil to the letter and to the best of his ability everything contained therein. This we have heard from those who knew him well personally. For these reasons I have always cherished and loved this holy prelate, being sure that all this was highly pleasing to God."

This was the testimony which Bede gave to Finan, though the difference of practice of the Irish church with regard to the celebration of Easter deeply rankled in the bosom of the Anglo-Saxon monk. He had certainly no reason to praise Finan, except the necessity he felt of upholding the truth. But even a rationalist philosopher will admit that a minister of religion having constantly before his eyes not only the precepts of the Gospel, but particularly the injunctions of the apostles (St. Paul, for instance, when he describes his indefatigable labors to bring up all his proselytes to the perfection of Christ Himself, and when he so powerfully enjoins the same to his disciples Timothy or Titus), could not receive into the Church a king and his nation without due preparation and proper worthiness.

In a second place, to prove it still better, it is proper to examine who were the missionaries other than the Irish who labored likewise in the same field of Anglo-Saxon proselytism. We do not take into consideration those who came from Italy or France, with Austin at their head. Not that we feel inclined to depreciate their labors in this great cause, but only because they do not seem to enter so strikingly in our line of demonstration. These *missionaries other than the Irish* were Saxons of every type from Essex, Sussex, etc., or Angles from every district of the country which was then called Anglia. These last had been mostly, at first, educated in Irish monasteries, until the Angles began to have convents and houses of study of their own. They invariably, according to Bede, tried to reflect in their own persons the chief features of such men as Finan or, better still, of the great Aidan, the preceptor of Finan himself. The reader will find in the "Monks of the West" many precious details on Aidan.

It is but natural that, this general Irish impulse having been given to the whole body of missionaries, the same mode of action was adopted by all; and this will render easy of comprehension the holiness which soon began to sweeten with its perfume the entire nation all over Great Britain. We possess, fortunately, a good example of it in the biography of Cedd or Cedda, whose name has been merely mentioned in a previous paragraph. He was by birth an Angle from Mercia, and became one of the four first priests sent to the Middle Angles by Bishop Finan. In course of time, after having evangelized this nation, he was called by King Sigebert to Essex, where the Christian religion, after having been preached and established under Austin and his monks, had been openly repudiated by the people, who obliged Mellitus, their bishop, to fly away. He also found time to preach the Gospel in East Anglia. A part of his biography will be found in the "Monks of the West;" but the curious reader will prefer to read the longer account given of it by Bede. The principal event connected with it, and appropriate to our present object, is recorded at the end of the twenty-second chapter (Book III.), where it is said that "in a place called Tilabury [Tilbury] he brought together a swarm of Christ's servants, among whom he established the discipline of regular life, such as people still rude in manners could practise."

This was a purely Anglo-Saxon monastery; and as it is said that the discipline of regular life in it was "such as people still rude in manners could practise," it is proper to look more closely at this "monastic discipline," which was in truth the greatest means of conversion used among the Angles and Saxons of Great Britain, and which in a very short time brought them up to the height of Christian perfection.

It is to be remarked that all those tribes of Great Britain, when they successively became Christians, had no other means of judging what was the Gospel's morality than the private and public conduct of their teachers. In this they were a great deal more favored than their German brothers who invaded Gaul, Italy, and Spain. In these European continental countries, besides the admirable bishops and priests who undertook their conversion, there was a very corrupt mass of people who professed Christianity and lived, many of them, like pagans. This was a stumbling-block for many of those rude tribes. In Great Britain the Saxons and the Angles found the country occupied by the Britons; all Christians, it is true, but in whom the new-comers found nothing to admire, and whom they fell directly to destroy. Nearly as long as this process of destruction lasted the Anglo-Saxons continued in their gross idolatry without bestowing a thought on the religion of the inhabitants. When they successively were exhorted by men of God to renounce their idols and worship a meek Saviour, they saw no other Christians but the monks, since they had driven away the Britons. Moreover, they must have thought that the Britons had no religion whatever, because the infatuated Celts, even the bishops and priests among them, had obstinately refused to bring to the knowledge of the true God the ferocious enemies who appeared only bent on their destruction. The only Christians, therefore, to whom they paid attention were the monks.

It was probably for this reason that St. Austin and his companions produced directly such an effect on the pagan inhabitants of Kent. They were struck by those austere strangers. It is known, nevertheless, that the Italian and Gallican missionaries, after their first success, found a great inconstancy and mistrust in their proselytes; and that the work of conversion became remarkable and of a permanent character only from the time when the Irish monks from the north labored among them all over the country.

We must, consequently, examine who were those monks; what perfection they practised; what was the character of the religion they came to announce—a character undimmed by the loose conduct of other Christians known to the Saxons. Then it will be easy to see that the perfection of monastic life soon became the almost universal aim of those nations, bringing supernatural holiness in its train.

The high personal sanctity of the Celtic missionaries from Lindisfarne, Iona, or Bangor has been admirably described by Bede in many passages of his *Historia Ecclesiastica*. It was the exact reproduction of Columba's life so graphically sketched by Montalembert. St. Patrick had given to Ireland the first spectacle of it; and it is in trying to copy it that the Irish people became so thoroughly Christian. The daily deportment of Aidan, of Finan, of Diuma, and so many others in Great Britain, became for the Saxons of Northumbria, Mercia, and Anglia the pattern they tried to imitate; and soon the monastic discipline was embraced by these tribes; at first *such as suited their rude manners*, but before long with all the heroism of holiness and the sweetness of the tenderest piety. So that the marvels witnessed primitively in Jerusalem, Egypt, and Rome were reproduced on the Humber, the Severn, and the Tyne.

Lingard, in our opinion, is the author who has given the best description of it, in his " Antiquities of the Anglo-Saxon Church," from Bede and other approved sources; and our easy task will consist in giving the substance of his sketch, with some textual quotations. God's grace will directly shine as the source of their holiness.

After having spoken of the different religious orders introduced among the Anglo-Saxons, he remarks that if in the distribution of time, the arrangement of fasts and prayers, etc., they differed from each other, "they all equally adopted the three engagements which are still considered as essential to the monastic institute: (1) an unlimited submission to the lawful commands of their superiors; (2) a life of perpetual celibacy; (3) a voluntary renunciation of private property."

We see, consequently, among them the same means of sanctification which have been previously proved as existing in the primitive Church among a number of the faithful, and which have been called the true path of perfection, established from the beginning by our Saviour and His apostles. This is altogether the working of grace.

I. Lingard demonstrates that obedience was strictly enforced by all the rules of religious orders which in course of time flourished in Great Britain from the very time of the Heptarchy. He finds those rules not only in the houses of the Benedictine order, such as St. Dunstan promulgated them in the tenth century, but likewise in the much more ancient order of St. Columba, which we have seen radiating from Iona all over Scotland and North Britain. " The obedience," he says, "which is required must be prompt and cheerful; it comprises the decisions of the judgment no less than the resolves of the will. But it admits of one exception. When the commands of the superior are contrary to the law of God, the monk is exhorted to throw off the shackles of obedience and boldly to hazard the frowns of his abbot, rather than incur the displeasure of the Almighty."

In the *Historia Ecclesiastica* of Bede there are often praises bestowed on those who were faithful to follow their superiors' injunctions. Thus of Fursy, the celebrated Irish abbot, favored with so many visions and supernatural gifts, it is related that " from the time of his childhood he had bestowed much care on sacred studies [*lectionibus sacris*], and on all holy monastic practices; but *what above all distinguishes pious people, he was most attentive to do whatever had been commanded him.*" *

Of the necessity of a monk obeying God rather than his abbot, there is a splendid example contained in the twenty-fifth chapter of the same Book III. After a long discussion on the proper time for celebrating Easter between Colman, an Irish abbot and bishop, who held for Columba's computation, and the young priest Wilfrid, who became later on the celebrated archbishop of York, and held for Rome, the decision given by King Oswy, who presided at the meeting, is most remarkable. For, Colman having tried to prove his side of the question by the former command of Columba, the great founder of Iona and apostle of the Scots, and Wilfrid having shown from Scripture that the government of the Universal Church had been given by God to Peter of Rome and not to Columba of Iona, and consequently that the Pope, the successor of Peter, was the mouth-piece of God, whom all must obey rather than the most holy man, Oswy exclaimed: "I tell you that I for one cannot think of disobeying the man who holds the keys of heaven. As much as I can, I wish to follow strictly his orders rather than those of any other holy man; for fear that if I ever reach the gates of paradise, no one could be found there able to open them against the authority of the gate-keeper himself." And all abided by this decision.

II. The writer of the "Antiquities of the Anglo-Saxon Church," speaking of monastic chastity, remarks that "to the Saxons, in whom during the time of conquest the opportunity of gratification had strengthened the impulse of the passions, a life of chastity appeared the most arduous effort of human virtue. They revered its professors as

---

* Bede iii. 19.

beings of a nature in this respect superior to their own, and learned to esteem a religion which could elevate man so much above the influence of his inclinations." And he gives proofs of it of which it will be our pleasing duty to speak before long. But it is proper to quote a few lines of his further observations: "To secure the chastity of their disciples, the legislators of the monks had adopted the most effectual precautions which human ingenuity could devise. The necessity of mortifying every irregular inclination was inculcated both by precept and example. The sobriety of their meals and the meanness of their dress perpetually recalled to their minds that they had renounced the world and its concupiscence, and had dedicated their souls and bodies to the service of the Deity. They were commanded to sleep in the same room; and a lamp which was kept burning during the darkness of the night exposed the conduct of each individual to the eye of the Superior. The gates of the convent were shut against the intrusion of strangers. . . . To the precautions of prudence were added the motives of religion. The praises of chastity were sung by the poets and extolled by the preachers. Its votaries were taught to consider themselves as the 'immaculate spouses of the Lamb;' and to them was promised the transcendent reward which the book of the Apocalypse describes as reserved for those 'who have not been defiled with women.'"

III. With regard to the voluntary renunciation of poverty, we prefer to quote Bede alone, as he is profuse on the subject, and his writings are not so accessible to the ordinary reader as the work of Lingard. There is particularly a passage of the twenty-sixth chapter of the Third Book which proves that the voluntary poverty of the Irish monks from Iona and Lindisfarne was not confined to each individual religious, but that everything around them, in their houses, their churches, their corporate dealings with the highest personages of the Anglo-Saxon kingdoms, breathed the very spirit of poverty—or *parsimony*, as Bede himself calls it. He speaks again here of Colman, the pupil of Aidan :

"How far he, following the example of his holy predecessor, carried *parsimony* is proved by the buildings of the very monastery which he governed. When he left it with his companion, there were besides the church a very few houses of the poorest kind which can be called decent. They had no money whatever; only flocks of sheep. If rich people happened to give them money, they directly distributed it to the poor. Not even for the reception among them of great and powerful people was there any need of coin or of splendid halls. The highest men of the nation never came to their church but to pray or to hear the word of God. The king himself when he thought proper to visit them took with him five or six attendants only, and after having said his prayers in the church withdrew. If by chance some refreshment had to be offered to the royal party, it consisted of the simple fare of which the brethren usually partook; and the visitors expected nothing more. The only solicitude of those holy doctors was to serve God, not the world. They paid attention to the souls, not to the stomachs, of those who applied to them."

This description is perfect; and the reader must conclude that since the community itself presented such an admirable spectacle of holy poverty, each individual monk could not think of treating himself better than were treated the king and his high officials when they came to the convent. St. Francis of Assisium carried almost to perfection the same religious principle in a far subsequent age; and his order has been admired by the whole world for the love of poverty which the founder had so highly recommended by precept and example.

This meagre sketch of monastic perfection can scarcely be supposed adequate to the task of rendering easy of comprehension the immense influence it obtained over the Anglo-Saxon mind and heart. Still, our present object is to explain how the same kind of holiness soon spread among the whole people.

For this object Bede comes directly to our help; and from his words it is easy to understand how the popular enthusiasm which he briefly describes was natural and simple, and how it excited them to a holy emulation. This comes directly after the passage quoted above: "It can be easily conceived that the simple habit [or costume] of religion became at that time an object of veneration. So that wherever any priest or monk showed himself, all received him with joy as a servant of God. Nay, if they simply met any of them on the public road, they ran to him, and bending the head, they felt happy if he touched them with his hand or blessed them with his lips. On Sundays they came in crowds to the church or the monastery, not to receive any bodily help, but only to hear the word of God. In case any priest chanced to appear in a village, directly the villagers expected to hear from him the word of life. For the priests and clerics had no other object in entering any town except to preach, baptize, visit the sick; in a word, attend to the souls of the people. The religious were so perfectly free from any taint of avarice that it required a kind of force on the part of rich and great men to make them accept land or property of any kind for the construction of their monasteries."

What could be the moral effect produced by the sight of such a disinterested virtue, if not to impress the rude Anglo-Saxons with a high esteem and deep love for the religious life. And as this was the invariable spectacle displayed by all the ministers of God, the people could not have any other idea of religion than the practice of the same virtues. For those simple souls, to be a Christian consisted in imitating those who preached to them Christianity by example better still than by word of mouth. In their good moments, therefore, when the natural ferocity of their souls was gradually tamed by what they heard or saw, they must have felt a sweet inclination to enter into the same kind of life. They could not at once aspire to the highest perfection of monastic discipline. For this reason it has been seen that when the Angle Cedd or Cedda was sent by the Celtic bishop Finan to preach in Essex, this zealous apostle of Middle Anglia and Essex thought of founding a convent where the natives themselves should be received as monks. He was, however, prudent enough not to require of them more than they could bear; and he only bound them to a monastic discipline such as their rude *manners* could submit to: *in quantum rudes adhuc capere poterant.*

Soon, nevertheless, the doctrine of humility, forgiveness of injuries, necessity of arduous labor, springing from a supernatural source, became possible for them, together with obedience, chastity, and poverty. Nay, more: it was not only in the lower or middle ranks of life that the Saxons and the Angles presented themselves as candidates in the path of perfection. The great, the powerful, the rich, vied with their humble brethren in devotedness and self-sacrifice. So that it is in Catholic England more, perhaps, than anywhere else in the Church that kings and queens, noblemen and noblewomen of every degree, from the duke to the simple knight, adorned the cloister during the Anglo-Saxon period with the most exalted religious heroism. And several of them even, who for some political or civil motive could not enter openly a convent, practised in the world the virtues of the monk or nun, after having bound themselves by a secret but most precise vow.

Of all the examples of this extraordinary life given out by Bede, that of Edilthrida* is no doubt most remarkable; and as Lingard copies it almost textually from the good Anglo-Saxon monk, it is but natural to give a few paragraphs of it, and for those who have already read it it can bear repeating: "As they [the Saxons] became acquainted with the maxims of the Gospel, their veneration for this virtue [chastity] increased; and whoever compares the dissolute manners of the pagan Saxons with the severe celibacy of the monastic orders will be astonished at the immense number of male and female recluses who voluntarily embraced a life of perpetual continency. Nor was the pious enthusiasm confined within the walls of convents. There were many who, in the midst of courts and in the bonds of marriage, emulated the strict chastity of the cloister. Of these Edilthrida may be cited as a remarkable example. She was the daughter of Anna, the king of the East Angles, and at an early period of life had bound herself by a vow of virginity. But her secret wish was opposed by the policy of her friends, and she was compelled to marry Tondberet, Ealdorman of the Girvii. Her entreaties, however, moved the sympathy of her husband; and compassion, perhaps religion, prompted him to respect her chastity. At his death she retired to a solitary mansion in the unfrequented isle of Ely; but her relations invaded the tranquillity of her retreat, and offered her again in marriage to Egfrid, the son of the king of Northumbria, a prince who had scarcely reached his fourteenth year. Notwithstanding her tears, she was delivered to the care of his messengers and conducted, a reluctant victim, to the Northumbrian court. Her constancy, however, triumphed over his passion; and after preserving her virginity during the space of twelve years, amid the pleasures of the palace and the solicitations of her husband, she obtained his permission to take the veil in the monastery of Coldingham.

"Absence revived the affection of Egfrid. He repented of his consent; and was preparing to take her by force from her convent, when she escaped to her former residence in Ely. After a

---

* Book iv. c. 19.

certain period her reputation attracted round her a sisterhood of nuns, among whom she spent the remainder of her days in the practice of every monastic duty, and was always distinguished by her superior fervor and superior humility."

Particularly in the family of Oswy, king of Northumbria, several princesses adorned the Church by the practice of the most arduous virtue in conventual life. There was first the sister of Oswy himself, Ebba, who became abbess of the monastery of Coldingham whither Edilthrida had retired from the court of Egfrid. Ebba received often the visits of St. Cuthbert, who was at that time evangelizing that part of the country, and a holy friendship continued all their life to subsist between them. There was likewise Elfleda, the niece of both Oswald and Oswy, and the very sister of King Egfrid, whom St. Cuthbert honored also with his friendship. She had for him such a veneration that, having been attacked by a severe illness and the physicians being unable to relieve her, she protested that if some object belonging to Cuthbert was sent her she would soon recover her health. The holy man hearing of it sent her a linen belt, which being placed around her waist brought her in a few days to a full recovery.

Ealdormen, dukes, and kings followed the examples afforded them by their female relatives. But this is so well known that it would be useless to insist longer on it. Thus, during the Heptarchy the Saxons practised all the humble and lowly virtues recommended by our Lord in His Sermon on the Mount. A few years before the irruptions of the Danes, which interrupted for a while this period of holiness and peace, Bede could use the words we have previously quoted, but which it is good to repeat here:

"This is [was] the present state of the whole of Britain in the year, . . . the seven hundred and thirty-first since the Incarnation of our Lord. In Whose name and eternal kingdom let the whole earth rejoice; let Britain congratulate herself that she has received His faith, and let the islands of the sea be glad above measure, and by their deeds bear testimony to His holiness."

Bede, therefore, was the witness (in the midst of the profound peace which he proclaims as reigning around) that the eternal kingdom of God had been established in the whole earth, Britain sharing in it not only by the precious gift of faith which she had received, but moreover by the holiness of her deeds, in which consists the true kingdom of God on earth.

4. *A Few Words on the Conversion of the Germans to Christianity.*

I. The previous narrative was intended as a test for the German and Scandinavian nations in general, particularly for those who were converted in consequence of their migration to other countries in which they met face to face the Christian religion and its ministers. The gradual steps by which the Saxons were brought in Great Britain from the coarsest paganism and the most ferocious manners to the practice of the highest Christian virtues suffice as an example to demonstrate the same for all the other tribes natives of the north of Europe. Those of them who passed first through Arianism, like the Vandals, have been cited as a proof that a fundamentally heretical Christianity such as Arianism was could not produce any great moral change in those nations as long as they remained Arian. But as soon as in the seventh century they unaccountably, as it were, professed to believe in Christ's divinity, and returned to the bosom of Catholicism, the road to holiness was immediately opened before them. This was remarkable for the Burgundians in Gaul and the Visigoths in Spain. It is impossible not to see in these historical facts the working of a powerful cause operating unceasingly in the bosom of the Catholic Church for the incessant production of fruits of holiness, all of them bearing the same character and reproducing the same type on the frozen shores of Scandinavia and in the burning clime of Egypt.

Who will refuse to acknowledge the finger of God in the stupendous concourse of so many events affecting nations of completely dissimilar characters, still giving to all of them the same form of sanctity? No one can suppose there could be any cause for it except the one assigned by St. Paul in the magnificent twelfth chapter of the first Epistle to the Corinthians, where he says: "There are diversities of graces, but the same Spirit; and there are diversities of ministries, but the same Lord. . . . All these things one and the same Spirit worketh, dividing to every one according as He will. For as the body is one and hath many members; and all the members of the body, whereas they are many, yet are one body; so also is Christ. For in one Spirit were we all baptized into one body; whether Jews or gentile, whether bond or free; and in one Spirit we all have been made to drink."

Turn as they may, reflect and think and write as they can, the rationalists will never be able to find as good a reason of the moral sameness of the highest type of virtue existing in all nations after their conversion to Christianity as this one; namely, It is the same God, the same Holy Spirit, the same Christ, who animates the whole body. Therefore the holiness produced by the effusion of this Holy Spirit must be of the same kind in all nations, however different they may have been originally in character, aspirations, habits, and customs. But because this great universal source of a sanctity alike in them all is no other than God Himself, it is consequently altogether supernatural; and it would be absolutely superfluous to look for it in the numerous catalogue of natural, rational, purely human and worldly causes.

In these considerations the facts adduced in proof were naturally confined to the primitive ages of the Church. It will soon be proved that the following centuries do not offer to the pen of the historian a different result. The same holiness has existed and shall continue forever to exist in the Church. If human instruments were used and human means adopted, they were absolutely inadequate to produce a general result, universal in its extent and bearing the same character in the most dissimilar nations, except through the Holy Spirit's inspiration.

II. But at this moment we must examine, very briefly indeed, the nations which remained in Germany after the powerful migrations of the fifth, sixth, and seventh centuries. Only a few words can be said on a subject naturally immense. But at least the circle prescribed to our inquiry will have been completed, and no link will be missed in the chain.

The irruptions of the German races into the Roman Empire were not caused chiefly, as has been pretended, by a desire of settling in more favored countries. A *barbarian* tribe has seldom been prompted to migrate by such a motive as this. It is now proved that if the whole of Germany threw itself over Gaul, Spain, and Italy in the centuries following the fourth, it was mainly because they were driven away from their own territory by more powerful nations coming from eastern Europe or Asia, such as the Huns, the Slavs, or the Sarmatians.

After the violent passage of so many hostile armies over that devoted part of Europe, Germany remained exhausted and at the mercy of any one powerful enough to occupy and colonize it. Whoever has read even cursorily the *History of the Huns*, by De Guignes, understands perfectly well the ground over which were undertaken the glorious missions of the Anglo-Saxon monks of Great Britain, and of the Irish missionaries of the Columban order, as they have been called by Montalembert. The gifted author of the "Monks of the West" has given in its pages such a brilliant individuality to the heroic agency of the great Columbanus that the Columban order of monks has become a fact which all must now admit. When they began their work of zeal in Germany in the seventh century, together with the missionaries led by Willibrord and Winfried from Anglo-Saxon England, who followed them in the eighth, Germany and Gaul were rapidly returning to their primitive savage state. The Merovingians in Gaul and the petty princes of Frisia and Thuringia in Germany were constantly at war with each other; and the Christianity which had already flourished to a certain extent in those countries had nearly disappeared, as well as agriculture and industry.

This must be insisted upon; for it must be admitted that the apostolic labors of the holy men who had previously preached the Gospel along the Rhone, the Rhine, and the Danube, as well as in the mountains of Switzerland and the Tyrol, had been nearly swept away by the devastating hordes which had ravaged those regions of central Europe from the fifth to the seventh century. Alzog acknowledges it when he says that "no full, satisfactory, and precise account of the conversion of the German people exists of a date anterior to the seventh century." Consequently the bishoprics established in Helvetia, in Rhætia, in Württemberg, etc., some of which dated from the second or third age, can scarcely be considered as belonging to the ecclesiastical history of Germany. And a new effort was to be made to plant again the Christian religion in those countries. This history begins, in fact, by the apostleship of Columbanus and Gall his disciple in Burgundy, Switzerland, and Upper Italy, as well as by the labors of Willibrord and Winfried in Frisia, Thuringia, Hesse, and other Germanic countries. Winfried particularly, better known as Boniface, is justly considered as the first apostle of those vast regions which extend north as far as Scandinavia.

Not only the previous Christian faith which a great part of those countries had professed, chiefly along the Upper Rhone, the Rhine, and the Danube, had nearly perished; but it would have been almost impossible for the new apostles to make any progress all over that vast territory, owing to the ferocity of the new inhabitants, had it not been for the Merovingian kings, who ruled over a great part of it when Columbanus and his companions came from Ireland, and also on account of the first Carlovingian rulers, who were in possession of that country at the arrival of Willibrord and Winfried from England. The whole territory was then occupied by wild tribes scarcely ever known before, all of them pagan and of a most ferocious character, such as the Frisians, Turingians, Hessians, Saxons, etc., to whom a religion was openly offered for acceptance which was altogether opposed to their instincts, and which they did not see at work around them. The missionaries had to go boldly to them, since these tribes did not intend to go farther south to the only countries in which Christians could be found. Thus a great number of those zealous messengers of God were destined to receive at the hands of these barbarians the crown of martyrdom as the most precious reward of their labors. These countries offer otherwise an almost unexplored field which few historians have labored to glean over.

The Irish missionaries—Columbanus, Gall, and their companions—met even with a difficulty which probably they had not expected. If some Merovingian rulers like the good King Guntran protected them effectually, others, the degenerate sons of the first Frankish Christian kings, persecuted them; and Columbanus himself was temporarily driven away from the country by Thierry of Austrasia.

The Carlovingians, however, became far more generous protectors of the Church than the Merovingians had been; and from Pepin of Heristal down to Charlemagne they all took the liveliest interest in the conversion of the northern tribes. But the best proof which can be afforded of the difficulty of the enterprise is that after many efforts had been made to civilize them through Christianity, by means of persuasion, it was found impossible to do so for some of them at least. Open coercion was adopted for that purpose only after all other means had failed with regard to the Saxons. Alzog disapproves of it; and all must admit that simple persuasion was the only natural and Christian way. But if the question is presented under another form, and reduced to inquire which was preferable, either to leave those tribes to enjoy a freedom necessarily accompanied with lawlessness, ferocity, and constant danger to their neighbors, or to bind them down to milder manners by the forced adoption of Christianity, perhaps the *policy* of Charlemagne toward the Saxons will not appear worthy of condemnation and irreconcilable with Christian ethics. But it was, after all, a State policy in which the Church was not concerned.

The author of the "Manual of Universal Church History" gives a succinct account of the chief *difficulties* which stood in the way of the conversion of German tribes. "The difficulties were," he says, "of a character peculiar to the people, and more numerous and appalling than those of any other nation. Among these were the deadly feuds and hereditary hatred of the various tribes; the apprehension, not unfrequently well founded, that foreign missionaries might disguise hostile intentions under pretence of a holy zeal; their aversion to everything Roman—a name which they associated with all that is vile and base; and, finally, their peculiar notions of morality and personal liberty. They carried their notions of personal liberty to such a length that they esteemed the privilege of bearing arms the most sacred of human rights, and felt bound, as a matter of honor, to take a bloody revenge on any one who should give them offence. Hence they could not comprehend and fully appreciate how One who suffered patiently and met death willingly and without resistance, could become the Saviour of mankind. The conversion of Germany was, therefore, a labor requiring time and patience, accompanied wih many difficulties and doubtful struggles, and was not brought to a successful issue till near the close of the eighth century."

Nay, it might be properly maintained that it would never have reached a "successful issue" if God had not by His grace changed the heart of these barbarians, and obtained at last from them that they should bow humbly under the yoke of the Gospel.

Under the Merovingian kings of Gaul, the missionaries who labored in France and Germany were chiefly Irish and Scotch. Besides Columbanus and Gall, whose names have already been mentioned, it is proper to glance a moment at several others. There was Fridolin, renowned all over Germany even at the present day. An Irishman by birth, he spent several years at Poitiers near the tomb of St. Hilary. "But in the year 511," says Alzog, "he arrived on the banks of the Upper Rhine, and founded at Sackingen [a town situated on an island of that river above

Basle] a nunnery and monastery of monks." From that retreat he visited all the tribes living on both banks of the Rhine.

Later than Fridolin, St. Trudpert evangelized the country around Freyburg in Breisgau as far as Schutern. Bishop Killian and his companions, Colman and Totnan, preached in Franconia. Together with Columbanus and Gall, a number of Irish missionaries, whose names have not been preserved, labored either in Burgundy, around the celebrated monastery of Luxueil founded by them, or in Helvetia and Allemania, which St. Gall entirely converted before his death in 646.

Bavaria, called at that time Noricum and Vindelicia, owed its conversion mainly to Frankish missionaries, the chief one among them being Emmeram of Poitiers.

But the man to whom after God was due the Christianization of the Germans was the Anglo-Saxon priest Winfried, better known as St. Boniface. Many of those who accompanied and helped him came likewise from Great Britain; and their labors began when the last Merovingian kings were giving way to the Carlovingians and Charles Martel was *de facto* king of the French. Boniface presented himself to Charles with letters' from the Pope in 723; and from that moment he began those arduous labors which have been fully described in several complete biographies written both in Latin and German.

It would be impossible to enter here into details, however important and interesting they might be. The Frisians were the first nation to which he carried the Gospel; and this took place before his first interview with Charles Martel. From Frisia he passed over to Thuringia and Hesse, where he received into the Church the princes Dierolf and Detdig, together with many thousands of the pagan inhabitants in the surrounding countries.

Then seeing the vast field which opened before him, he directly thought of founding monasteries and nunneries, as the best means of spreading holiness and light over an immense region given over so far to superstition and darkness. He called on his Anglo-Saxon friends for that purpose; and, says Alzog, "of those who answered his call, Burchard, Lullas, Willibald, his brother Wunibald, and Wita are the best known. Many female religious also came over, among whom were the learned Anigilde and her daughter Berathgit, Cunitrude, and Thecla, who belonged to the nunneries of Kitzingen and Ochsenfurt, on the Main; Lioba, who was at Bischofsheim, on the banks of the Tauber; and Walpurgis, at Heidenheim in the Saulafield."

The intention cannot be to go through the whole life of this great man, who died at last a martyr at the hands of barbarous, unconverted Frisians. But he left at his death the Church firmly established all over Germany. Most of the celebrated bishoprics which in the course of the following ages formed the main web of Church history in the north of Europe had been founded by him, or through his instrumentality; particularly those of Mentz, Wurtzburg, Eichstadt, Baraburg, Erfurt, Utrecht, Tongres, Cologne, Worms, and Spire.

It would also be too long to speak in detail of the monasteries which were then built in every part of the country. It must suffice to mention that of Fulda, "which when completed," says Alzog, "was placed under the charge of Sturm, the most beloved of Boniface's disciples. Like St. Gall and Reichenau, Fulda was for a long time the nursery in which the bishops of Germany were educated and trained, and the home of the arts and sciences."

It would be but a repetition of what has been said of Anglo-Saxon England, both as to the obstacles it offered to conversion and the height of holiness it at last attained, to rehearse again the various steps through which those wild nations along the Rhine, the Danube, the Elbe, and the shores of the Baltic Sea, passed gradually from the rankest idolatry and the coarsest customs of barbarism to ordinary Christian life at first, and finally to the practice of the virtues which our Lord had openly proclaimed in His Sermon on the Mount.

It is particularly known to what degree the Saxons carried at first their opposition to Christianity. It is likewise known that if at various times they appeared to give way to conviction after the severe defeats inflicted on them by the Carlovingian kings, it was but a feint on their part, and on the other side "the Franks," says Alzog, "*forced* them to profess Christianity and receive baptism."

It is the only time this happened during the whole history of the Church; and it could not be expected that holiness should be established among the Saxons by such measures as these. This strange fact must be regarded as a simple expedient of policy on the part of the Carlovingian kings, in which the Church could take no part. Consequently it is not surprising to hear from Alzog that "this policy was continued [by Charlemagne alone] without interruption and with untiring perseverance for a period of thirty-three years, and *was uniformly resisted with the most hearty and determined obstinacy.*" It was not, therefore, by Charlemagne's armies that the Saxons were converted. The more severely they were defeated the more obstinate they remained, even when they appeared to yield and consented to be baptized.

Their conversion began only after all these attempts had been made in vain; and it was chiefly due to St. Ansgar, archbishop of Hamburg, to whom it was, as Alzog says, "a work of love." With Ansgar the bishops of Osnabruck, Paderborn, Minden, and Verden labored assiduously with the same ardor; and at last the Saxons were converted as all the other barbarian nations of the north have been before or since, by God's grace.

Details cannot be given here. They are found, however, in all ecclesiastical histories. The only thing of importance is to merely mention the remarkable degree of holiness introduced among all those nations of Bavaria, Austria, Saxony, and the Baltic coast. Nay, there does not seem to be any need of describing it at this moment. For it culminated in Germany and France under Charlemagne and his successors. Every one is aware that this was precisely the period of history known as the Middle Ages. The following chapter will be entirely devoted to the description of that peculiar piety and exquisite sanctity which has always been the characteristic mark of the "ages of faith." If there are shadows in the picture, they will not be of such character as to render that name unsuitable; and it will be easy to prove that with all possible shadows and drawbacks they cannot be called "dark ages."

CHAPTER VI.

CHRISTIAN HOLINESS DURING THE MIDDLE AGES.

1. *Difference of Opinion on the Subject.*

THE appreciation of the middle ages, so conflicting and contradictory in our day, may refer to government, polity, customs, ideas, science and art; what is called civilization, and public opinion may more or less vary on these various subjects. But this cannot be the object of inquiry at the present moment. There is only question here of the morality prevailing at that epoch; and many authors in treating of it fall into the mistake of bringing together subjects of a quite different nature like those just mentioned; whence arises an unlucky confusion, the cause of many false views.

Writing simply on the Church's holiness, we must strictly confine the present investigation to facts bearing on Christian ethics; but even on this very subject there is a total disagreement between Protestant and rationalistic writers on the one side and Catholic authors on the other. Luther, Calvin, and in general all the prime movers in the sixteenth century's heresies, openly accused the whole Church of having fallen before their time into the grossest immorality. Their followers have continued to this day repeating their assertions; and the middle ages have invariably been represented by them as dark, corrupt, abominable. In the rationalistic camp the same has likewise in the main been the case till very recently, when this historical subject has been studied with more impartiality and attention. Alzog in the second volume of his "Manual of History" quotes passages from Galle, Jacob Grimm, Daniel, Bohmer, and Kraus (American edition, *sub initio*), which prove a great change of opinion outside of the Catholic Church.

The perversion of history on this important question had been formerly so complete that a large class even of Catholic writers had adopted something akin to Protestant views, chiefly in France, owing no doubt to Gallican principles. M. de Montalembert justly says on this subject in the introduction to his "Monks of the West:" "The clergy itself [in France] felt ashamed of those ages, which its own writers called *barbarous*, and during which, nevertheless, the Church had been so powerful and prosperous, so free and respected, so much obeyed and loved. Yes, historical ignorance—or, if you prefer, thoughtlessness—had so far invaded the sanctuary itself that the clergy, exclusively preoccupied with the frailties and scandals of those times which we willingly acknowledge, did not hesitate to sacrifice the purest glories of its Order to the dislikes and prejudices of worldlings. Yes, it must be said, in order to show the progress we have lately made, that with regard to the most heroic conflicts of the Church we have [in France] during two centuries accepted on trust the open lies of our enemies and persecutors, and we have re-echoed them. Many have been the Christians, and among them priests and Catholic doctors, who, taking side with the strongest in those former conflicts, have openly advocated the bad against the good cause, and described in their books lay tyranny as being the innocent victim of the Church. Scarcely a hundred years have passed since French bishops in their circulars expressed the wish to see 'the plots of Gregory VII. buried in an eternal oblivion'! Fleury, so long our oracle in point of ecclesiastical history, prostituted his extensive learning and his undeniable talent to the service of Rome's enemies; and when he came to write of the time which elapsed from St. Benedict to St. Bernard, he dared indite these very words: *the golden age of the Church is now gone!*"

It is doubtful if a single Catholic writer would in our day coincide in the least with those French authors of the last two centuries. Discoveries have been made in the field of history which preclude the possibility of such an extraordinary blindness. And it is scarcely conceivable for us that men who professed to believe that the Church is "the kingdom of God," that not only she has received the promise of inerrancy in point of faith, but likewise the privilege of purity in morals (such as becomes the Bride of Christ), still imagined that there was a time when both these gifts had been well-nigh lost by her. To us devolves at this moment the grateful task of proving that not only this was not the case, but that, on the contrary, the middle ages were principally a period of sanctity in spite of all the moral drawbacks of that epoch.

M. de Montalembert says again with justice: "This new and

salutary impulse given to history which the last forty years have witnessed, and which has so much benefited the Church, was not the work of clergymen. They have rather followed than inspired this moral rehabilitation. But it has been commenced by Protestants [in France, M. Guizot; in Germany, John von Müller, Voight Leo, Hurter, and both Menzels]; it has been helped by neutrals sometimes by open adversaries; it has been chiefly continued and carried on by Catholic laymen" (and here he quotes K. Digby the author of "Ages of Faith").

Since this was written by Montalembert more has been found out than even he believed. For after having said, a little farther on, that "since the first great defiance thrown down by the establishment of Christianity to the triumph of evil in the world, never perhaps has the empire of the devil been so much shaken and contested" as in the middle ages, he adds, nevertheless: "They have been called the ages of faith, and they have been justly so called, for faith was then more supreme than at any other epoch of history. But there we must stop. This is much, but it is enough for the truth. We cannot venture to maintain that *virtue and happiness* have been throughout these ages on a level with faith." Thus he himself believed there were dark shadows in those times, in point of morality.

Perhaps indeed virtue and happiness at that epoch have not been quite *on a level with faith*. But they have been superior to whatever was witnessed in all Europe before or after. This is certain, and this begins to be known to impartial students of the past. But it cannot yet at this moment be a subject of discussion. It must result from the facts themselves, and these will soon be forthcoming.

Though, however, many prejudices against the mediæval Church have so far given way before the light of history, the whole truth is still far from being known on account of the extraordinary delusion created in all classes of society by the ardent hatred of the first reformers against Catholicity. And this great cause of all modern prejudices must be examined somewhat attentively, to know better the true source of the fallacy, and to render more striking the intended demonstration when it will be time to furnish it.

Christ had plainly spoken when He announced the Church's perpetuity. He clearly foretold, it is true, there would be scarce dals. Still, the Church was never to perish, and, to use His own expression, "the gates of hell should not prevail against it." Consequently, to secure its permanency, there would forever remain in it an interior principle of purification, renovation—*reformation*, to employ the term generally used. To declare that the Church had altogether disappeared, and that there was need of building up a new one from without, was not only blasphemous, as being an open contradiction given to Christ, but it was absolutely senseless and absurd, since it would have required in the new *reformers* an authority for rebuilding it equal to that of the Son of God. Had the *reformers* been consistent, they would have felt bound to put forth such an extravagant claim. They did not dare openly so to do; still, they maintained that they had actually received a mission from heaven to that effect. They were, therefore, in fact the apostles of an altogether new gospel, since very soon indeed in tracing up the source of the corruptions of which they complained, they had to go up as far as the first apostles themselves. Did not Luther declare that the Epistle of James was an epistle of straw?

No separatists had ever before assumed such pretensions as these. In the eyes of former heretics the Church's history previous to their unfortunate separation was their own church history; and they treated with reverence everything connected with ancient traditions and old records. But the position taken by the Protestants from the very start made it a necessity for them to depreciate everything anterior to them. Whenever there had been, since the beginning of Christianity, any antagonism between two sets whatever of doctrines, opinions, or customs, it had never amounted to the total opposition which immediately appeared between the new Protestant faith and that of the middle ages. This opposition was as strongly marked as that which exists between light and darkness. Every one can judge of it by comparing what the Christians of the middle ages believed with the pretended faith imposed by the new teachers. Consequently these new teachers could not but hate and despise the epoch that had just preceded them; and the most violent abuse was the best expression of that hatred and contempt. But why did the whole world admit it in the wake of the reformers? Why did the middle ages become at once almost infamous? It would be long and difficult to state all the reasons there were for this. It will be sufficient to mention briefly the chief ones.

There had been real abuses in the Church; and these were taken advantage of to prejudice a great number of men against an age which few, if any, had known in its purity. M. de Montalembert again points out some of those objections: "A thousand incontrovertible witnesses rise up to recall the general insecurity (at that time), the too frequent triumphs of violence, iniquity, cruelty, deceit, sometimes even of refined depravity; they seem to demonstrate that the human and even diabolical element then reasserted, only too strongly, their ascendency in the world. By the side of the opened heavens, hell always appeared; and in juxtaposition with those prodigies of sanctity, which are so rare at other times, were to be found ruffians scarcely inferior to those Roman emperors whom Bossuet calls 'monsters of the human race.'

"The Church, which is always influenced up to a certain point by contemporary civilization, allowed to exist many abuses and scandals the very idea of which would to-day horrify both her subjects and her enemies. They proceeded sometimes from that corruption which is inseparable from the exercise of great power and the possession of great wealth; sometimes, and most frequently, from the invasion of the lay spirit and temporal power. Yes, cupidity, violence, and debauchery rebelled often, and with success, against the injunctions of the Gospel, even among its own ministers; they often infected the organs of the very law which had been intended for their repression. We can and must acknowledge it without fear, because all these excesses were redeemed by marvels of self-denial, penitence, and charity," etc.

This being undoubtedly true, it is not difficult to imagine how the reformers could not only persuade their own followers that those ages had been profoundly corrupt, but likewise suggest to many Catholics doubts, at least, as to the reality of the holiness which then prevailed. These doubts would soon give place to a certainty as to the existence of universal depravity. The only process required for this was to throw in the shade the innumerable proofs of the sanctity of millions living at that time, and to give prominence to the monstrous corruption of a few desperate characters of whom alone the new historians would speak. And this policy was certainly adopted by Protestant ecclesiastical writers from the beginning, as the "Centuries of Magdeburg" abundantly prove. It is surprising that for a long time the

Catholic controversialists scarcely perceived the importance of remonstrating against this most unfair proceeding. Baronius, in the preface to his "Annals," complains that he was the first to undertake it on a large scale, and in his time the evil had fearfully spread. The first page of his great work shows how unblushing was the partiality exhibited, particularly by the Centuriators of Magdeburg, though they always affected a great show of veracity. Many unwary Catholics, no doubt, imbibed the tempting poison, and even in the true Church the traducers of the morality of the middle ages became numerous.

To fully understand the fatal effect this must have produced on so important a subject, one has only to remember what a single man, Pascal, did for the defamation of the Jesuits, his enemies. His "Provincial Letters" are now well known, and acknowledged as being full of calumnies, slanders at least, and unjust aspersions. Still, on some minor points, as, for instance, the *morale relachée* of two or three casuists, there is some truth, since their works have been censured by the Holy See. And this has sufficed to hoodwink millions of men who from that time to this have considered the majority of the members of the Society of Jesus as dangerous men, morally fatal to those simple souls who placed themselves under their direction. The Protestant historians of Magdeburg had given the first example of these treacherous tactics.

A second cause which powerfully contributed to the same result was the deleterious action of the numerous body of men called *humanists*, which was brought into existence by what has been called the revival of learning. Even before Protestantism arose they had already predisposed a great number of people against the pretended rudeness, nay, grossness and vulgarity of the times which immediately preceded them. Much has been written of late concerning their character and influence over a great part of Europe. Though admired by many modern writers, they have been openly accused by others of wishing to restore paganism; and several facts mentioned by Cantù in his *Reforma in Italia* seem to prove it for a few of them. In general, however, they were simply, in our opinion, conceited pedants, most fastidious in their classical taste, extremely narrow in their petty vanity, and altogether incapable of judging rightly of their immediate predecessors, whom they despised and abused. They must have been considered great oddities by the simple men by whom they were still surrounded, because the middle ages were yet in full vigor when they appeared. Imagine a class of literati, bookworms, searchers after old Greek and Latin manuscripts, worshippers of the exquisite taste of Greece and Rome, and ardent revilers of Gothic art and literature. For them purity of style had replaced purity of morals; for it is unfortunately proved that the majority of them were fearfully corrupt, if one can judge from their habitual thoughts and many productions of their pen. Their Catholic faith, consequently, hung rather loosely on their shoulders, though only few of them ever thought of *reviving* paganism and actually worshipping Jove and Athene. The discovery of some old parchment, perhaps on cookery or gymnastics, which was thought to have been lost and suddenly came to light was far more interesting to them than the preservation of many useful arts openly practised during the middle ages, which they allowed, about that time, to perish; so that they are now perfect enigmas, or at least puzzles. Their inner life was spent among authors two thousand years old or more, and they profoundly despised the many great and noble things they saw around them. The grand cathedrals, just finished in their day; the proud Gothic castles; the beautiful and artistic bridges over rivers and lakes; the solid and brilliant furniture of the houses; the rich and substantial dresses of lords and ladies, burghers and simple citizens, were in their eyes full of bad taste, because they were not constructed on the models of the four old orders of architecture, nor copied from classic paintings, nor made on the pattern of Etruscan vases, Greek tripods, and Roman lamps. If so they judged and misjudged in point of art, they were not proof against misjudgment in point of morals and holiness. The stern stoicism of Cato or Thraseas was a far higher virtue in their eyes than the valor of the crusader, the devotedness of the Christian nun, and the austerity of the Christian monk. There is no need of expatiating any longer on the subject. It must be admitted by all impartial thinkers that they were not justified in despising the artless candor and modest purity so prevalent even in their time. Still, they were instrumental in passing on to us a false judgment on those high themes.

But the reformers, when they came, eagerly welcomed to their bosom that humanists' mania for pure style, of which they had in general rather a small share. Who can admire the refined taste of Luther in his Latin or of Beza in his Greek? Still it was a great help to prop up their own hatred of Catholic morality by the undisguised contempt the humanists had felt for the same. Every one must now recognize the combined effect of both to the detriment of what began to be called the *Dark Ages.* Morality, according to them, must have been at a very low ebb, since people had then so different a look from the proud Roman or the sprightly Hellene. And this opinion became in course of time more confirmed still by the care each European nation took to conform its arts, its literature, its ordinary life to the former classic model, and to leave mediæval patterns in the background.

A third reason must be briefly mentioned to explain the universality of the opinion adverse to the cause herein advocated by us. This is nothing else than the weakening of faith, which soon became a source of almost complete estrangement between modern times and the preceding centuries. Everybody is aware that antagonism in point of art and literature between various epochs of history is the greatest source of unreliable judgments from the one to the other. The middle ages were principally ages of faith. Our own is chiefly an epoch of disbelief. All the motives which so powerfully acted on the Europeans of those times appear delusions and childish errors to the men of our own. The sanctity which then prevailed is called a vain superstition, and the biographies of the greatest saints living at that epoch are supposed to be legends, or rather ridiculous tales. It is not possible to expect a fair appreciation when there is such a difference between the ideas and aims of both periods. This could be indefinitely developed; it is sufficient to leave it to the reflections of the reader. But evidently no one need be surprised that the opinions of our contemporaries differ so widely on the subject. There remains only to discuss a simple question, namely: Was it true virtue which then governed society, or rather superstition, error, nay, brutality and vice?

2. *The First Period of the Middle Ages Consisted on the part of the Church in a Rude Training of Wild Tribes. Hence Violence, Crime, Immorality could still be Expected from the Greatest Number. The Ages of Faith had not Really Commenced.*

In speaking of the Anglo-Saxons in Great Britain, the fact has been pointed out of a great difference between the first period of their ecclesiastical history and that which followed. Directly after their conversion the immorality and cruelty they had brought with their paganism from Scandinavia, and which obtained among them the whole time they remained pagan in their new country, frequently reappeared in their manners. They were rude—*rudes*—even in their first monasteries. Particularly their warfare continued to be cruel and barbarous.

This was unavoidable, and proves only the indefatigable care taken by the Church in forming her children on Christ's pattern by slow beginnings and with an accommodating spirit. She never was disheartened by the arduous labor required for the protracted education of some of the rudest tribes known to history, as were the Anglo-Saxons. The same happened for all the German, Sarmatian, and Hunnic nations which invaded the south of Europe from the fifth century to the tenth. And this has been precisely the great mine of objections worked out by the Church's accusers.

Yet it is evident, when the whole history of those times is examined, that the Church was constantly hard at work to prevent frightful evils before they occurred, or to heal the wounds inflicted on society, after they had suddenly burst out and horrified mankind. Because the bishops never despaired of those they were training, and because, after a long life of exhortation, instruction, threats, and correction, each of them often saw his efforts reduced to naught by the obstinacy and brutishness of barbarians, it has been concluded that this very obstinacy was the result of the religion itself in which they were instructed. At least the reflection is often made that this was the Christianity of those days, and this suffices for drawing the conclusion that *such a Christianity was bad.* It is important to insist also on the difficult task imposed not only on bishops, but likewise on innumerable missionaries, Gallo-Roman, Irish, English, and Gallo-Celtic, who stood face to face, on the coming of these hordes from the north, with no other weapon than a crucifix, and no other means of persuasion than God's word. It will then be easily understood that this period of transition must necessarily have been an epoch of violence or crime, and cannot be properly included among the ages of faith, which began undoubtedly afterwards; and that the disorders of those times cannot be attributed to the Church.

The most arduous labor on the contrary, fell on both *bishops* and *monks*, whose lives are well-nigh unknown, owing to the almost total want of contemporary chronicles. The devastations were so horrible, universal, and protracted that no one could think of devoting his time to the writing of records. The only resource left us is a general description which, however, is so well attested by the current events of those times that it must be respected by the most severe critics. Those nations will be first examined who were still pagan when the invasions began; afterwards the Arian tribes, which immediately followed or accompanied the first, will come up for discussion. The Franks in all their subdivisions; the *Allemanni*, or All-men (pure Germans), in their various tribes; the Huns and Tartars, coming from the extreme end of Asia, were the chief pagan nations which swept like a besom of destruction over the fairest portions of the Roman Empire. They seemed at first to have no other object in view than to destroy. Still, some of them soon seemed inclined to settle in a more favored country than their own, after having decimated the native population. The greatest number, however, were driven from behind by more powerful and barbarous tribes; and in order to escape from the blast in the East they fell upon the populous, rich, and civilized countries of the West. Finally, the most terrible and destructive of all were those who, like the Huns, seemed to be led only by an unconquerable impulse toward a useless and thorough devastation. Pagans or Arians, it made no difference.

Strange to say, the leading pagan hordes, even the worst among them, did not appear to have had the deliberate intention of killing and destroying everybody and everything they met in their way, as did the first Arian Goths and the Vandals who followed them. The Franks and Allemanni particularly would have been apparently satisfied with living in contact and settling quietly among the Greeks, Romans, and Celtic nations which previously occupied the territory. All they asked was a sufficient quantity of land and the full liberty to follow their native customs. Still the commotion they produced, chiefly among the Gallo-Romans, was at first as terrible as the sudden opening of a volcano in the midst of a rich agricultural country. There was an abrupt interruption of all the ordinary ways of life common during many ages under Rome's authority. The political, social, and municipal habits prevalent in the west of Europe from the time of Julius Cæsar down to the fifth century—that is, during four or five hundred years—were so totally upset that the most acute and learned historians and antiquarians have been unable so far to decide if the municipal laws which resulted from the establishment of the *communes* in the twelfth century among the former barbarians had anything in common with the old Roman *municipia*. The most ordinary opinion is that this Roman institution had altogether perished during the invasions; and that the priceless freedom bestowed upon the cities of western Europe by the communal system in the twelfth century was altogether of mediæval origin. If the primitive municipal laws which had regulated the daily life of Gallo-Roman citizens thus totally disappeared, how could anything remain of their former political and social customs? This reflection can give a more exact idea of the devastation caused by the barbarian invasions than the most sweeping description of all their horrors could do.

But in the midst of those elements of terror, a totally different spectacle strikes the attention, and inspires the hopes of better things. All the institutions the barbarians met in their way were destined to perish, except the Church. Strange indeed; the uncouth and devastating northern tribes appeared at once struck with awe and became respectful in presence of the sacred ministers of religion, *except the Arians*. To pretend that because these were Christians they felt well disposed toward the Catholic Gallo-Romans (as some modern writers have thought) argues a total ignorance of history. A remarkable example, it is true, is insisted upon, that on one occasion the Arian Visigoth army led by Alaric spared the churches in Rome in 410. But the well-attested facts of the total ruin of Gaul, Spain, and Africa by Arian troops throws altogether in the shade this momentary relenting of a single army at the command of its chief.

Of all the pagan tribes, on the contrary, which took a part in those expeditions, the northmen from Scandinavia were the only ones who took pleasure in pillaging and burning churches as well as palaces and monuments, in killing bishops and monks together with patricians and citizens. All the other pagan nations acted differently.

It can at least be said in general that the Franks, Allemanni, and Suevi, though they often plundered churches, respected clergymen everywhere; and it is of them that we must first study the Christian education. This, as was said, was brought about by bishops and monks, and the reader's attention must now be called to it.

From the day that Constantine gave freedom to the Church, he honored its rulers in a particular manner, and entirely left them the control of spiritual affairs. His noble conduct at Nicæa is particularly well known. But some of his sons, Constantius chiefly, adopted the policy which was afterwards followed by many European princes. They simply wished to make themselves supreme in Church and State. To this pretension must be mainly attributed the extension and baneful influence of Arianism in the whole extent of the Roman Empire. The ministers of religion would, in consequence, have become mere tools in the hands of the State rulers had it not been for the opposition of the popes supported by the great majority among the bishops. When the first barbarians came, the whole framework of the civil government fell almost at once; and it would have been the same with regard to religion had the schemes of Constantius and his abettors succeeded. Fortunately for Europe, what has been called, much later on, Erastianism did not prevail; and the bishops remained in possession of their rightful authority. This alone saved society from entire ruin. For, on account of the respect invariably manifested at that epoch by the rudest soldiers toward the Christian priesthood, "government, administration, public order, civilization, everything of a saving nature took refuge [at the coming of the barbarians] under the pastoral crozier." These are the very expressions of M. de Riancé in his *Histoire du Monde*,* and they perfectly express the solemn fact.

Chateaubriand in his *Études Historiques* has developed the same idea in so masterly a manner that we cannot do better than translate the whole passage. It is, however, proper to state that this took place in its entirety only in course of time, and was simply beginning when the first invasions burst out in all their fury. With this

---

* Vol. vi. p. 456.

qualification the description is perfect, and suffices to give a thorough idea of those times. "A bishop baptized, heard confessions, preached, imposed private and public penances, placed sinners under anathema, or raised from them the sentence of excommunication, visited the sick, was at the bedside of the dying, buried the dead, redeemed the captive, fed the poor, the widows and orphans He founded and endowed hospitals for ordinary diseases and for lepers, managed the church property, pronounced as a justice of the peace between individuals, and as an arbiter between cities. He published at the same time treatises on morals, on discipline, or theology, wrote against heresiarchs and against philosophers, studied science and history, dictated letters to those who consulted him on religion, corresponded with the various churches and with bishops, monks, hermits. He took his seat in councils and synods, was called to the cabinet council of the emperors, and entrusted with negotiations in state affairs, and often he was sent to usurpers or to barbarian chieftains in order to disarm or repress them. Thus the three powers, religious, political, and literary, were concentrated in the bishop's hands."

All this and more is undoubtedly true; and no one can be surprised that Attila refrained from attacking Rome at the simple word of Pope Leo I., and that "the Scourge of God" withdrew from Gaul at the sight of St. Lupus and St. Germanus. The title of *defensor civitatis* became attached to the episcopal dignity, and it is unheard of in the history of those times that any bishop ever feared to boldly present himself before the hardy conquerors who had come from the wilds of Scythia or Germany.

When the first invasion took place (Franks, Allemanni, Suevi etc.) nearly all the Gallic bishops were Gallo-Romans; and many were distinguished by the noblest qualities of mind and heart. Three of them, however, especially attract our attention: Sidonius Apollinaris. bishop of Clermont; Remigius, of Rheims; and Perpetuus the fifth successor of St. Martin to the see of Tours. They were all contemporaries of Chlovis, and witnessed his wars first against the Romans commanded by Syagrius, and afterwards against the Allemanni, the Visigoths, and Burgundians.

As soon as the Roman power disappeared with all its institutions —social, political, and municipal—a large part of Europe became the theatre of internecine wars between uncouth tribes contending together for the possession of the disputed territory. Then the episcopal dignity remained alone standing; and the bishops, though Gallo-Romans and belonging, consequently, to the conquered race, became the mediators, or rather *arbiters*, between the vanquished and the conquerors.

Sidonius Apollinaris felicitously expressed it in his speech at Bourges, on the occasion of the election and consecration of Simplicius, a new bishop who was to replace the late one :* " Do you look at the age of the candidate, this one has the vivacity of youth and the maturity of years. Do you think of genius and literary attainments, it is doubtful if he possesses more native talent or a greater amount of acquired knowledge. . . . If you reflect on the necessity imposed now on bishops of frequently assuming the duty of *legates* in behalf of the people, this man has already appeared more than once in the presence of kings covered with furs [barbarian chieftains] or before princes adorned with the purple [Roman rulers].",

Sidonius Apollinaris was not only a great writer for his age; he was not distinguished alone for his virtue and holiness; he belonged to one of the noblest families of Gaul, and was related to Avitus and Majorian, who became emperors of the West. The renown for virtue, talent, and wealth distinguished also both St. Remigius, who converted Chlovis, or rather the French nation, and Perpetuus, who, at the same epoch, was bishop of Tours. Both were very rich, though they did not belong to any imperial family.

It is to be deplored that few documents remain by which we might judge of the private lives of those great prelates who presided at the creation of modern Europe by their mighty influence over their age. There are, however, some delightful relics of their time, of which we cannot refrain from furnishing at least one example. This is simply the last will and testament of Perpetuus, of which we possess still an authentic copy.† I deeply regret, however, that I cannot give the whole of it, on account of its length. It deserves to be written in golden letters, and shows better than anything else how Europe was saved by the charity of the bishops. The preamble alone is worthy of a saint:

"In the name of Jesus Christ. Amen. I, Perpetuus, a sinner, priest of the church of Tours, cannot consent to die without having written my last will. This neglect would defraud the poor

---

* Epist. ix. lib. 7. † Spicil. Acheri, vol. v.

of those goods which the grace of God has so liberally and lovingly bestowed upon me, though undeserving, and I do not wish that the property of a priest should pass to others than to the Church."

The wealth of this holy bishop was immense, and the greatest part of it, if not the whole, was his personal property, inherited from his ancestors, and used during his life for the needs of his diocese.

To the priests, deacons, and clerics of his church he leaves the *peace* of our Lord Jesus Christ, and wishes them to remain steadfast in the faith, avoid schism, and follow only the Gospel's rule. At the end of the paragraph he exclaims: "Peace to the Church! peace to the people in cities, in country places! the peace of God the Father, of the Lord Jesus Christ!" None of his property went, therefore, to the priesthood.

Of the disposition to be made of his body this is what he wrote: "Ye priests, deacons, and clerics of my church, I permit you, after having taken advice with Count Agilo, to bury my corpse wherever you choose. This is perfectly indifferent to me. I know that my Redeemer liveth, and that in the flesh I will see my Saviour. Still, if you do me the favor to listen to me, though unworthy of it, I would wish you should let me rest until the day of judgment at the feet of holy Martin. See to it, however, judge yourselves, and decide; whatever you will do I approve."

Then, after having given their freedom to his servants (for slavery was not yet abolished), who must have been very numerous, he devises to the cathedral of Tours two extensive villas: the one called *Saponaria*, with its mills, its sheep-walks, meadows, and ponds; the other called *De Bertiniaco*, with its woods and arable lands, which he had bought himself from a rich deacon called Daniel. And he concludes this paragraph with the declaration that whatever shall be due him on the day of his death shall be considered as paid, so that his debtors could not be sued for it.

His relatives and friends were then remembered, and they were presented with small gifts; his property was not to go to them; he left them only reliquaries, gold or silver crosses, chalices, and vestments if they were priests. But what he did in behalf of his two sisters deserves to be quoted in full: "To my sister Julia Perpetua I leave the small golden cross in which there are relics of our Lord" (some piece of the holy cross, no doubt). "I, however, beg of her that if she happens to die before Dadolena, she will leave the cross with her. As to thee, sister Dadolena, I will that at thy demise the cross passes to any church thou choosest, that it may not fall into unworthy hands. But in case Dadolena dies before thee, dearest sister Fidia Julia Perpetua, it will be thy duty to leave the cross to any church thou likest. Remember me, my most beloved. Amen."

After these and some other legacies comes finally the disposal of the bulk of his property in the following words, which evidently come from his heart:

" As for you, my soul and love, my dearest brothers, my crown of joy, my lords and masters, my dear children; ye, the poor of Christ, reduced to indigence, to the begging of your bread, to a life of sorrow; ye, widows, orphans, waifs abandoned on the roadside; I declare you my heirs and successors. After having disposed of the previous legacies, I will that whatsoever else I possess in fields, pastures, meadows, groves and forests, vineyards, manses and farms, gardens, ponds, rivers and lakes, mills and barns; and besides in gold, silver, garments and linen, everything else of which I have not otherwise disposed, shall go to you, my sole heirs. And that everything may be done properly, conveniently, promptly, I will that as soon as possible after my demise all this property shall be reduced into money, of which three equal parts will be made. Two of these shall be distributed to the male part of the population entitled to it by their indigence—under the care and supervision of the priest Agrarius and the Count Agilo. The other third part is to be divided among the widows and poor women, at the discretion of my sister Dadolena."

I read nowhere that Dadolena bitterly complained that after having received, of all the immense property of her brother, only a small golden cross, which she was simply to keep during her life, she had besides the trouble of distributing among poor females unknown to her a full third of the property of which herself and her sister Julia were, after all, the only rightful and natural heirs. Modern civilization and jurisprudence have given us very different ideas on the subject of inheritance from those which prevailed among our Christian ancestors of fourteen hundred years ago. But the view Perpetuus entertained of the use of his wealth was more calculated to make an impression on the Franks and Burgundians, and convert them, than the modern idea of strict justice, which is at this time the rule universally followed. Charity was a new virtue of which the barbarians scarcely had any notion, and they could not but be struck with admiration when they perceived how wealthy bishops practised the precepts they inculcated. Had we the text of the last will and testament of St. Remigius and of other Gallo-Roman bishops of the sixth century, it would be, no doubt, a repetition of the one which has just been noticed. For the perfume of the most heavenly charity which exhaled from Perpetuus' heart must have been the usual way good bishops expressed their interior feelings at that epoch. Gregory of Tours speaks of a great number of them in his works, and often mentions that they were men *eximiæ charitatis;* though his great object everywhere was to extol their power in heaven by the recital of the miracles performed at their sepulchres.

There lived, no doubt, at the same time men unworthy of their high calling, who scandalized the Church by their ambition and avarice. The writer of the *Historia Francorum* does not fail to speak in proper terms of those blots on the ecclesiastical body. But a close persual of that history and of his other writings will convince the reader that greed among bishops was the exception and liberality the rule. And this makes it easy to understand how the barbarians were converted, though for a long time still they retained their former ferocity.

A strong exception to this, however, is taken by Mr. Lecky in his "History of European Morals."* He speaks precisely of St. Gregory of Tours, who was undoubtedly one of the best Gallo-Roman bishops of the sixth century. He quotes passages of the saint's writings which to a modern reader appear to justify him in his conclusions that "Gregory's ethics sometimes exhibit the most singular distortion," and that "the moral judgments of this unhappy age [the sixth century] were distorted by superstition." To discuss the whole subject would require many pages of a strict criticism. For, the facts adduced in proof are numerous, and apparently conclusive. I doubt not that the author of "European Morals" has himself examined the texts, and has not been satisfied with second-hand quotations. It is sure, nevertheless, that he was not the first to propose these objections. In France M. Ampère (the younger) in his *Histoire littéraire, etc.*, and M. Fauriel in his *Histoire de la Gaule méridionale,* had previously brought forward the same texts of Greg-

---

* Vol. ii. p. 240 *seq.* 261, 277.

ory of Tours, and taken very nearly the same views of them. But the Abbé Gorini in his *Défense de l'Église* * has strictly demonstrated that the texts can very well bear totally different conclusions, and that the meaning of the holy bishop has been entirely misunderstood by both M. Ampère and M. Fauriel. The same must be said of Mr. Lecky in the eyes of any one who has read attentively the book of Gorini, to which I am reduced to refer. The only truth that remains is that the bishops were holy men, but the barbarians were monsters of cruelty and lust, and could not immediately practise Christian virtues in their purity.

But the bishops were not alone working for their conversion. We have spoken of monks who heroically labored for the same object. Gallo-Roman, Irish, British, and Celtic missionaries, as was said, faced at once the hordes coming from the North, but could not directly inspire them with the spirit of exalted holiness. This is to be briefly seen. There were monasteries in the West at a very early age, long before that of Benedict. Montalembert has proved it in his "Monks of the West." I do not allude here to the primitive examples of asceticism in Rome, going as far back as the apostolic age, when delicate young girls, like Agnes and Cæcilia, embraced a life of prayer and virtue, and consecrated their virginity to God. These holy women lived in their families because there were not as yet any monastic establishments either in Italy or in Gaul and Spain. Near Milan there was a house of this kind at the beginning of the fourth century, since the young Martin, afterwards ،bishop of Tours, coming back from Pannonia to Gaul, spent a short time in it, and began there his long life of austerities. He directly after, founded at Ligugé near Poitiers the first house of cenobites in Gaul under the direction of Bishop Hilary, so well known by his opposition to Arianism. The monastery of Marmoutier was the second of the foundations of Martin.

St. Honoratus landed in 410 on the island of Lerins near Toulon, and soon gathered around his attractive person a multitude of men desirous of devoting their lives to God, and to the conversion of pagans. The virtues practised until that time in Upper Egypt began to flourish on this far shore of the Mediterranean Sea. Many bishops of Gaul received their apostolic training in it; and it is well known that St. Patrick did so likewise before he went to convert the Irish.

---

* Vol. ii. p. 140 *seq.*

Cesarius of Arles had been brought up at Lerins, and powerfully contributed to the propagation of monasticism, by the celebrated rules he wrote both for monasteries of men and convents of women.

In the very centre of Gaul, in the former country of Vercingetorix, the only worthy foe of Julius Cæsar among the Gallic Celts, a branch of monasticism altogether independent from Lerins is seen already flourishing early in the third century. Austremonius, sent to Auvergne by Pope Fabian, had built in the midst of those towering mountains, for the most part extinct volcanoes, a number of holy houses, several of which continued down to a very late period. Issoire was one of them. Sidonius Apollinaris, in his time bishop of Clermont, speaks particularly of another near his episcopal city, which was generally called *Suburbanum Arvernorum monasterium*. It is from those ancient fountain-heads of proselytism and holiness that came forth the apostles who primitively evangelized the central part of Gaul, long before Maur, St. Benedict's disciple, arrived for the same object.

Farther east, in the Jura Mountains, Romanus, who had been brought up in a religious house near Lyons, established himself as a simple anchoret in the thick forests which bordered on Helvetia, and founded the monastery of Condat, better known under the name of St. Claude. Soon the holy institute spread so rapidly that all those rugged chains of mountains in eastern Gaul were literally covered with holy houses, ready to meet the ferocious Burgundians and other Germanic tribes when they should come to devastate the country.

In those establishments the majority of the inmates were Gallo-Romans, among whom Franks, Burgundians, Goths, Vandals, came to live after their conversion; so that a large number of men belonging to those barbarian tribes became also missionaries in course of time, and continued the previous work of Gallo-Roman apostles. Finally, Irishmen came with · Columbanus; British Celts with Gildas and Samson; Anglo-Saxons with Wilfrid, Willibrod, and at last Winfried, better known as St. Boniface.

To have a sufficient idea of the extent to which the monastic houses had multiplied at the time of the first great invasions, when the Franks arrived led by Chlovis, or shortly after, we have only to refer to the most interesting memoir of M. Mignet quoted by Montalembert, under the title *Mémoire sur la conversion de l'Allemagne par les moines*. The celebrated French historian ascertained by his researches that throughout the sixth century there were eighty monastic establishments in the valleys of the Saone and Rhone; ninety-four from the Pyrenees to the Loire; fifty-four from the Loire to the Vosges Mountains; and finally ten from the Vosges to the Rhine. Still the Benedictine monasteries were few in number at the end of this period of time. The majority of the monks must therefore have belonged to the anomalous orders previously mentioned, whose rules have never been known, or rather which had no other rule than the abbot's will. It is but gradually that St. Benedict's rule penetrated among them; but in course of time it supplanted the archaic or arbitrary laws of each of those houses; but it is not known at what precise epoch this happened for any of them. The Benedictine order found no difficulty in absorbing all the others, except that of Columbanus, which resisted for a long time, because it had received from its founder more precise rules than any ancient institution.

After these preliminaries, the process of conversion in the barbarian world can be easily followed. It will directly be seen that it must have been very slow, surrounded with difficulties, and that holiness, if gradually increasing, must have been hampered by the previous vices of those nations. It must have taken a long time for the true ages of faith to begin.

Without the bishops the monks would have been unable to succeed in their arduous undertaking, because every grace must come originally through the hierarchy. There was, besides, a particular reason it should be so at that time. This was nothing else than the absence of strict rules among the monks, which necessitated the supervision of the bishops over them, and many councils in Gaul decreed it at that time as being of absolute necessity.

Both bishops and abbots, therefore, concurred in the great work of the formation of Christian Europe. In the "History of the Franks," by the Bishop of Tours, are found everywhere convincing proofs of the immense authority religion then acquired even over pagan savage tribes. The various Merovingian kings submitted almost constantly to that authority. Still, every one is now aware that even after their conversion they remained for a long time slaves to the same violent passions, and scarcely appeared to differ from what they were when pagans. But there was for them a kind of fascination in the episcopal or monastic character, derived from its holiness. Thus, although Thierry, king of Metz, often received the most severe admonitions from Abbot Nizier, on account of his immoralities and cruelties, he insisted, however, on having him raised to the dignity of bishop of Trèves, though he knew that the holy man would thereby become still bolder in his denunciations and threats.

Most of those holy men who acquired such a power over barbarian chieftains were, for a long time, Gallo-Romans only, and belonged to the conquered race. The first Frankish abbot, known to history under the name of Marculph, died in 558, and it is only much later that barbarian names become common among bishops and abbots.

The Celtic monks from Wales who landed in Armorica, being driven away from Great Britain by the Anglo-Saxons, and whose immigration lasted a full hundred years—from 450 to 550—met likewise with a stubborn resistance from the Celtic Armoricans, whom they found pagans, but whom they at last converted so thoroughly that the name of Breton and Catholic in France is still synonymous. The monks were more instrumental than the bishops in the conversion of that part of Gaul; hence the whole peninsula of Brittany became toward the end of the sixth century a huge bee-hive, as it were, in which the monks' incessant labor did for that country what the colaborers and successors of St. Patrick did for Ireland. It is possible that the identity of method in both cases produced an identity of result. If in modern times seldom or never whole nations are at once converted, so that missionaries have now to be satisfied with a larger or smaller number of neophytes in the midst of an alien population, the cause of this partial failure is, perhaps, that the former method is never adopted at this time. The most zealous missionaries of our age seldom think of planting numerous monasteries among their converts. This is very different from the question of a native clergy which produced such a sensation in Catholic Europe thirty years ago, and of which nobody now speaks.

The conversion of western Europe by bishops and monks, the obstacles it met, the length of time it required to overcome previous habits and prepare the northern nations for holiness is now sufficiently known. There remain only a few words to add on the Arian tribes of Goths, Vandals, Lombards, etc., who came together with the pagan German nations, and offered almost unsurmountable obstacles to their conversion to Catholicism. We are acquainted with their ferocious manners, and know that their pretended profession of Christianity made the case less hopeful than if we were considering only their former barbarism. Their total reduction to the dogmas and discipline of the Church during the sixth and seventh centuries is one of the most remarkable facts of ecclesiastical history.

The persecuting spirit of the Arians became first a most serious drawback everywhere to the general advance toward holiness, and it was only after their conversion that sanctity became at last conspicuous in the ages of faith. As was previously seen, a great part of Gaul, the whole of Spain, and the Latin portion of Africa were completely devastated under the scourge of this heresy. It went so far in Numidia and Mauritania that, the rule of the Vandals being immediately followed by that of the Saracens, Christianity entirely disappeared from those countries which zealous missionaries at this time find it so difficult to bring back to Christ. People do not sufficiently reflect that it is the only occasion when the Cross absolutely disappeared before the Crescent. Everywhere else except, perhaps, in farthest Asia, many Christians and even Catholics remained in the midst of Mohammedans; in north-west Africa it was a complete extirpation, though so many bishops' sees had formerly existed in the country. This alone is sufficient to prove the extent of the evil brought by Arianism.

The only northern Arians who, for a considerable time, did not persecute the Catholics were the Visigoths of north Italy. Theodoric in particular, left the Church, and even the Pope perfectly free. At the end of his reign, however, he began to adopt the policy carried out everywhere by his coreligionists; so that the universality of the fact remains uncontested.

Persecution, however, was resorted to by the Arians only after some attempt at proselytism had failed. Those heretical chieftains and bishops pretended to be theologians, and could prove from Scripture and tradition that Christ was not consubstantial with His Father. The Catholics never refused the contest, though they knew their theological victory would be followed by the prison, the rack, and death. Striking examples of this are found in the writings of Gregory of Tours, Sidonius Apollinaris, and Victor Vitensis. This fury for both arguments and blood proves the tenacity with which those nations held to their errors in point of faith. For on such occasions as these it is not reason which is consulted, but passion which is obeyed; and in general the more the radical fault of an argument is pointed out, the more is it adhered to on the mere strength of empty words. In our days it is still obvious particularly in the obstinacy of Protestant Sacramentarians, who pretend they entirely rely on the words of the Gospel, yet refuse to admit the dogma of the real presence in the Eucharist, although the expressions of the Saviour are so precise.

But the Arianism of German nations lasted but a century or two, when it suddenly gave way nearly at the same time in Spain, Gaul, and Italy. The Franks took a noble part in effecting it; some holy princesses married to Arian kings became most efficient agents of the grace of God; and the incessant zeal of Catholic bishops and monks was also instrumental in bringing on this happy result. Still, the rapid action of those causes is almost unexampled in the Church's annals. Let us ascribe it to the benevolent designs of Providence. Arianism in the West was an immense obstacle to the introduction of holiness among the lately converted tribes. Europe could not run rapidly in the path of evangelical perfection before it was first united in the profession of a single faith, and the middle ages could not begin before this took place. God, therefore, swept Arianism away.

From these considerations a strict conclusion follows: The period of violence, passion, and crime which is comprised within the whole Merovingian epoch in Gaul, and even a part of the Carlovingian, must not surprise any one and seem inexplicable to anybody. This was to be expected from all the circumstances of the case, and the study of our proper subject begins from the end of these troublous times.

3. *Formation of Christian Congregations, in Cities mainly by Bishops, in the Country particularly by Monks.*

It seems unfit to attribute holiness — namely, the highest development of the inner Christian feeling — to a period when Europe, divided into small fragments, was cursed with the worst features of feudalism, deprived apparently of self-action under a growing despotism, and on an evident return to barbarism, or rather savagery. The more so that those states which still preserved some strength in these primitive feudal times, and were not altogether deprived of material prosperity, showed already

signs of rebellion against the Church; as it soon happened to
the dukes of Normandy and the kings of England, previous to the
Cæsarian pretensions of the German emperors. Still, it is perfectly true that at this very time of an apparent disorganization
the deep foundation was laid of modern Catholic Europe, and all
the elements of her grand destiny were already at work in the
deep feeling of faith which became then pre-eminent, and in the
pure principles of the highest morality, infallibly leading to holiness, which were broadly and effectively taught to the people by
bishops and monks.

For we are not speaking here of princes, emperors, and kings,
but of the mass of Christians, "*the people*," who were soon gently
taken in hand by bishops and counts in cities, and by monks of
the Benedictine order in the rural districts created, in fact, by
their industry. It has been seen that the bishops became the
protectors of cities, and in general they were helped for this by the
counts who had the civil management of townships. In the country the converted barbarians found immense forests that had
been allowed to grow and invade the cultivated districts, first by
the wretched policy of the latter Roman Empire, which took
notice only of cities by its municipal system, and afterwards by
the constant commotions of the Merovingian epoch. The German tribes had brought from their respective countries a great
attraction and fitness for cultivating the land, but they were at
first frightened by the intolerable labor necessary for clearing
it of woods. The Benedictine monks gave them the example,
founded their monasteries over the burnt remains of the forests
they had cut down, and invited the people to come and build their
huts around their own bee-hives. This was the origin of many
villages in the Europe of a later period, and even a large number
of cities have had no other derivation. This was the true source
of modern civilization, and it must be brought to view somewhat
in detail. It is in the large aggregate of common men belonging
to all the northern races, more than in their feudal rulers, that we
must look for the elements of faith and virtue which became the
chief characteristic of the following centuries. The Christian
people—*populus Christianus*—is the strong and pure individuality
which must attract all our attention. In our way we may meet
with several emperors or kings, dukes or barons, worthy of those
heroic times. We will, in such cases as this, consider them as

belonging to the mass, and there is no distinction to be made, for instance, between Louis IX. of France and the most obscure of his subjects to whom he administered justice under the shade of the renowned Vincennes oak.

How this *Christian people* was formed is the first question to be examined. A remarkable text taken from the *Études Historiques* of Chateaubriand has already placed before our eyes the various functions, ecclesiastical or civil, which were considered at that time as essentially belonging to the episcopal office. It can be easily seen that all those functions had for their object the spiritual or temporal good of the people. By analyzing that comprehensive paragraph of the great French writer, and taking each phrase of it apart, it would be easy to illustrate the whole subject by a great number of facts taken from the history of that epoch. This would be a strict demonstration of its truth; but it would result in a large volume. Every one can do it for himself by taking a single author belonging to that epoch in whose writings the action of bishops is concerned. For the incipient stage of it, which we consider at this moment, Gregory of Tours would suffice. For besides his "History of the Franks," he has written a book, *De gloria Martyrum;* another, *De gloria Confessorum;* and another remarkable one, called *Vitæ Patrum.*

Many of the stories related by him have no reference to the present subject. But there are numerous details which powerfully confirm all the assertions of Chateaubriand. It is impossible to quote here more than one or two, and they are given as being mere samples of many others. In the Life of St. Nicet, bishop of Lyons (chap. viii.), a curious example is pointed out of the way a bishop could help the poor when he had no more money to give. Nicet merely wrote a note by which he recommended this poor person to the charity of the faithful. It is what is often done in our day; but there were circumstances at the time of Gregory which do not frequently happen in this age. One of those notes had procured for the man to whom it was given a comfortable living during the life of the saint, and after his death the alms were still more abundant, on the presentation of the note, on account of the dear memory of the holy man. The mendicant found himself at last the possessor of six gold pieces (*sex aureos*) besides the note, which was indeed the hen with the golden eggs. A thievish Burgundian became aware of it, and, following the mendicant in the woods, assaulted him and robbed him of his treasure and of his note. In his extremity the poor man begged of the barbarian to give him back at least the piece of paper, which could be of no use to him. This was done without difficulty, and the new bishop of Lyons, successor to Nicet, being apprised of all the circumstances, placed the whole case in the hands of the count of the city. With the help of his police the count had the Burgundian apprehended, but he openly denied everything of which he was accused, until the bishop requested him to swear to his statement with his hand raised over the signature of the saint at the end of the note. He boldly endeavored to do it, but was struck down with a violent attack of epilepsy. After a fit of two hours' duration he came to himself, acknowledged his crime, and, the Lyons bishop interceding for him with the count, he was only condemned to return the money with two additional pieces taken from his own purse.

Daily facts of this kind happened in most dioceses of western Europe, and it is difficult to exaggerate the influence the bishops acquired by the constant practice of justice and charity. What power must they have obtained over the minds and hearts of those entrusted to their charge! How different was their position in Church and State from what we witness in our day over the same countries in western Europe!

Gregory of Tours, directly after relating this touching story, exclaims with confidence in the presence of numberless witnesses ready to confirm his assertions: "How many prisoners loaded with chains in the *ergastulum* have been set free by this holy bishop! How many heavy chains of iron have been broken down by him under the hammer! To have an idea of it one has only to look at that ponderous mass of metal which is still preserved in his cathedral, and was composed altogether of instruments of torture. Quite lately I have heard Syagrius, the bishop of Autun, relate in the presence of King Guntran, that in one single night during his life the holy man entered unbidden seven prisons of the city and let free all the prisoners therein confined, and the judges did not dare to have them arrested again."

Bishop Nicet had, no doubt, previously ascertained the innocence of those who had been incarcerated and whom he restored to freedom. Acts of this kind necessarily suppose a perfect holiness of life on the part of him who boldly performs them; and the generations in the midst of which they are enacted not only admire them and bless them, but they are ready to fall prostrate at the feet of those benefactors of mankind, and will implicitly obey and follow them.

Another Nicet, bishop of Treves, is celebrated with the same enthusiasm by Gregory of Tours in his *Vitæ Patrum* (chap. xvii.). He was first a simple monk in a monastery, in the north of Gaul, of which he was elected abbot. And so remarkable was the reformation he effected among the brethren that Theodoric, king of Metz, venerated him, and allowed him often to remonstrate against his own crimes. This dissolute prince, who had experienced some inclination toward a change of life at the instigation of the zealous abbot, could not rest satisfied at the death of the archbishop of Treves unless Nicet was appointed his successor. The people and clergy assented with pleasure, and a troop of lords and grandees of the kingdom were appointed to go to Nicet's monastery and bring him to Treves. Toward the end of their journey these gentlemen prepared to spend the night in the midst of rich fields where the corn was ripening, and after sunset they had their tents erected and began to let loose their horses, who directly rushed among the wheat of the poor people. "Call back your horses instantly," cried out the blessed Nicet, "or I shall excommunicate you." But these lords replied with indignation: "Thou art not yet a bishop, and thou already speakest of excommunication!" "I tell you," retorted the holy man, "that the king in having me taken by force from my monastery intends to place that burden over my shoulders. But if I become a bishop, it is the will of God that I intend to do; and if the king's will is opposed to it, I shall certainly defeat his evil purposes." And at the same moment the good man ran into the fields and brought back the horses before they had destroyed the crops. Thus he entered the city of Treves in the midst of the admiring crowds of citizens.

Under the reign of Theodebert, the son of Theodoric, the same bishop proved still better that he was no respecter of persons. For the king, naturally excluded from the offices of religion by his criminal conduct, dared to enter the church on a Sunday, with a large number of attendants, all more or less under the Church's censures by the infamy of their lives. The bishop ordered them all out with circumstances which deserve to be read in the text of

Gregory himself; and in spite of the resistance of these proud courtiers and princes, he succeeded in his purpose, and celebrated the divine mysteries as soon as the sacred edifice was purged from their presence.

But these extraordinary displays of zeal, though well calculated to form the character of new and rude nations, could not happen every day. The constant action of the bishops by preaching, administering the sacraments, visiting the sick and poor, educating the children, and performing all the ordinary functions of the holy ministry, served better still for the grand purpose, so well described by the author of the *Études Historiques*. This cannot be proved in detail, but results from all the circumstances of those times. The frequency of the intervention of Providence by miraculous agency, so constantly alluded to by Gregory of Tours in all his works, might be likewise enumerated as a powerful source of morality and holiness among the new converts from barbarism and idolatry. We prefer not to insist on it, though we think most of the time their truth cannot be questioned when they are weighed by the scrutiny of simple human reason. But there is another circumstance which not even a rationalist can set aside, because it is in itself a grand historical fact of daily occurrence in those ages. We are speaking of the early formation of the Christian character in mediæval cities by bishops. They had been Gallo-Roman cities, and were then being transformed into Frankish, Gothic, Burgundian, or Lombard towns over a great part of western Europe. But the most striking exterior fact of these apparently barbarous times was the constant building up of innumerable churches in all cities. Any reflective mind is deeply surprised at the reading of Gregory's works. Everywhere there are contentions and feuds, and spilling of blood, and enormous crimes, as if society was on the point of dissolution. But in the midst of that moral darkness, not only the virtues of the bishops shine strangely and beautifully, but they appear everywhere the greatest church-builders that the Church's annals ever witnessed. These holy edifices were not only the consecrated spots in which religion could proceed in peace in the performance of her holy functions; they were likewise sanctuaries of refuge whither the oppressed and afflicted could run in time of danger, and were sure to find sustenance and protection. They were just adapted to the best formation of the character of those rude tribes.

Such were the most remarkable causes which contributed to the building up of modern Europe, and prepared the advent of the middle ages; rendering at last holiness possible in a world apparently convulsed and ready to perish in disorder and anarchy. But to complete the picture, the action of the monks for the same great object, in country places and hamlets, in mountains and plains, forests and wild deserts, must be examined, if but for a moment. With the bishops in cities, they prepared western Europe for its high destiny.

Montalembert has, fortunately, achieved this very task in the second volume of his " Monks of the West." This is the chapter entitled *Les Moines et la Nature*—The Monks and Nature—and the reader must be content with the simple translation of a few paragraphs:

"Picture to yourself the whole of Gaul and the surrounding countries—that is, the France of our day with Switzerland, Belgium, and both banks of the Rhine"—he might have made the enumeration longer—"covered with forests such as are scarcely seen in America at this time, whilst not a vestige of them remains in the ancient world. Look at those vast agglomerations of woods, gloomy, impenetrable, spread over mountains and valleys, the highest places as well as the low marshy grounds, going down as far as the mouths of rivers and the sea itself; furrowed here and there by deep-water streams wildly running through the roots and prostrated trunks of gigantic trees; cut up by swamps and morasse where animals and men could be swallowed up and perish; the dark abode, in fine, of numerous beasts of prey unused to flee at the approach of man, and of which several species have now disappeared

"To penetrate into these dreadful jungles, and confront ther monstrous animals, remembered still in an universal tradition, an whose remains are often exhumed, required a courage which is neve put to the test in our actual world. Nothing of the kind exists eve in the forests and deserts of America. . . . Yet the monk altogethe unprepared, without arms, without sufficient tools, often without eve a companion, plunged headlong into those deep solitudes. He cam from an old world which the surfeit of civilization and the onset o barbarians had unnerved and made decrepit, to dive at once into th unknown. But he felt within himself a strength which nothing ca surpass or even equal, the strength communicated to man by faith a living God, and on account of it he was full of contempt for m terial enjoyment, and looked only toward a supernatural and future life. . . .

"Behold them, therefore; look with attention; they know only prayer and penance; they are the hardy pioneers of Christian civilization and of modern society. . . . They penetrate into those dark recesses, carrying with them a light which shall never be quenched—*Ibunt de claritate in claritatem*. . . . They boldly walk in, sometimes only with a hatchet, followed occasionally by a troop of faithful new converts, or by a mob of astonished and indignant pagans who boil over with rage at the sight of their sacred trees, the great object of popular superstition, uprooted and lying on the ground unhonored. . . . No obstacle, no danger can make them desist; the deeper is the gloom of those dark forests, the stronger is the attraction. . . . Sometimes they had to creep under the low and intricate branches of trees, to discover at last a narrow and dim cavern blocked up by rocks or briers; at this sight they felt ready for the occasion. It was just at the entrance of such a den that the Burgundian priest Sequanus, creeping on his knees and entering in a hole from which ferocious beasts would have recoiled, addressed to God this prayer: 'O Lord, who hath created the heaven and the earth, who listeneth to the prayers of those who implore Thee, from whom everything good cometh, and without whom human weakness can do nothing. If Thou commandest me to dwell in this solitude, give me some sign of it, and bring to perfection this beginning of a holy intention.' Then, feeling consoled at the end of his prayer, he began to build on this very spot the cell which became the origin of the abbey and of the actual town of St. Seine."

The author of the "Monks of the West" relates then how those holy anchorites were often followed by multitudes of people, rich or poor, learned or ignorant, who wished either to become monks under their rule, or at least to dwell around them and cultivate the ground the same as they did. And thus were numerous Christian congregations formed in the most forbidding localities of western Europe. He then describes the clearing up of the woods, the tilling of land, and the settlement of farms over that immense territory:

"The clearing up of woods, which in our day has become a calamity, was the most urgent necessity of those times. It was, however, carried out with prudence and discretion. Ages and ages passed by before the penury of timber was felt in our southern provinces, where the growing of trees seems now impossible. During those ages the monks incessantly continued the process of cutting up regularly wide furrows through the huge standing mass of woods. They divided them, they brought light into them, they formed of them large fields which constantly grew in size, and were now forever given to cultivation. . . . They spent their whole lives in transforming into meadows and arable lands a soil previously occupied by oaks and briers. . . . Occasionally they had to open themselves a way by fire, in order to do away with useless wood. But oftener they used the spade, the pick-axe, the shovel, to prepare at last the ground for receiving the seed and being changed into a meadow. This process began just around the primitive cell, which was generally built near a water-course. By and by the light of heaven penetrated under the thickest foliage. The gigantic oaks fell down, and gave place to a field of waving corn. Most of those monks who had read the Latin poets could remember the beautiful lines of Lucan:

'Tunc omnia late
Procumbunt nemora, et spoliantur robore sylvæ. . . .'

"These examples of industry soon acted on the rural populations of the neighborhood. Many went to look at these wonders; and not a few practically set at it themselves. . . . Thus is naturally explained the rapid increase of the population all round the monastic establishments, as well as the immense amount of labor undertaken by the cenobites, whose results subsist still and are for us a subject of wonder. The richest agricultural districts of modern France have had no other origin than this. . . .

"The monks were not satisfied with inculcating habits of labor, and teaching improved processes of agriculture, among the Frankish population of Gaul. They attached still much more importance to spiritually cultivate so many souls precious in the eyes of God. By their examples and exhortations, by their active charity as well as by their oral teaching, they deeply penetrated into those rude natures, and planted in them the germs of virtue and eternal life. It is owing to their influence, no doubt, that must be attributed the solicitude which several provincial councils of Gaul manifested at that time for the spiritual instruction of the rural inhabitants. 'The priests,' said the council of Rouen in 650, 'will give notice to their parishioners that it is the duty of farmers to send to mass, at least on Sundays and holidays, the men that they employ as laborers or keepers of their flocks and cattle, all those, in fact, who spend their lives in the fields or in the woods and there are exposed to become beasts among beasts. Those who neglect that duty will be severely called to account. For our Lord on coming among us has not chosen for His first disciples learned and noble men, but fishermen and lowly people. It is not to those of a high intellect, but to poor shepherds, that the angel first announced the nativity of our Redeemer.'

"To provide for the spiritual needs of these graziers and laborers, the monks either helped or replaced the secular clergy by building in the most remote and out-of-the-way places their cells or oratories. These in course of time became churches. Around them the peasants' cots were erected. . . .

"The monks, often in spite of themselves, became the fathers of numerous spiritual progeny. Thus the monastic community and the rustic village were soon united in the same bonds of faith, labor, and common prayer. Everywhere, in the midst of those woods so long inaccessible, of those former deserts now teeming with multitudes, was heard the hymn of joy, of thankfulness, of adoration. Isaias' prophecy was fulfilled under their eyes, for them and by them: 'The mountains and hills shall sing a canticle, and the trees of the forest shall applaud,' etc. . . .*

"Are we not occasionally tempted to lend an ear and listen, expecting that at least a faint echo of this bewitching harmony shall reach us through the long waves of former ages? Never, certainly, did a more harmonious concert go up to heaven from our earth than was heard when the wonderful symphony of so many pious and pure voices, rising at once from the clearings in the woods, from the declivity of rocky hills and the precipitous sides of cascades and torrents, broke out in unison to celebrate the happy birth of a new era. So at morn we hear the birds hidden under the thick foliage, or, better still, our own babes and infants just awakening from sleep, warbling with joy their innocent carols, to welcome the dawn of day, without so much as thinking of its storms or its declining hours.

"The Church has known more solemn and brilliant epochs, times more worthy to excite the admiration of sages. the fervor of pious

---

* Chap. lv. 12.

souls, the unshaken confidence of her children. I doubt if she ever exhaled a sweeter perfume than during this first period of monastic life.

"Gaul had during five hundred years been oppressed under the ignominious yoke of the Roman Cæsars. During the barbarian invasions the whole country had been a battle-field where blood-shedding, arson, carnage, had reigned supreme. Now, on the contrary Christian virtue under the discipline of penance and self-sacrifice was budding forth, and faith was expanding as the leaves and blossoms of shrubs after winter. On all sides moral life was reviving, the same as do the green boughs of trees in the spring; and already under the hoary branches of the former Druidic forests the youthful espousals of the Church with the Frankish—say European—people were being celebrated."

The ground was at last prepared for the "new creation;" Europe was Christian and no more barbarous. Holiness could flourish, and the middle ages had begun.

4. *The True Foundation of Holiness Laid Down in Redeemed Europe*

This had been set down firmly by Christ Himself in the Gospel, and its conditions were afterwards explained by Popes and the Fathers of the Church. But it was time the whole of it should be authoritatively summed up and placed entirely before the redeemed barbarians, so that all classes of men could understand the true value of life, and direct their steps in a clear path illumined by the sun above, and leading to the high regions of moral heroism and sanctity. It had been done formerly for civilized people in Rome and Greece. It was to be done for rude people in the ninth century, when the Carlovingian line in Gaul was expiring, and Europe was at the point of being parcelled out in a immense number of small states; all, however, united by the same faith and bearing the general name of Christendom. Of all the books that were then written for the guidance of the faithful nor became so fruitful of good results, for public morals, as those of Jonas, bishop of Orleans. From their publication we date the true origin of the ages of faith, though these ages were already born and would have accomplished their providential destiny without the help of any book whatever. The works of Jonas, fact, were the fruit of the times, and they came at the best m ment for fulfilling thoroughly their work. It cannot be questioned that their salutary agency was pre-eminent, and from their publication dates a new era in the moral world.

Jonas succeeded Theodulph to the see of Orleans in 821, died in 842, and during the twenty-two years of his episcopate he rendered immense services to Church and State. His first literary production, *De Institutione Laicali*, and the one which followed, *De Institutione Regia*, may be considered as having been of paramount importance for the promotion of virtue in Europe at that epoch. We do not speak of his other book, *De Cultu Imaginum*, which does not enter into our scope. To fully understand the moral value of these writings, it is proper to remark that so far what is called here the basis of holiness, which is merely its code, had been contained only in the Gospel and the writings of the Fathers. The whole subject was undoubtedly treated in full, both in the inspired records of the New Testament and in the authoritative explanations given by Heaven-appointed teachers. Still, the whole matter had never been before embraced in any systematic treatise. The great schoolmen who were to do it, both for dogma and ethics, had not yet appeared; and each particular teacher of religion—nay, each one of the faithful—had to extract the substance of the Christian code from texts apparently disconnected, chiefly from the Saviour's teaching which came from His lips, as every one knows, on all possible occasions arising during His diversified missionary life. This, however, had been sufficient, together with the interior grace of God, to produce those abundant fruits of holiness which have been previously described both in the East and in the West. To the highly impressive Orientals and Greeks the process was easy, and their hearts were moved to a deep feeling of piety, making them susceptible of a great degree of sanctity, by any passing word or action of our Lord or His Apostles. But the systematic and logical mind of Europeans, such as it was destined to be developed and expanded, required in the teaching imparted to them a greater connection between the different parts, so as to bring under view, if possible, the whole subject at once.

This Jonas of Orleans did first in his work *De Institutione Laicali*, so as to anticipate the moral theologians of every possible age. Luke d'Achery, who gave the first edition of it in modern times, calls it *aureum opus;* and it is indeed a golden book which

can highly edify a Christian of the nineteenth century as it did
the Franks of the ninth. It is one of those productions which
never grow old and appear always appropriate to one's needs; so
that I am firmly convinced that if a good translation of it was
now made in some modern language it would be devoured with
avidity by all solidly pious people; more, perhaps, than the "Devout Life" of St. Francis of Sales, to which it has been compared.
It is in those entrancing pages of the Orleans bishop that all mediæval Christians were destined to dig deeply, in order to find
out the nutritious root of holiness contained therein. I cannot
give here even an abridgment of the work. But although French
ecclesiastical writers, such as Fleury, Rohrbacher, and the authors
of the *Histoire Littéraire de la France*, have highly praised the logical
character of the book, adding that, *as usual*, the author merely
comments on texts of the New Testament and of the Fathers, they
in fact do not in the least give any idea of it. This strict method
had never been *usual* before Jonas of Orleans, and he truly anticipated the great schoolmen of the following centuries. He was
the first to collect not only a few but all the passages of Scripture
bearing strictly on his subject; and it is wonderful how he chose
only those whose meaning was most clear and striking, leaving
aside the dubious ones because they wanted precision and force.
The comments of the Fathers, also, which he gave were always
opportune and felicitous; and as the Latin style is truly elegant
though simple, the book is always read with relish and pleasure.
It is in truth a masterpiece; and this was the moral code which
was to be henceforth in the hands of all prelates and priests to
whom the moral education of the people was entrusted.

There is not a single important question of Christian morals
which is not there explained and illustrated, and the casuists of
the following centuries would not do better than read it constantly and explain it efficiently. It is there, no doubt, that the spiritual food on which the mediæval Christians were fed is found in
its wholesome purity, and it may be called the moral *vade mecum*
of the ages of faith. But if I cannot enter into details, there is at
least one peculiarity which must be mentioned. It is alluded to
in particular at the end of the First Book,* and it can give us a
perfect idea of Jonas's intention in writing this work, and also of

---

* Chap. xx.

the state of morality in the Christian world at that epoch. He there asserts several times that his great object was to bring back the people of his day to the full practice of heroic sanctity, such as it was carried out in the church at Jerusalem under the apostles, because faith and charity had in his time grown cold in the hearts of *some*, and it was important to revive it in *all* the followers of Christ. The quotation of a few passages will render his meaning perfectly clear: "If we read again the Acts of the Apostles, and attentively examine the devotion that prevailed among the Christian people in the apostolic age, we will find that the piety of the faithful at this moment is very inferior to it. *All* those ancestors of ours were full of ardor and devotion to duty; a *certain number* (*nonnulli*) at present lag far behind them in good works. At the very birth of the Church faith shone brightly in the deeds of *all* believers; now faith is dim in *several* (*apud quosdam*), because the practice of good works is often neglected. In the words of St. Augustine, 'Christ is the same for us that He was for them; but if we have the same belief, we have not the same ardor of devotion. By them brotherhood in Christ was more valued than brotherhood by blood. *All* having the same faith, property was the same among *all;* and since Christ was common to them, they thought that wealth must be common too.'

"In those young days of God's Church the ardor of faith was such that 'they were persevering in the doctrine of the apostles, and in the communication of the breaking of bread, and in prayers; and they had all things common, and they partook of food with joy and simplicity of heart, praising God.' But the Christians' devotion in our day is far from being so ardent, because secular business is preferred by *some* (*a quibusdam*) to the apostles' doctrine," etc.

The same remark is made whenever in this book the author compares his time to that of primitive Christianity. The evil of his epoch consisted, according to him, in the lukewarmness of a *certain number;* and he wished to repair the evil, so as to bring the practice of religion among all up to the initial point at Jerusalem. Nothing can be plainer in the whole text of Jonas, and the strict conclusion is evidently that in fact, in his time, a great number of the faithful lived so piously that they did not appear in their conduct to have degenerated from the first Christians. This, after all, is a great praise bestowed upon an age which immediately followed centuries of social convulsions such as the world had never witnessed before. A second conclusion is likewise derived from the same fact; namely, that the conversion of the barbarians had not been a failure but, on the contrary, a great success so far. The only thing that remained to be done consisted in giving them a friendly impulse toward the height of holiness, which is the ultimate goal and object the Christian religion on earth has always in view.

It is important to dwell a moment on this consideration, for this particular reason, namely, that the epoch of the Carlovingian line in Europe is generally considered as being scarcely less barbarous than the Merovingian (both showing, it is said, how little the Christian religion had so far acted on the human mind and heart). This is in general the verdict passed upon those ages, and it is a verdict most unjust, nay, preposterous, which the work of Jonas of Orleans, *De Institutione Laicali*, absolutely disproves.

For you have in the three short Books of that masterpiece a code of morality which had never yet been given to mankind in its entirety, clearness, and systematic arrangement. Let Mr. Lecky expatiate at length (as he has done with great justice and force) on the principles of his intuitive code of morals. Let him show that the rule of action (*regula agendorum*, as it has been called by Ferraris) is in fact eternal, has always been the same for all nations, does not depend on climate, racial leanings, hereditary habits, etc., but is imprinted in the heart of all, as St. Paul says; the author of the "History of European Morals" must, nevertheless, admit that this rule of action, so truly divine, though in the reach of human reason, is often powerless against the voice of passion and prejudice, has not prevented many nations from running a career of vice and crime, and often can be made a pretext for excusing the greatest excesses of immorality. In fact, it is extremely difficult to extract practically from those great principles composing the moral world in man an unimpeachable and unimpeached code of morals. Plato, Aristotle Cicero, have not done it in the old world; all the philosophers of the "intuitive school" in modern times, as quoted by Mr. Lecky, disagree about it; and if we look in our day into the doctrines of the greatest professors of moral science in England, Germany France, etc., whenever they take no account of the Gospel, we find the same want of unanimity, the same inability to succeed in giving us a code acceptable to all, and capable of directing our great-grand-children for many generations in the same path of virtue and sanctity.

Yet soon after the troublous times of the Clothairs and Theodorics and Dagoberts; immediately after the disgraceful quarrels of Louis the Pious with his children; under Charles the Bald, and directly before the time of Hugh Capet and his rude contemporaries, a simple bishop of Orleans writes a book of moral theology which at once decides broadly all the questions which the old philosophers of the "intuitive school" were unable to clear up. The doctrine is unassailable. The only objection that some might prefer consists in a certain severity of morals which no one would expect after such a period of lawlessness and violence. Few strict Christian moralists of our day would express so forcibly as the book does the rules prescribed, for instance, for the sins of thought and the sanctity of the marriage-bed. Still, this noble work is immediately accepted by the whole Christian world as the code which is to be proposed to the young, the ignorant, the poor, as well as to the learned, powerful, and wealthy. Is not the conclusion manifest that the barbarians had been truly converted, and that before long they would aspire to a heroic holiness to which they were at last invited?

But Jonas did more. He wrote another work as wonderful as this first one, and he called it *De Institutione Regia*. The rulers of the Christian world, the emperors, kings, and princes, were to have their code of morals as well as their own subjects. For it was not only individual piety which was to flourish, but the political bonds of the various nations were henceforth to be consecrated by religion. Holiness as a guide was to replace expediency, ambition, the wiles of diplomacy, and the crushing action of might, which had been so far the only rules followed by sovereigns. A hasty glance must be given to this extraordinary production.

Some rules had been promulgated in the Mosaic law* with regard to the future conduct of kings in Israel when the time should come for the election of hereditary rulers among the Jews, and several texts of the Old Testament prescribed to them the observance of equal rights, justice, mercy, and truth.† But a

---

* Deut. xvii. 14, *seq*.
† See Eccl. xxxii. 1, Prov. xx. 28 and xxix. 14.

much higher conception of the kingly office was to be the privilege of Christian times. With Constantine we observe already the supremacy and total independence of the sacerdotal office in spiritual matters. His successors, however, profoundly disturbed the mutual action of the two powers spiritual and temporal, and when the barbarians came it was to be feared that, even after their conversion, the rulers of the new kingdoms would insist on proclaiming the slavish obedience of all to their despotic will on matters civil and ecclesiastical. It required, in fact, the constancy and heroism of many great bishops to vindicate the rights of the Gospel over the fierce passions of Merovingian monarchs, and it would have seemed a wild and impossible project to devise for them any Christian rules of conduct based on the noble principles of the new religion. How could they ever be brought to admit that the meanest of their subjects was their equal before God; that their authority should be enforced only in accordance with justice and right; that their individual conscience required from them a strict daily examen and a still more strict restraint of every hour; that, finally, they were accountable to a superior power for all their actions and thoughts? And this was reduced to the practical rule that popes and bishops were appointed over them as not only advisers but positive directors and guides, whom they were bound implicitly to obey in all spiritual matters.

Charlemagne was the first who came to an open acknowledgment of all these new principles of action regulating the policy of the state rulers in the new dispensation. But nothing was yet written on the subject, and every individual case was left to a fair understanding of the Gospel laws as they were given out in the New Testament. It is not surprising, therefore, that Louis the Pious, his son, a man Christian to the core and more careful of his soul than of his authority, should submit blindly to his fate, when his sons rose against him, and should agree to his own degradation at the dictation of unworthy prelates, whose great aim was to meddle merely in political matters. This was forbidden them by the constitution of the Church, and in all doubtful cases they could not act without consulting the Pope, to whom they did not even apply; but no precise code existed yet.

Jonas of Orleans was one of the few Frankish bishops who stood firmly on the side of the unfortunate emperor against his unnatural children. He had not taken part in the pretended council at Compiègne in 833, presided over by Ebbo, archbishop of Rheims, by which Louis the Pious was deposed and subjected to public penance, and he was one of the most active prelates in the council of Thionville in 835, when the previous sentence against Louis was reversed and Ebbo was compelled to resign his see. It is needless to say that Pope Gregory IV. confirmed the action of this last assembly.

Jonas was thus the man most competent to prescribe the rules by which Christian kings should be governed in their administration without giving up any of their just rights, so that State and Church should help each other and both benefit human society. This was done in the book *De Institutione Regia*, which settled the principles of monarchical government such as they were understood during the middle ages. It can be said, in a single sentence, that thereby *holiness* was made the governing principle of courts, as the same had been firmly established the guide of common citizens in the previous work, *De Institutione Laicali*.

This new book was addressed to Pepin, king of Aquitania, with whom Jonas had lived on terms of intimacy. The preface is a model of simplicity and good breeding, and the repeated expressions of tender affection and regard for the unaffected virtues of the young sovereign attract at once the attention, and display to the eyes a new political world unfolded by the mild doctrines of Christianity. It is a very strong proof that the Gospel indeed had brought together all ranks of society almost on the same moral level, without interfering with the hierarchy of ranks and offices. This was done by instilling into all minds suavity of manners and a courteous respect for whatever is worthy of it. True politeness was born with the new religion, and never before in the most refined circles of Greece or Rome had anything been seen or heard comparable to it in simple good taste and cordial sympathy. And this is the more remarkable that it happened so soon after the rough explosion of savagery which had devastated Europe. It is a fact almost inexplicable except through the supernatural action of Christianity.

But if the expressions are redolent of suavity and of the mildest spirit, the tone is earnest and the doctrine most strict if not severe: "Oh, my most serene lord and king, in thinking of what I must do for your salvation, which indeed I desire above all things, . . . I humbly remind your highness to consider attentively how swiftly time carries everything in its course; that its joys end invariably in grief; that worldly honor and love and pomp and sweetness engender finally bitterness, because every son of Adam is destined as food to the worms and the rottenness of the sepulchre. The voice of God has declared it to our first parent: 'Thou art dust, and unto dust thou shalt return.'"

The whole of it is written in the same warm style, breathing always affection and a most tender sympathy. As to the book itself, which is much shorter than the one destined for laymen, it must be sufficient here to give the headings of a few of its chapters. The first and second speak of the sacerdotal authority and of its functions with regard to the spiritual guidance of temporal rulers. Constantine had acknowledged it when he said to bishops: "God has made you priests and given you the power to judge us; and it is with justice that you undertake to do it." The third chapter explains at length "what a king is, what he must do and avoid." In a few words the ruler's power is broadly distinguished from that of the tyrant; and many texts of Scripture and of the Fathers are brought out to describe the virtues he must practise and the excesses he must abhor. The fourth chapter speaks of the "kingly ministry;" that is, of his special functions as a Christian ruler; and it may be said that this was kept constantly before the eyes of kings during the middle ages, even when they were most unwilling to listen to the admonition: "The ministry of the king consists especially in governing God's people with equity and justice, and in securing peace and concord. He is first and foremost the defender of the churches and of the servants of God. For it belongs chiefly to his office to provide for the safety and peaceful ministration of the priesthood; and employ, if necessary, his soldiers to protect and secure from harm the Church of Christ; namely, all those members of it whose helplessness requires it, such as widows, orphans, and the poor in general. His great care must be to see, if possible, that no injustice is perpetrated, and in case any wrong is done that it be set to rights, and that its authors do not escape from justice either by hiding themselves or securing their impunity by boldness and force of arms. . . ."

The abuse of authority was provided against in the fifth chapter, which prescribed to the king the choice of upright judges and faithful officials to prevent public infraction of the kingly office, and to watch over the peace and contentment of the subjects. It is curious to see the rules the king had to follow in making his choice of officials, and what kind of men he was directed to select: "The men constituted in authority for such an object must know that Christ's people, over whom they are placed, are in fact their equal by nature and in the eyes of God. The power they receive is only intended for the good of the community, and does not authorize them to domineer over inferiors. Let them not suppose that the men over whom they preside are *their* people, and are in their hands mere tools for promoting their own glory and securing their purposes. This would not be the reign of justice, but the unjust sway of tyranny. . . ."

It is remarkable that this was written when the maxims of feudalism were spreading all over Europe. It might be called a solemn protest against the radical injustice of the new system.

The three following chapters represented the kingly authority as coming from God, and consequently requiring the most faithful obedience from the subjects. But no one must imagine that this amounted to the acknowledgment of the "divine right of kings" as preached subsequently by James I. of England and all Protestant theologians. There is, hovever, no time and space to show the difference of both.

The other chapters, from the ninth to the seventeenth, speak of the law of God in general, as imposed on monarchs as well as on their subjects. The details are exactly like those given in the book *De Institutione Laicali;* and the main object is to intimate that the kings are men like all others, and could not enjoy privileges with regard to God's laws.

It is important to mention at the end of these short abstracts that this second book of Jonas of Orleans attracted immediately so much attention, and exerted so powerful an influence, that the whole of it, except the preface and the last chapters, was inserted among the canons of the Sixth Council of Paris, which took place in 829. It thus became a public document acknowledged by the ecclesiastical authority; and consequently formed a part of the canon law, at least in France. There is no need of alluding again to the importance it immediately acquired for imparting to the middle ages a special feature which could not but lead to holiness in high places—that is, in the princely courts and political circles of those times—as the work *De Institutione Laicali* had done for the common class of society.

Europe, being provided with a code for kings and another for the people, could rapidly progress on the road to sanctity. The more so that another code had already been given to a powerful branch of the social world at that epoch. This refers to the rules of St. Benedict by which all the monasteries of Europe were at last governed. A word has been said on the gradual absorption of all the religious orders existing previously to that of St. Benedict. At the precise epoch which is now under consideration—the end of the ninth century—the transformation had taken place. There was but one rule for all the ascetic establishments; and this rule in its primitive simplicity has always been regarded as the embodiment of the most strict spirit of Christianity. Holiness reigned in the cloister; it was rapidly acquiring the preponderance in society. This must be seen in the following section, as briefly as the copiousness of the subject will allow.

5. *The Ages of Faith were likewise Ages of Holiness.*

Kenelm Digby in his *Mores Catholici* has treated this subject *in extenso*. To give the substance of this great and admirable work would far exceed the limits assigned to ours. Besides, it would be impossible to condense a book which merely consists in the narration of an immense number of facts; chiefly because the strength of the demonstration depends entirely on that number and their circumstances and connection. The dark side of those times, moreover, is but slightly given by Digby, and this has subjected the work to a just criticism which it is intended here to avoid. Another plan must therefore be adopted.

The general idea followed by the author—to represent the evangelical beatitudes as eminently practised during the middle ages—is no doubt excellent and to the purpose, since the essence of holiness consists in the strict practice of the virtues preached by our Lord in His Sermon on the Mount. But to adopt the same plan would necessarily bring on the same length of details, or at least something of it. It is preferable to suppose that the reader knows sufficiently the work entitled *Mores Catholici*, but that his conviction requires to be strengthened, particularly with regard to its weak points; and this cannot be done better than by a simple, short, but exact description of those most abused ages extending from the tenth to the fifteenth centuries. Europe formed then a powerful commonwealth which was called Christendom. All nations composing it had common features which they had received from their common religion; and the simple recital of these universal peculiarities will ensure the conviction that a high degree of sanctity must have everywhere flourished, simply from the whole array of circumstances then existing on the whole western continent. For this object it will be sufficient to consider the public worship of those people, their charity, general manner and morals, family habits, and finally their death. The objections consequent upon what is known of simony and incontinence among the secular clergy, and the prevalent state of war, will be briefly reviewed and answered at the end of these considerations.

I. The Catholic worship, in its public character, wore then a peculiar aspect which had not been seen in the previous Roman world; which has passed away in our cold age; and probably will never again appear. At all times this adoration of God has been holy and fostered holiness in the Church; during the middle ages it was eminently so. It is important to glance at it in the numerous monasteries then flourishing, and in the innumerable cathedrals, parish churches, chapels, and oratories with which Europe was profusely and literally covered.

After a long period of superstition and heathenism on the whole earth, which had followed the simplicity of the patriarchal age, a worship worthy of God was at last introduced everywhere by the religion of Christ. The Father in heaven was finally adored through the mediation of His Eternal Son and under the wide-spread influence of the Holy Spirit, Who had taken possession of the universe and dwelt in the heart of each of His creatures. Whatever has ever been devised by the ingenuity of man, in his rashness to invent rites which Heaven had not revealed, and were intended to supplant the true religion, has invariably ended in a miserable failure. The Christian rites alone have survived all the attempts of deists or rationalists, so as to satisfy the cravings of the human heart toward the propitiation of Heaven, and the deep sense of dependence of the creature on his Creator. The burst of piety which astonished mankind on Constantine at last granting liberty to the Church was for that enlightened age the proof that it came from heaven. Ceremonies so noble, so grand, so full of majesty and power, could not but take their rise in the action of God teaching His children how to adore Him. No Greek, no Roman could imagine that the efforts of man to reach heaven by his prayers could take a higher and holier form. As long as the Empire stood the Christian heart remained satisfied that human godliness could never go farther. And with respect to the essentials of the worship this was true, and there could be no change since the new dispensation was to be the last.

But soon after the untold calamities which followed this first triumph of religion, when it seemed that a terrible barbarian outbreak had for a long time silenced the former Christian solemnities, a sight was revealed to the eyes of men which the spectacle of religious pomp in all former Greek and Roman cities had certainly never equalled.

An immense number of large monastic establishments have just been constructed as if by magic, not only in populous centres, but in the wilderness of the forest or on the top of hills and mountains. The rivers of Italy, Africa, Spain, Gaul, Germany, England, are lined, as it were, by these monuments of religion and industry. But the most eminent feature of those noble piles is always a vast church edifice, rising above the low cells and long cloisters, where hundreds, nay, thousands of cowled monks or pious rustics are standing or kneeling in profound adoration. Though the fields around are tilled with care by swarms of laborers, the service of God goes on unceasingly under those arched vaults, along those spacious naves and aisles, chiefly in the dim-lighted and mysterious sanctuary. Yes, the night as well as the day is devoted to a worship which must represent that of Heaven, since there is no intermission in the praise, and the love, and the songs of angels and saints. Splendid storied windows speak to the humblest and the most ignorant of the life of Christ, the providence of God, the sweetness of Mary, the constant ministrations of pure spirits in their flight from heaven to earth. Hear the deep and soft tones of that new instrument unknown to the highly artistic Greeks of old, but invented by a monk and played upon by another. Listen to those deep-cadenced voices intoning the noble songs of an inspired poetry, and telling in distinct accents the story of the earth's creation, the fall of the first man, his redemption and sanctification, and the high destiny to which he is called. Almost every day long processions of priests, children, and deep-praying men come from a distant shrine and enter the sacred edifice with song and litany; all with their eyes intently looking on the highly wrought tabernacle which rises in the midst of the mystic altar where the Holy of holies resides.

But the bell has ceased tolling, the voices are hushed, the organ either murmurs softly or is silent. It is the most solemn moment on earth, for **Heaven** has come down. The Eternal Son is present; Angels and powers surround Him; the crowd in the nave is prostrate on the ground; and all hearts are lifted up to heaven. It is the only sacrifice worthy of the Divine Majesty. The Man-God Himself adores in the midst of His adorers, and offers to His Father the blood He shed on the cross. A drop of it would have sufficed to cleanse the whole world; and man can consider himself redeemed.

This was the firm belief of all those mediæval Christians; and the strongest human intellect may without fear be defied to show that a higher and holier worship could be devised. God alone, through His infinite love, had designed it; and as it is His last and eternal covenant with man, nothing can be added to or taken away from it.

This was at that time taking place daily in the most remote and wild parts of western Europe. In the cities a still more solemn pomp surrounded the divine mysteries. For each city had its bishops, and each bishop his cathedral. The mind is bewildered when those solemn edifices are considered with attention: their immense size, their artistic beauty, their lofty vaults and loftier pinnacles; the endless groups of statuary surrounding the sanctuary; the large number of dignitaries standing or kneeling around the prelate, all clad in the most costly vestments, all deeply engaged in prayer or song; the multitude of people, to the number of ten or twenty or thirty thousand, sending to heaven a stream of harmony which resounds through the thick forest of columns and pilasters; the brilliant windows illustrated with biblical scenes or legendary stories; the incense filling the aisles with perfume, and the soft and colored light reflected from walls and woodwork tracery. Where on earth would anything like it be seen? Yes, the age that saw the building of these piles was an age of wonders; and the most incredulous is obliged to confess that the mediæval worship of God has surpassed in grandeur and sanctity whatever has been seen before or since.

But neither monastic churches nor cathedrals could cover every rood of ground in mediæval Europe, on account of their costliness and the time required for building them. Still, the people had then solemnly declared with the prophet of old that "the earth was the Lord's, and the fulness thereof." Every hamlet, therefore, must have its church; every turn of the public roads its oratory; every crag and nook and corner in mountains or hills its shrine; every house its statue; every tree, almost, its holy symbol. Men were then proud of their religion. They did not wish to conceal it as something to be ashamed of. Rural solemnities were devised to encircle the whole year round. The village parish had its priest, the smallest oratory its pious chaplain; and, because man needs rest, it was universally thought that one day in the week was not sufficient. I will not attempt to describe all the saints' feasts, all the holy seasons of religious festivity. Think of Christmas and Easter and Pentecost and the Lady days and Midsummer Night and Michaelmas and All Saints!

Here I am reminded that it must have been a priest-ridden age. So it was indeed, but the people liked it. Some pretend still at this late hour that poor men could not then earn their bread, being prevented from working a great part of the year. But it has been lately proved that the reverse was true, and the poorest of the rustics were then as comfortable as well-to-do farmers in our day. Happy they were that the clang of the hammer in factories was often silent, and the hard labor at the plough suspended. Do the economists of our age imagine that working men are now more happy because their labor is incessant, and because their poorly rewarded toil, in many cases, does not know any intermission? If so they think, let them ask the opinion of our proletarians, as they are called, and they may be at last enlightened.

But this is indeed too long a digression. The question at hand seems to have been forgotten, and we must return to it. The few details just given, with which we must remain satisfied, have proved beyond question that in mediæval times the worship of God was peculiar; and that at any other epoch the earth has never seen anything like it. A few reflections must be devoted to proving that it was calculated to foster holiness; since there are men who pretend that the highest morality, holiness consequently, is independent even of the belief in God, independent consequently of a more or less pure worship.

Yes, our ears are stunned by the clatter of many voices eulogizing atheism itself, and pretending that those even who "have felt constrained to abandon their former faith in a Creator' not only may be, but actually are, exemplary men practising all the virtues of the sage, which they say are the same as those of the Christian. It seems, therefore, that we were mistaken in counting the pure worship of God during the mediæval times as the proof of a high degree of holiness. Mr. Mallock has thought proper to discuss this very question, and to disprove the new pretension of modern thinkers, in his excellent work, "Is Life Worth Living?" I could simply refer to it; a few words, however, will not delay us long, and may be sufficient for the purpose, independently of the strict reasoning of that gifted writer.

I will confine myself to a short line of argument; remarking first, as a preliminary matter, that the question must not be one of persons, but of tendency. That there are some *persons* whose moral character is pure though they do not believe in God is irrelevant to the present question. The object is to inquire if the *tendency* of atheism is to foster a holy life. Reduced to these terms, the question cannot offer any difficulty.

Mr. Mallock believes that the present originators of atheistic thought in England are men of exemplary lives; and we are ourselves persuaded that Lalande in France, a pronounced atheist of last century, was eminently what is called a good man. Can any one conclude from this that their disbelief in the existence of God was or is their main reason for practising what is called virtue? Would there not be still a better reason for it, were they firmly convinced of the contrary? Is it the same with regard to morality, to have no fear of a future judge; or to be fully convinced of a strict accountability to God? Individual men are acted upon by a thousand motives in the performance of their actions. The question is *not*, Is individual atheism absolutely incompatible with morality?—the word holiness would be misplaced here—but *it must be* the general one, Which is the best motive for a pure life, a firm belief in God or the reverse? We are right, therefore, to say that it is a question of tendency, not of persons. This being admitted, we proceed in our line of argument.

The very essence of the matter under consideration refers to a large mass of people, since it embraces the whole of western Europe and includes nations of various races, aptitudes, and leanings. They have to be brought, at least in a great number, to the perfection of holiness. What will be the best motives to conduce to it? There may be several; but one of the strongest must be the fear and love of God, and consequently His pure worship. There is question here of the multitude, not of a few individuals among them. No one can hesitate to say that the more ardent the religion of the multitude will be, the higher they will rise in holiness. First, they have constantly before their eyes the highest pattern of it, since God has said: *Perfecti estote sicut et Pater vester cœlestis perfectus est.* Our Saviour knew what holiness must be, and He declared that the first and greatest commandment was to love God above all things. Pure worship must be, therefore, the highest and most effective inducement to good morals. Again, Moses brought down from Sinai the two tables of the law; and the first contained only the precepts of religion. To strike these off at a blow is to deprive morality of its better half. And this is not only Christian teaching; it is the natural teaching of the human heart; because those precepts of the first table were inscribed on it before they were engraved on the stone. It is only at this late hour in the course of time that sophists pretend the contrary. The pagans themselves admitted it, since they invariably inculcated the fear of the gods as the beginning of wisdom and the first inward utterance of our moral sense.

But even in our day this is perfectly well understood by the common-sense of the people. No one believes that the worshippers of God in any Christian temple can be put down on a level, in point of morality, with those who never darken the door of a church. There may be a few hypocrites among the worshippers; but those who are sincere are universally considered as far better morally than men who have no religion whatever. Go and inquire of those who have under their charge the peace of the community, and ask them if when a burglary or murder takes place they look first in a Christian congregation to find the criminal.

But if this is true at all times and in our own in particular, it was eminently so at the epoch under consideration. All are aware of the low morality of the barbarians when they first rushed on southern Europe; and a description has been attempted of the efforts required from bishops and monks to tame them and instil into their hearts the most common feelings of humanity. In the course of a few centuries the success was complete. This was chiefly because the Huns as well as the Franks, the Burgundians as well as the Vandals, worshipped the same God, had their children baptized in the same fount, and were themselves fed with the same Eucharist. It was a wonderful change, which, however, need not be described in detail at this moment. So late as the Carlovingians even, directly after the frightful outbreak of the Northmen, if many Europeans were on the road to sanctity, they had not yet attained it. Many crimes, on the contrary, continued to horrify mankind. Still, when during the centuries which followed we contemplate the solemn worship of the Christian religion spread at last among them all, and offering the wonderful features which have been so briefly and so inaccurately portrayed, have we not reason to say that they were already holy people? The new habits of piety, of tender devotion, of universal dependence on God, they had so remarkably acquired, could not but foster in their hearts the most strict moral sense, the strongest attachment to duty; in fine, what we Christians call the perfect fulfilment of the whole Decalogue, with the addition besides of the virtues preached by our Lord in His Sermon on the Mount. This is far superior to the highest morality taught by any philosopher of the "intuitive school," and particularly superior to the moral tendency fostered by *positivism;* and this was eminently the result of the religion they had been taught to honor and practise, which culminated in the grand display offered by their noble worship of God.

The great misfortune is that people in our day do not like any more to speak of "holiness;" they prefer to use the words "pure ethics." The only thing we must require of them is to admit that holiness comprises all the pure ethics known to the moral philosopher, besides something far above them; namely, a certain *consecration* of the whole subject to heaven. This is to be considered a moment.

Let any moral philosopher point out, if he can, a single article of "ethical science" which is not already prescribed by "revealed doctrine." He will be brought to acknowledge his inability to do so, for the very simple reason that "ethical science," if exact, is nothing but the voice of conscience promulgating the external and unchangeable principles of the moral order. But in the precepts of the Mosaic decalogue, as well as in those of the Christian religion, this is always presupposed, because *grace* supposes *nature*, and as the *decretum Gratiani* said many centuries ago: "In principle the natural law is the same that is contained in that of Moses and in the Gospel."

But the natural law such as it is, when brought out from the inner world of the human conscience and dissected by the scalpel of the mere philosopher, seems to be only a part and parcel of our poor humanity, such as are its other faculties of body and mind, and can scarcely be imagined to contain anything holy, since holiness belongs, after all, to heaven. The revealed doctrine, on the contrary, appertains to the order of grace, which is altogether heavenly; and consequently it must impart to ethical matters what has been called a sort of consecration. This consecration, the result of God's grace, is the only thing which is added to the practice of natural virtue; that is, to the power of doing good derived from the native moral strength of man. Can the philosophers of the "intuitive school" object to this? Must they not admit, on the contrary, that the supposition is far from being absurd, and that if it really takes place it will be very beneficial for morality, and give it a true title to the quality of holiness? For "the true light," as St. John says,* "which enlighteneth every man that cometh into this world," is the natural light of reason, which does not come precisely to the soul by a direct ray from the Eternal Word but, as it were, in a reflex manner through our human faculties. Though coming originally from heaven, it does not receive a heavenly *consecration*, but can produce only a human virtue having no claim to true holiness.

But as soon as "the Word was made flesh, and dwelt among us," as St. John maintains farther on,† then "we saw His glory, the glory . . . of the only begotten Son of the Father, full of grace and truth." Here the ray of light is direct, and can reach the soul in a supernatural manner. No wonder that the virtue produced is no more a human virtue, but a heavenly one, carrying holiness with it. It is the result of the direct action of the Son of God on the soul, and explains perfectly the inborn sanctity of the Christian, who himself deserves to be called Son of God by adoption.

It is, therefore, in a strict sense that the Christian can be called *holy* when his life comes up to his profession. His sanctity is not a *cloak* like the imputation of Luther, leaving the sore of his sins festering inwardly in the eyes of God. The soul has been thoroughly cleansed, and the smile of heaven approves the purity of the new-born creature.

---

* Chap. i. v. 9. † Ib. v. 14.

It seems now easy to understand that the sublime worship of Almighty God so prevalent during mediæval times, being the outgrowth of grace imparted by the God-man, was altogether calculated to engender true virtue in the heart of those people, and was at the same time a proof that they were holy. Their virtue was not natural only. It came from God and went back to Him.

If, on the contrary, you dissever morality from religion under the pretext that even some atheists can recoil with horror from injustice, robbery, adultery, murder, etc., and can also be unselfish, charitable, patient, etc., you commit the imprudence of leaving the mass of mankind at the mercy of their unruly passions. It is safe to deny that this mass is capable enough of self-restraint to avoid rushing into the most deplorable excesses. Deliver them from the fear of God, as Lucretius wished to do for the men of his generation, and the earth will become the fit image of Tartarus. Virtue will be derided and crime eulogized. This would certainly have happened to Europe at the epoch of which we treat, if the barbarians had learned from the degenerate Romans that the fear of hell and the hope of heaven were pure bugbears. They learned, on the contrary, that the love of God is the basis of all virtues, and that His holy worship is the greatest concern of human life, and the surest means for any one of becoming holy, as a step to an eternal reward; they placed their reliance chiefly on the grace of Christ, who had established the kingdom of heaven in their hearts. After this first characteristic of the mediæval period the consideration of the second is likewise of great importance; and this is the admirable spirit of charity which then prevailed.

II. The difficulty here consists in the copiousness of matter. It would require a large volume, with a great care taken for condensation, to bring forth only the most remarkable facts connected with the subject. It would be worth while to do it, since no better description of the middle ages can be made than to go through a mere rehearsal of their unbounded benevolence. Still, it cannot be done here. Fortunately, Mr. Lecky in his fairness has drawn a picture of it which, though condensed in a few pages, is, I think, one of the best of its kind that has ever been written.

The admirable generalization of the gifted author begins from the epoch immediately anterior to the mediæval times, and that part of it does not seem to enter into our actual scope. But as this first branch of the subject seems to be very useful at least to appreciate what follows, it seems far from irrelevant to have the whole of it presented at once:*

"The active, habitual, and detailed charity of private persons, which is so conspicuous a feature in all Christian societies, was scarcely known in antiquity, and there are not more than two or three moralists who have even noticed it." Here he quotes Cicero, *De Officiis.* "Christianity for the first time made charity a rudimentary virtue, giving it a leading place in the moral type and in the exhortations of its teachers. Besides its general influence in stimulating the affections, it effected a complete revolution in this sphere, by regarding the poor as the special representatives of the Christian Founder, and thus making the love of Christ, rather than the love of man, the principle of charity. Even in the days of persecution, collections for the relief of the poor were made at the Sunday meetings. The agapæ, or feasts of love, were intended mainly for the poor, and food that was saved by the fasts was devoted to their benefit. A vast organization of charity, presided over by the bishops and actively directed by the deacons, soon ramified over Christendom, till the bond of charity became the bond of unity, and the most distant sections of the Christian Church corresponded by the interchange of mercy. Long before the era of Constantine, it was observed that the charities of the Christians were so extensive—it may, perhaps, be said so excessive—that they drew very many impostors to the Church; and when the victory of Christianity was achieved, the enthusiasm for charity displayed itself in the erection of numerous institutions that were altogether unknown to the pagan world. A Roman lady, named Fabiola, in the fourth century founded at Rome, as an act of penance, the first public hospital; and the charity planted by that woman's hand overspread the world, and will alleviate, to the end of time, the darkest anguish of humanity. Another hospital was soon founded by St. Pammachus; another of great celebrity by St. Basil, at Cæsarea. St. Basil also erected at Cæsarea what was probably the first asylum for lepers. Xenodochia, or refuges for strangers, speedily rose, especially along

---

* Hist. of Europ. Morals. vol. ii. p. 79.

the paths of the pilgrims. St. Pammachus founded one at Ostia; Paula and Melania founded others at Jerusalem. The Council of Nice ordered that one should be erected in every city. In the time of St. Chrysostom the church of Antioch supported three thousand widows and virgins, besides strangers and sick. Legacies for the poor became common; and it was not unfrequent for men and women who desired to live a life of peculiar sanctity, and especially for priests who attained the episcopacy, to bestow their entire properties in charity. Even the early Oriental monks, who for the most part were extremely removed from the active and social virtues, supplied many noble examples of charity. St. Ephrem, in a time of pestilence, emerged from his solitude to found and superintend a hospital at Edessa. A monk named Thalasius collected blind beggars in an asylum on the banks of the Euphrates. A merchant named Apollonius founded on Mount Nitria a gratuitous dispensary for the monks. The monks often assisted by their labors provinces that were suffering from pestilence and famine. We may trace the remains of the pure socialism that marked the first phase of the Christian community in the emphatic language with which some of the Fathers proclaimed charity to be a matter not of mercy but of justice, maintaining that all property is based on usurpation, that the earth by right is common to all men, and that no man can claim a superabundant supply of its goods except as an administrator for others. A Christian, it was maintained, should devote at least one tenth of his profits to the poor." —Mr. Lecky may have somewhat misunderstood the bearing of some of the numerous authorities he quotes here.

" The enthusiasm of charity, thus manifested in the Church, speedily attracted the attention of the pagans. The ridicule of Lucian and the vain efforts of Julian to produce a rival system of charity within the limits of paganism emphatically attested both its preeminence and its catholicity. During the pestilences that desolated Carthage in A.D. 326 and Alexandria in the reigns of Gallienus and of Maximian, while the pagans fled panic-stricken from the contagion, the Christians extorted the admiration of their fellow-countrymen by the courage with which they rallied around their bishops, consoled the last hours of the sufferers, and buried the abandoned dead. In the rapid increase of pauperism arising from the emancipation of numerous slaves their charity found free scope for action, and its resources were soon taxed to the utmost by the horrors of the barbarian invasions. The conquest of Africa by Genseric deprived Italy of the supply of corn upon which it almost wholly depended, arrested the gratuitous distribution by which the Roman poor were mainly supported, and produced all over the land the most appalling calamities. The history of Italy became one monotonous tale of famine and pestilence, of starving populations and ruined cities. But everywhere amid this chaos of dissolution we may detect the majestic form of the Christian priest mediating between the hostile forces, straining every nerve to lighten the calamities around him. When the Imperial City was captured and plundered by the hosts of Alaric, a Christian church remained a secure sanctuary which neither the passions nor the avarice of the Goths transgressed. When a fiercer than Alaric had marked out Rome for his prey, the Pope St. Leo arrayed in his sacerdotal robes, confronted the victorious Hun as the ambassador of his fellow-countrymen, and Attila, overpowered by religious awe, turned aside in his course. When, two years later, Rome lay at the mercy of Genseric, the same pope interposed with the Vandal conqueror, and obtained from him a partial cessation of the massacre. The archdeacon Pelagius interceded with similar humanity and similar success, when Rome had been captured by Totila. In Gaul Troyes is said to have been saved from destruction by the influence of St. Lupus, and Orleans by the influence of St. Agnan. In Britain an invasion of the Picts was averted by St. Germain of Auxerre. The relations of rulers to their subjects, and of tribunals to the poor, were modified by the same intervention. When Antioch was threatened with destruction on account of its rebellion against Theodosius, the anchorets poured forth from the neighboring deserts to intercede with the ministers of the emperor, while the Archbishop Flavian went himself as a suppliant to Constantinople. St. Ambrose imposed public penance on Theodosius on account of the massacre of Thessalonica. Synesius excommunicated for his oppressions a governor named Andronicus; and two French councils in the sixth century imposed the same penalty on all great men who habitually ejected the poor. Special laws were found necessary to restrain the turbulent charity of some priests and monks who impeded the course of justice and even snatched criminals from the hands of the law. St. Abraham, St. Epiphanius, and St. Basil are all said to have obtained the remission or reduction of oppressive imposts. To provide for the interests of the widows and orphans was part of the official ecclesiastical duty, and a Council of Macon anathematized any ruler who brought them to trial, without first apprising the bishop of the diocese. A Council of Toledo threatened with excommunication all who robbed priests, monks, or poor men, or refused to listen to their expostulations. One of the chief causes of the inordinate power acquired by the clergy was their mediatorial office; and their gigantic wealth was in a great degree due to the legacies of those who regarded them as the trustees of the poor.

"As time rolled on, charity assumed many forms, and every monastery became a centre from which it radiated. By the monks the nobles were overawed, the poor protected, the sick tended, travellers sheltered, prisoners ransomed, the remotest spheres of suffering explored. During the darkest period of the middle ages, monks founded a refuge for pilgrims amid the horrors of the Alpine snows. A solitary hermit often planted himself, with his little boat, by a bridgeless stream, and the charity of his life was to ferry over the traveller. When the hideous disease of leprosy extended its ravages over Europe, when the minds of men were filled with terror not only by its loathsomeness and its contagion, but also by the notion that it was in a peculiar sense supernatural, new hospitals and refuges overspread Europe, and monks flocked in multitudes to serve in them. Sometimes, the legends say, the leper's form was in a moment transfigured, and he who came to tend the most loathsome of mankind received his reward, for he found himself in the presence of his Lord.

"There is no fact of which an historian becomes more speedily and more painfully conscious than the great difference between the importance and the dramatic interest of the subjects he treats. Wars or massacres, the horrors of martyrdom or the splendors of individual prowess, are susceptible of such brilliant coloring that with but little literary skill they can be so portrayed that their importance is adequately realized, and they appeal powerfully to the emotions of the reader. But this vast and unostentatious movement of charity, operating in the village hamlet and in the lonely hospital, stanching the widow's tears and following all the windings of the poor man's grief, presents few figures the imagination can grasp, and leaves no deep impression upon the mind. The greatest things are often those which are most imperfectly realized; and surely no achievements of the Christian Church are more truly great than those which it has effected in the sphere of charity. For the first time in the history of mankind it has inspired many thousands, men and women, at the sacrifice of all wordly interests, and often under circumstances of extreme discomfort and danger, to devote their entire lives to the single object of assuaging the sufferings of humanity. It has covered the globe with countless institutions of mercy absolutely unknown to the whole pagan world. It has indissolubly united, in the minds of men, the idea of supreme goodness with that of active and constant benevolence. It has placed in every parish a religious minister who, whatever may be his other functions, has at least been officially charged with the superintendence of an organization of charity, and who finds in this office one of the most important, as well as one of the most legitimate, sources of his power."

In this admirably condensed sketch, Mr. Lecky does not seem precisely to recognize the middle ages as having been the most prominent in the practice of charity; and he appears even to intimate that it was a "dark period" in the history of the Church, only illumined by many remarkable instances of that sublime virtue. Still, he has written at least a sentence which, in its comprehensiveness, restores in fact to that much-abused epoch its true character and its substantial glory, when he said that "by the monks the nobles were overawed, the poor protected, the sick tended, travellers sheltered, prisoners ransomed, the remotest spheres of suffering explored." It is almost impossible to say more, and the legitimate development of these few words would embrace the whole subject, and present a picture which has never been seen even in the history of the Church, glowing with more splendor, and expressing with more fidelity the true portrait of Christianity and its Founder.

Frederick Hurter in his *Tableau du Moyen Age*, translated from the German by J. Cohen,* had long before Mr. Lecky fulfilled the same task, and given still more details, all derived from the history of the middle ages. A few words of this long description will make amend for some deficiencies in the English author, due mainly to the brevity of his generalization: "It was not only in monasteries that travellers, the poor, the necessitous, found an asylum and met with people ready to help and serve them; it was not only near cathedral churches that houses had been constructed for that purpose. But charitable establishments of every degree

---

* Tom ii. p. 492, *seq.*

had been founded, and were profusely scattered over Europe. Sometimes they were entrusted to the care of religious orders; sometimes they were given in charge to men who consented to live under certain obligatory rules, though they were not religious. On a river bank, where no bridge had yet been constructed; in a lonely valley, where the traveller might lose his way in the darkness of the night; on the top of mountains, where no human habitation was near and no refreshment could be procured, Christian benevolence had erected houses for no other object than to offer shelter and food to the pilgrim. From the eighth century down to a much later epoch, chapels and oratories had been built for the simple purpose of furnishing to the poor of the neighborhood a weekly allowance of the provisions they needed. . . . "

But the author of the "History of European Morals" has qualified his description by the enumeration of other facts of a totally different character, and calculated to represent the middle ages under a rather repulsive aspect. He confines, however, his derogatory remarks to only two points, one relating to the insane, the other to a want of judgment in the charitable distributions. Nothing is more simple and easy than the answer to the first objection. The healing art had made but little progress since the time of Hippocrates, and Christianity is not responsible for it. The causes of the terrible maladies by which man is deprived of his reason were totally unknown, and have remained so until our age; remedial agents could not be properly applied, and it is difficult to see how this could be attributed to any want of charity on the part of the Church. It is true that, as Mr. Lecky insists, insanity was considered to a certain degree as having often supernatural causes; and how can it be proved that it has not? The ideas of "witchcraft and diabolical possession" may have been occasionally unjustly connected with it, and some deplorable results, no doubt, were the consequences of it. But how can it be maintained that this argued any hardness of heart on the part of Christians, when there are so many brilliant proofs of the contrary? A simple error of judgment and its painful consequences leave the admirable spirit of charity then existing absolutely entire, since nobody could think that there was the least connection or opposition between the two. They were most charitable, but they believed in the power of the Evil One so clearly indicated by Jesus Christ Himself.

As to the supposed injudicious use of charity which, in the opinion of Mr. Lecky, "directly increased the poverty which it was intended to relieve," this is a mighty question which cannot be discussed here. It affects in no way the holy virtue of which we treat, since people at that epoch could not perceive that they were "injudicious." They implicitly followed the impulse which they felt inwardly for the literal fulfilment of the precept and the perfect imitation of the example of Christ, and in this they truly practised that sublime virtue which is the only important consideration for us at this moment. But without entering into the question which Mr. Lecky discusses at length, it is not out of place to remark that political economy, whose teachings he seems to consider of great importance, is now regarded by the best sociologists as having completely failed in the great object its supporters had in view; and it is not from the principles either of Adam Smith or of the Manchester school that the Christian charity of mediæval times can receive its condemnation.

The ground is now prepared for the special consideration of the active bearing this charity had on holiness in the case under review. And, first, it is seen at once that if the worship of God, such as it was then practised, imparted to the virtues of those Christians a heavenly consecration alone capable of giving them a truly holy character, the same was the result of their ardent love for their afflicted brethren, for the lowly, the poor, the sick, the friendless, the needy. As has been justly remarked in the long passage quoted from the "History of European Morals," "the Christian Church has indissolubly united, in the minds of men, the idea of supreme goodness"—that is, of holiness—"with that of active and constant benevolence." Since holiness in man must consist in the imitation of God carried to a heroic degree, according to Christ's recommendation, *Perfecti estote sicut et Pater vester cælestis perfectus est;* and since mankind, in its worship of God, has always called Him not only the Greatest—*Maximus*—but also and chiefly the Best—*Optimus,*—man to be holy must actively work to the advantage of his fellow-men, the same as God does incessantly by His providence for us. The Church, consequently, in calling the religious state one of perfection, declares that its members must not only attend to their own salvation—that is, their own good—but also to the salvation—that is, the good—of others. There are, no doubt, some religious orders which are called contemplative and do not practise exterior benevolence. They are often accused, on this account, of being useless to mankind; but every one of us knows that through their prayers heavenly graces are daily obtained, often far preferable to any temporal blessings.

In the Christian scheme, therefore, charity is a great part of holiness; and thus because the middle ages were eminently charitable they must be called eminently holy. For this reason, probably, all men, unless they are barbarians, feel an instinctive reverence for those who devote themselves to their neighbors' service. It is universally felt that there is in them something of God's holiness which calls for veneration; and often, indeed, barbarians—since the name has been used—have fallen prostrate at the feet of a benefactor who had rescued them from misery and death.

This must not be considered as an unfounded instinct derived from unreasoned feelings, and deserving to be classed among many other amiable weaknesses of our human nature. There is a real foundation for it, and it is not difficult to find it out. Christian charity, when it reaches a certain degree, supposes that the intense selfishness which crops out of our nature at every moment of our lives has been overcome; and not only it seems to be dead in those who are ardently benevolent, but it is replaced by an inward feeling of self-sacrifice which does not belong any more to this earth, but assumes immediately the highest supernatural form. There have been men, it is true, who have given even their life for their country, their children, their friends; and their motives may have belonged altogether to this world. Ancient history is full of examples of this kind, and every educated man knows at least some of them. But this is very different from the self-sacrifice of the Christian when he devotes his whole life to the service of his neighbor. This is to be seen.

The virtues of the pagans were not sins, as Luther pretended; they were real natural virtues, which St. Augustine believed God had often rewarded by great temporal blessings. They consequently supposed self-sacrifice, and required real efforts to overcome selfishness. But the sphere in which they were embraced was limited to the low grounds of this world, and could not possibly rise above it. The highest act of virtue, probably, ever performed by a pagan was that of Regulus when he surrendered himself to the Carthaginians; that is, devoted himself to a most cruel death in order not to break his word. It is very doubtful if he attached to it the idea of duty in our modern sense, and it may have been only the result of a stoical pride which none of us can call a virtue. But even in the more charitable and probable supposition, there is no proof that, even at this early time of the Roman republic, the idea of a duty of this kind was in any way connected with the idea of God and religion. It is rather very likely, if not altogether certain, that this connection did not exist. Consequently there could be nothing supernatural in the highest virtues of the heathen, as there is nothing above nature also in the highest virtues inculcated by the modern "intuitive school of morals." But it has been seen that this is only the practice of "pure ethics," not of holiness, for the reasons formerly assigned.

The mediæval Christians took a widely different view of the subject. In sacrificing themselves to their neighbors they sacrificed themselves to God. They positively intended to honor and imitate the God-man by their charity; and being thus intimately united to Him, they absolutely belonged to the supernatural world of which Christ is the centre. Their ideas of virtue, consequently, were as high as heaven itself; and thus their actions received that consecration of holiness of which a word has been said

For this reason it was not only a high but also a wide-spread virtue; because, since the birth of Christianity, the Holy Ghost has taken possession of the universe; and as He is the source of our moral strength, it must be widely diffused over the earth Remark well the difference between that universal diffusion resulting from the Christian scheme and the few sporadic examples of it that the pagan world ever furnished. Among the ancient heathen these heroic acts can be counted by the dozen; among the mediæval Christians by the million. And there is another difference between them which is most remarkable. All the noble actions recorded of the Greeks and Romans took place as it were, on the spur of the moment. In the vehemence of a generous enthusiasm they threw their lives away. But the self sacrifice of the monk, of the nun, of the simple Christian, lasts most often during the whole span of their existence, or at least the best part of it. It is a slow martyrdom, whose reward cannot be seen but at a great distance, whilst their constancy is every day tried by the obscurity of labor, the violence of temptation the wearisomeness of common duty.

Such a virtue as this has never been seen in the world except among the followers of Christ. It belongs, consequently, to the transcendental order, and can be called true sanctity. It may appear presumptuous in the eyes of the world to use such a word as this; it was but simple and natural, however, in their especial position. Hence if any one of them habitually recoiled from calling himself holy, they did not scruple to admit that they belonged to a generation of saints. The name was openly taken by the Christians of the very first ages, and was publicly sanctioned by the apostles themselves. In mediæval times this was more true than ever, as there was a large number of them spread over the whole of Europe, all engaged in the same holy avocation. Look at them everywhere " protecting the poor, overawing the nobles, tending the sick, sheltering the travellers, ransoming the prisoners, exploring the remotest spheres of suffering in order to assuage it. Every monastery has become a centre from which charity radiates." These words of Mr. Lecky cannot be too often repeated, and they express the simple truth. But all this is done at the expense of an immense amount of self-sacrifice; and the bestowers of the benefit are almost as numerous as the recipients of it. Who can refuse to admit that holiness reigned then supreme in redeemed Europe?

III. The next point promised for discussion may well seem superfluous, but is not. This is the consideration of mediæval morals as a third proof of holiness. Christ has said that His law consists only of two precepts, the love of God and the love of the neighbor. Both have just been satisfactorily discussed with regard to the middle ages, and it could be directly concluded that nothing more to prove in them a high morality is needed. But the great objection raised against this epoch refers precisely to the morals or manners of the people, which are said to have been gross, vulgar, violent, barbarous, so as to have impeded for a long time the progress of civilization. If such were the fact, it would be preposterous to call that time a Christian age, much less a holy epoch; and in spite of all the possible worship of God and display of charity, it would be, perhaps, proper to consign it to the obscurity and obloquy that shrouded it a century or two ago. This has to be examined.

The word *morals* includes often in modern English a great deal more than is strictly understood by it. It refers not only to the human acts dependent on the control of conscience, and essentially belonging to the moral order; but it often relates simply to exterior forms of conduct perfectly indifferent to virtue or sin, and which are much more exactly expressed by the word *manners*. This has introduced into the English tongue an unhappy confusion of ideas which is to be carefully guarded against in the matter under consideration. Manners which are to a certain degree indecorous, owing to our modern ideas of taste, are directly pronounced immoral, though conscience cannot be affected in any way by them; and thus holiness is supposed to be impossible without culture.

In judging of the middle ages and of the morals of the people during their continuance, a great attention must be paid to this difference of meaning. It shall soon be proved that there was real refinement in the thoughts and habits of the mediæval Christians, and that the age which originated chivalry was not barbarous. But this is not precisely the state of the question; and in speaking of the exquisite holiness prevailing at that time, we must be very careful to understand it in the Christian sense as the reign of a heroic virtue, not the paragon of a fastidious culture, which certainly did not exist at that time.

To do this *in extenso* would transcend our limits. The task has been admirably accomplished in the *Mores Catholici* of K. Digby. It is impossible to go through those volumes without experiencing a keen delight at the sight of so many charming pictures in which true heroism partakes of a childish simplicity, and the splendor of heaven seems to be blended with the primitive scenery of an earthly paradise. We must be content with a few flowers culled in that delightful garden. To understand their importance it is fair to remark that it is easy, if somewhat unprofitable, to ransack the annals of any nation of the highest moral character and find in it examples of a startling corruption. The author of *Philosophumena* has represented the papal reign of Zephyrinus as one of bribe, intrigue, and foul crimes, and has attributed the lowest passions of greed and hypocrisy to men who have been until our day honored by the Church as saints. The loose reputation of the fifteenth century has also been rendered still much worse by the wild gossip of a Guicciardini, whose conjectures and calumnies have been taken as facts by many modern historians. So, likewise, captious critics have taken the trouble of selecting with care scandalous stories of every description, true or not, and have placed them on record as the best picture which could be given of the ages of faith. Simple readers imagined that the question had been sifted to the bottom; and public opinion openly condemned the morals of those times because the manners of men widely differed from ours. Until Kenelm Digby undertook the heavy task of collecting innumerable facts of a very different nature, belonging to the same epoch, no one supposed that so much could be said in favor of the *darkest period of history;* and it turns out that it was one of the brighest in the moral order that ever blessed this earth by its sanctity.

To begin directly with it, one of the worst features of that period consisted, as was believed, in its violence and disposition to shed blood. All cities were said to have been at war with each other, and in each of them factions of the most inveterate character divided the citizens into furious groups, intent only on their mutual destruction. But the author of *Mores Catholici* has given on his side pictures of peace, tranquillity, civic virtues which it would be difficult, or rather impossible, to find in our boasted era of refinement and mild manners. We will quote one or two of them, taking care to select only a few traits in each story for the sake of brevity.

The first is taken from a celebrated work of Antonio Ferrari, surnamed Galateo because he was born in Galatina, in Apulia, toward the end of the fifteenth century. Near that town there was another called Gallipolis, whither he retired when he left the court of the King of Naples, to follow his taste for a quiet life. It is in that city that he wrote all his works, which have always been placed in Italy among the best of that age. His *Descriptio urbis Gallipolis* is still read with the keenest delight by all lovers of good Latinity. Paul Jove compared its style to that of the best authors of antiquity. In this book Ferrari or Galateo describes what he had seen during many years among the quiet people of the city and its neighborhood; and there is no doubt that the same picture could have been drawn of many other places in Italy, though the end of the fifteenth century was far less irreproachable than the two previous ones. We suppose that Mr. Digby's translation is correct:*

"Here men are most pure, most moral; not liars, not rapacious, not seditious, not intemperate, not ambitious; and what Plato ascribed to maritime cities, not unjust, not fraudulent, but vera-

---

* Dolman, London, 1846, vol. ii. p. 37.

cious, faithful, abstemious, contented, charitable; and notwithstanding their sea-life and the multitude of mercenary troops and the influx of foreigners, preserving their integrity and constancy: In peace mild, tractable, and humane; and of their bravery in war the Venetians, Spaniards, and French can best speak. The education of boys and young men is liberal and modest. Arrogance and insolence are not found among our youth, who are full of love for one another, and benevolence. But what is above all important, the people are not negligent of religion and the divine worship. St. Agatha, patroness of the city, they piously venerate; and what we have such difficulty to persuade other people to do, these people, whether about to live or die, of their own accord have constant recourse to the sacraments. The virtue of the women corresponds to these manners; they are chaste, industrious, and obedient. On holy days they stay much at home; on other days they spin. . . . At thirteen you will find few unmarried. Good men and lovers of truth cannot pass over in silence the virtue of an enemy. Thus though the Venetians are not styled most Christian, yet, when they took our city, as true Christians and Italians they respected the women, and guarded them diligently in the church of St. Agatha. . . . Upon the whole, my dear Summonti, I know of no city more capable of serving the purposes of a happy life, if one knows how to enjoy it; none more fit for a sweet and tranquil existence. . . . Here is the image and shadow of that holy city which will be in heaven, and which from heaven has never yet descended."

Another description, by Bernardin Gomez, of the manners prevailing among the Valencians and Catalonians during the reign of Diego I. of Arragon, in Spain, would deserve to be copied in full; but, unfortunately, this is impossible, through want of space. The same is also true of what the annalists of Salamanca and other cities in Spain would furnish. But with regard, again, to those of Italy, the emphatic declaration of the Puritan Milton in his "Second Defence of the People of England" cannot possibly be omitted; and, fortunately, it is concisely expressed in a comprehensive phrase: "I fled to Italy, not as the place of refuge to the profligate, but because I knew and had found before that it is the retreat of civility and of all polite learning."

But the best and shortest proof that can be given of the Christian feeling of remorse, the keen qualms of conscience so easily aroused in those simple souls by the voice of religion, and the reformation instantly effected in their manners when they had disobeyed the voice of duty, is the tremendous effect of the preaching of St. Francis and St. Dominic in the thirteenth century.

The brief sketch of it given by Digby,* to which are added many scenes of the same nature following the exhortations of Jordan of Pisa, Berthold of Ratisbon, Anthony of Padua, John d'Avila, and others, would suffice to prove that those times were holy because, when negligence had crept in, it was the work of a moment to bring back the inhabitants of a populous city, of a large district, sometimes of a whole kingdom, to the most heroic resolutions carried out to the letter. These are a few of the words of a monk living at the time in the convent of St. Justina at Padua, who described the moral revolution in Lombardy effected by Francis and Dominic: "All began to fear and obey God, to forgive one another, to forget injuries, to bury hatred, to renounce usury, to make restitutions, to avoid pomp and plays and every kind of luxury. . . . At Cortemilla the country people left their ploughs and implements in the fields and flocked in to hear Francis' discourses on the vanity of the world which passes away, the penalty that awaits sinners, and the everlasting beatitude of the just. The hardest hearts were split like the rocks of the desert, and the waters of contrition flowed from them."

It cannot be too often repeated that this argues a keen perception of the supernatural, and a profound reverence for the doctrine of holiness even when it had been neglected. People were then deeply impressed with the idea that the heavenly world was the country prepared for man, and that he could by righteousness have a foretaste of it in this vale of tears ; that all the beauty of nature was only a pale reflection of that of heaven, and heaven could come down in the heart of man by the practice of Christian virtues. This made holiness at the same time simple and easy.

This sublime theory of the espousals of heaven with earth, which it is so difficult for men of this day to comprehend, was easily understood and put in practice by the simplest men of that period. There is a most beautiful passage of Hugo of St. Victor in his *Institutiones Monasticæ de Vanitate Mundi* lib. ii.) which renders

---

* Vol. ii. p. 156.

this palpable, and places at once the middle ages on a level with the most refined in point of what is called *spirituality;* that is, the intercommunication of a superior world with this. The holy writer takes for his text these words of the Gospel: "Unless you become like little children," etc., and he says:

"What are the manners of a boy, of a simple child? He is not solicitous nor covetous. He exercises himself in simple and innocent play. . . . He knows his father's grounds; now he is in the field, . . the garden, . . . the orchard, . . meadow, . . . vineyard. He knows the peculiar delights which belong to each season of the year. In the spring he follows ploughing, . . . in the summer reaping, in the autumn the vintage. . . . He loves to gather the new fruits, to roast the unripe corn, to pick out the first ripe grape. . . . If he knows that his father is about to go to any town or castle, . . . he wishes to go with him, that he may see new and unaccustomed things, so that on his return he may relate what he has seen. . . . But if in going out he were not to hope for a quick return, . . . he would not leave his father's house without lamentable groans and great sorrow. He is glad to find diversion abroad, but he wishes to have no permanent abode anywhere, except in his father's house, with his domestics, among whom he was born and with whom he was bred. . . . He would not be separated from them even in death. Nothing beyond this he seeks, nothing more does he desire.

"Like this boy, let us study to converse in the house of the Lord, and we too shall find peace and rest and pleasure. Let us be simple, not desiring foreign things, loving more the delights which God hath prepared for us and which are found in His house, rather than the blandishments of this world. Here we have transparent fountains, flowery meadows, wide and swelling fields, rich vineyards, irrigated gardens, abundant flocks, fertile crops, fruitful trees, delights of every kind; all, in short, that the soul can desire or possess. Do you ask what are these fountains, meadows, and gardens? They are the examples of the just, the sources of wisdom, and the sweets of all virtue. For we have our feet directed in the ways of the commandments of God in order that, remembering His mercies which have been from all generations, we may exercise our heart and enkindle our desire in His love. We can indeed contemplate all the works of our restoration and redemption from the beginning to the end of the world, according to the course of time, the events of things, and the deeds of men."

It is impossible to express more happily the facility with which holiness can be attained in this world, when this world is considered as the house of God. In the middle ages this was an elementary knowledge which all possessed, and no one can be surprised that so many at that time reached a high degree of it. How could these ages be called barbarous, cruel?

And the sanctity peculiar to that age was accompanied with a nobleness of thought, a delicacy of feeling, nay, a poetical spirit which are precisely the reverse of the grossness and vulgarity generally attributed to that epoch. Here is a last passage, taken this time from Petrus Blesensis, copied by Frederick Hurter in his *Tableau des Mœurs de l'Église au Moyen Age.** It is doubtful if many of the best writers of this century could carry to a greater perfection this nobleness of thought, delicacy of feeling, and true poetry. Still, no one accustomed to the style of mediæval writers is surprised to find it on this occasion, because it was then natural, frequent, and often expected. It is addressed by the writer to a young lady of a high parentage, who preferred a cloistered life to the hand of the Duke of Burgundy's nephew, promised her in marriage. Her name was Anselma.

"This young prince undoubtedly excels in comeliness of form; his bravery and gracefulness are admired by all without exception. All the gifts which can attract a young woman he possesses: the most charming conversation, an unbounded generosity, and perfect dignity in his bearing. But your wisdom has chosen the better part, and if the struggle has been painful, and its issue doubtful for a moment, the final victory has been on this account more glorious. If you were still in the world, it is true, men of the highest rank would surround you preferably to other noble ladies; diamonds and jewels would give *éclat* to your beauty; you might some day feel justly proud of the number of your relatives and children; every one of them would constantly consult your wishes to gratify them. Instead of all this, the narrow walls of a convent contain the world in which you move; there is not any more for you the freedom of quitting it; no worldly joys, no worldly pleasures, no boisterous festivities; your dress is coarse and invites you to mourning; dry bread

---

* Vol. iii. p. 272.

and boiled herbs your fare. But how uncertain and short-lived are the pleasures of this world! After them follow occasionally repentance and often suffering. Anxious care is inseparable from wealth and honors; pomp and popular favor are dreams. Remember that a woman cannot become a mother except through dangers and pangs; sickness, confinement in a dungeon, revolutions worse than death, can deprive her of a son in whom she concentrates her happiness. Watch over your heart, keep yourself holy. Nothing is so valuable as the treasure of virginity; the Lamb follows her alone; alone she makes us like unto the angels of God."

Was it a barbarous age in which such lines as these were written? And how many pages of the same nature would we have to transcribe in order to give an exact idea of the refined holiness common then in all classes of society, but particularly among the poor?

It was seen previously that holiness properly consists in the voluntary fulfilment of the religious vows; that they contain the very essence of the *beatitudes* preached by our Lord on the Mount; and, in fact, the only perfection attainable in this life consists in the rigorous practice of obedience, chastity, and voluntary poverty. Those alone who have bound themselves by these holy obligations, and are faithful to them, can practise the pure charity of the Christian toward his neighbor, and assure themselves that they have attained the height of self-sacrifice, in which consists the true imitation of Christ. It is at least very difficult, if not impossible, for people in the world to devote themselves entirely to a life of good works continued unceasingly till death and the grave.

If ever this has been the case on earth, it was during a time when the whole of Europe was covered by monasteries and convents which had not yet degenerated from their primitive fervor, whose inmates daily sacrificed themselves to the good of their fellow-men. The sanctity which flourished in those holy houses spread its fragrance all over the country, and was soon the welcome guest in the hut of the peasant. The rustics themselves became, as it were, transfigured. The universality of this fact during the middle ages must strike every one who peruses the contemporary writings, and Mr. Lecky has been brought to acknowledge it, though he attributes it entirely to a secondary cause which alone could not have produced it. He imagines that it was only the sight of the pictures and images placed everywhere at that time under the eyes of all beholders which transformed entirely the character of the peasant class and rendered their manners so gentle and often refined, as if the constant sight and conversation of the monks was not a still more powerful inducement. The passage, however, deserves to be quoted, because it is as true as graphic:

"The grateful beings with which the creative fancy of paganism peopled the universe—in ancient Greece and Rome—shed a poetic glow on the peasant's toil. Every stage of agriculture was presided over by a divinity, and the world grew bright by the companionship of the gods. But it is the peculiarity of the Christian types that while they have fascinated the imagination they have also purified the heart. The tender, winning, and almost feminine beauty of the Christian Founder, the Virgin-mother, the agonies of Gethsemane or Calvary, the many scenes of compassion and suffering that fill the sacred writings, are the pictures which for eighteen hundred years have governed the imaginations of the rudest and most ignorant of mankind. Associated with the fondest recollections of childhood, with the music of church-bells, with the cloister's light, and the tinsel splendor, that seemed to the peasant the very ideal of majesty; painted over the altar where he received the companion of his life, around the cemetery where so many whom he had loved were laid, on the stations of the mountain, on the portal of the vineyard, on the chapel where the storm-tossed mariner fulfils his grateful vow; keeping guard over his cottage door, and looking down upon his humble bed, forms of tender beauty and gentle pathos forever haunt the poor man's fancy and silently win their way into the very depths of his being. More than any spoken eloquence, more than any *dogmatic* teaching, they transform and subdue his character, till he learns to realize the sanctity of weakness and suffering, the supreme majesty of compassion and gentleness."

There was certainly a transformation effected in the European peasant by his religion. Henceforth the halo of holiness was to surround him as long as he remained faithful to its teachings. But though the beautiful objects Christianity placed under his eyes had a great effect in softening his passions and purifying his heart, the spectacle of the living saints that he saw constantly, and their gentle admonitions or stern rebukes, produced a greater still, principally because the *dogma* was never absent, and the images he saw were only the symbols of it.

IV. Holiness in the family is the next topic; and it is with sincere regret that I am compelled to pass by the delightful descriptions of domestic manners profusely scattered over the third chapter of Digby's sixth book. A short and comprehensive sketch is all that is possible here; and as the whole depends on the idea of marriage entertained by the mediæval people, it is proper to consider it first. This was essentially and totally a new and Christian idea, and for the first time in man's history the chief aspect of it was that of sanctity. Marriage was a sacrament, a holy thing, not only blessed by the Church, but containing mysteries of the highest order in human conception. St. Paul had clearly declared it.* There is, perhaps, nothing more sublime in the doctrine of this eloquent apostle than what he says repeatedly of the union of God with man through Christ, of the function of the God-man in the economy of salvation. The Church is a body through which a divine life circulates as blood in the human frame. Christ being the head, it is from Him that flows the stream which vivifies the whole. This is the grand image by which we are enabled to understand the text of St. Peter, where he says that we are "partakers of the divine nature."

But, according to the same apostle, Christ is the bond of another union; namely, that of husband and wife, through the sacrament of marriage. They are united together as the God-man is united with the Church, and for this reason must the husband love his wife and the wife her husband. Can anything holier be conceived? Is it not true that sanctity must henceforth be associated with the idea of a wedded pair's union?

No doubt this was known to Christians long before the middle ages; in fact, from the very beginning. But it may be fairly maintained that it was not universally understood and acted upon as thoroughly as in mediæval times. Those noble ideas must have but slowly entered into the mind of the greatest number of converts in Roman and Grecian countries. Such of them as had reached a high degree of spiritual refinement rushed with ardor into celibacy, which the apostles praised still far above the married state. The mass was but slowly trained to adopt the most sublime social views of religion, particularly about marriage; precisely the same as it took a long time to wean them over from

---

* Eph. v. 32.

the superstitions of polytheism. To exculpate them from adhering still to many pagan practices, as it is known was the case, it is now proposed by Christian antiquaries* to distinguish between what was entirely indefensible in idolatry, which was forbidden, and what belonged to natural religion which could not be absolutely condemned. Thus habits of a doubtful orthodoxy continued to exist in Rome and Constantinople among Christians.

The same was the case with the purity of morals taught by the new religion. Its sublimity was not at first entirely understood and put in practice by a great number of neo-Christians; and though the essentials of morality were certainly adopted, because enforced by popes and bishops, still the sweetness of its perfume vaporized in a socially corrupt atmosphere. It became worse still during the barbarian invasions. So that the precise moment when Europe was thoroughly Christianized was also the epoch when perfection of manners must have been reached; and this was toward the end of the ninth century; that is, at the very date of Jonas of Orleans' episcopate, though the full effect of it was somewhat retarded by feudalism.

This is fully confirmed by all contemporary writers, as is proved by Kenelm Digby's great work. It could not, in fact, be otherwise, owing to the devotion they all felt henceforth for the Holy Family. Mary and Joseph with the divine Infant were constantly before their eyes; and even rationalists must admit that this picture of a model household was calculated to act profoundly upon the whole framework of society. Christ was the pattern of children, as Joseph and Mary were those of married people and parents. It is proper to consider apart each of these social elements.

The Holy Infant of Bethlehem, who soon became the youth of Nazareth, was the Son in eternity of the Eternal Father and in time of the Virgin Mary. Heaven and earth embraced each other in His divine person; and if the heavenly element was known to be unfathomable, the earthly fell under the senses and acted most sweetly on all human emotions. All the particularities either of his birth in an abandoned cave or of his laborious life as a mechanic in Galilee were treasured up in the heart of hearts of all mediæval Christians. The Christmas carols, particularly,

---

* See the London *Month* for October, 1879.

that were then sung all over Europe would fill a large library if they all had been printed since the fifteenth century. Some partial attempt at it has been made lately for France; and it is indeed wonderful to see the multitude of those *noels*, as they are called, which have survived, though they are, no doubt, but a small number compared to those that have perished. The extremely popular legend of the translation by angels of the Nazareth house from Palestine to Italy proves that the youth of our Lord was always, also, an object of tender devotion in those ages of a holy simplicity. All knew then that almost the only fact recorded in the gospels during so many years of a divine life was that Christ "was subject to his parents." Was not this the most eloquent teaching of subordination in families? There was then no captious interpretation of a clear text. All firmly believed what they read. A God had been obedient not only to Mary, his mother, but to a man, Joseph, who was not his father. In ancient pagan Rome there was a fierce authority given to the father over his children: he could sell them into slavery or put them to death. This terrible legislation was thought necessary in so important a matter as family concord and subordination. It must be maintained that the Christian submission of children to parents during the middle ages was still far better enforced by the sweet picture of Bethlehem and Nazareth than it could be in Rome by the odious sway of *patria potestas*. Filial piety had a meaning in Christian Europe which it could not have near the Tarpeian rock.

But since we speak of marriage itself and not of its surroundings, it is particularly the union of Mary and Joseph which should be considered here, because it was this chiefly which gave to conjugal love in mediæval times its truly divine character. It could never be presented under a more alluring and graceful form than the one it took during so many years under the humble roof of Nazareth; and this was the standard of purity and holiness which was daily offered to the contemplation of any wedded pair. The senses had no part to bear in it, and precisely on that account love burned brighter in the heart for being altogether spiritual and above the senses. It was the first time marriage was declared to exist in essentials independently of sexual union. Few would carry the ideal of it to the perfection of the pattern offered to all; but all at least should understand that Christian wedlock was principally a union of hearts. A holy and spiritual love, a most tender but chaste affection was the essential prerogative of the Christian institution of matrimony. Everything else of a physical nature became lawful on account of the ultimate object, the procreation of children; but the aim of the Christian must always tend higher than mere sensuality, otherwise how could any one look without a blush on Mary and Joseph's household?

A divine religion alone could offer such a teaching as this to mortal man; and it is surprising how many examples the middle ages furnished of a perfect imitation of the proffered pattern; whilst the immense majority were at least induced to refrain from an excessive indulgence, which in modern times has become almost the rule. Kenelm Digby gives a list of some "illustrious queens who lived a cloistral life upon the throne. Such were the wife of Charlemagne; Cunegonde, wife of Henry the Second, Emperor of Germany; Agnes, wife of the Emperor Henry the Third; Elizabeth, wife of the Emperor Albert; Radegonde, wife of Clothair; Adoere, wife of Chilperic; Bathilde, wife of Chlovis; and Agnes of Bohemia, wife of Frederick the Second." Digby does not mention the emperors or kings; but Mr. Lecky does not forget the names of Henry II. of Germany, Edward the Confessor, of England, and Alphonso II. of Spain.

Since mention is made again of the author of "European Morals," it must be incidentally remarked that by a strange error of judgment he brings this as a proof that in the middle ages "it would be difficult to conceive anything more coarse and more repulsive than the manner in which they regarded marriage." And the reason he gives of it is that "the tender love which it elicits, the holy and beautiful domestic qualities that follow in its train, were almost absolutely omitted from consideration." This is as unaccountable as untrue, when the previous reflections are minded. Not only the view taken of it was not "coarse and repulsive," but it was eminently refined and pure, as has been proved. The eminent author of the "History of European Morals" finds fault likewise with the occasional abstinences from marriage intercourse either prescribed by the ritual of those times or consented to by both parties for pious purposes; and he condemns it because he seems to think that one of the parties was always unwilling. But from all the accounts which refer to such cases as these it is evident he is mistaken; and with regard to the propriety of those ascetic usages a Christian will always be satisfied with the advice* of St. Paul on which they were mainly based.

---

* 1 Cor. vii. 5.

The Christian ideal in marriage evidently transcends everything that human legislation has ever invented to give it stability and dignity. The Mosaic law, though divinely revealed, allowed the *libellus repudii*, which was simply a divorce *a vinculo*. Our Lord declared that this had been granted to the Jews only "because of the hardness of their heart,"* but "it had not been so from the beginning;" and in the new dispensation the husband and wife were to be "two in one flesh," and "what God had united man should not presume to sunder." This was perfectly well understood and accepted in the middle ages; and the popes invariably stood firm on that point against the wild passions of several kings and emperors. In those contests the people always sided with the spiritual authority, even in the last case of Henry VIII. For if he carried his point by force, history has recorded how the cause of Catherine of Arragon was dear to the popular heart.

In treating the general subject of sanctity with regard to other times and countries, the main object has been to show in detail how the Christian religion early developed in Jerusalem and Palestine, in Egypt and Syria, and finally in Rome and the West, the highest possible pattern of morality offered to man by the doctrine of the Sermon on the Mount. An effort also was made to concentrate the whole of it into what has been called "the religious vows." Here this matter of holiness takes a somewhat different aspect. In this very chapter scarcely anything has been said of the branch of asceticism in which voluntary poverty, religious obedience, and unsullied chastity were openly professed, though there were many monasteries at that time. The reason of the difference is plain, and redounds to the honor of the middle ages. In other times and countries Christianity had undoubtedly effected an immense revolution in the morals of nations. It would be idle to deny it in the face of the latest discoveries in the field of history. But it is proper to give more development to some reflections which have already been made in too condensed a form. The corruption of polytheism had been of so universal and thorough a character that it required centuries to raise the whole mass of mankind to the high level of Christian purity. The conversion of so many nations to a better faith, and the adoption by them of at least tolerable moral habits, was a most surprising fact which God alone could bring about. But the grossness of many habits contracted

---

* Mark x. 5.

during so many ages of a rank idolatry opposed a sturdy resistance to the undimmed purity of the moral doctrine preached by Christ and His apostles. The opposers of Christianity object often this looseness of life which strikes the reader when he finds in the historians of the fourth, fifth, and sixth centuries proofs that the neo-converts or their children of the next generation were still addicted to many vices which appeared to disgrace their religion. Read, they say, the strictures of St. John Chrysostom against the Christians of Antioch in his time, to whom he preached some of the finest homilies ever written; and go through many other testimonies of the same purport. The mass indeed of the people was still very corrupt, though they believed in Christ. This is the objection.

But the irrefragable proof that this was not due to their new religion, nay, that it was in spite of it that they continued, many of them, to wallow in vice, is the undeniable fact of the vast number of ascetics, either in the cloister or in the world, who practised to the letter the highest virtues which ever honored humanity. At the same time, therefore, that the Antiochian Christians were every day shouting in the circus, proclaiming their admiration or their contempt for the many-colored charioteers, and engaged in factions and broils, often to the extent of bloodshed, there were in the suburbs of the city many monasteries where pious monks devoted their lives to the practice of the most arduous virtues, and filled the world with the perfume of their sanctity. This was the spectacle offered nearly everywhere during the first five centuries of our era. Consequently, in describing the exquisite character of the primitive Church, the writer is mainly bound to present to the reader's admiration that part of the Good Shepherd's flock among whom the moral doctrine of Christ bloomed in all its beauty, and this is sufficient for the purpose, because it was there only that it had attained its true ideal. During the middle ages Christianity had finally prevailed not only in many individuals, but generally in the mass. Paganism had entirely disappeared; and if some remnant of its superstitions lingered still in Europe, it was only in a few remote and sequestered spots which can be entirely neglected in the general account, and ascetics were not the only true Christians.

An objection, however, can be urged as to the epoch which is assigned here for the beginning of this happy period. The ninth century and the first quarter of the tenth are known as the darkest period of Catholic history. The Supreme Pontificate itself was at the mercy of profligate noblemen in Rome, the highest offices in the Church were invaded by rapacity and violence, simony rampant, and incontinence in the secular clergy already prevalent. The objection is not without strength; an answer shall be given, after the present subject is concluded in the next paragraph.

V. The last consideration, previously announced, refers to the way people generally ended their life during the middle ages. This will be the work of a few moments. Faith was their chief characteristic, but they particularly firmly believed in a future state of rewards and punishments. The least doubt or misgiving never affected their mind on this subject; and such was the impression it made on them that during their sleep they often saw vividly what was to them a personal proof of the torments of hell or the joys of heaven. This has been objected to those ages as if it were a proof of superstition. It was simply the attestation of a deep-seated conviction of the Gospel's truth; for the words of our Lord are a sufficient evidence in the eyes of the Christian. Many details of those dreams, created undoubtedly by imagination, might be subject to criticism. They all were, however, more or less warranted by the sentence which the Saviour predicted would be pronounced at the last day on the wicked.

So profound must have been the effect produced on those simple and impulsive souls that it must have kept them, most of the time, in the strict observance of God's commandments. It was only in their unguarded moments that they fell into those irrepressible excesses of which the chronicles of that epoch have preserved the memory.

Some of them, no doubt, were during many years the slaves of violent and disgraceful passions. It could not have been the case for the great majority of them, who were constantly kept within proper bounds by the fear of the Lord and of His judgments. Scripture says that it is "the beginning of wisdom;" and whoever is strongly impressed by that holy fear is at least on the way to holiness, and will surely reach it by the means of sanctification the Church gives him. If the great mass of mankind is now almost beyond the pale of hope, it is mainly on account of their contempt for the threats of God and of their own conscience. When no one thinks of his last end, but only of present enjoyment, there can be scarcely any prospect of reformation. For mediæval Christians the door of amendment was always open before their eyes, and the worst of them felt constantly impelled to knock at that door, let it be on account of dreams or not; to them it was a reality.

Consequently there is no wonder that the greatest profligates returned at last to the path of virtue, occasionally long before the end of their life. It became one of the characteristics of the times; and it is so often recorded in contemporary writings that it is always expected by the reader whenever darker crimes than usual are unveiled and shock his feelings. When this happened the simple and holy people around expressed no surprise at hearing that some great lord, known for his abominable excesses, had suddenly disposed of his estates and his titles to enter an austere monastery, where he soon began to edify his brother-monks by the severity of his penance and the practice of the most exalted virtue. There is now no country in Europe, no district of any size in France, Italy, Spain, Germany, or England, where some tradition does not exist of a reformed baron, a converted viscount, some repentant knight, at least, who spent long years of self-inflicted expiation either as a recluse in a church or as a lay brother in an austere community. This alone argues a high standard of virtue in the nation, because it supposes a keen sense of remorse in the vicious, whilst, on the contrary, if a holy life is unknown among the multitude, the most guilty men can scarcely feel the need of reformation.

6. *The Dark Side of the Middle Ages is briefly Explained.*

From the time of the last Carlovingians in Germany and Gaul—the latter half of the tenth century—down to the permanent settlement of the Capetians in France during the eleventh, western Europe was given over to an almost complete anarchy. The state constitution established by Charlemagne was replaced by pure feudalism; and Hugh Capet is justly called the first feudal French king. Such a political revolution in the midst of the devastations of the Northmen in the West and of the Huns or Magyars in the East could not but bring in its train almost a social disorganization. The Church suffered in her discipline as the State in its welfare. Still, this is precisely the period when, in our opinion, the ages of faith began. The frightful disorders which convulsed Europe are now attributed to the barbarism of the people, though they were then for the first time in history thoroughly Christian; and some even of the best Catholic writers assert that "virtue was not then on a level with faith." They remind us with justice that there were at that epoch "great abuses in the Church, awful crimes in society, a constant state of war," etc. This must surely be admitted; but we complain that in the terms in which this is stated there is an unfortunate confusion. All this is attributed to the middle ages in general, and as Catholicity was their true spirit, the reader naturally infers that even religion was compromised by the public evils of those times, and that the period which has been justly called the golden age of Christendom was far less happy and virtuous than ours, for instance.

To do away with this delusion it is proper to point out what were the causes of those abuses, disorders, crimes; and it will be easy to perceive that they came entirely from the pagan barbarism of the Northmen and the Huns, from the political institutions that those savages brought with them, and from the social anarchy necessarily caused by the sudden dissolution of the Frankish Empire founded by Charles the Great. Not only the Church was completely irresponsible for all those calamities, but she alone directly after regenerated and totally Christianized those new pagans in an incredibly short period of time. Nay, as long as the evil continued there was always in the people everywhere a deep spirit of holiness such as has been described. The abuses were in the main confined to the upper classes of society; and even these, instead of being altogether corrupt, offered occasionally the spectacle of eminent virtues. This is to be examined somewhat in detail.

The full extent of the moral and social corruption prevalent at that epoch can be referred to the unchastity of the secular clergy, the scandalous excess of simony, and the constant state of war. Each of these subjects of inquiry must be studied apart. But to fully understand their bearing on the question of holiness in the Church it is important to speak, though very briefly, of the true origin of those extraordinary abuses. This was undoubtedly a three-fold fact; namely, the pagan barbarism of the new invaders of Europe (the Northmen and Huns), the feudalism which they brought with them, and the anarchy that followed the dissolution of the Frankish Empire.

I. Attention is not sufficiently paid to the remark that the sudden arrival of the Northmen and the Huns, almost at the same moment, was a new invasion of paganism, this time greatly worse than that of the former German nations. When the Church had fully obtained a victory which all subsequent ages have admired; when, with an untiring labor lasting fully four hundred years, she had finally transformed and civilized them and brought them to a holy life, she saw with dismay swarms of other barbarians bringing with them the revolting worship of Thor, Wodan, and Freya. These were not German divinities, but the new mythology came from Scandinavia. Of all the tribes which had devastated Europe during the previous four centuries, the Anglo-Saxons were the only ones who sacrificed human beings to the monstrous Trinity of the North; and the Anglo-Saxons had not ravaged any other country than Great Britain. They had become at last devout Christians like the Franks, Burgundians, and Goths. The Danes, who came a little later on and professed the same kind of idolatry as the Anglo-Saxons, had only ravaged England and Ireland, and had also embraced the worship of Christ. But now from the dark north of the Baltic Sea other tribes were coming more ferocious still, and worshipping the same murderous gods. They arrived when, all former barbarians being already converted, the ages of faith had fairly begun everywhere their mild sway; and the student of history is aware of the devastations by the Northmen which ensued in Gaul, Holland, Germany, Spain, and Italy itself directly after the splendid reign of Charlemagne. It is known that the fury of those savages was chiefly directed against whatever bore the character of Christ. Churches, asylums, monasteries, convents of women, were the great objects of their rage. They were not awed into respect at the sight of pontiffs or monks, as the Franks, Germans, and Goths had been. This is proved by all the records of those times. If the Church discipline became relaxed, if monks left often the walls of their convents and forgot their ascetic rules, can a reproach of it be made to Christendom, to the Church which had just given such proofs of holiness and zeal during several centuries? Is it not, on the contrary, wonderful that these new savages themselves were so soon converted and entered also in the path of holiness? Must we not believe that sanctity, indeed, had all the while continued to flourish among the new apostles who performed again such wonders?

The Huns, who likewise contributed powerfully to the disorders prevalent in the tenth century, did not, probably, belong to the nation which had been led by Attila five hundred years before. At least there was no connection between both events. The ancestors of the Hungarians, called also Magyars, are the only ones with whom we are now concerned when we speak of Huns here. Nothing positive is known of their religion, which must have been a most crude superstition, since their manners were, according to all historians, most cruel and barbarous. But the confusion into which they invariably threw all the countries they invaded must have been as pernicious as that which resulted from the Northmen's incursions in the West. Between both the whole of Europe was convulsed to the very centre, and the few reflections just suggested in the case of the Scandinavians need not be repeated with regard to those ferocious Magyars. It is indeed wonderful that the mediæval Church did not perish altogether; and there must have been in it a great development of sanctity to have resisted the shock.

But it is particularly through the institution of feudalism that the door was open to the abuses that crept in at that time in the form of concubinage and simony; and this subject must be clearly laid bare and explained.

II. Modern writers in general do not agree as to the true origin of feudalism. Some go so far as to attribute it to the Romans; but they are evidently wrong. Many believe that it was a direct importation from Germany, and that it had spread in Europe long before the tenth century. With the single exception of the Anglo-Saxons in Great Britain, this is not true. The tribes of the Jutes and Angles, who destroyed or drove away the Britons from their native country, were truly Scandinavians, and had introduced feudalism in Great Britain several centuries before the period now under consideration. But they had not spread this institution on the continent, where the Carlovingians established, on the contrary, a governmental system totally different from the feudal, since it was highly centralized. This is a positive proof that the Germans and Franks of Pepin and Charlemagne did not know feudalism in their native country; and the contrary case of the Anglo-Saxons confirms the opinion of those who trace the origin of feudalism to Scandinavia. It is undeniable that under the heptarchy in Great Britain Scandinavians had established in that island a social system which was essentially feudal; and that as soon as the Northmen (Scandinavians likewise) made settlements on the continent in Germany, France, and Italy, pure feudalism began to prevail everywhere, whilst it had not before to any extent. The conclusion is evident.

To understand it more thoroughly, it is good to examine with some care a few facts which cannot but strike the reader. The system followed by Charlemagne had been essentially one of centralization; but as soon as the Capetians appear, principalities almost independent *de facto*, and organized under the feudal form, show themselves everywhere. To speak of France in particular, as soon as Hugh Capet is acknowledged king (A.D. 987), "the country is divided into a number of fiefs, of which those immediately dependent on the crown were the *four dukedoms* of Francia, Normandy [including Bretagne], Aquitaine or Guyenne, and Burgundy; and the *three counties* of Toulouse, Flanders, and Vermandois." *

Normandy and Flanders were the centres and starting-points of these new political organizations, because these countries were the first conquests of the Northmen on the continent. A simple look into the history of that epoch would offer the same spectacle in Germany and Italy. The former central system of Charlemagne was everywhere replaced by a fragmentary society under numerous chiefs, and it is then that *fiefs* begin to appear.

It is true that there was some plausibility in the opinion of those historians who formerly attributed the origin of feudalism to the social disorganization consequent upon the breaking up of the Frankish Empire, of which there will be occasion to speak shortly. In the midst of a universal anarchy, they said, chieftains arose everywhere who took possession of a smaller or greater territory, according to their individual power, and would acknowledge in the sovereign only a nominal authority. Hence this division of Europe in an infinite number of small fragments. It was not a system that had come from Scandinavia, but it sprang from a universal decomposition of society. So they said plausibly, and their opinion prevailed.

Had this been the case, however, the new fragmentary states would not have been modelled everywhere on exactly the same pattern such as they invariably were afterwards. Feudalism was abso-

---

* Alzog, Univ. Church Hist., vol ii. p. 309.

lutely the same in Sicily and the Abruzzo as in Flanders or southern France; and feudalism was a very complicated system.

This could not have happened unless there had been a central starting-point from which it had originally come, to insure unity in the whole; and there is no other supposition which satisfies the mind except when looking to Scandinavia for it. Let this be seen a moment.

The essence of feudalism, it is well known, consisted in this, that the possession of land was originally vested only in the king, who had primarily distributed it in the form of *beneficia* or fiefs, to his followers (*fideles*), under the obligation of obeying his summons to war whenever he called them. An act of disobedience on those occasions cancelled the *beneficium*, which returned to the crown. But the king's great vassals, as long as they remained faithful (*fideles*), had the same power of conveying a part of their own territory to other lower vassals, under the same condition of military service. Hence in purely feudal countries the king alone possessed the land *jure proprio;* the beneficium or fief ennobled the recipient as long as he kept it, and made him a freeman. A man, therefore, was free and noble who had a parcel of land, though his possession of it depended only on his fidelity to the king. Those who were not land-owners were not freemen, could not be called citizens, were of no account in the state, except as serfs on the parcel of land which they were entitled to till. Whence could such a system as this have originated?

It is known from history that in pagan Scandinavia whenever, from outlawry or from inability to subsist on a frozen land, a Viking looked to the south for booty or, better still, for making a new settlement, he engaged a number of adherents to his cause, who promised to obey him absolutely, in the hope of sharing in his success. Either in a fight at sea or in a pillaging expedition on land, the Viking's authority was considered absolutely paramount. No one among Scandinavians would have dared to complain of the portion he had received from his lord, and scarcely considered himself as possessor of it unless he continued faithful to his trust. This became a universally received principle whenever a permanent settlement was effected by them on some devoted point on the coasts of France or of Italy. Dudo of St. Quentin in his rude poem admirably describes the survey and division of Normandy made by the order of Rollo, after all the inhabitants had been either destroyed or driven off. Bretagne was afterwards added to Normandy by a cunning treaty, but was not so easily disposed of. It is wonderful how soon this system was adopted everywhere in Europe, with scarcely any modification. All lands were henceforth subject to feudal rules; and no one could be landowner without promising personally military service. It was only two or three hundred years later that this obligation contracted by a vassal of following his superior lord to the wars could be changed into a tax; so that henceforth money replaced personal attendance on the battle-field. This was the main source of all the abuses that crept into the Church, as will be presently seen.

Though wonderful it is not difficult to imagine how this system spread so rapidly over western Europe. There had been constant invasions following each other for the last six hundred years. No one could be sure that other irruptions would not follow. On two occasions a highly centralized government had not resisted the shock. The Roman power with its former prestige had succumbed ingloriously. The brilliant Carlovingian Empire had not obtained a better success. On this last occasion anarchy had been so complete that every small community, either district or township, was reduced to its own resources in every case of present danger. The fierce spirit of Scandinavia had embodied itself into a multitude of small armies with a most striking organization never before seen on earth. It had succeeded in overturning the empire of Charlemagne in less than a century. Was there need of looking anywhere else than on feudalism for a bulwark against a foreign foe? And in case any one had looked for something different and equally serviceable, would he have found it? There was evidently no other resource than this strange military system for enjoying peace; and hence every one rushed to it.

It has been remarked, in fact, that the feudal system was admirably organized for war. One single chieftain at the head; strict military service required from all subjects; the steel battle-axe superior to any Roman sword; iron plates for a covering of the body; and strong castles, with walls twelve feet thick, as the only sure refuge for women and children under the protection of valorous knights. Who can be surprised that Europe then adopted the feudal system against all further invasions?

It was, however, a barbarous institution, in which society was reduced to its most simple elements. Had it not been for the Church, which placed the pope over the head of kings and obliged them to admit that he was their natural adviser, the judge of their morals, the reprover of their iniquity, the protector of the weak, and the refuge of the oppressed, Europe would have certainly returned to barbarism and perished in blood and flames. The feudalism of the thirteenth century under St. Louis in France was exteriorly that of Scandinavia, but interiorly that of a Christian nation. The maxims of the Gospel had overcome and tamed the selfishness and coarseness of the former chieftains. But we are concerned here with the first outcome of this system of government, and must examine what effect it had naturally on mediæval morals, and who was accountable for it.

III. We must first consider, though but for a moment, how far moral disorder had followed the state of anarchy introduced by the new invaders, and see if Christians had on account of it forgotten their religion and lost all their claims to holiness of life. This is so far from being true that it was precisely at that moment that Germany flourished under the Saxon emperors, and France began to revive under the Capetian dynasty. The excesses of simony and unchastity had not yet penetrated to any considerable extent north of the Po and the Danube. Henry the Fowler, Otho the First and the Second, and particularly Henry the Second, acted powerfully with the German bishops, and generally with the popes, to preserve morality pure and faith entire. The celebrated monastery of Cluny in Burgundy spread its influence over all the monastic establishments in France, Italy, and the north, and thus contributed to restore discipline well-nigh destroyed during the Norman and Hungarian invasions. Under the rule of St. Majolus and St. Odilo, Cluny became the admiration of the world. Bishops, cardinals, popes, visited it together with kings, dukes, rulers of nations. In spite of this extreme prosperity the monks continued fervent in their ascetic rules, and spread far and wide the odor of sanctity. When the history of this epoch is studied with attention, people are surprised that there was still such an exuberance of piety; and it must be inferred that the mass of the population had remained pure, though a few years before they were subjected to such unheard-of calamities. This will become more evident when the depth of the evil, which soon extensively broke out, is examined more attentively.

IV. This has already been resumed under the three-fold heading of unchastity, simony, and a universal state of war, and to this we must turn our attention in order to vindicate, to a great extent, the character of the middle ages from these wholesale accusations.

a. With regard to the first—unchastity—it is important to examine when it began, because many writers often speak as if it had been a universal plague whose origin was lost in a fabulous antiquity, going back almost to the first days of Christianity in the West. It is very fortunate that a man so learned as the Benedictine Mabillon has thoroughly studied this question, and expressed succinctly and clearly his opinion of it in his *Acta SS. Bened.** We translate a short paragraph of it: "When Gregory VII. openly attacked clerical unchastity, there were more than a hundred years since the celibacy of the clergy [until that time undefiled, consecrated by the practice of so many centuries, and by the authority and virtue of so many great men in the Church] had been impugned and openly assailed by a certain number [*quibusdam*] of corrupt and dissolute church ministers. At that moment [the tenth century] unworthy pontiffs occupied the Roman See, and the evil finally broke out so violently that some priests [*quosdam presbyteros*] dared to contract publicly marriage. One of the first examples of it that we find in history" (here Mabillon quotes his own *Analecta* †) "was that of a certain parish priest of Châlons in Gaul by the name of Angelricus, who had taken a wife in the presence of his own parishioners. After the ceremony, when he prepared to take her to his house, the pious and faithful people of the place stood in his way to prevent the accomplishment of his nefarious purpose, and at the same time lodged against him their complaint with the Châlons bishop, named Mancion. The priest was summoned to appear before his superior in a synod convoked for the nones of May. There he humbly acknowledged his fault, and was sent by the bishop to his metropolitan, Fulco [archbishop of Rheims]. Mancion had taken this step because he was in doubt what kind of punishment it was his duty to inflict for such a new and perverse disposition in a clergyman. Nothing is known of Fulco's answer; but from Mancion's letter, which we still possess, it must be inferred that the crime of the parish priest was a new one, altogether unheard of at that time."

---

* Præf. ad part ii., Sæculi iii. p. 41.   † Vol. iii. p. 438.

From Gams' tables, *Series Episcoporum Ecclesiæ Catholicæ*, it appears that Mancion the bishop of Châlons, died in 893, and Fulco of Rheims had been assassinated (*occisus*) a few years before. It is permitted, therefore, to conclude that cases of this kind did not happen in France before the beginning of the tenth century. It is known from other sources that in Germany the same happened only under the Hohenstaufens: later, consequently. In Lombardy, particularly at Milan, under the Lombard dynasty, and owing probably to the neighborhood of Rome, the evil was at first greater; but the citizens opposed to it a sturdy resistance, of which it shall be our duty to speak presently.

The evil, which increased rapidly until the popes, particularly St. Gregory VII., put a stop to it, was unfortunately greatly promoted by the political state of Rome at the very beginning of the tenth century. The Lombards, who, coming from the banks of the Elbe and even, it is thought, from the shores of the Baltic Sea, had long before settled in northern Italy, to which they gave the name of Lombardy, had brought feudalism with them as the Anglo-Saxons did in Great Britain. It may not have been of so strict and barbarous a character as the subsequent feudalism of the Normans; still, the country had been divided in a great number of small duchies and counties, whose chieftains enjoyed a despotic power. This system was gradually introduced into Tuscany and the Roman states; and at the end of the ninth century the Margrave Albert of Tuscany considered Rome and the country around as his fief. Theodora the Elder, a celebrated courtesan, obtained under him an immense power which passed over to her daughters, Marozia and Theodora the Younger. In all feudal countries the ecclesiastical dignities soon became simple fiefs which were granted by the sovereigns to their creatures; and this became the great source of simony, as shall soon be seen in detail.

It was natural that the Church preferments (which until that time had depended on the free election on the part of clergy and people, and latterly in many cases on chapters of cathedrals and monastic assemblies) should henceforth mainly depend on the arbitrary choice of the head of the State. This had already been often the case in Merovingian Gaul, though feudalism had not yet appeared. Immense evils had resulted from it, as may be seen in the "History of the Franks" by Gregory of Tours. A remedy had been applied to this abuse under the Carlovingians with a full understanding and consent on the part of Rome. But as soon as feudal law became universal in Europe, the sovereigns everywhere insisted on appointing bishops, abbots, prelates of every degree, down to the very parish priests, because all these preferments had become *fiefs* and could not escape from the consequences.

The election of the popes, therefore, at the beginning of the tenth century was openly vested in Albert of Tuscany, and three infamous women became all-powerful in the choice of the Supreme Pastor of Christendom. It could be naturally expected from this that the Roman pontificate should have suddenly become a sink of iniquity; and it is the conclusion immediately drawn by many writers of the last century, and by Protestant or rationalist authors of this age. Mr. Lecky himself, generally cautious and fair in his statements, does not hesitate to say that "the Papacy during almost the whole of the tenth century was held by men of infamous lives."* This is altogether untrue; and it is now easy to prove that scarcely two or three popes during the whole extent of that period deserved to be stigmatized by anything like this bold assertion.

Not less than twenty-five popes governed the Church during the tenth century, so that the average length of each pontificate was only five years. Of the whole number it can be broadly stated that John XII. alone deserves a thorough condemnation. He was the son of Alberic Duke of Tuscany, the husband of Marozia, and Alzog cannot be accused of injustice when he says of him that, "though young in years, this unworthy occupant of the papal chair was old in profligacy, and brought disgrace upon his exalted office by his many vices and shameful excesses. *But the Church,*" he adds, "*then in a most humiliating state of bondage, cannot be made responsible for the outrageous conduct of this young debauchee.*"

Of John XI., son likewise of Marozia and of Alberic, her first husband, the record is rather dark, because he was throughout his pontificate under the influence of his mother and brother. But scarcely any other pope of that age can be compared to either this one or to John XII. Luitprand, bishop of Cremona, has accused several others of open crimes; but his testimony is openly contradicted by that of Flodoard and Deacon John, who disculpate entirely Sergius III.; and is proved to be unreliable in the case of John X. Luitprand is, in

---

* Vol. ii. p. 329.

general, too favorable to secular princes as against ecclesiastical rulers. He was in point of time one of the first admirers of the system called afterwards Cæsarism; and perhaps he was the very first writer who employed the words "sacred majesty" as applied to the emperors of Germany. Whenever Flodoard is opposed to him—and this is often the case—his assertions must be discarded as unworthy of trust.

On the other side, many of those unfortunate pontiffs of the tenth century were worthy of sitting in Peter's chair. Among them we can only name John IX., Benedict IV., Anastasius III., Leo VI., Leo VII., Stephen VIII., Marinus II., and Agapetus II. It is useless to say that the last pope on the list, Sylvester II., was one of the greatest and best pontiffs that ever ruled the Church; and it is indeed hard to say how the author of the "History of European Morals" could write the short phrase which has given rise to this very imperfect discussion.

It is, nevertheless, indubitable that the odious state of bondage in which many popes of the tenth century were held by the Tuscan and Roman tyrants acted most disastrously with regard to the morality of the clergy during those troublous times. How could the supreme pontiffs fulfil their high duty of supervision over the whole Church whilst they were mainly occupied with the constant disorders of the city in which they lived, and whose civil and religious control escaped almost from their grasp? Several popes died of violence; many sat a very short time in the chair of St. Peter. It is indeed surprising that they did so much for Rome, for Italy, for the whole world. For their records are not altogether void of great and glorious events. But our limits prevent us from even mentioning them in particular. Meanwhile it is true that feudal Europe was left almost without a head. Clerical discipline could not but become relaxed. Ignorance of the most important religious truths increased; and it is said that Christian people scarcely knew anything more than the Lord's Prayer and the Creed. It seems, therefore, that Europe had indeed fallen into barbarism; that holiness of life not only had disappeared, but could not possibly retain a name in such a disorganized society. This is what is generally believed.

But in the first place, if this had been truly the case, the Church at least could not be reproached with having been the cause of it. The great importance many modern writers attach to a full description of the dark side of this epoch consists in fastening on the Christian Church the blame of what is odious in it. They find a kind of delight in placing her on the stool of repentance as guilty. But the reader understands that at least this is not true. The Church was the victim of the passions of men; she was altogether irresponsible for the evils of those times, which were all mainly derived from feudalism.

In a second place, the picture must not be taken as being altogether without any redeeming features. We will quote but two of them. The first was a complete reformation of monasteries, those fertile sources of holiness which can be called in the history of the Church a well-spring of constant regeneration, in spite of occasional drawbacks. Cluny has been named; it is proper to return to it for a moment. Rohrbacher in his *Histoire de l'Église Catholique** says of it without any exaggeration, and in a rather too concise form: "The virtues practised at Cluny brought to its solitude a great number of men distinguished by their birth and high station in life. Not only laymen of illustrious blood came thither to embrace a life of penance, but often canons and even bishops left their churches to devote the remainder of their days to asceticism. Counts and dukes vied with each other in introducing into the monasteries dependent upon them the rule of Cluny, in order that the holy abbot [Odo] might reform them. Soon Odo did not confine his zeal to the walls of his convent, but labored assiduously to re-establish the monastic discipline in the whole of France and in Italy. The most renowned monastic houses to which he succeeded in giving his rule were Fleury-sur-Loire in the diocese of Orleans, St. Pierre-le-Vif at Sens, St. Julian of Tours, Carlieu in the Mâcon diocese, St. Paul at Rome, and St. Augustine at Pavia."

Alzog goes still farther. Speaking of Odo's successors he says: "Under Aymar, Majolus, and particularly Odilo and Hugh, this asylum of holiness and learning (Cluny) went on steadily increasing in importance and influence, till finally toward the close of this epoch (1048) there were to be found many monasteries even in Spain and far-off Poland, which recognized the jurisdiction of the abbot of Cluny. William, the worthy disciple of Majolus, labored effectually for the reformation of monasteries and the establishment of schools in Normandy and northern France; and Richard, abbot of Vannes at Verdun, was equally successful in correcting the abuses which had crept into the

---

* Vol. xiii. p. 30.

monasteries of Belgium." From these holy houses chiefly was to come the reformation of the clergy in point of morals.

A second redeeming feature of this epoch is the number of great personages who practised the highest Christian virtues. At the beginning of these reflections we thought we were authorized to say that in the middle ages holiness prevailed at least in the lower classes of society, and that the disorders and crimes which now are made a subject of virulent reproach against the ages of faith were confined to the feudal nobility. We thus appeared to have given up the justification of the highest classes as a complete impossibility. But this was not our formal intention; and here it is proper to qualify our meaning. Höfler in the *Dict. de Théol. Cath.* (art. *Empire d'Allemagne*), speaking of the German emperor Henry II. and of his time, which coincides with the period under review, says with justice: "No emperor of Germany ever carried out more completely than Henry II. the wise design he had formed of placing excellent bishops at the head of the various dioceses. Later on his successors thought they could derive an abundant source of revenue from the sale of bishops' sees, and transformed simony into what they called a royal tax [*jus regale*]. Henry II., on the contrary, kept always in view the spiritual interest of the Church, and gloriously ended the period of the Saxon emperors. This period was rich in princes, bishops, abbesses, great military men, statesmen, and saints, all of them of royal blood. None of the kingly races that followed Henry II., and obtained the imperial crown, produced so many rulers distinguished by a righteous will, a devoted heart, a life altogether given up to the accomplishment of the noblest designs. As soon as the empire was founded [by this Saxon race] the Germans obtained the hegemony of the world, and the venerable empire of Charlemagne kept anew the leadership of peoples and kingdoms as long as it remained faithful to the principles of its origin."

This is perfectly true, and could be proved by an infinity of details. But this alone would suffice to show the incorrectness of the prevalent opinion with regard to the pretended loose morality in mediæval times. It cannot be said absolutely that "virtue was not then on a level with faith;" the proposition must be corrected at least by the remark that there were then a great number of men of the highest rank in whom virtue was fully on a level with faith, though it could not be said of a certain number of others. Would to God the same might be true of our age!

In a third place, having previously traced up the origin of unchastity in the secular clergy, and proved that it was not older than the beginning of the tenth century, it is important to look at its extent and at the various checks it received. The conclusion must be that the evil was not so wide-spread as is generally supposed, and that its existence is far from arguing a deep corruption in society.

For a long time—most of the time, in fact—it was almost confined on the continent to a part of France and to Lombardy. Germany during the reign of the Saxon and Franconian emperors was totally exempt from it. Most of the measures taken against it in several councils referred to France and northern Italy alone. Simony was spread much more extensively, as will be presently seen. England, however, was touched by the evil as early as the epoch of the Heptarchy, for a short period of time. St. Dunstan, acting with energy and prudence, sufficed for bringing on in Great Britain a complete reformation. The history of Gregory VII. proves that he experienced a much greater difficulty in suppressing avarice than lust. It follows that the general idea on the subject is greatly exaggerated, particularly if we look at the checks the evil received.

We will mention only two of these checks; namely, one that came from the people, the other from the Church's rulers; but both suffice to vindicate the truth that in mediæval times holiness reigned to a great extent.

It would be a great error to imagine that clerical immorality was ever looked upon with indifference both by the faithful in general and by the ecclesiastical rulers. The fact above mentioned, taken from Mabillon, which, he says, was one of the first examples of this vice recorded in history, is yet fresh in the reader's memory. The action immediately taken by the people of the parish where it took place is most remarkable. They were evidently shocked at this sudden display of priestly corruption so far never heard of in their neighborhood, at least. The bishop of Châlons-sur-Marne, to whom they carried the culprit, was himself so much surprised that he did not know what punishment the canons of the Church inflicted for this degrading vice, and referred the case to his metropolitan, the archbishop of Rheims. But what is most important here is the feeling of horror excited in the citizens of an ancient city, such as Châlons was, at a sight which none of them could have expected. If the records of those times were thoroughly sifted for such a purpose, it would no doubt be found that the same was the case for a great many other localities ; and the annals of the Church of Milan furnish, we may say, the proof of it.

It has been already remarked that northern Italy, and Lombardy in particular, was one of the most noted parts of Europe where clerical unchastity spread earlier and was carried to the greatest excess. This might be attributed to the feudal customs which were introduced along the Po by the Lombards as early as the fifth or sixth centuries. All the dioceses and parishes were fiefs, and the lords of fiefs were independent. The open abuse of concubinage, however, did not break out in northern Italy much earlier than in France; and suddenly we are the witnesses of a spectacle which undoubtedly proves that the people were not disposed to look on it with indifference, and that their own virtue made them indignant at the sight of it. What rendered the evil worse in the archdiocese of Milan, in particular, was that for several years the archbishop himself was openly guilty of that crime; and it may be fairly supposed that on this account the greatest number of inferior clergymen rushed into it. The Council of Pavia in 1022, presided over by Pope Benedict VIII., passed a number of decrees against clerical unchastity; but Guido archbishop of Milan, took no account of them, and his clergy followed his example rather than obey the Church. They were supported in their contumacy by the bulk of the Lombard aristocracy; but the people instinctively recoiled at the sight of these excesses. They required only an organization with leaders at their head to prove their stern determination of upholding virtue.

Two good priests, Ariald and Landulf, became ostensibly their chiefs; and although this new party was composed mainly of the lower classes of society, they soon grew bold enough to express their firm determination of putting an end to the scandal. The aristocratic party was at first amazed at the audacity of this rabble, and thought that ridicule would suffice to put it down. They called them *patarini*, from *pataria*, which in the Milanese dialect meant a popular faction of good-for-nothing fellows. But the new organization, instead of being cowed down by this vulgar insult, accepted the name and boasted of being patarini indeed. They grew bolder and more numerous every day, though they had no political power on account of their inferiority of caste, and used only the influence of religion and virtue to obtain their end.

It is most remarkable that they obtained it at last; and this apparently ridiculous insurrection of the rabble against the wealthy, the influential, the powerful classes of Milanese citizens, compelled the body of the clergy in 1057 to subscribe a document by which they promised to faithfully observe the rules of celibacy.

If in the most corrupt parts of Christendom the people thus openly checked the spread of unchastity in the clergy, it will be easily admitted that in places less tainted by vice they exerted likewise their efforts for the same object, though scarcely any records of it have remained.

That the rulers of the Church also did not, on their part, remain indifferent to the same evil is abundantly proved by all the ecclesiastical history of that age; and to render the proof of it striking it would be necessary only to bring forward a multitude of facts well known by this time, when the middle ages have been so thoroughly studied. The life of Gregory VII., in particular, would suffice to demonstrate that the highest virtue, rising often to heroism, was displayed for this object by many popes, cardinals, prelates, to whom the Church's purity was entrusted. The scope of the present volume does not admit of such a vast historical development; and it is not needed, because many special books of great ability and learning have been written on this subject. We must pass on to the next stage of the present discussion.

b. The second class of accusations directed against the middle ages refers to simony, which, as has just been said, spread at that epoch in the Church much more extensively than unchastity. And simony being a much nearer outcome from feudalism than the other vice, many other disorders connected with it, which evidently grew from feudal customs (such as the open disrespect of canonical laws which debarred ecclesiastics from engaging in war, from meddling with temporal concerns, oppressing the poor, and the like), must be considered at the same time. It will be plainly evident that had there been no simony, the other excesses would not have afflicted the Church; but with feudalism it was not possible that it should not prevail. Gregory VII., therefore, and many other popes who fought valiantly against this vice of simony were in fact attacking feudalism in its most essential features. This has not been sufficiently remarked, or rather has seldom been even noticed by historians, and will give to this part of the discussion an interest of its own, at the same time that it will effectually free the Church from the excessive obloquy she has been subjected to on this account.

The meaning of the word simony is sufficiently well understood. It arose from the fact recorded in the Acts of the Apostles, when Simon Magus offered money to St. Peter in return for a purely spiritual gift.* To exchange some temporal advantage—money or anything else—against a spiritual gift of any kind is simony. This crime has often been attempted in the Church, even in primitive ages; but it can be maintained that under the feudal legislation it was *unavoidable*. A very able article written by M. Alphonse Callery in the *Revue des questions Historiques* (for October, 1879), entitled *L'Impôt du Roi*, has spread an extraordinary and altogether new light on many feudal transactions. And though the writer does not speak of simony in his paper and intends only to discuss the origin of *impôts* particularly in France, he has completely explained, without even thinking of it, the strange fact of the most unblushing simony which suddenly appeared everywhere in Christian Europe at the very beginning of the middle ages. This vice must be now admitted as being inherent to feudalism; and the popes, in order to preserve the Christian principles in the matter of investitures, for instance, had to move heaven and earth, as it were, to enlighten the Christian conscience on so vital a question, and to insist on the strict limits which feudal princes could not transgress in granting their *beneficia*. From the very principles of feudalism, all ecclesiastical dignities had gradually become so many fiefs, which could not be granted to any one unless he promised military service or—at a later epoch—gave a compensation for it in disbursing a sum of money. From this it is evident that, bishop's sees being strictly fiefs granted by the prince, no bishop-elect could take possession of his office, before or after his consecration, without binding himself towards his lord—the emperor, king, or duke—to a strictly personal military service whenever called for it, or without purchasing a change of this obligation by a sum of money commensurate with the importance of his new functions. The feudal laws at that time were considered binding in all Europe; the Christian conscience was naturally brought to believe that there

---

* Acts viii. 19.

could not be a crime or fault in obeying them. But the worst part of the whole system was the singular fact that these feudal customs were not grounded on natural or divine or ecclesiastical right, but only on national prejudices which had originated in northern Europe during pagan times and had taken possession of all Christian countries. M. Alphonse Callery, probably without wishing it, has touched here the most fatal sore of that old gangrene so long admired by many excellent men; namely, the feudal power. This must be seen more attentively.

As previously remarked, feudalism essentially consisted in the promise of military service to a lord by his vassal, as a compensation—a *quid pro quo*—for the granting of a benefice or fief—*feudum*. In course of time—for this took place very gradually, as M. Callery shows—military service was replaced by a sum of money, which at last was turned into a tax; and the special object had in view by the writer of *L'Impôt du Roi* is simply to render an account of the various steps by which taxes were introduced in France, and thus free the kings, particularly Philip the Fair, from the odium of having acted arbitrarily in imposing many of them. But to elucidate the subject under all its aspects, M. Callery is bound to remark that feudal laws were never considered as founded on strict right—that is, on natural or Roman law—but they were only national customs whose origin, according to him, cannot be pointed out.

To prevent an unhappy confusion on the subject M. Callery, therefore, calls public attention to the fact that many modern writers on feudal laws, particularly the more modern ones, are altogether unreliable, because, in their anxiety for explaining everything according to legal principles, they often have recourse to the natural, or Roman—and, we ourselves would add, the canon—law, whilst, as he justly says, there was not the least connection between all these branches of jurisprudence and feudalism, which was simply a collection of national customs irrespective of right or wrong. He ends these considerations by stating in a note that it was "the Roman law which in fact killed outright the feudal *régime*," by making right prevail over absurd customs.

We perceive, therefore, at the very beginning of the middle ages, among nations fundamentally and radically Christian, a pagan code ruling them by simple customs in which even the natural law was not consulted, to which even in many cases it was opposed. No one, surely, will pretend that the Church had introduced it. Still, no one appeared to be aware of this serious anomaly; and it was with a perfectly good conscience that the feudal prescriptions were followed. Hence when a man of noble blood, having entered the career of Church preferment, was offered by his lord a benefice, such as a bishop's see or a rich abbey, he did not feel the least scruple in taking his oath that he would follow his lord in all his wars, fight for him against all comers, and shed blood in torrents to prove his fidelity to his sovereign. If this sovereign wanted money rather than a soldier, the new bishop or abbot could not even see any difficulty in giving money instead of military service. And by this very simple process, in the matter of ecclesiastical preferments, simony directly spread as far and wide as feudalism itself went. Is this a proof that the middle ages were a very corrupt epoch?

Before examining this last question, however, it is proper to qualify what has just been said. In the crudity with which it has been presented, owing to M. Callery's blunt exposition, it seems it must be supposed that the feudal ideas then prevalent had extinguished the moral sense in people subjected to them; and that whatever the Gospel and canon law prescribed against simony and the shedding of blood by ecclesiastics had been entirely forgotten. This, surely, could not be. When the pagan Northmen embraced Christianity, they received a new code which enlightened their consciences on many points, and gradually civilized them and prepared them for holiness. It is known how those nations became finally alive to and susceptible of the most refined moral ideas. The various steps they passed through in this spiritual progress could be easily ascertained by historical researches; and it would be easy to distinguish by a higher moral pattern the age of St. Louis of France, for instance, from that of Hugh Capet and his immediate successors. The feudal laws regulating the duties of the vassal toward his lord, and expressing the hierarchical rights of the lord toward his vassal, were gradually cleared up and fundamentally changed by the Christian code which all Europe obeyed. So that when the popes remonstrated against the abuses engendered by feudalism, they struck in the public conscience a key which awakened Christian feelings that otherwise would have remained dormant. Consequently the execution of feudal laws must have left the Christian conscience in a state of

It is nevertheless undeniable that the temptation to prefer the prescriptions of that strange code to those of the Gospel was on many occasions very strong. The feudal ideas had during many ages entwined themselves with the whole life of the people; for they embraced all the phases of life, and recurred at every moment of it. Those nations could not even understand a state of society different from the one under which they lived; and for this reason it required many centuries to abolish feudalism. If the Roman law, according to M. Callery, killed it, it took many centuries to accomplish the measure. In fact, when a long-established custom is in opposition to any law, human or divine, a very long period of time is necessary for the human and even divine law to prevail. There are always, in such cases as these, wretched compositions with the human conscience which appear lawful to the great number of men; and it is only among those in whom the moral sense is most keen that the sophism on which the custom rests will be directly perceived and opposed.

Thus it is very probable that when a German emperor of the Hohenstaufen race required of a high dignitary in the Church the oath of a vassal, as it was then understood by all classes of society, the vassal scarcely reflected that, the investiture of the office being given through the proffer of the crosier and the ring, the emperor in fact assumed the right of granting spiritual authority itself, together with the temporalities attached to the office. So the popes understood it directly, and opposed the attempt with all their energy. But the temporal interests connected with this feudal ceremony were of so attractive a nature that many churchmen succumbed to the temptation. Nearly all the sees in Germany were soon filled with prelates who had surrendered the rights of the Church, and acknowledged the State as the source of spiritual power. There was directly an inextricable confusion created between the temporal and spiritual authority. If military service or money was required as compensation for the *beneficium*, the new canonists pretended that it was granted only in view of what was of a temporal nature in the transaction, and not in view of the spiritual office. It was, however, impossible to distinguish between the one and the other. Thus simony had crept in under false colors, and Europe was soon infected by it; for it did not long remain confined to Germany.

Any one who has read the history of those times knows with

what zeal the popes opposed the granting of investitures with the circumstances resulting from the feudal code. For a long time this was attributed to ambition and pride on their part. Modern researches have completely justified them. Nay, at this day their heroic struggles followed by a well-bought triumph is the best vindication of the Church's holiness at that time. No one can pretend that all members of the Church must be holy in order to secure that character to the organization itself. It is sufficiently upheld when the interpreters of Christ's will, those who have been entrusted with His authority, are faithful to their trust. It is not the conflict that obscures the principle; it is the end that clears it up. It just happened that this conflict did not begin in France, under Philip the Fair, before it had terminated in Germany by the triumph of right; and France, in her turn, by the brutal victory of Nogaret over Boniface VIII. failed at last in her purpose, because she thereby raised the indignation of Europe against her. Dante himself, the pretended Ghibelline, sang it in verse that shall never perish.

For the popes were not unsupported in their conflict against wrong. They had on their side human conscience, which proved its soundness in the general result. How could the pontiffs alone have carried on the warfare for so long a time, and brought it at last to a happy issue, had they not been supported first by the whole mass of the people, and then by a great number of princes, prelates, warriors even, together with heroic women like Mathilda of Tuscany? Let the reader reflect that the contest was essentially a moral one. The question was: Which of the two sides would prevail, virtue or vice? Innocent III., among other pontiffs, settled the question, and no one can pretend to-day that the heart of the Christian world at that time was corrupt, since without necessitating the fall of the skies the reign of justice was at last established. To those who would refuse to acknowledge the Church's holiness at that epoch on account of the prevalent scandals, the strong antagonism against those scandals on the part of the people and their spiritual rulers can be successfully opposed as a proof of moral soundness at the core. The more so that right at last prevailed, and the thirteenth century, with its admirable virtues and transcendent heroism, bringing in its train a most remarkable prosperity among European nations, will ever be a cause of just pride for Catholicity, and a sufficient answer to all its accusers. It was a period of excessive activity for good as well as for evil, but in the end good preponderated, and the Gospel's precepts at last ruled over society. If at that time, as Montalembert has said, " by the side of the opened heavens hell always appeared," the key of the abyss remained in the hand of the Supreme Pontiff, who would have closed it by a last victory had it been time for the world to come to an end.

c. The last indictment against the middle ages, and the strongest in appearance, is the universal state of war which then prevailed in Europe. It is useless to describe it here, since it can be found in hundreds of books which, nevertheless, often exaggerate it and overcharge the picture. It can be easily proved, on the contrary, that, admitting all the facts well known by this time, it was emphatically an age of peace, particularly if we compare it with our own. The last but one of the beatitudes proclaimed by Christ on the Mount was the blessing He bestowed on peacemakers, and mediæval Christianity bore eminently that character.

The complete demonstration of this apparently strange proposition has been furnished by Kenelm Digby in the admirable work from which we have often quoted. And as it would be impossible to perform the task more satisfactorily, it will suffice to give a short abstract of the headings prefaced to his ninth book, in which he fully discusses the subject. Unfortunately the delightful and most convincing details in which he indulges as usual must be altogether passed over. No one, however, is prevented from consulting the original, and it is undoubtedly one of the most agreeable pastimes any one can afford himself.

The eminent author furnishes ample proof that the love and desire of peace prevailed in the ages of faith, and that nations in general assumed a pacific character. Peace was extolled, war regarded with horror. The *demon* himself, in whom all then firmly believed, and whom they all strongly hated, was known chiefly as the enemy of peace. The people detested war, and warriors often felt deep remorse for engaging in it.

The heart-felt yearning after peace was expressed in the prayers, hymns, and regular offices of the Church. No object of hope or desire was oftener repeated. Devotions, public supplications, processions were of frequent occurrence for the same purpose.

The peace invoked by the people and promised by the Prince

of peace was, above all, internal—peace of the heart. It was enjoyed, first, as against internal disorder, for men were then at peace with God, and therefore at peace with the evils of life, with death, with the grave itself. Secondly, they were at peace with themselves, hence they had the spirit of wisdom. Thirdly, they were at peace with men, even with the enemies of truth. But they renounced an evil peace which is often looked for in wealth, in honors, in the world's vanities. Particularly would they have felt horror for the cold peace of the unbeliever, which in our age is called indifference. The internal peace of the middle ages, on the contrary, is well expressed in all the paintings and statues they have left us as the pure emblem of an undisturbed tranquillity.

From internal peace followed that of domestic life. The simple manners of these ages promoted it. There was then peace between all the members of the house. The patriarchal character of Catholic families indicated it. As there was then invariably peace in marriages, often family feuds were put an end to by the happy union of two of their members.

From domestic peace followed peace through society. Catholic life always bore a pacific character. Litigation was denounced and shunned. The legal profession was sanctified; still, a holy horror prevailed against lawsuits. Men then preferred suffering loss. Hence civil causes were often referred to the arbitration of the clergy. The trial by battle, another baneful fruit of feudalism, was condemned as contrary to peace. To all disputes men were averse; ambitious desires were repressed; they were excluded by the prevailing taste for natural joys. Hence cheerful life in cities and in the country. Truly the spirit of peace had descended through religion upon men.

From the domestic and social elements peace passed to all the details of the political constitution. The ideal of all government in the ages of faith was essentially pacific. This was seen in the ritual of coronations and the representations of monarchy; in the pacific education of princes; in the pacific symbols of power; in the pacific instructions given to kings; in the dispositions required of their councillors; in the softening intervention of women in the government. The judicial character of a monarch was preferred to his warlike spirit. The action of parliament and of all administrators was mainly pacific. Peace also was greatly promoted by the harmony between the temporal and spiritual powers. The desire of establishing a unity of empire in Europe arose from the desire of peace. The pacific ideal of subjects was implied in the views of government, and the good of the people was recognized as essential to states.

The pacific ideal of government was realized to a great extent, as is proved by the great number of pacific kings, princes, and nobles. The funeral monuments we still possess of those ages bear testimony to it. The middle ages enjoyed more peace than modern writers pretend. This is also proved by the origin and nature of the truce of God.

Peace naturally ensued from the union of all nations promoted by the Catholic Church. . . . Political peace was desired and ratified on religious grounds.

The general character of warlike operations in the middle ages is to be attentively considered. Wars in general were commenced, conducted, and terminated in the spirit of peace. The calamities of war did not fall on all men, and multitudes enjoyed exemption from them. Wars did not interrupt works of peace. Destructive modes of warfare were prohibited. Pacific instructions were given to soldiers. Chivalry was instituted with a view to counteract their vices and promote peace. Three kinds of wars were sanctioned: wars of justice, wars for mercy, the crusades to rescue oppressed brethren.

The object of border wars was to repel invaders. That of internal wars was to put down disturbers of peace. The only wars liable to objection were those of the tyrannical feudal lords, cooped up in their monstrous castles. But the Church always cried out against those local tyrants. Brotherhoods were instituted to defend the country against them. The royal power was invoked. Italy succeeded in subduing them. The French kings always fought against them, and greatly curtailed their power. The clergy used the temporal power they had acquired, and in order to defend the people erected castles themselves. The German bishops warred against the castles of the robber-knights.

Finally, a review is made of the blessed peace-makers, including kings, princes, feudal lords, knights adverse to duelling in the modern sense; obscure men and women; the clergy generally, who condemned tournaments as contrary to peace, the sovereign pontiffs, the papal legates, the great prelates; the monks and friars.

This sketch includes the whole subject of wars in the middle ages, and ends in what can be called their complete justification. Being in the form of a table of contents, it seems at first sight to be a mere array of assertions. But that these assertions are made good by the eminent author will be readily admitted by any one who will consent to read the entire ninth book of *Mores Catholici*. The most important part, however, is the chapter on the "tyrannical feudal lords," which precisely enumerates most of the facts objected to the mediæval epoch. It is doubtful if a stronger case against the evils of those times could ever be made by any reviler of the middle ages. The substance of all the usual outcries against feudalism is certainly brought forward by Mr. K. Digby. But he victoriously proves that this ugly feature, however detestable in itself, instead of detracting from their pacific character, confirms it on the contrary, and places on record the best possible proof that the Christian spirit reigned supreme in the midst of those feudal disorders and crimes. With these few reflections we close the discussion on the character of holiness fostered by the Catholic Church during the three or four centuries which have been most unjustly called the darkest period of human history. The picture would be greatly enhanced if besides the religious and moral questions involved in it, the social, civil, and material aspect of Europe at that time could be sufficiently illustrated. But this would go beyond our scope. It has been done lately by some eminent writers; and the more this epoch of history is studied in authentic documents and the true sources, the more impartial men become convinced that a great injustice has been done by previous authors in the invariable description they drew of what they called the "dark ages." Even economists now admit that the well-being and happiness of the lower classes of society at that time was far superior to what it is at the present day; and if social economy continues to progress on the road on which M. Le Play was the first to place it, the well-wishers of the people in this age will insist on a return to many of the institutions which have been misrepresented and abused since the beginning of the sixteenth century.

CHAPTER VII.

SUPPLEMENTARY.

1. *A Short Summary of Facts so far Unfolded.*

THE Church's beneficial action on the morals of men has thus far been described from the beginning of Christianity down to the end of the middle ages. To complete our task, it must be briefly sketched for modern times. The stream of holiness flowing from her lips and heart can suffer no interruption as long as the kingdom of God is to continue on earth.

Is it not wonderful to see how invariably she has brought all nations to the practice of the most exalted virtues? Among the Jews, Egyptians, Syrians, Persians, and the innumerable tribes of the far Orient, as well as among the Greeks, the Romans, and the Celts in the West, this was most remarkable primitively on account of the superstitions and vices prevalent among them all. But the conversion of the barbarian world, and the introduction among them of the most sublime morality, was more wonderful still, owing to their savage ferocity and their former indulgence in the most unbridled passions. Still, the Saxons in Great Britain, the Northmen in central Europe, the Huns along the Danube and farther east, became, through the Church's exertion, the humble followers of a meek Saviour, and placed their glory in the thorough performance of the mild virtues inculcated by Christ in his Sermon on the Mount. Could the Church have succeeded in such an extraordinary task had she not been herself eminently holy? The blemishes appearing in some of her spiritual rulers, as recorded by the impartial historian, must have been at that time rare exceptions resulting from the weakness of human nature, of which the Church cannot be made responsible, since they were so clearly opposed to her own teaching. But it is important to remark that those *exceptions* were, no doubt, but comparatively few, since they did not prevent the establishment of true holiness among so many millions of simple hearers and beholders. With corrupt leaders the Church would have spread corruption, not virtue. New converts must have generally practised not precisely what they heard, but chiefly what they saw. If the inner life of the Redeemer grew up so quickly and so brightly among the new Christians as history teaches it did, there could be no other reason for it except that it was also conspicuous in the teachers, and the simple chronicles of those fourteen centuries abound with a further proof of it in the numerous biographies they have left us of those primitive apostles, bishops, and monks. What an expansion of charity, of piety, of self-sacrifice, is spread over the pages in which the candid recital is written! The annals of the world present no other spectacle comparable to this; and the sanctity of the Christian Church blooms as eminently and exclusively in human history as the brightness of the sun in its noontide splendor outshines all other sources of light.

It evidently culminated during the middle ages; because the Church's influence was then paramount, and her moral direction was in the main heeded. It was only from a comparatively small number of emperors, kings, and princes that an emphatic voice of disobedience was occasionally heard. But because the doings of those *great men* in the world formed then the main staple of history, the reader of those simple and primitive records is occasionally induced to believe that contumacy was then rife and the Church's power closely restricted and ineffectual. But it is fair to remember that besides the Fredericks and Henrys of Germany, the Philips of France, the Plantagenets and Tudors of England, there were millions and millions of fervent Christians not only in the cloister and in the wilderness of the forests, but in towns and cities, in hamlets and farm-houses, whose lives were spent in the constant praise of God and the fulfilment of the most arduous duties. Yes, great virtues were then practised not only in Italy and Spain and Gaul, but in England and Scotland and Germany and Sarmatia, and in Scandinavia itself. Have not all these countries, which then comprised an immense number of smaller states, a surprising list of saints inscribed in their respective hagiographies? Each province of France, to my knowledge, enjoys at least the advantage of a numerous array of holy people who have embalmed the mediæval epoch by the perfume of their virtues. In Brittany, where I was born, several folio volumes have been published containing the biographies of a small number of them. The great majority of them will never be known but to God. The same is true of all European countries which have to this day remained Catholic; and among those which are now Protestant the memory of the former heroes of holiness is still vividly kept by many among the people.

This is intended only to introduce the special subject of this chapter. The continuance of that sublime privilege in the Catholic Church must be proved even for modern times—nay, for our very day—in spite of the universal lowering of the moral standard.

2. *How far did Corruption Invade the Sanctuary previous to the so-called Reformation?*

On the threshold of these considerations we are met by a universal reproach addressed to the Church itself. Popes, bishops, monks, it is said, had become excessively corrupt in the fifteenth century, so that on every side a reformation was called for and never effected. The Roman Church received the name of the new Babylon even from Catholic writers; and the pontiffs, though they all promised a change at their accession to the chair of Peter, invariably demurred from undertaking it as soon as they were seated on the pontifical throne. Details are not necessary here, since they are found in all modern histories; and the conclusion first openly proclaimed by Luther is drawn indistinctly by ardent foes and pretended friends, that the Church had lost her privilege of sanctity.

In the exaggerated picture which is generally sketched of those deplorable times, one feature is invariably left out; namely, the zeal displayed by a great number of other popes, bishops, and religious who actually prevented corruption from spreading deeply among the people, so that the bulk of the Church was not affected by it. Impartiality alone would prompt any writer to bring this forward. But before doing so, as our duty prescribes, it is important to examine leisurely the extent and limits of the evil, and also to look into the most vital question connected with the whole matter under consideration. This is the important inquiry concerning the Church's moral teaching at that time. For the reformers, when they came on the stage of action, wished to spread the belief that immorality as well as superstition had become the main doctrine preached to the people. This was not true; and the most unworthy of spiritual rulers at that time never failed to teach what they did not practise themselves, and their exhortations were invariably those of true successors of the apostles. The principles of holiness, consequently, remained as firm and were as strongly upheld in the darkest period of the fifteenth century as they had ever been previously. This alone would be a sufficient proof that the Church never forfeited her right to be called the moral teacher of mankind.

But before anything else, the total measure of moral evil must be accurately inquired into and ascertained; and it is important afterwards to examine if around the immorality generally prevailing in higher circles there was not a large field which had not been tainted by corruption, and which reproduced still the Christian virtues of a former age.

To judge well of the plague-spot in its nakedness, its chief causes must be first briefly stated. The main one was a reproduction at that time in Rome of the disorders resulting from feudalism in the tenth century. The papal elections, it is true, had been placed by Gregory VII. in the hands of the cardinals, and there was no more fear that the tools of ambitious margraves and of corrupt women should sit on the papal throne. But because in the middle ages the popes, generally siding with liberty, had never seen fit to centralize their power, and had left a great political freedom to the people and their barons, this at last degenerated into frequent disorders bordering sometimes on anarchy. The petty chieftains of villages or towns around the holy city became almost independent, and the state of war between them was nearly incessant. Rome itself was the prey of factions ruled by a few families. The papal temporal power dwindled almost to nothing, and the pontiff's spiritual authority suffered immensely from it. They could scarcely remain in Rome.

This brought on the transfer of the papacy to Avignon, which the popes could not avoid, and, the Great Schism of the West being the consequence of it, Christendom was almost disorganized, because people were left in doubt as to the origin of power in the Church.

If the unity of the Church appeared broken, the Empire itself was in a state of disorganization, and the kings of Europe refused to acknowledge a suzerain in His Imperial Majesty. Each of them claimed a paramount authority in his dominions.* They soon began, in consequence, to oppose the mandates of the sovereign pontiffs as the German emperors had done; and the kings of France particularly, beginning with Philip the Fair, resumed in their limited spheres the policy of the Hohenstaufens. Legists were pitted against canonists, and the principles of right itself became tainted. The Catholic Church had rigorously no share in all those causes of demoralization.

The deleterious effects of those sources of disorder were, however, immensely magnified by the wealth of the clergy, which had been accumulated during the whole of the middle ages, and which then became the origin of untold abuses and of a too-visible corruption.

Wealth had come unbidden to the clergy, who morally suffered from it though not guilty of its introduction. But the multiplicity of benefices bestowed on single persons, and the number of monasteries given *in commendam* to secular prelates, cannot be so easily excused, and form almost the total amount of facts from which pernicious effects followed. The heart bleeds, however, in mentioning these deplorable facts, chiefly on account of their consequences. How could the dioceses, the parishes, the monasteries, be duly supervised and administered, when the one who had the title and enjoyed the revenues either could not but neglect them entirely, owing to their multiplicity in one single hand, or gave them to hirelings with an insufficient salary? Hence from every side bitter complaints arose. Those who had at heart the good of the Church remonstrated against such glaring abuses. The popes as loudly as any others. It is said that Benedict XII. proposed to the cardinals to resign all their benefices except one, and he promised as a supplement to fund a rental of a hundred thousand golden florins, besides half the revenue of the papal states; the project failed because the majority of those interested did not think it sufficient to support their state. Zealous men at last, like Jerome Savonarola, inveighed openly against the corruption which had invaded the sanctuary. For a long time good men applauded him, until at last he appeared to reject all superior authority; and though it seems that he acknowledged his error at the last mo-

---

* See Cantù.

ment, and accepted his fate as an expiation, it remains doubtful if he can be numbered among those who called for a legitimate reform.

Meanwhile, among other deplorable circumstances, many monasteries had been given *in commendam*, and in consequence disorders crept into those establishments from which the Church could have expected a great help for her regeneration. It is unfortunately true that in the fourteenth and fifteenth centuries they had in general degenerated from their primitive fervor. If the vile calumnies of Aretino and Capilupo in Italy against them cannot even be read, much less trusted, the reproaches addressed to many religious by holy men of that age are too precise and pointed to be set aside. It is indeed a sad picture of houses which have always been the glory and the joy of the Church. Still, in the midst of these lamentable evils it can be maintained that holiness had not disappeared, and it must be proved.

3. *The Moral Teaching of the Church was at that Time as Firm as Ever.*

Had Christianity been only a human institution, in the midst of this moral decomposition the worst theories in ethics would certainly have prevailed. The Roman pontiffs themselves, not having in this supposition the privilege of inerrancy, the consequence would have been that in the decisions of councils, in the bulls of the popes, in some at least of the authoritative documents which were issued so copiously at that epoch, proofs would have been afforded that many streams in the Church's life being corrupted, the source itself was corrupt. Nothing of this ever appeared even in the worst period of the fifteenth century. No Protestant reformer has ever been able to point out any article of moral teaching as being evidently opposed to God's law. The Calvinists were reduced to inveigh against the worship of images and the veneration rendered to the Pope as to a God! The more sensible among the Protestants confined themselves to drawing fanciful and odious pictures from well-ascertained facts such as those which have been just described. They concluded that the teaching must have been bad since the life of many among the clergy was so reprehensible. They were soon answered, however, that our Lord had commanded His disciples to do what the priests of the law prescribed, but not what they did. He had given them infallibility, not impeccability.

To quote a single example of this most remarkable feature of those times, the *Bullarium* of the pontiffs who governed the Church in the fourteenth and fifteenth centuries exists still and has been published. It is impossible to find any difference in its tone, in its moral directions, in its enforcement of virtue, from similar documents of the best ages. Among the bulls of Alexander VI. the only one that has been openly attacked is precisely the one which has been most unexceptionably useful to mankind. It is the drawing of the line of demarcation between the Spanish and Portuguese possessions in America. Had it not been for this papal decision it is certain that there would have been a constant state of wrangling or open war between those two nations in the New World; whilst, on the contrary, disagreement between them has always been both slight and rare. This is one of the last acts of arbitration of the popes; and it would be difficult to find another more pregnant of good for humanity.

But the best proof that the Church did not then fail in her moral teaching is derived from the strict continuance of the same doctrine in ethics as well as in dogma from the previous ages. It is known that from the time of Jonas of Orleans there have been a long succession of great teachers authorized by the Church and devoted to her service. They have been called the schoolmen. St. Thomas Aquinas was the greatest of them. If in their writings there were occasionally some points that the Church disapproved and others which the Church left every one free to accept or reject, the main substance of them was authoritatively sanctioned, and formed a complete body of what was to be believed and practised—*credendorum et agendorum.* It was this which gave to the middle ages their peculiar character of faith and holiness.

Had there been later on any change in the moral doctrine of the Church, a new set of pretended doctors would have appeared, and the previous schoolmen would have been attacked by these new teachers. The loose manners of the epoch would have been fostered by what was taught in universities, academies, and schools, and the disorders of the clergy would have been at least palliated by a new interpretation of God's law. Nothing of the kind ever appeared; and the good men who constantly and earnestly called for reform did not cease to refer to the old ecclesiastical law as existing still and forming always the basis of duty. The popes never objected to their remonstrances, and often approved of them. Savonarola himself was never opposed by Alexander VI. except when the infatuated monk dared to deny papal authority. These are well-ascertained facts which suffice for a complete demonstration.

To give it the last and highest degree of power, it is not inopportune to remark that the Protestant *reformers* in their violent reproaches addressed to the Catholic Church embraced the schoolmen in their reprobation as well as the theologians of their time. It is from their wholesale abuse that the mediæval period began to be misunderstood and vilified. By attacking the scholastic philosophers and theologians, they knew they were striking at the Church of their time; and consequently they identified with justice the doctrine of St. Thomas with that of the more modern doctors flourishing in the fifteenth century. The old universities founded formerly by the popes continued to exist; they followed the same methods and supported the same propositions in faith and morals. The strictures, violent abuse, and gross satires of Luther and other reformers were even chiefly directed against the founders of scholasticism, and Thomas Aquinas was particularly abused by them. And the main reason of it was that the immortal writings of the primitive schoolmen were only commented on by the more modern professors, and were found in the hands of all philosophical and theological students. Luther, who certainly had received the same instruction in his Augustinian convent of Wittenberg, was perfectly well acquainted with this fact; and he would not have committed the blunder of ascribing the disorders of his day, of which he spoke so violently and which he habitually exaggerated, to a change in the teaching of the old masters; that is, of the Church herself, who had approved and sanctioned them. He attacked both.

This suffices to establish the truth under consideration. The Catholic Church, even in the most deplorable times, continued to be the teacher of the nations, and imparted to them the wholesome doctrine of the Redeemer in all its primitive purity; and the principles of holiness never were departed from or even obscured.

4. *A Large Array of Facts Prove that the Principle of Regeneration in the Church was always Active in the Midst of a Widespread Corruption.*

The residence of many popes at Avignon during the fourteenth and fifteenth centuries has been pointed out as one of the great causes of the prevailing evils. Still, a false impression on the subject prevails which must be removed. It is generally supposed that the whole was a dark period. But from 1305, when Clement V. was elected, till 1378, when an antipope who took the name of Clement VII. was placed in opposition to Urban VI. (the precise origin of the schism), nine pontiffs governed the universal Church, and resided at Avignon. All of them were recognized as legitimate by all Christians; fulfilled their duty; and most of them maintained a strict discipline in the secular and regular clergy, as well as among the people. Some of them, even, can be considered among the best successors of St. Peter; and one particularly, Benedict XII., not only lived on the throne as an austere Cistercian monk, but eventually became an ardent reformer of all abuses. Rohrbacher in his *Histoire de l'Église** has demonstrated it in the admirable sketch of the life of this pope, which he drew from authentic documents. It is wrong, consequently, to suppose that the whole fourteenth century was a corrupt age. A great part of it can be compared to some of the best periods in the history of the Church. In the impossibility of reproducing all the facts brought forward by the painstaking and loyal French historian, a few points at least must be mentioned to vindicate particularly for Benedict XII. the title of a true reformer and a great pope.

And first, his policy towards kings and princes, if conciliatory, was always firm and based on duty. It can be at once appreciated from the answer he gave to Philip of Valois in 1337, the third year of his pontificate, in the city of Avignon, whither the French king had come to visit him: "Sire," he said, "had I two souls, I would willingly give one of them to do your pleasure and satisfy your wish; but I have only one, which I must preserve from sin. Whenever you desire to ask me anything, see first that there is nothing in it contrary to God's law, nothing that I cannot grant without injury to my conscience and danger to my salvation. What you ask me to do is not such as would

---

* Vol. 20, p. 229, *seq.* French edit. 1858.

be safe for me; and I am compelled to say that I cannot consent to it and gratify you." This was said to a powerful monarch, a short time after Philip the Fair had well-nigh destroyed the temporal power of the Holy See, and Pope Benedict was then living in the midst of the French possessions and, as it were, at the mercy of the king.

In a second place, with regard to his own court, at the very beginning of his pontificate he announced publicly in a great consistory that all ecclesiastics and prelates not attached to his person must withdraw from Avignon and return to their respective benefices within a month, under the pains prescribed by the canon law; unless there was for any of them some peculiar reason, of which he himself should be the judge, to remain longer at his court. As to the collation of benefices, it is known that he was always opposed to their accumulation into one hand, and if he could not obtain from the cardinals that they should resign those they possessed, keeping one only, he imposed it severely on other dignitaries. He was, besides, most careful never to grant any benefices except to worthy persons, and he preferred to leave them vacant. As to his own relatives, he never was guilty of prefering them to others, and nepotism could not be laid to his charge. He himself said that a pope must be like Melchisedech, "without father, mother, genealogy."

In a third place, he very early set at reforming the secular and regular clergy. The canons of the cathedral of Narbonne were known for their scandalous life; he applied himself vigorously to their reformation a few months after his accession. He appointed at the same time visitors to institute inquiries in the various chapters of the provinces of Narbonne and Arles, and recommended them also to look into the affairs of the monks of St. Benedict and of the Premonstratenses in the same districts.

He did not neglect his own order, that of the Cistercians, and issued a most remarkable bull to strengthen the bonds of discipline in all the branches of the Benedictine brotherhood. The Annals of Raynaldi, the *Bullarium Romanum*, besides Baluze and the *Histoire de l'Église Gallicane*, give most precious details on those important matters. Yet, strange to say, neither M. de Lépinois, in his *Gouvernement des Papes*, nor Cesare Cantù, in his *Reforma in Italia*, speak of it. They must have been ignorant of it, for neither of them can be suspected of wilfully concealing anything advantageous to the popes. Cantù speaks openly of the successful efforts made by many holy men and women for the reformation of Benedictine monasteries in Italy, without a word in reference to the decrees of Benedict XII., which must have been still more powerful for the intended effect than all individual action. The pope sent the original document to the abbots of St. Denys, near Paris, and of St. Columba of Sens, with the order to publish it in a provincial chapter which met the following June, 1336, in the abbey of St. Germain des Prés at Paris. This day was the origin of a new regeneration of the order, which began directly to set about the people's reformation as monks knew so well how to do. The document itself has been known since as the "Benedictine Bull."

Another was soon issued with regard to the mendicant orders, which were at that time beginning to fall off from their primitive fervor. A number of those religious preferred to appear at the papal court in Avignon rather than reside in their convents or apply to works of zeal. They were first sent back to their regular avocations, the same as secular ecclesiastics and prelates had been previously ordered to go. The bull destined for them revived the strictness of their rules with regard to public offices in their churches, to the prescribed modesty and humility in their dress and intercourse with the people, and warned them against too ardent a zeal, which had already been the cause among them of many disorders and disputes. This papal decree was published in a general chapter of the Franciscans held at Cahors in June, 1337.

Several less important injunctions were likewise laid upon the members of the Dominican order, and the friar-preachers applied with a new ardor to their missions which Vincent Ferrer was soon destined to render forever illustrious all over Europe. All this was effected in less than three years after Benedict XII.'s installation into office; and the purity of religious life, which was the main result of it, contributed powerfully to the reformation of manners among the people and to the introduction of sacerdotal virtues in the secular priesthood. Cantù in his *Reforma in Italia* does not spare his vituperations against the parochial clergy at that time. He openly accuses them "of gross ignorance, of simony in the administration of the sacraments, of frequent intoxication, of unbridled passions." He does not allude to any positive facts of this character either in his text or in his notes, and his accusations are too general and too sweeping to be believed in their entirety. Still, there can be no doubt that a thorough reformation was sorely needed. The zeal of the bishops was kindled by the pope's exhortations and fostered by the renewed energy of the monks. Rohrbacher remarks that under the pontificate of Benedict XII. provincial councils were celebrated at Rouen, Salamanca, Bourges, Château Gontier, Tarragona, Treves, Avignon, Aquileia, Toledo, Barcelona, and Canterbury. It is known that on those occasions decrees are always issued, not only for the moral good of the people, but chiefly for the revival of piety and virtue among all classes of the clergy.

The reader must not imagine that Benedict XII. was the only Avignon pope who labored earnestly and effectually for the good of the Church. It has already been asserted that of the nine supreme pontiffs who resided at Avignon, from Clement V. to Urban VI. (that is, previous to the Great Schism of the West), not a single one of them can be accused of open dereliction of duty. But if time and space allowed, interesting details could be furnished of the constant efforts made by Innocent VI. to continue the reforming policy of his great predecessor; of the whole life of Urban V., one of the best popes that ever governed the Church. He labored ardently for the reunion of the Greeks with Rome, revived Catholicity in all the Danubian provinces, did not forget the Chinese, to whom he sent Minorites as missionaries, and finally returned to Rome in spite of the popular factions which continued to disgrace it. He would probably, had he lived longer, put an end to the terrible wars between France and England which lasted a hundred years. In the expressed intention of reconciling the two kings he went back to Avignon, where, unfortunately, he soon died, so that his successor, Gregory XI., was naturally induced to remain in that city. The residence of the popes in Rome was still well-nigh impracticable on account of the violent and constant feuds which raged in the papal states, particularly in the city, where the Colonnas and Orsinis continued to wrangle among themselves, and often shed blood in torrents. Cesare Cantù and other impartial historians mainly assign to this cause the prolonged exile from Rome of the pontiffs, many of whom sincerely wished to occupy again their see, but were frightened by the violence of feudal barons.

It is only from the time of the schism—namely, from the pontificate of Urban VI. in 1378—that the popes of Avignon deserve severe censure; and as the schism was effectually extinguished by the election of Martin V. in 1417, the dark period of that epoch extends only to about forty years. This remark is important and in point, because nearly the whole of this very time was occupied by the fruitful missions of St. Vincent Ferrer, carried on over a great part of Europe. It is, therefore, almost preposterous to suppose that the Church remained at any moment without an active principle of regeneration working in her. To this we must now turn our attention.

The schism originated from the election of Clement VII. As to the virtues of the true pope, Urban VI., the only thing objectionable in them was his too great severity, which the dissolute manners of many men could not brook. He wished to bring down the cardinals to the austere life he had himself adopted, and to oblige them, for instance, never to have more than one dish on their table. This, together with other sumptuary laws he proposed to enact for the sacred college, frightened them so that they pretended they had not been free on the day of his election. They had, however, during three months acknowledged him as pope, announced his accession in letters sent by them to all the courts of Europe, and received favors and dignities from him. Still, they maintained they had not been free, and meeting together at Fondi, in the Neapolitan kingdom, they proceeded to another election and chose Robert of Geneva, who took the name of Clement VII. and went to reside at Avignon. Urban VI. remained in Rome, as all his successors did after him. As three cardinals only remained faithful to him (the only Italians of the sacred college), he directly promoted twenty-six prelates to the cardinalate, and thenceforth there were two papal courts, one at Avignon, evidently schismatical, the other at Rome, regular and legitimate. France, Scotland, Naples, Arragon, and some minor states followed the Avignon pope; the remainder of Christendom submitted to the Roman pontiff. There was properly no schism among the people, because even those who acknowledged Clement VII.—the schismatical pope—were fully persuaded he was the true pope, having universal authority, and they never thought of forming only a fragment of the Church.

This remark of Abbé Darras is in point, and gives a less gloomy view of the state of the Church at that time. Still, it cannot be denied that the authority of each of the two popes was seriously lessened by these unfortunate events. Their chief occupation was often to attack each other, either by mutual sentences of excommunication or by exciting their princely and kingly friends to war against their respective antagonists. They, moreover, felt less free to address boldly reproaches to the bishops and inferior clergy who favored them; and this was the main cause of the moral disorders that spread over Europe during the whole time of the schism, and furnished the subject of many eloquent pages to Catharine of Siena, Bridget of Sweden, Antoninus of Florence, Vincent Ferrer, and many other friends of the Church of Christ.

These disorders, however, did much more injury to good morals in the districts ruled by the Avignon popes than in those under Roman rule. The long schismatical pontificates of Clement VII. and Benedict XIII. (Peter da Luna) became a fruitful source of corruption in France, Naples, and Arragon, and caused the previous attempts at reformation to be disregarded. The moral life of cardinals, prelates, inferior clergymen, chiefly in those countries, became deplorable. Still, it must be repeated again that the Church was at no time left to the wild guidance of the passions of men. The apostolic life of Vincent Ferrer is alone a sufficient proof of it.

5. *Holiness continued in the Church during the Darkest Period of the Great Schism.*

Vincent Ferrer was born in 1350. He died in 1419, two years after the election of Martin V. His life, therefore, was coextensive with the dark period under consideration. His apostolate, particularly, embraced the worst part of it, and he reluctantly held high offices under the antipope Benedict XIII. His biography is perfectly well known, and the Bollandists have cleared up all the difficulties which could throw some obscurity over it. They mainly follow the work of Ranzano, a Dominican like Ferrer, which they publish in full. But many other sources of information were consulted by the authors of *Acta Sanctorum*, and the most severe criticism cannot find fault with their conclusions.

The field over which Vincent labored embraced a great part of central Europe; and no better test than his life could be applied to the important question: How far had moral corruption extended?

and to the other: Did this attempt at regeneration succeed? He began to preach in 1398, and continued until his death in 1419. Consequently his labors lasted twenty-one years; and he was not alone in those holy expeditions, but he was always accompanied by at least twelve of his Dominican brethren and a great number of prelates and priests, besides many pious laymen and women. Thousands, in fact, helped him in producing the extraordinary reformation in morals he effected everywhere.

The Bollandists give copious details and proofs of his extensive travels, according to the chronological order, and they point out the successive steps of his apostolate year after year, month after month, and occasionally even day after day. It is not possible to copy this most interesting but necessarily long sketch; and our purpose does not require it. It suffices to state in general that he evangelized successively: 1st. All the provinces of Spain, including the kingdom of Granada, whither he was called by the Mussulman prince Mohamed Aben-Baba, and converted thousands of Arab Moslems and Jews. 2d. All the provinces, likewise, of France, from the most southern—namely, Provence and Gascony—to the farthest north—that is, Champagne, Picardy, and Lorraine. 3d. The independent dukedoms west and north of France; namely, Brittany, Normandy, and Flanders. 4th. Henry VI. of England sent purposely a vessel to Gallicia and brought him to Great Britain, where he spent more than a year (1406) in England and Scotland, whence he passed over to Ireland. 5th. In northern Italy he evangelized Savoy, the republic of Genoa, Piedmont, and Lombardy. 6th. In central Italy he preached among the Florentines, the Pisans, the Sienese, and in some of the papal provinces along the Adriatic Sea. 7th, and last. Several other countries of minor importance could not be mentioned in this hasty enumeration, such as the Balearic Isles, Switzerland, the valleys of the Alps particularly, where he converted many Waldenses, Cathari, and even some pagans who worshipped the sun. He does not seem to have penetrated into Germany; and though he was twice invited to Constance on the borders of it, by the fathers of the Council, he found good reasons to be excused. His only motive seems to have been that he did not wish to interrupt his missions in order to concern himself with the affairs of Church and State, which were then thrown into an utter confusion. He thought, with justice, that the best way to oppose the evils of the times was to labor effectually for the reformation of morals among clergy and people.

The effect he produced among both was indeed wonderful. To use the words of his last biographer, the Dominican Andrew Pradel: "The moment St. Vincent entered a city it immediately wore the appearance of Ninive when Jonas preached penance to it. People wept when they heard the saint's mass; but their tears were most abundant when he exhorted them to repentance. It was then that sighs, groanings, and lamentations filled the air. It might have been thought that each one mourned the death of a first-born, or of a father or a mother. The spectacle of the vast plains which alone could contain his auditory gave an idea of the universal judgment. It anticipated, in fact, the future terror and lamentation of all the tribes of the earth when they shall be gathered together in the valley of Josaphat. But as Nicholas of Clémangis, an eye-witness, observes, the most lukewarm souls and hearts of stone were softened, and gave vent to their sorrow in tears and accents of the bitterest anguish.

"We may, moreover, picture to ourselves the extraordinary confluence of people. The saint's hearers were not only the inhabitants of the city where he preached; there were frequently gathered around his pulpit more than fifty thousand people, even when he spoke in small villages. They gladly went several leagues to hear him. During his sermons all the artisans of the place abandoned their labor, and the merchants their warehouses. In cities where there were schools the masters suspended their lectures. Neither the inclement season, wind, nor rain prevented the multitudes from collecting in the public squares where the saint was to preach. The sick who had sufficient strength to walk left the hospitals, others were bodily carried; all hoped to enjoy, by simply hearing Vincent, the health of body and soul at the same time, and this hope was frequently realized.

"As to the general fruit of his apostolate, we must quote from an authentic document; namely, a letter written by the Council of Orihuela to the Bishop of Carthagena in Spain: 'The arrival of Vincent Ferrer has produced immense good in this country; it has been a grand occasion of salvation to all the faithful. This city in particular, at the close of his preaching, and by God's grace, is delivered from every vice and public sin. . . . All noisy entertainments have been given up. . . . On Sundays and feasts of obligation all go to mass with devotion, such as no one believed could have happened, much less expected to witness. . . . There no longer exists in this city either rancor or enmity against any one; but each one, spontaneously and for God's honor, pardons the other. We have counted more than one hundred and twenty-three reconciliations; sixty-six deaths and a host of broken limbs have been pardoned. Now every one lives in peace and concord. In the great city of Tolosa all the women of abandoned character have renounced their disorders.'"

What is said here of Orihuela and Tolosa in Spain could be repeated of all other cities where St. Vincent preached; and in the extensive sketch given by the Bollandists the great majority of Spanish towns are particularly mentioned. In the compendium previously given of it, nothing more could be said than that Vincent "evangelized all the provinces of Spain." Further details were necessarily omitted. But in Arragon, Castile, Navarre, Andalusia, Valentia, and Murcia the general process of reformation took place. It is even remarkable that Vincent was not satisfied with going once through every locality in those provinces; but subsequently he returned once, twice, three times, to cities where he had produced such a remarkable change during a first "mission." The same was true, likewise, of many provinces of France; and he even went twice to Brittany, so distant and insignificant a country, at the urgent solicitation of the duke and duchess. He died at Vannes during his second appearance among his dear Bretons; and he is on this account more particularly honored by them. No French or foreign priest who enters the little city of Vannes forgets to say mass at least once in the humble but most holy room where he lived and died. It has been changed into a chapel, and has continued during nearly five hundred years to be the most devout spot in all Brittany after St. Anne d'Auray.

When reflecting on all these circumstances, the mind is struck by the fact that of all the countries which he succeeded in regenerating morally, the only ones which were in the following century permanently invaded by Protestantism were England, Scotland, and a few towns of Switzerland, such as Geneva. All the Latin nations were by him evangelized; he successively visited and revisited them several times, and bestowed on them his most arduous labors. On the contrary, he spent in England and Scotland only a little more than a year, and appeared in Geneva but once, I think, and for a few days. Modern writers assign several causes to the steady adherence of the Latin nations to Catholicism in the time of Luther, and to the defection in general of the northern countries. Would it be presumptuous to think that the labors of St. Vincent Ferrer had their little share in this strange fact? If the wonderful effects of his zeal had disappeared at his death, nothing could be concluded from it with regard to what took place a hundred years later, when Protestantism arose. But it is certain that his own order at least, the Friar-Preachers, had helped him along all his life, and were animated with the same spirit. They continued very active after Vincent's death during the whole of the fifteenth century, and their monasteries were profusely scattered among all Latin nations. Besides the Dominicans, the biographers of St. Vincent speak of prelates and priests of other orders—that is, abbots and monks—who accompanied him everywhere in great numbers. These were, no doubt, Franciscans, Carmelites, and Augustinians, who must have concurred afterwards with the Dominicans in rendering permanent the good effected by the apostle—for thus St. Vincent was called.

This proves that the reformation effected by the bulls of Benedict XII. in the religious orders had persevered and continued until Protestantism appeared. The Jesuits, who came later on, were destined not to prevent but only to check its progress permanently, as has been recorded by modern historians. Meanwhile the popes who governed the Church after the Great Schism (some of whom, unfortunately, were more politicians than high priests) never forgot, however, that they were the successors of Peter, and that they possessed his prerogatives for the spiritual good of mankind. Their *bullarium* affords the proof of it; and if some of them did not contribute personally to the sanctification of Christians by encyclicals and dogmatic or moral treatises, as the Leos, Gregorys, and Innocents had done before them, they nevertheless allowed full liberty to the religious orders to carry on the great object of their institutes by their constant labors in the field of moral regeneration. No more striking case in point can be adduced than the preaching of the great Dominican monk Jerome Savonarola, who would have been cheered even by Alexander VI. himself on account of the reformation he brought about among the Florentines, had he not, as it seems, shown at last a rebellious spirit against lawful authority. Can there be found, we repeat, a single moment when the Church appeared shorn of her prerogative of sanctity?

A curious proof that the answer to this question must be negative is given by Cantù in his *Reforma in Italia*. He begins thus his *Discorso XI* on the *politician popes*, and *Alexander VI.* in particular (we translate from the French version):

"The moral evils just described—under Alexander VI.—were enormous;* the providence of God opposed against them an ardent zeal, a solid piety, a ripe science. No one can hesitate to recognize that the spirit of truth and sanctity which must animate the Church until the end of time gave them a clear proof of its perseverance. It was principally in the religious orders that men arose ready to revive the Christian spirit; and all those orders during that time present at once—if any one looks attentively for them—an array of eminent personages distinguished by their virtues, noted for their learning. Bernardine of Siena was then travelling through Italy, promoting peace among its citizens, scatter-

---

* This was already written and sent to the press when I became aware that a book had lately appeared in Italy which completely disproves the calumnies accredited during the last two hundred years, or more, against the character of Alexander VI. The author is a learned member of the religious congregation called "the Pious Schools." His name is A. Leonetti, and the title of his work is *Papa Alessandro VI. secondo documenti e carteggi del tempo*. From irrefragable documents and letters written at the time of Alexander himself, and without any ulterior view to publication, the conduct of this pope is thoroughly vindicated. Nay, more; the origin and cause of the fables published and believed in aftertimes is presented with details which must carry conviction. The writer spared neither time nor expense to discover in the chief libraries of Italy and France manuscripts which had been buried in oblivion since they were written. No one had yet undertaken to examine the question thoroughly; and mendacious authors in the pay of Florence chiefly, whose government at that time was bitterly opposed to the grand policy of Alexander, had an open field to spread their slanders over all Europe.

The *Civiltà Cattolica*, in its number for August 21, 1880, resumes its opinion of this book in the following words, which we translate from the Italian: "All the arguments and judgments of the author will not appear equally evident to all readers. Still, any one who will go through the work must experience the conviction that a like farrago of absurd and impudent calumnies, of lies and falsehoods, invented by human passion and believed by human credulity, such as the pretended history of this pontiff exhibits, has not found its parallel in the case of any other man."

Had I known this book sooner, several passages of this chapter would have taken another form.

ing alms among the needy, building churches, convents, hospitals, and founding bee-hives of missionaries whose swarms took wing directly and were wafted over the whole world. Bernardine of Feltro enraptured the people by his eloquence and holiness, by his readiness to hear the complaints of widows and orphans; he labored to propagate *monti di pietà* (pawnbroking establishments), a new institution designed by Barnaba, a Franciscan of Perusia, to save the poor from the extortions of usurers. Giacomo of Montebrandone, in the *Marchie;* Pietro di Moliano and Antonio di Stroconio, in *Umbria;* Pacifico di Credano, in the Novarese territory; Angelo di Chivasso, revered by the people at Cuneo; Giacomo d'Illyria, in a convent near Bari; Vincenzo d'Aguila, known by his austere life; and many other Franciscans obtained for their sanctity the honors of public veneration. The Dominicans were kept in their primitive fervor by Antonio of the Roddi family, and by St. Antonine, archbishop of Florence. This great man lived as a monk; and when he travelled used only a mule; but his palace his purse, and his granaries were freely opened in times of scarcity and pestilence. To those who pretended that a great prelate like him must inspire respect by exterior pomp he simply answered, without uttering a word, by going to Rome dressed in a monkish cowl, astride an old mule, with a small and poor retinue; still, wherever he went the greatest honors were paid him by all classes of society; people knelt in the public streets to receive his blessing, whilst proud bishops and cardinals blushed to see themselves neglected as soon as he appeared among them."

To copy the full enumeration of holy personages living at the time of Alexander VI. and given out by the accurate Italian historian would go beyond our scope; particularly because the list of celebrated and holy women living at the same time, which immediately follows in Cantù's book, is still longer than that of the men. But it was proper to make this short mention of it on account of the misconception under which many labor in our age, with regard to the epoch of Alexander VI. in particular. It seems to be admitted that the Church had then sunk into a universal state of moral decomposition for which there was no other remedy than the fearful shock of heresy which soon followed. It can be, on the contrary, maintained that the mass of the people not only had kept the faith, but were preserved in the practice of all Christian virtues by the zealous exertions of bishops, monks and nuns, many of whom belonged to the highest families of the Italian race. The same would be found to be true of Spain, France, and other European nations.

These were the conclusions drawn by me from a close study of ecclesiastical history during the time of the Great Schism and the short period immediately following. It was indubitable that the Latin nations had been preserved from corruption by the great and zealous preachers who then arose.

But it seemed also that the northern nations of Europe, particularly Germany, had not participated to a great degree in the blessings of this true reformation. They must have remained corrupt, and thus the success of Luther was rationally explained. Still, all this was a misconception which a powerful work lately published in Germany has altogether disproved. Germany was no more corrupt at that time than the southern races, and owing to M. J. Janssen, professor at Frankfort, we now have most copious proofs of it. Under the simple title of "A History of the German People from the End of the Middle Ages"—a most serious and learned work in six large volumes—he gives such a complete demonstration of the morality and well-being of Germany at that epoch that it has created an immense sensation, and elicited the applause of all learned men, Protestants as well as Catholics. M. Janssen begins his labors from the second half of the fifteenth century, because he thinks that modern German history commences from that epoch. It is precisely the worst time of the Great Schism. Still, the most copious and conclusive documents he possessed enable him to draw an astonishing picture of prosperity and Christian civilization. He gives thorough details on instruction and education, on science and art, on agriculture, industry, commerce, on political, social, and domestic economy, on everything, in fine, which make a nation prosperous, moral, and happy.

All this, he says, was the consequence of the deep religious feeling which had prevailed during the middle ages. The spirit of that golden age had not died out. It was deeply implanted in the German nation, and burst out afresh under the influence of Nicholas de Cusa. This great cardinal was, he thinks, for the north the restorer of science and piety, and he alone succeeded in doing in Germany what many holy men had effected in the south. It is a pity that we cannot, at this moment, enter into more details on a work which is destined to effect a complete revolution in the ideas which have so far prevailed on that much-abused epoch the middle ages.

But the most important point to be considered is the conclusion M. Janssen draws with regard to the Protestant rebellion which soon followed. Not only he does not think that the pretended reformation was the natural result of a deep-seated corruption; he is fully persuaded that "the revolution of the sixteenth century did not embrace only religious questions, but was effected chiefly on economical, social, and political grounds. The more I advance, in my studies," he says, "the more I become convinced that this revolution consisted in the total abandonment of faith operating through good works. The works of faith and justice being once abandoned as a useless doctrine, the natural consequence was the destruction of social order such as the middle ages had created it."

Before long Protestantism in Germany will be fully understood, owing to the mighty efforts of her great writers, as the character of the French revolution will be known from the works of M. Taine and other candid inquirers.

But this most imperfect sketch of M. Janssen's work could not give any idea of its importance with regard to the state of morality in the German Church during the worst period of the fifteenth century. It is important to furnish a few more details particularly concerning the religious and moral character of the people. The Church, the school, and the family combined their efforts for this mighty object. The whole of Germany was covered, as it were, with popular schools, independently of the universities, in which Nicholas de Cusa had promoted a high development of theological, philosophical, classical, and mathematical studies, which still continued to flourish a long time after his death. But the important point, at this moment, regards the primary schools for the people, and the results of the combined efforts of both the Church and the family for the moral improvement of the lower classes. The author minutely describes the popular morals at a time which was considered by modern writers as mainly characterized by ignorance and vice. He shows, on the contrary, that the domestic circle was distinguished with the greatest suavity of manners. He gives the titles of many ascetic books full of the most tender piety written for the common people.

He enters into many details on the ordinary way of preaching, and proves that sermons in the churches were as frequent as in our age, and a stricter obligation was made on all classes to hear the word of God in the pulpit. More than fifty editions of the Bible in the vulgar language, and an immense number of books destined to instruct the people on their religion, such as catechisms, tables of sins, etc., prove that not only religious instruction was not neglected, but that it was pursued with as much zeal as in the most flourishing times.

He gives many details on the activity prevailing in literary circles. Directly after the invention of printing an immense number of editions of ancient and modern authors came out from the German presses. There was then among printers a sort of Christian apostolate such as had animated the monks when they wrote their splendid manuscripts. From 1457 to 1500 more than thirty thousand works were published, some of them in several folio volumes, and no one could then foresee that printing would ever be used for evil purposes.

But what is more wonderful still is the extraordinary development of art which then took place. Architects, sculptors, painters, musicians vied with each other to spread morality and religion among all classes. The author passes in review the names of many great masters in art, such as goldsmiths, painters on glass, engravers on wood and on copper or steel, embroiderers, musical composers, and admirable performers on every kind of instruments. And at the end of all these considerations he devotes an entire chapter to describing " popular life" (*Volks Wirthschaft*) so as to carry the admiration and enthusiasm of his readers.

It would be, after this, useless to repeat that even the fifteenth century was an age of virtue and happiness not only among the Latin nations, but even in the heart of Germany and the north of Europe.

6. *The Catholic Church in the Present Age Continues its Work of Regeneration with the Ardor of Renewed Youth.—Conclusion.*

Considered from any possible stand-point, the Catholic Church has given us unmistakable proofs of its divine origin. Its preparation by Gentilism and Judaism carries it back to the first appearance of man on earth, and demonstrates its adaptation to human nature both in the unity of the design and the variety of its applications. Its early spread all over the globe at the coming of Christ, by the preaching of a few Jewish apostles, is a sure voucher of the divinity of its Founder, and of a providential working in its establishment. The sudden turn in human history, and the immense improvement in morals which makes of its birth so remarkable a feature in mankind's annals, proves that God Himself directs the spiritual affairs of men, and in the matter of moral goodness does not leave our race to the feeble guidance of reason. But particularly the sublime holiness that has distinguished it, during the whole extent of the nineteen centuries which go to compose its glorious records, is the most complete demonstration that at this day, as well as in the previous ages, the Holy Spirit animates it and renders it fruitful in good works.

This last proof of its heavenly origin—the continuance to this day of its sanctity—must be the most convincing for us all because we all are the witnesses of it, and any one who reflects cannot but be struck by the spectacle. To develop it in all its details would require a long work, and only a few pages remain at our disposal. Let a last faithful statement, therefore, as compendious as possible, be made of the Church's action at this moment for the moral regeneration of mankind; namely, for what has been called the spread of God's kingdom on earth.

I. The first consideration of importance here is the immense number of human beings within the Church's precincts whom God inspires with the thought of sacrificing themselves for the moral improvement of their fellow-beings. This has always been a characteristic mark of the Catholic Church, and is at this moment as prominent as at any previous epoch. It is known that in all communities of men, whatever may be their state of civilization and enlightenment, whatever may be even their religion and their belief in a hereafter, a certain number are found with a greater keenness of conscience than others and a better appreciation of the moral sense, which all indeed have, but a' few only feel deeply. Still, it is a prerogative peculiar to the Church of Christ that in its bosom this is not confined to a simply natural and individual leaning, having scarcely any reference to others. It is derived from a supernatural source, and directly thrives to expand as broadly as the soul itself, whose aspirations can be called infinite. These chosen people instinctively feel that they have received a peculiar call from God Himself. To obey Him they must first sanctify themselves and enter the path of the evangelical counsels, in order to be ready for an apostolic life and raise others after them to the height of sanctity. This is found in the Catholic Church alone.

From this holy band women are not excluded. They are often the most ardent. They are the Church's crown and glory; but precisely on account of their instinctive impetuosity under the divine impulse they are severely placed under a strict direction, which becomes sweet to them because they understand the need they have of it. For in this most remarkable galaxy of choice souls, in the women as well as in the men, everything must be ruled by reason and good sense; nothing must be left to eccentricity, extravagance, fanaticism. Strange indeed! the motives are the highest, the prospects the brightest, the feelings the keenest; still, the working of the whole is the most rational, sober, almost demure. Is there anything on earth comparable to this? Could anything of this kind be devised and arranged by human skill and ingenuity?

Look at their number and their variety of temperament. It would not be, we think, an exaggeration to say that in the whole Catholic Church there are at this moment at least a million of human beings who have felt this call to holiness and realize it in the way just described. They belong to all classes of society; there are among them children of princes and lords, and there are also children of poor people and of simple rustics. They are scattered among all nations; many in the most refined countries of southern and central Europe; a good number in the frozen regions of the north or in the forests of the New World. Asiatics as well as Europeans and Americans are often desirous of embracing that holy state, and the Catholic virgins of China are as devoted as those of Syria or Palestine.

But though they belong to races of so many different leanings and adaptations, they all follow the same rules, which can be reduced to two: To look first after their own moral improvement and perfection, and then to ardently labor for the sanctification of others. And in their enumeration it must be said that at this time particularly the secular clergy hold a most honorable place. The time has gone by when seculars and regulars were antagonistic. Look at both in Germany, in France, in Italy, in Spain, and all over this continent, and say if they are not a band of brothers engaged in the same holy work of bringing back the nations to Gospel sanctity. In case any exceptions are found here and there, they are so few and insignificant that they may be passed over as of no account in the general result.

All this has been the effect, after God, of the wise provisions and decrees of the Council of Trent. From that time down to this the reformation effected in the secular and regular clergy has been constantly increasing and brightening till our own day, when it is as perfect as human weakness permits. Look at the hierarchy particularly, and you will try in vain in the whole history of the Church to find an epoch when it was more submissive to the Holy See, more learned and zealous, more animated with the spirit of a tender piety reflected in the purity of their lives.

It is in the hands of those servants of God that the distribution of the Church's charities is entrusted. And it may be doubted if there has ever been an epoch when that golden virtue flowing from the heart of Christ has produced more abundant fruits than in this age. At the origin of Christianity St. Paul collected alms in Macedonia for the faithful in Jerusalem; in our day the needs of the most distant nations in India, China, and the heart of Africa are supplied by the Christians of the great cities of western Europe and of this continent. The Catholics of New York, for instance, are not satisfied with the numerous calls addressed to them in behalf of their destitute fellow-citizens; they find besides the means to help the famine-stricken Irish, the destitute Indians of the north-west, the struggling Catholic communities of Palestine, of Algeria, of all countries from which the cry of distress is heard. But in the absolute impossibility of an adequate description we must pass on to a second consideration.

II. The Church, not satisfied with practically teaching the doctrine of holiness to her submissive children through her orders and hierarchy, holds aloft before the eyes of all mankind the only standard of morality acceptable to human reason. Its code is not veiled in mystery; its moral doctrine is not esoteric and destined only for the private ear of the catechumen. The great voice which proclaims the true principles of action (*agendorum*) resounds through the whole earth, and can be heard by whomsoever listens, even among outsiders.

The councils, based on the word of God, have in all ages declared that the teaching body in the Church, with Peter at its head, is infallible in point of morals as well as of faith. Peter alone is the source of it, and communicates it to his successors. In this scheme there can be no question of opinion, hesitation, doubt. The pronouncements of simple philosophy in ethics are too often of that character. Moral philosophers of the strictest class, when they do not call to their help the Church's authority, form only *schools* which always differ from each other in many important points. Reason alone, though in theory able to reach the truth, is often in practice biassed by prejudice and passion. If this is true of those non-Christians who admit eternal principles of right, the case is greatly worse for those who endeavor to found morality on a basis independent of God. The doctrine they proclaim is necessarily unreliable; their principles once admitted would leave every one at the mercy of his passions; and if this deflection from both reason and faith became general, morality would entirely perish among men, or its shifting code would be a most unsafe guide. This, fortunately, shall never happen universally, because the Church has the promise of perpetuity; and its doctrine must ultimately prevail. Meanwhile, though in the midst of enemies, opposed by discordant teachings of mere opinion and fancy, it holds firmly in its grasp the standard of right, of true morals, of holiness itself. Suppose that at this moment the Church's voice proclaiming the true axioms of divine law was suddenly silenced, what would become among men of the sacred institutions of marriage, of the family, of the right of property, of social truths and political constitutions? Every bond through which the framework of human society is held together would snap like a tube of glass, or vanish like a soap-bubble. Every one acquainted with the wild theories advocated to-day by large associations of men is aware that this is neither a bugbear nor even a simple exaggeration.

Look well around you, and endeavor to find which is the institution on which alone rests the hope of the future; and few among men will refuse to admit that the Church is that institution more at this time perhaps than ever before.

III. After these general reflections it is proper to come to some particular points of great importance in the present discussion. An attentive observer will easily remark that the Church sows the seed of holiness, and reaps its most abundant fruits in all classes of society. It begins with the child to whom through its parents it first imparts the knowledge and the love of God's law. Among the admonitions invariably given in the tribunal of penance, the most important consists in ascertaining if married people fulfil their duty in this regard. Not only this is always inquired into, but directions are also given particularly to the uneducated with regard to the method they have to follow. It is a most powerful means of securing to future men and women the habits of a Christian life at a time when their tender age disposes them to receive readily the most lasting impressions. But religious instructors are not satisfied with advice given to parents. They soon take the young in charge; and who cannot see how powerful for good must be the usual preparation for confirmation and communion? What care is not taken in our day to form good habits in baptized infants as soon as they become conscious and capable of sin? What means are not adopted to root out from their young hearts the first growth of sinful habits?

Look, further on, at the Church's action on young people when they reach the adult period. All moralists, even if not Christian, must confess that the time of life comprised between fifteen and twenty-five years is the most critical and perilous. The majority of those whose career becomes a wreck, and are destined either to perish early or to drag a miserable existence, a prey to shameful passions, owe, undoubtedly, their moral loss to a want of proper direction at that dangerous period of human life. But the question may be fairly put, Where and by whom is youth properly, tenderly, and actively cared for, taken in hand, and saved from moral snares and pitfalls? There can be but one answer to these questions, because the Catholic Church alone undertakes this most delicate and important moral work. In its bosom only is there a safe harbor for those who are tempest-tossed and at the moment of perishing. At the time of the fiercest temptations there is always hope for the young man or young woman who chooses to secure and receive the help of the Church's sacraments. It is in this particular case that the well-known adage is fulfilled literally: "Out of the Church there is no salvation."

Within its precincts, on the contrary, not only the young are saved, but after an almost complete shipwreck the vicious, even if advanced in age, can be rescued from the waves. In every mission given in the Catholic Church numerous examples always occur to prove that God truly receives to reconciliation the most obdurate sinners. Death-bed repentance is often derided, and is always insecure; still, true reconciliation with an offended God at the last moment is a thing of daily occurrence in the Church of Christ.

IV. Not satisfied with securing the salvation of her own children, the Catholic Church undertakes to reclaim from superstition and vice those innumerable nations who walk still "in the shadow of death." What is the object of those "foreign missions," so remarkable at the precise time this is written? It is exactly the same the first apostles had in view; namely, to spread the "kingdom of God," or the reign of virtue and holiness, on earth. It is impossible to attempt here even a slight sketch of it. Either in the decaying churches of the East, among the former Christian populations trampled upon during so many centuries by the barbarous Moslem power; or in the midst of the heathen Hindoos; or among the Buddhistic tribes of China, Mongolia, Tibet; or still more, all over the dark continent of Africa, from its whole circumference toward its now renowned centre, the country of its great lakes, and the sources of its mightiest rivers, men and women are seen at this moment with only one aim, guided by one single directing hand. That aim is to restore to the blind their eyesight, and to those morally dead the life of conscience. The directing hand is that of the Supreme Pontiff, the successor of Peter, the one the middle ages loved to call "The Apostolic." Except directly after the discovery of the road to India, and of the vast continent called the new world, the Church never had such a mighty occasion of showing her activity and zeal as at this day. All the obstacles to her universal action and sway are now thrown down; the whole globe embraced now by commerce is open to a far higher object in which ardent apostles—men and women—throw their whole soul. They are decimated by death, but their ranks, as in a mighty army on the battle-field, are immediately reformed and reinforced. The heroes of to-day were unknown ten years ago, and in ten years more nothing shall remain of them except their souls in heaven and their imperishable memory on earth. But the work will continue to go on until its completion, which is sure to arrive, because that "the earth is the Lord's, and the fulness thereof," was predicted by David, and must sooner or later come to pass.

It would be, however, futile to insist here on a description which a full volume could scarcely succeed in detailing. It is simply expressed by the mere words of the heading to this section: "In this work the Church to-day displays to the world an ardor of renewed youth." It is good, however, to mention briefly some characteristics of that "ardor."

V. To carry on this work of regeneration at home and abroad, the Church spares neither labor nor solicitude nor material means. The labor is incessant, arduous, heroic. But no one complains that there is no intermission, no softening down, no place for the satisfaction of simple human feelings. It must forever *continue*, or no satisfactory effect could be produced. It is always a *hard climbing up* without the prospect of a softer life in a gentle declination to lower ground, because whatever is great is always arduous, looking constantly to higher regions. It is consequently of its nature *heroic*, and no noble heart can ever murmur against the necessity of becoming a hero, chiefly when the victory secures "glory to God in the highest, and peace on earth to men of good-will." This is our short commentary on this incessant, arduous, and heroic labor. A word must be said, in a second place, on the solicitude displayed by the Church for the inward formation of Christ in His members.

Those who know anything of the untiring activity which distinguishes the Church of Rome in the choice of means adopted for the obtaining of its mighty end cannot choose a better word to characterize it than by calling it a motherly solicitude. Look at it in the selection of its agents, in the instructions forwarded to them, in the various steps it takes for their encouragement, proper reward, or, on the other side, remonstrances, correction, disapproval, and you will distinctly recognize the feelings of a true mother. It extends to everything: to the proper education of the young; to the holiness of the sanctuary; to a truly angelic life in women's convents; to the strict observance of the rule in men's monasteries; to the decency, nay, splendor of divine service; to the needs of Christ's poor; to the conversion of sinners, the perseverance of the just, the extension of God's kingdom among the heathen; and, last not least, to a stern opposition against every form of error or vice. In all those branches of a divinely inspired activity, the Church after St. Paul becomes a true mother in its incessant solicitude. Moderation, tenderness of heart accompanied with firmness and uncompromising adherence to duty, form the character of its polity. It is not, certainly, in this age that the life of its rulers is a sinecure. They know that they are appointed by Almighty God to continue among men the ministry of His Son; and as the public life of Christ is their pattern, they do not expect rest in this world, and look only to heaven for repose and enjoyment.

In a third place, the material means at their command deserve a moment's consideration. The time has gone by when the gratitude of mankind had placed in their hands all that was requisite for securing their object. Many reproaches have been formerly addressed to popes, cardinals, prelates of every degree, as if the immense wealth they enjoyed had been mainly used for their selfish gratification. No doubt, owing to human weakness, abuses had crept in, and the life of Christian pastors was not always conformable to the evangelical precepts. Still it must be repeated, since people seem to have forgotten it, that in the worst times there was at least a great part of the wealth bestowed by the pious for the good of the Church, which could not be touched by the most ambitious and greedy among the clergy. It is indubitable that, even at that deplorable epoch, charity at least abounded; and there was not a single human misery which was not relieved. Hospitals, asylums, reformatories, houses of education, all funded and apparently forever secured against greediness and rapacity, furnished abundant means for systematized relief and the alleviation of all human distress. But our present concern regards only the means left at the Church's disposal in our day. In every country she has been despoiled, and left bare of every shred of property. More than this, legislation has everywhere interfered to prevent her from becoming rich again; and in case means of importance were again accumulated in her hands, the prospect is never absent from her sight that confiscation by the State would be again resorted to. Still, the needs required for such a gigantic work as the Church must necessarily undertake are enormous, and mankind would suffer if it was deprived of them for a single day.

Fortunately the providence of God is inexhaustible; and in the total absence of permanent wealth, the Church's children are inspired with an irresistible desire of coming to their mother's help. For daily wants daily alms are required; and not a day passes that the purse of individual Christians does not become the treasury of a universal Institution. Remember how the process of it has been already for many years going on among the Catholics of France, of England, of this country. See how it begins to operate among those of Spain, Portugal, and Italy. Germany is now learning how to do it in the unutterable distress of persecution and spoliation. Details are unavoidably excluded here; but it suffices to remind the reader that as the Church is thus resuming the way of life which distinguished the beginning of its career, the same holiness must prevail in its *head* and *members* which struck the eyes of the pagan world around its cradle in Jerusalem and Rome. This, thank God! must be the concluding word of this volume.

VI. During the last two hundred years and more, the progress in the path of sanctity has been steadily going on among the pastors of the flock of Christ. It has never been more remarkable than at the present day. The development of these two propositions would necessitate details which every one can easily ascertain by referring to this most modern phase of history. Who does not know that at least from the reign of Louis XIII. in France (a longer period would be unnecessary) the see of Peter has been occupied by a series of pontiffs highly impressed with the holiness of their office, and attentive only to the call of duty? Under their rules at once mild and strict, prelates, bishops, and clergy have been gradually brought to the practice of a truly evangelical life. Some decline may have been perceptible, in spite of the popes, among the French during the last century, and in the German episcopate under the Josephine vexations. But it was only a temporary check, extending but slightly to other countries. The scourge of persecution and war has purified at last the whole Church from this last dross; and the result has been what all sincere Christians must perceive with admiration. Is not holiness at last triumphant in the Vatican, turned almost into a prison; in nearly every bishop's house throughout Christendom; in the humble residences of secular clergymen; in the pious houses of religious men and women devoted to the service of God? This is, in very few words, the spectacle offered universally throughout the world. Insignificant anomalies, redressed as soon as perceived, cannot mar the general beauty of the scene which surrounds every temple raised to God on earth. The sanctuary is nowhere polluted, but everywhere worthy of its destination. Around the altar of Mary pure souls can meet without fear of desecration. The statue of Christ opening His bosom to show His divine heart to the faithful calls them all to the purity He brought on earth. Canticles of praise and thanksgiving resound night and day from the lips of innocent children, of pure women, of men full of faith, and never recoiling from its profession.

This description might be indefinitely prolonged. It is not necessary, particularly for those who know that it is but the effect of the infinite love of Christ for His Church, Who "delivered Himself up for it, that He might sanctify it, cleansing it in a bath of water by the word of life; that He might find in it a glorious Church without any spot or wrinkle, but that it should be holy and without blemish."*

---

* Eph. v. 25, *seq.*

www.ingramcontent.com/pod-product-compliance
Lightning Source LLC
Chambersburg PA
CBHW051847300426
44117CB00006B/296